CW01649330

The Illustrated Directory of

HOUSE PLANTS

The Illustrated Directory of

HOUSE PLANTS

A practical guide to growing over 500 plants for the home

Compiled by
WILLIAM DAVIDSON

AURA BOOKS

This 1991 edition published by
Aura Books plc, Unit 1, Fairway Drive,
Greenford, Middlesex UB6 8PW,
United Kingdom.

ISBN 0 947793 99 2

Credits

Editor: Geoff Rogers

Designers: Roger Hyde,
Mark Holt, Tony Truscott Designs

Colour reproductions: Bantam Litho Ltd, Rodney Howe Ltd, Magnum Graphics Ltd, David Bruce Graphics Ltd, Scansets Ltd.

Filmset: SX Composing Ltd.

Printed in Belgium by:
Proost International Book Production,
Turnhout, Belgium

The beautifully fragrant blooms of Freesia

Compiler/Author

William Davidson is involved with all aspects of house plants, and has been employed by Rochfords, Europe's leading growers, for most of his working life. His interests encompass growing, exhibiting, writing, consultancy, lecturing, as well as radio and television programmes. He is the author of many successful books on house plants.

Contributing Authors

Keith Andrew has a special interest in breeding phalaenopsis and miniature cymbidiums. A commercial orchid grower for 25 years, he has given papers at conferences in California and exhibited orchids in Germany and the UK.

Ray Bilton is an acknowledged expert on cymbidiums. He has given papers on the breeding of cymbidiums at the World Orchid Conferences in Australia and Thailand and has contributed to orchid periodicals throughout the world.

Peter Chapman has been an enthusiastic grower and collector of cacti and succulent plants for more than 20 years. He has co-authored several books on the subject and contributed many articles to magazines. He is also an accomplished photographer.

Peter Dumbelton has spent the whole of his professional life growing orchids and for the past 14 years has been working for a commercial orchid company, where he is now nursery manager. He lectures to a wide range of societies and often judges at orchid shows.

Alan Greatwood has grown orchids for over 30 years, having learned his trade from one of the established orchid growing firms. His main interest today is growing species on into specimen plants, for which he has won many awards.

Margaret Martin is a very experienced grower of cacti and succulent plants. She has passed on this experience in magazine articles and has co-authored several books on her favourite plants, often illustrated with her own photographs.

Paul Phillips is one of the foremost breeders of paphiopedilums in the world, and Chairman of the British Orchid Growers Association. He has lectured on paphiopedilums in many countries and has written for orchid magazines in Australia, America, Britain and Germany.

Wilma Rittershausen is Editor of the *Orchid Review* and the author of several orchid books. She frequently contributes articles to orchid and gardening magazines. Her brother Brian runs the family orchid business set up by their father P R C Rittershausen.

David Stead is an experienced professional grower with a particular interest in breeding odontoglossums. Formerly Chairman of the British Orchid Growers Association, David Stead is a regular contributor to orchid journals and international conferences.

FLOWERING PLANTS

The fiery brilliance of a scarlet begonia can brighten a whole room with its dazzling display. And such is the range of beautiful flowering plants available today that every season can be alive with their colour. Give them plenty of light and remember to feed and water them well when they are in bloom and they will reward your attentions a thousandfold with natural vitality and charm.

Catharanthus roseus

Strelitzia reginae

FOLIAGE PLANTS

Whether you favour the cool freshness of ferns or the flowing lines of a stately palm, foliage plants have much to offer in the home. Try grouping several plants together, combining different heights, shapes, colours and textures for added impact. This will not only produce an attractive display but also help to create a beneficial zone of high humidity around the plants.

Cryptanthus bromelioides tricolor

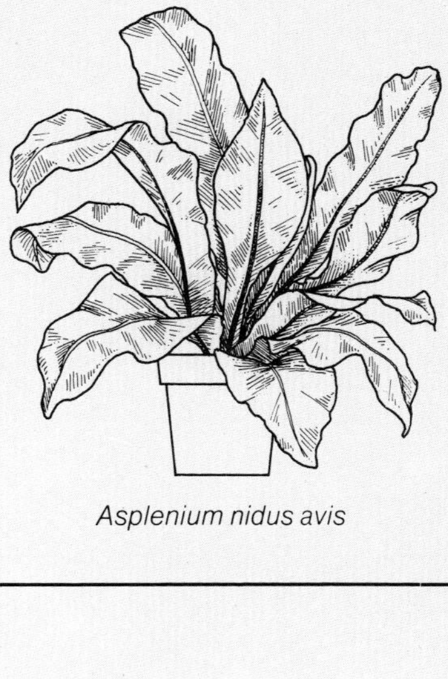

Asplenium nidus avis

ORCHIDS

Orchids are not as difficult to grow as is sometimes imagined; some can be raised in the home with ease and a great many can be grown in a greenhouse and brought indoors when they are in bloom, where they will usually last for several weeks. Orchids can be divided into three temperature ranges: cool, intermediate, and warm. The species and hybrids described in this book are clearly classified according to these ranges; the temperatures quoted are winter night minimums. Read the descriptions carefully and try to grow a few orchids for yourself. You could become hooked!

Miltonia Peach Blossom

Cymbidium lowianum

CACTI and SUCCULENTS

Size for size, some of the cacti produce relatively huge flowers; tiny rebutias and lobivias are literally smothered with beautiful satiny blooms during the summer. And even those cacti and other succulent plants that do not bloom so readily offer growth patterns and spine formations that never fail to fascinate. Most cacti and succulents need a bright window and a cool winter rest.

Parodia aureispina

A

B

C

D

E

Acanthocalycium violaceum

A practical hint
When shopping for plants choose those suited to the intended spot; most plants will have tags attached indicating their requirements.

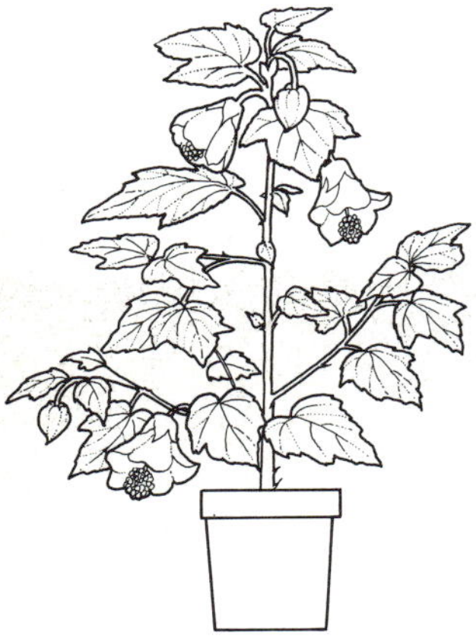

Abutilon hybrids

- **Good light**
- **Temp: 10-18°C (50-65°F)**
- **Keep moist and fed**

There are numerous varieties, with pendulous bell-shaped flowers in a range of colours, and some have colourful foliage. Many of the abutilons are worthy of a place in the houseplant collection for their foliage alone.

Most are of vigorous habit, and capable of attaining a height of some 1.8m (6ft) with their roots confined to a pot of about 18cm (7in) in diameter. However, pruning of over-vigorous growth presents no problem and can be done at almost any time of the year. Firm top sections of stems will not be difficult to root in a fresh peat and sand mixture. Feed well when they are established.

Light, airy and cool conditions suit them best, and they will be the better for spending the summer months out of doors in a sheltered position. Use a loam-based potting mixture.

Above right:
Abutilon 'Boule de Neige'
One of the many named varieties of abutilon hybrids. All are charming.

A practical hint
Check plants offered for sale to ensure that they are free from pests and dead or dying leaves. Try to avoid purchasing pre-wrapped plants.

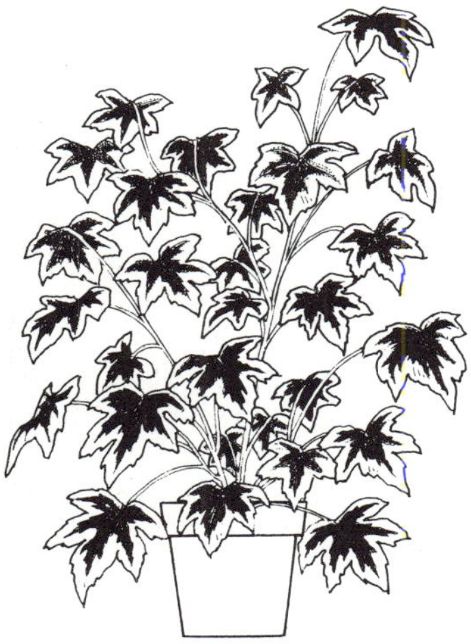

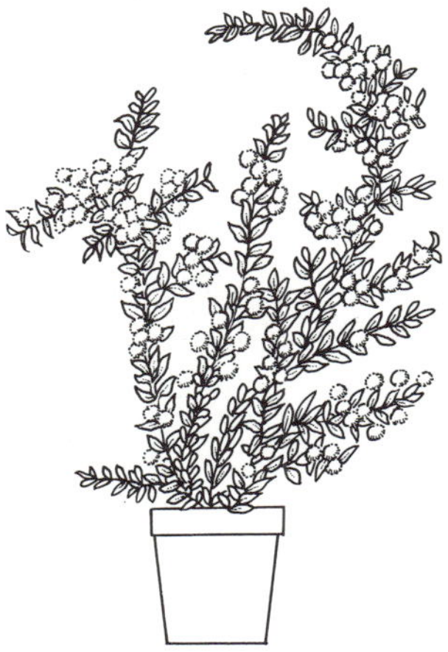

Abutilon sevitzia

- **Good light**
- **Temp: 13-18°C (55-65°F)**
- **Frequent feeding**

Vigorous growing plant for cooler conditions that offer good light, but not full sun when close to glass. Has attractively variegated maple-type leaves and pendulous orange-coloured flowers not unlike a small single hollyhock.

A loam-based mixture is essential when potting plants on – a task that must not be neglected if plants are to do as well as they can. While in active growth feed at every watering, to keep colour. Firm cuttings about 10cm (4in) in length will root readily in peaty mixture if placed in a heated propagator; when growth begins, remove the growing tip of the cutting. When well cared for, individual stems will put on 90cm (3ft) of growth in one season, but pruning can be undertaken at any time to limit growth. Never allow plants to stand in water for long periods, but water copiously while fresh leaves appear.

Soft growth attracts many pests, so a careful and frequent check is advised, especially under the leaves.

Acacia armata

- **Good light**
- **Temp: 13-18°C (55-65°F)**
- **Keep moist**

Native to Australia, *A. armata* develops into an attractive shrubby plant that does well in a conservatory, but may in time become too large for smaller rooms. However, pruning of over-vigorous growth can be undertaken in the early part of the year, which is also the best time for potting plants into larger containers. A loam-based mixture is necessary if plants are not to become too soft and lush.

New plants are made by sowing seed in spring, or by taking firm, but not old, cuttings in midsummer. Older material is too woody and less likely to succeed.

The principal attraction of this plant is the yellow flowers, which appear in spring. During the spring and summer, plants require to be fed regularly and watered freely; they need less water and no feeding during the winter months.

Left: **Abutilon sevitzia**
A colourful, free-growing plant that thrives in moderate temperatures. Prune to shape at any time.

Right: **Acacia armata**
Where space permits, this free-flowering shrub will bring welcome colour to a cool indoor location.

A practical hint
In all weather conditions, particularly winter, ensure that plants are properly wrapped for the trip home. Frost is fatal.

Acalypha hispida

- **Good light**
- **Temp: 13-18°C (55-65°F)**
- **Keep moist and fed**

These striking plants, with their large leaves of mid-green colouring, grow to a height of some 1.8m (6ft) in ideal conditions. Drooping beetroot-red bracts develop from the axils of leaves to create the principal attraction of this fine plant.

The best time to purchase these plants is in the spring when the fresh young ones will get off to a better start. Keep them moist at all times, giving a little less water in winter, and feed well when they are established. When they have filled their existing containers with roots, use a loam-based potting compost to pot the plants on and help to develop them to their full potential.

Keep your acalypha in good light but avoid strong sunlight. Remove the dead bracts regularly and keep a watchful eye for pale leaf discolouration, which is a sign that troublesome red spider mites are present. Treat the undersides of leaves with insecticide at the first signs.

Right: **Acalypha hispida**
At its best when young, this fine plant is adorned in late summer with distinctive red catkins. Renew plants each year from cuttings.

Acanthocalycium violaceum

- **Full sun**
- **Temp: 5-30°C (41-86°F)**
- **Water with care**

Acanthocalycium violaceum is a cylindrical plant about 12cm (4.7in) in diameter. During summer, it produces large numbers of beautiful violet flowers, about 5cm (2in) across. Even during winter the plant is attractive, and the stout yellow spines show up well against the dark green of the stem. This cactus does not offset easily, certainly not as a young plant; many apparently solitary plants do occasionally form offsets with age.

A good potting mixture is two parts of loam- or peat-based material to one part of sharp sand or perlite. *A. violaceum* should be watered with caution even during the summer growing period. Always allow it to dry out between waterings and if possible water on a sunny day. Feed every two weeks with a high-potassium (tomato) fertilizer when the buds form. If it should lose its roots, allow the plant to dry for two or three days and repot in fresh, well-drained mixture. Keep in a well-lit position.

Above:
Acanthocalycium violaceum
A most attractive globular cactus, beautifully spined and producing splendid colourful blooms.

A practical hint
A simple precaution in winter is to put plants in the body of the car, not in the boot, where temperatures are much lower.

Achimines hybrids

- **Good light**
- **Temp: 13-18°C (55-65°F)**
- **Keep moist and fed**

One of those cheap and cheerful plants that will go on flowering throughout the summer, and can be raised from early spring-sown seed, from cuttings, or by peeling off and planting some of the scaly rhizomes. They are fine as conventional pot plants situated in good light on a windowsill or, perhaps more splendidly, as hanging-basket plants growing overhead.

After the flowers and foliage have died down the plants should be allowed to dry out and rest throughout the winter. They can be started into growth again in the spring. At this time the rhizomes can be peeled apart so that more plants are produced. Place the rhizomes in hot water before planting, and they will generally do better.

Keep the plants moist and avoid a very dry atmosphere, which will encourage red spider mites to the detriment of the plant.

Above left and left:
Achimenes hybrids
These two colourful varieties show the range available in this popular houseplant. Avoid strong sunlight.

Acorus gramineus variegata

- **Grows anywhere**
- **Temp: 7-13°C (45-55°F)**
- **Keep moist**

Not particularly attractive as an individual, but a fine plant for grouping with others. Well suited for inclusion in a bottle garden or converted fishtank, the acorus has a distinctive shape and is not invasive. Grassy foliage is green and gold in colour and produces neat clumps that may be divided at almost any time in order to produce new plants.

Very much the average indoor plant, it will respond well to a modicum of attention, but abhors hot and dry conditions and too much fussing over. A light location with protection from strong sun is best, and it will not object to some fresh air from open windows on warmer days.

Few pests seem to bother this plant, but in hot and dry conditions red spider may make an appearance and should be treated with one of the many available insecticides as soon as detected. When potting on, a loam-based mixture is best, but one should avoid putting plants into very large pots.

Above: **Acorus gramineus**
An easy-care, grassy-foliaged plant that does well in low temperatures if kept moist and in reasonable light.

Ada aurantiaca

- **Cool: 10°C (50°F)**
- **Easy to grow and flower**
- **Winter/spring flowering**
- **Evergreen/no rest**

This species belongs to an extremely small genus of only three species, which are allied to the odontoglossums. It is an epiphyte from Colombia, where it grows in the same location as many of the odontoglossums and therefore requires similar cool house conditions. Although *Ada aurantiaca* is allied to odontoglossums, very little hybridizing has been achieved and the species is grown for its unusually brilliant orange flowers, which appear on compact sprays during the winter and spring. The individual blooms are small and are not fully opening, but produce bell-shaped flowers which are most attractive on the spray.

The plant is a neat, compact grower that can be easily raised from seed and is therefore plentiful. It produces small pseudobulbs, which are partially protected by the base of the outside leaves. The flower spike comes from the base of the leading bulb when it has completed its growth. Pot in an open, well-drained bark compost. Do not overpot. Best when grown on without division.

Above: **Ada aurantiaca**
This is a cool-growing species with a compact growth. It blooms in the winter and spring.

Adenium obesum var. multiflorum

- **Full sun**
- **Temp: 13-30°C (55-86°F)**
- **Keep almost dry in winter**

Although it is a succulent plant in its native habitat, this adenium cannot produce the massive water-storage stem as a small specimen. It is one of the most beautiful flowering succulents, but not one of the easiest to grow, mainly because of the higher, draught-free winter temperature needed. However, given the right conditions, it will produce masses of red or pink blooms over a relatively long period during spring and summer. Plants can start to flower when only 15cm (6in) high. The thickened branching stems bear glossy bright green leaves; these normally fall during winter, when the potting mixture should be kept only slightly moist.

Grow in a good potting mixture, which can be either loam- or peat-based; to ensure the necessary free drainage it is worth mixing in about one third of sharp sand or perlite. Water can be given freely when the plant is in full growth and flower, and an occasional feed with a high-potassium fertilizer is beneficial at this time. Propagation is possible from summer cuttings.

Right: **Adenium obesum var. multiflorum**
This tender succulent thrives in warm bright conditions all year.

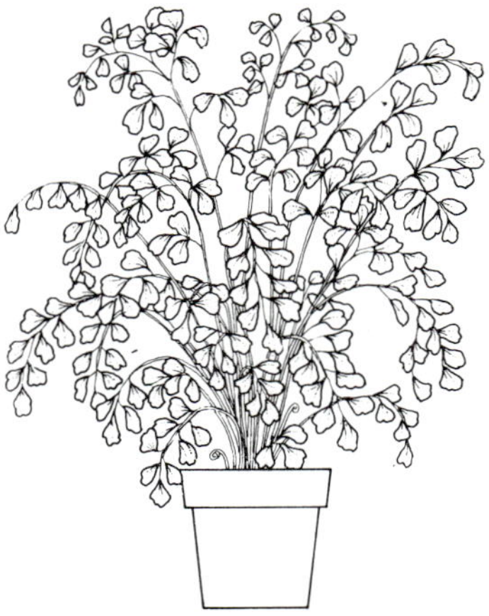

Adiantum

- **Light shade**
- **Temp: 18-21°C (65-70°F)**
- **Moist surroundings**

Numerous varieties are available of these most delicate and beautiful foliage plants, whose pale green foliage contrasts with their black stems.

Bright, direct sunlight and dry atmospheric conditions will prove fatal. Offer these elegant ferns lightly shaded positions in a warm room: place plants in a larger container and surround their pots with a moisture-retaining material such as peat. Misting of foliage is often recommended, but this exercise can have undesirable effects if the surrounding air temperature is inadequate. It is therefore better to use the mister to wet the soil surface.

Avoid use of chemicals on foliage. When potting on, a peaty mixture is needed, and once plants have established in their pots weak liquid feeding will be needed every time the plant is watered. During winter, feeding is not important and watering should be only sufficient to keep the soil moist.

Above: **Adiantum**
These come in many varieties, mostly with delicate foliage that is a perfect foil for other plants.

Aechmea chantinii

- **Good light**
- **Temp: 13-18°C (55-65°F)**
- **Avoid overwatering**

Among the bromeliads this one has a reputation for being tough. It has very vicious spines along the leaf margins, which makes careful handling, and positioning, essential. The green-and-silver banded foliage itself makes a striking plant, but when the red-and-orange coloured bract appears one begins fully to appreciate the intricacy and remarkable spectacle that this splendid plant displays.

Like all the more majestic plants in the bromeliad family, this will take several years to produce bracts following the purchase of a young plant. New plants can be started from offshoots that appear at the base of the parent stems of an older plant that has produced bracts. These should be planted individually in a loam-based potting mixture to which some prepared tree bark has been added. Pot as firmly as possible to prevent the plants toppling over, and keep out of direct sunlight until new growth is evident.

Aechmea fasciata

(A. rhodocyania)

- **Good light**
- **Temp: 13-18°C (55-65°F)**
- **Keep urn filled with water**

The silvery-grey leaves have a light grey down on them that adds much to the attraction of this most excellent of all bromeliads. Its grey leaves are broad and recurving and form a central chamber or urn, which should be filled with water. There are spines along the leaf margins, so be careful when handling. Also avoid touching the grey down on the leaves if the plants are to be seen to their best effect.

Young plants can be raised from seed, in which case bracts take some five to seven years to appear, or from basal shoots of mature plants, in which case bracts develop in two to three years.

The bract is a delightful soft pink in colour and, as if this were not enough, small but intensely blue flowers will also develop in the spiky pink bract. This is a truly fine plant that is easy to manage and will remain in 'flower' for up to nine months.

Above: **Aechmea chantinii**
Frequent misting will maintain the humid conditions all aechmeas prefer. Bloom may last for months.

Above right: **Aechmea fasciata**
This is the most beautiful and popular of all aechmeas. The pink 'flower head' is truly striking.

A practical hint
Avoid draughty areas such as doorways and corridors when locating plants indoors, and keep them out of cold window spots at night.

Aeonium arboreum 'Nigrum' ('Zwartkop')

- **Full sun**
- **Temp: 5-30°C (41-86°F)**
- **Water occasionally in winter**

An attractive, robust succulent with almost black glossy leaves arranged in a rosette that can be as much as 20cm (8in) across. The stem carrying it is about 1.5cm (0.6in) thick and as it gradually elongates one is left with a rosette of leaves on about 30cm (12in) of bare stem, any lower leaves having fallen off. Cut off the leafy top with a short piece of the stem, let it dry for a couple of days and then just push it into the surface of fresh potting mixture. It will soon rot to form a flat, compact plant once more. Keep the old stem; it will send out many small rosettes, which in their turn can be removed and rooted.

This aeonium makes a good houseplant but needs plenty of light or the leaves will tend to lose their beautiful dark colour and turn greenish. Although it will withstand a lower temperature, it does not need it and will thrive in a normal living-room. Use any good standard potting mixture.

Above left:
Aeonium arboreum var. **nigrum**
The almost black leaves of this succulent make it most unusual.

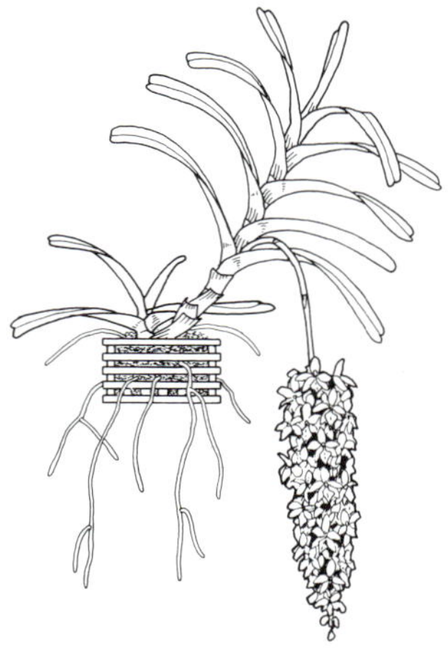

Aerides fieldingii

- **Intermediate/warm: 13-18°C (55-65°F)**
- **Easy to grow and flower**
- **Spring/summer flowering**
- **Evergreen/semi-dry rest**

A popular orchid from tropical Asia. About 50 species have been described. This epiphytic plant grows and flowers well in the intermediate or warm section of the greenhouse. Because it makes many aerial roots, a high degree of humidity is an advantage, with frequent spraying during the summer months.

This is one of the most free-flowering species of the genus, with drooping, branching spikes often up to 60cm (24in) in length. The flowers, which appear in spring or summer, are about 2.5cm (1in) across and are pinky-white suffused and mottled with rose-mauve. This species is also commonly known as the 'foxtail orchid', as are others (for example *Rynchostylis*), that bear their flowers in a similar way. The flowers are sweet-scented, and will remain in perfect condition for up to four weeks if the plant can be kept in cooler conditions while in flower.

Young plants are occasionally produced from the base. These can be removed when ready but ideally the plant should be undisturbed.

Left: **Aerides fieldingii**
This is an easy species to grow in the intermediate or warm greenhouse. Fragrant and spring flowering.

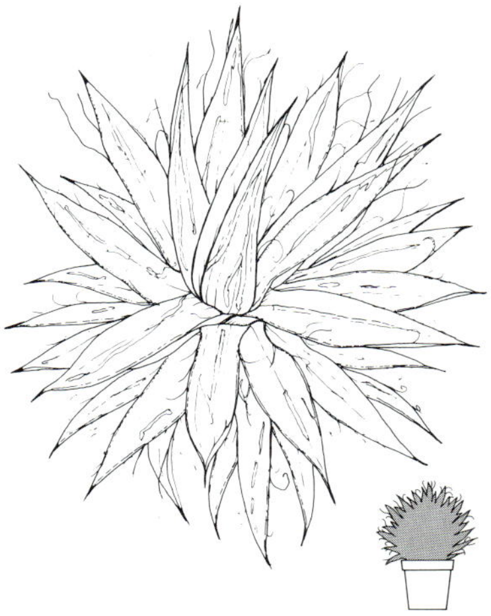

Aeschynanthus lobbianus

- **Light shade**
- **Temp: 16-21°C (60-70°F)**
- **Keep moist and fed**

These are temperamental plants that will produce exotic red flowers with seeming abandon one year, and in spite of having had identical treatment, will produce very little the next year. One of the supposed secrets of getting them to flower more reliably is to keep the plants very much on the dry side in winter and to lower the growing temperature. It is a procedure that works for many of the similar gesneriads, such as the columneas. During the warmer months, they should be kept out of bright sunlight.

The plants have glossy green leaves and have a natural pendulous habit, which adds considerably to their charm. New plants are easily started from cuttings a few centimetres in length that may be taken at any time during the spring or summer months. Arrange several cuttings to a small pot filled with peaty mixture and this will ensure that full and attractive plants develop. It will also help if the growing tips of young plants are removed to encourage branching.

Above: **Aeschynanthus lobbianus**
Bright red tubular flowers emerge from 'lipstick cases' during the summer. The pendulous habit of this plant makes it ideal for growing in a hanging basket. Avoid draughts.

Agave filifera

- **Full sun**
- **Temp: 5-30°C (41-86°F)**
- **Water with care**

Agave filifera forms a rosette 65cm (26in) across; each leathery leaf is 3cm (1.2in) wide and ends in a stout spine. The leaves are dark green in colour with white threads along the edge. This agave will eventually throw up a flower stem 2.5m (8ft) high, on the end of which are purple and green bell-like flowers. The main rosette dies after flowering, but new rosettes will form at the base of the old plant. The lifespan of the main rosette is 8-25 years.

Because of its tough leaves, *A. filifera* is very resistant to a dry atmosphere. If it is kept indoors during the winter months, place it outdoors during the summer. It needs sun during the growing period to keep it a good colour and shape. It is ideal for a patio or veranda.

This agave will grow in any loam- or peat-based medium. Water generously during very hot weather but keep only slightly moist during winter or periods of cloudy, damp weather.

Right: **Agave filifera**
Although a potential giant, this succulent is slow-growing, and it makes a very distinctive specimen when small. The narrow leaves have sharp spines at the tips.

A practical hint
Aloe variegata (the partridge breast aloe) is one of the easier plants for a light windowsill and can be propagated from offsets.

Agave parviflora

- **Full sun**
- **Temp: 5-30°C (41-86°F)**
- **Do not overwater**

One of the smallest of the agaves, *Agave parviflora* is ideal for a small greenhouse. The adult rosette is 18cm (7in) across, and the slender dark green leaves have white edges and white marginal threads. Eventually the plant will flower and die. The flower stem is about 1m (39in) high and carries pale yellow flowers. The agave will probably be over five years old when it flowers, and young plantlets will form around the dying rosette. These should be removed and potted up. Because of its attractive form, *A. parviflora* makes a good houseplant. When warm weather comes, put the plant outdoors in full sun; this will keep it in good health.

A good loam- or peat-based medium will suit this plant. It should be repotted annually. During hot weather, water freely: but keep it just moist during the winter and wet, cloudy weather. Agaves, with their tough leaves, present a problem to any insect pests.

Agave victoria-reginae

- **Full sun**
- **Temp: 5-30°C (41-86°F)**
- **Water with care**

Agave victoria-reginae is the most beautiful of the small agaves. It is a densely leaved rosette: the leaves are 15cm (6in) long, dark green in colour with beautiful white markings. Each leaf ends in a terminal spine, which should be treated with respect. *A. victoria-reginae* can withstand a very dry atmosphere and may be used as a houseplant during the winter months, but in the summer growing period it needs full sun to bring out its beautiful colouring.

Like all agaves, this species has a long flower stem, 3-4m (10-13ft) in height. The flowers are cream. After flowering the rosette dies, and unfortunately there are unlikely to be any offsets. But you may well have had the plant for 10 years before it flowers.

Any good loam- or peat-based potting mixture is suitable for this plant. It should be repotted annually. The plant may be watered freely during hot sunny weather but should be kept fairly dry at other times.

Left: **Agave parviflora**
This is one of the smaller agaves and makes an attractive addition to any collection. Offsets are usually formed around the base. It is an easy plant to raise from seed.

Above left: **Agave victoria-reginae**
Probably the most beautiful of all the agaves, this slow-growing succulent does not usually form offsets, but is readily raised from seed. The leaves are tipped with sharp spines.

A practical hint
When locating plants, read care tags and position accordingly, as many are suited to shaded positions whereas others must have light.

Aglaonema crispum 'Silver Queen'

- **Light shade**
- **Temp:18-21°C (65-70°F)**
- **Keep moist**

There are numerous aglaonemas that form central clumps that increase in size as plants mature, but the variety *A.* 'Silver Queen' is superior in all respects. Individual spear-shaped leaves are produced at soil level and have a grey-green background colouring liberally spotted with silver.

New plants are made by separating the clumps at any time of year and potting them individually in a peaty mixture in small pots. As plants mature they can be potted on into slightly larger containers, and will in time produce offsets of their own. For the second and subsequent potting operations, use a potting mix that contains some loam, but it should still be very much on the peaty side. Warm, moist and shaded conditions are essential if leaves are to retain their texture and brightness. Watering requires some care; plants must be moist at all times, but not saturated, especially in winter.

Above right, centre: **Aglaonema crispum 'Silver Queen'**
The beautiful variegation of the leaves will be maintained if the plants are kept in light shade.

A practical hint
Hanging plants are fashionable but need careful positioning – never so high that their needs may be neglected. About head level is ideal.

Aglaonema pseudobracteatum

- **Light shade**
- **Temp: 18-21°C (65-70°F)**
- **Keep moist**

A demanding plant, best suited to the experienced grower; the principal difficulty is the high temperature, which must be maintained. A height of 1m (39in) is not unusual in mature specimens. Leaf perimeter is green with a centre of whitish yellow.

New plants are propagated from top sections of stems with three sound leaves attached. Severed ends are allowed to dry for a few hours before being treated with rooting powder; plant in peaty mixture in small pots, and plunge in moist peat in a heated propagating case; to ensure success the temperature should be around 21°C (70°F). When potting cuttings for growing on, put three cuttings in a 13cm (5in) pot, using a potting mixture with 50 percent loam.

These plants are not much troubled by pests, but mealy bugs are sometimes found where the leaf stalks curl round the main stem. In this situation, thorough saturation with liquid insecticide will be needed.

Allamanda cathartica

- **Good light**
- **Temp: 16-21°C (60-70°F)**
- **Keep moist and fed**

The allamanda is better suited to the conservatory or sunroom than indoors. Using a loam-based potting compost this rapid grower will require ample moisture at its roots and frequent feeding while in active growth in spring and summer.

For best effect, train the active growth as it develops to a framework of some kind so that when the golden-yellow trumpet flowers appear they are set off to maximum effect. Although the flowers are sometimes sparse, there will generally be more of them if the plants are fed with a fertilizer recommended for flowering plants – something with a fairly high potash content, rather than nitrogen.

In winter, the amount of water given can be reduced and the plants can be severely pruned back to create a better shape and more manageable size.

Above:
Aglaonema pseudobracteatum
An interesting subject for adding height and colour to collections. Must have warmth to thrive.

Left: **Allamanda cathartica**
In spacious, warm and humid surroundings this tropical vine bears trumpet-shaped flowers in summer. Dwarf forms are available.

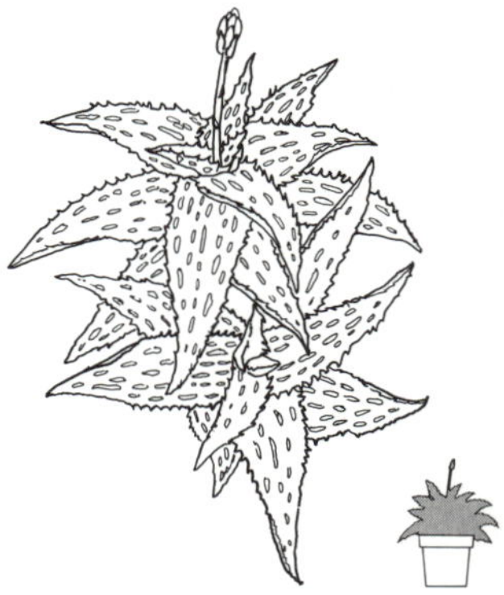

Allium neapolitanum

- **Good light**
- **Temp: 10-16°C (50-60°F)**
- **Water freely while growing**

This member of the onion family can be increased by sowing seed in spring, or by removing offsets from around the parent bulb.

Bulbs are planted in shallow containers using loam-based open mixture, with bulbs almost touching. After planting, bulbs are plunged in ashes or peat in a cold frame or cold greenhouse in cool conditions, or they may be plunged out of doors and removed to greenhouse conditions when growth is evident. If you raise the temperature to a little over 16°C (60°), flowers will be produced at an earlier stage. After flowering the soil should be allowed to dry off; store the bulbs in this condition until the new seasonal cycle begins. At the start of the new season, fresh soil is needed.

Alocasia indica

- **Light shade**
- **Temp: 18-24°C (65-75°F)**
- **Keep moist**

One of the more exotic and temperamental members of the Araceae family. There are numerous cultivars, all with exotic velvety appearance and arrow-shaped leaves.

Their most important needs are for a temperature of around 24°C (75°F) and for a humid atmosphere. The soil in the pot must be kept moist at all times, and it is essential that the surrounding atmosphere is also moist; this will mean placing the plant on a large tray filled with gravel, which should be kept permanently wet. The tray can contain water, but the level should never be up to the surface of the pebbles so that the plant pot is actually standing in water. Plants allowed to stand in water become waterlogged, and will rot and die. Feeding is not important, but it will do no harm if liquid fertilizer is given periodically.

Aloe jacunda

- **Partial shade**
- **Temp: 5-30°C (41-86°F)**
- **Keep slightly moist in winter**

A true dwarf succulent plant, this is one of the most attractive of the aloes. It consists of prettily mottled fleshy leaves, forming a compact rosette 8-9cm (3.2-3.5in) across. Individual leaves are up to 4cm (1.6in) long and 2cm (0.8in) broad at the base. This delightful little aloe branches freely from the base and soon forms an attractive clump. Excess heads can easily be removed, complete with roots, for propagation. Typical small, tubular aloe flowers, rose-pink in colour, are produced on stems up to 30cm (12in) long.

Any good potting mixture is normally well enough drained for this aloe. Grow it indoors by all means, keeping it in a light window, but avoid full sun. It can even be planted out in the garden during spring and summer. It should be watered freely in spring and summer. Indoors in winter it will need more water than in a greenhouse.

Above: **Allium neapolitanum**
Ball-shaped clusters of sweetly scented white flowers adorn this plant during the summer months. These flowering stems can be cut and placed in a vase of water. Cool conditions are recommended.

Above right: **Alocasia indica**
This plant needs high humidity and constant warmth and is better suited to the greenhouse than the home. The veined leaves are its special feature. New plants can be obtained by carefully dividing the rootstock.

Centre right, right: **Aloe jacunda**
This very attractive dwarf succulent soon produces offsets from the base to form a group, and is free-flowering. Its need for partial shade makes it ideal as a room plant, for a not too sunny window.

A practical hint
Plants that are grouped together will often look superior to a collection of pots scattered about the room. A gravel tray is fine for plants.

Aloe variegata

- **Partial shade**
- **Temp: 10-30°C (50-86°F)**
- **Keep dry in winter**

This is certainly one of the best-known succulent plants. It thrives on many windowsills in homes and offices, and its success indicates the chief cultivation tip – it is better as a houseplant than in a greenhouse environment. The surprising thing is how little water the plant seems to need, even indoors. The leaves have a thickened 'V' section and are up to 15cm (6in) long in mature plants, though most specimens are much smaller. They are bright green, marbled with whitish bands. Although so common, this is a delightful plant, enhanced occasionally by the appearance of bright pink, tubular flowers on a stem up to 30cm (12in) long.

Although this aloe seems to thrive on neglect, it is possible to go too far in this respect, witness the miserable, dried-up specimens sometimes seen! Add about one third extra sharp sand or perlite to any good potting mixture, either loam- or peat-based.

Above left: **Aloe variegata**
The very well-known Partridge breast aloe is ideally suited to the living-room as it thrives in shade. Pink flowers are sometimes produced at the end of a long stem. Very little water is needed.

A practical hint
Yellow-bracted aphelandra plants need lots of water (a little less in winter), and must be fed at every watering while active.

Alpinia sanderae

- **Light shade**
- **Temp: 18-24°C (65-75°F)**
- **Avoid overwatering in winter**

One of the many ornamental members of the ginger family, Zingiberaceae, but at present they are generally in short supply. The ginger plant discussed here has highly coloured, upright stems of silver and green foliage, but is made very limited use of as a houseplant.

One of the problems is that it is slow to propagate, as one has to wait for plants to mature and then to divide up the clumps into smaller sections in order to produce additional plants; this is too slow for the commercial grower, who, on account of high energy costs, must have plants that can be put through his greenhouses in the shortest possible time.

To do well indoors, *A. sanderae* will need a minimum temperature of 18°C (65°F). It will also need careful watering and must never remain saturated for long, especially in winter. Feed in frequent weak doses rather than occasional heavy ones, and not in winter.

Above right: **Alpinia sanderae**
Narrow, green-and-white variegated leaves are carried on tall, slender stems. Careful cultivation is necessary to retain colouring and to prevent loss of leaves.

A practical hint
Long-lasting fragrant flowers of the orchid *Angraecum sesquipedale* appear in winter, and the plant needs warm, moist, light conditions to thrive.

Ananas bracteatus striatus

- **Good light**
- **Temp: 13-18°C (55-65°F)**
- **Keep on dry side**

The best of the South American bromeliads, the green form of which, *A. comosus*, is the pineapple of commerce. There is also a white variegated form, known as the ivory pineapple.

In good light the natural cream colouring of the foliage will be a much better colour, but one should avoid very strong sunlight that is magnified by clear glass. Wet root conditions that offer little drying out will also be harmful. Feed occasionally but avoid overdoing it. New plants can be produced by pulling offsets from mature plants and potting them individually in a mixture containing leaf mould and peat. In reasonable conditions plants can be expected to develop small pineapples in about three years; although highly decorative, these tend to be woody and inedible. However, as pineapples are developing, the central part of the plant around the base of the leaves will change to a brilliant reddish pink.

Left: **Ananas bracteatus striatus**
An extremely ornamental member of the bromeliad family that will develop dazzling colour in good light. Be wary of the spined leaf margins. Suitable only when young and small.

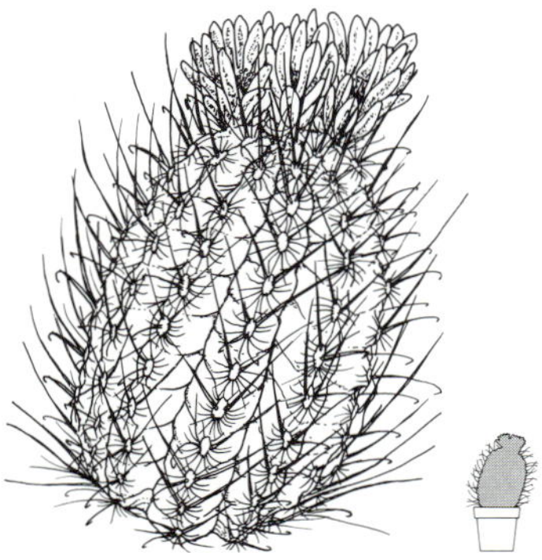

Ancistrocactus scheeri

- **Full sun**
- **Temp: 5-30°C (41-86°F)**
- **Keep dry in winter**

A beautifully spined, very attractive cactus that is well worth the little extra attention needed to cultivate it. The roughly spherical stem, which does not normally form offsets, carries strong yellowish spines, sometimes as long as 4cm (1.6in). A good specimen is around 7cm (2.8in) across. The funnel-shaped flowers, yellowish-green in colour, are about 2.5cm (1in) wide.

Admittedly, this is not one of the easiest of cacti to grow, but it should thrive if its requirements are understood. The main difficulty is that it has large, fleshy roots that have a tendency to disappear at the slightest amount of excess water, and for this reason some specimens are grown grafted. But all should be well if you use a very open potting mixture, made by using equal parts of sharp sand or perlite and a standard loam- or peat-based mix; water only in spring and summer.

Above: **Ancistrocactus scheeri**
A slow-growing cactus with very beautiful spines and flowers. As it has a thick, fleshy root, it is prone to rotting and needs very careful watering. Offsets are not usual.

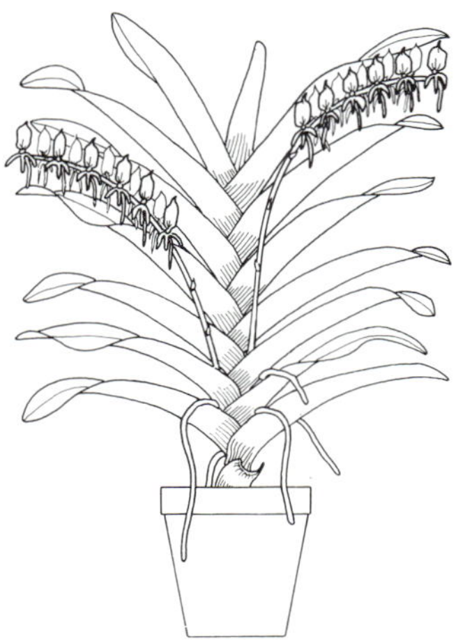

Angraecum eburneum

- **Warm: 18°C (65°F)**
- **Easy to grow and flower**
- **Winter flowering**
- **Evergreen/no rest**

There are over 200 species of angraecums, although very few are seen in cultivation. They come mainly from tropical Africa.

This winter-flowering species resembles *Angraecum sesquipedale* in plant habit but the flower spikes are often longer, producing nine to 12 flowers about 10cm (4in) in diameter. The sepals, petals and spur are green and the lip pure white. Curiously, the flowers appear on the stem as if upside-down.

The plant thrives in generous conditions and should be watered throughout the year. During the summer months regular overhead spraying of the foliage and aerial roots is beneficial. The plant can also be foliar fed in the same way for nine months of the year. Although it likes a position in good light, the leaves are all too easily burnt if it is allowed to stand in bright sunlight for any length of time. A good position for this plant is near to the glass (which should be shaded in summer) suspended in a hanging basket. Not suited to indoor culture.

Right: **Angraecum eburneum**
Two varieties of this warm house species: superbum (top) and grimaldi (below). Long sprays of fragrant flowers are produced during the winter months.

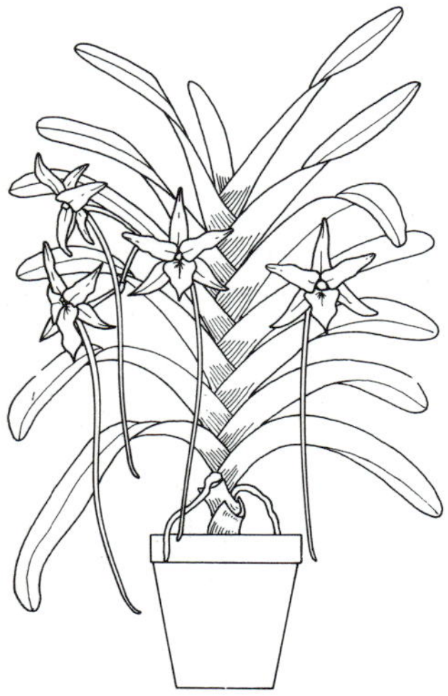

Angraecum sesquipedale

- **Warm: 18°C (65°F)**
- **Easy to grow and flower**
- **Winter flowering**
- **Evergreen/no rest**

This is the best-known of the large angraecums and produces one of the most majestic of all orchid flowers. The plant, which can grow to a height of 90cm (36in), has strap-like, leathery leaves that equal the plant's height in span. The star-shaped flowers, produced two to four on stems that arise from the leaf axils, are 15-18cm (6-7in) across and a beautiful creamy-white in colour. Their most distinctive feature is a greenish spur that may be up to 30cm (12in) in length. The flowers appear in the winter months. They are long lasting on the plant and very fragrant.

Even though this epiphytic genus is restricted to parts of Africa and the island of Madagascar, some 200 species are known.

Angraecums are subjects for the warm house, and being without pseudobulbs require moist conditions and plenty of light. However, some of the smaller-growing plants should be protected from full sun, and for all plants frequent spraying can be a great advantage for healthy growth.

Above: **Angraecum sesquipedale**
A magnificent species for the warm greenhouse, where it requires good light. Large waxy flowers in winter.

Anguloa clowesii

- **Cool: 11°C (52°F)**
- **Easy to grow and flower**
- **Early summer flowering**
- **Deciduous/rest in winter**

This is a small genus of about ten species, which grow naturally as epiphytes and terrestrials. They are high altitude plants from South America.

This large and beautiful species is commonly known as the 'cradle orchid' owing to the ability of the lip, which is loosely hinged, to rock back and forth when tilted. The lip is fully enclosed by the rest of the flower, which gives rise to a further popular name of 'tulip orchid'. The plant will grow well with lycastes but is considerably larger when in leaf.

Plenty of water and feed should be given during the growing season, when the plant is making up its large pseudobulbs. Water should be withheld when the leaves are shed at the end of the growing season. The flowers, 7.5cm (3in) across, appear singly from a stout stem at the same time as the new growth. They are a lovely canary yellow with a strong fragrance.

This lovely orchid originates from Colombia and today nursery-raised plants are usually available. Suitable for cool greenhouse culture.

Right: **Anguloa clowesii**
The large and beautiful cool-growing 'cradle orchid'. The fragrant yellow blooms appear in early summer.

A practical hint
For maximum effect the best location for *Aporocactus flagelliformis* is a hanging container, so that drooping stems and flowers stand out.

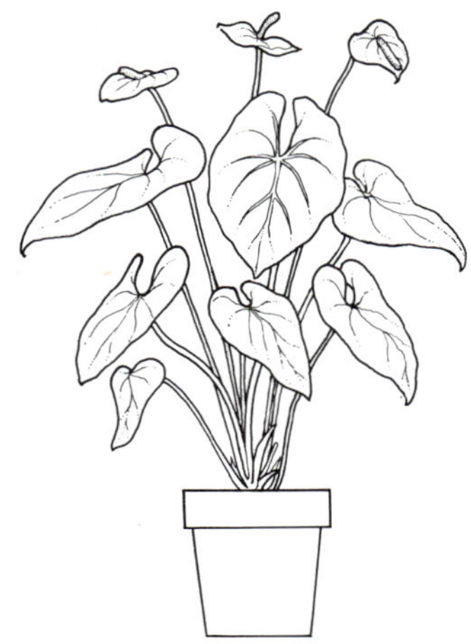

Anthurium andreanum

- **Light shade**
- **Temp: 18-24°C (65-75°F)**
- **Keep moist and fed**

One of the most spectacular of all the flowering plants grown in pots, this needs a temperature in excess of 18°C (65°F) and a high degree of humidity to give of its best. Flowers may be pink, white or red, with the latter being the colour most frequently seen.

As cut flowers *A. andreanum* has no peers. Flowers are borne on long stalks and from the time they are cut they have a full six weeks of life when placed in water, and will last much longer if left on the plant. Obtaining plants may be difficult, but they can be raised from seed and germinated in a temperature of not less than 24°C (75°F). However, it will be several years before the plants produce their exotic flowers. Leaves are large, carried on long petioles, and have an arrow-shaped appearance. Use an open leafy mix when potting on, and keep the plants well watered, misted, and away from direct sunlight.

Left: **Anthurium andreanum**
Warmth and moisture will encourage this plant to produce its stunning flower spathes, mainly in summer.

A practical hint
There are numerous astrophytums that have a stately, symmetrical form that will enhance the appearance of any collection.

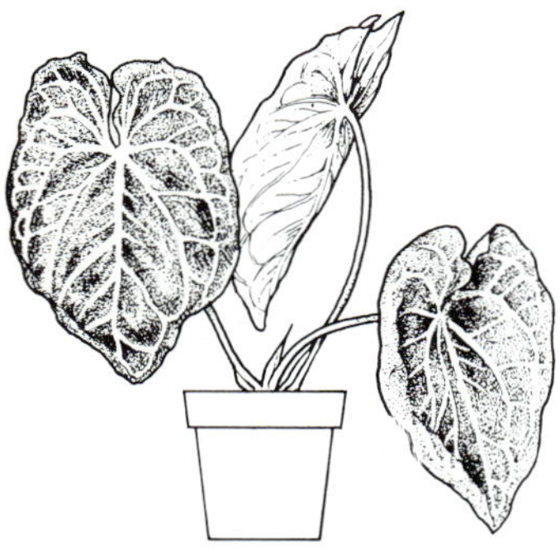

Anthurium crystallinum

- **Light shade**
- **Temp: 18-24°C (65-75°F)**
- **Moist atmosphere**

This plant is among the more temperamental foliage plants. It does produce a flower, but this is in fact a thin rat's tail. However, the rat's tail has the important function of producing seed, from which new plants can be raised relatively easily in a high temperature. The patterned, heart-shaped leaves are very large and spectacular and usually have to be supported if they are to show to their best advantage.

High temperature, lightly shaded location and humid atmosphere are their principal needs. Roots should at no time dry out. Regular feeding will maintain foliage in brighter colour and better condition. Potting mixture containing 50 percent loam should be used and the pot should be provided with drainage material. Although plants must not dry at their roots, it is essential that water should drain away freely.

Pests are not a problem. Avoid handling, or cleaning the leaves with chemical concoctions.

Anthurium scherzerianum

- **Light shade**
- **Temp: 16-21°C (60-70°F)**
- **Keep moist and fed**

This is the baby brother of *A. andreanum,* but is much better suited to average room conditions, in both space requirements and care. Green leaves are produced on short petioles from soil level, and flowers are generally red in colour and produced over a long spring and summer period. The spadix in the centre of the flower has a natural whorl to it that gives rise to one of its common names, 'piggytail plant'.

All anthuriums require an open potting mixture, and one made up of equal parts of peat and well-rotted leaves will be better than an entirely peat mix, or a mix containing loam. Once established, plants need regular feeding to maintain leaf colouring and to encourage production of flowers with stouter stems – weak-stemmed flowers will require support. Like *A. andreanum* this should be kept out of direct sunlight.

Above: **Anthurium crystallinum**
The large, boldly veined leaves of this plant are impressive and best supported. A subject for very warm, humid, lightly shaded conditions.

Above right:
Anthurium scherzerianum
At up to 30cm (12in) tall, this anthurium is well suited to the home. Propagate by dividing clumps.

A practical hint
Be selective when purchasing plants such as azaleas, and ensure that flowers are not too far advanced. A few open flowers and lots of buds is best.

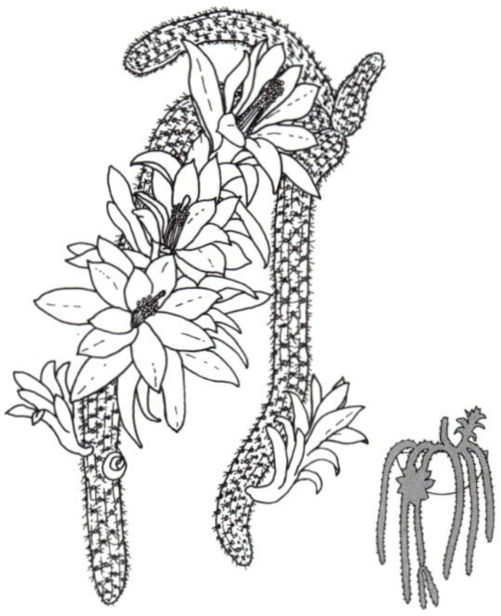

Aphelandra squarrosa 'Louisae'

- **Light shade**
- **Temp: 16-21°C (60-70°F)**
- **Keep moist and fed**

The aphelandra has two fairly obvious common names, 'zebra plant' and 'saffron spike', relating to different parts of the plant – one to the grey-green leaves striped with silver, and the other to the saffron-yellow spike that forms the bract produced in midsummer. It is equally attractive with or without flowers, and reaches a height of about 60cm (2ft) when grown in a 13cm (5in) diameter pot. Larger pots will produce taller plants, usually in their second year.

When in good health all aphelandras will produce a wealth of roots and, consequently, require frequent feeding and potting on as soon as they have filled their existing pots with roots. Peaty mixtures are not much use to this plant; try a proprietary brand potting soil that contains a good proportion of loam. In spring and summer established plants must be fed with every watering.

Aporocactus flagelliformis

- **Diffuse sunlight**
- **Temp: 5-30°C (41-86°F)**
- **Keep moist all year**

A beautiful plant for a hanging basket, this cactus will grow happily in a window. The long slender stems may reach a length of 2m (6.5ft); they are closely ribbed and densely covered with small brown spines. In early spring, the stems are covered with vivid cerise flowers; these are tubular, 5cm (2in) long, and last for several days.

A loam- or peat-based mixture is suitable for this plant. Feed with a liquid tomato fertilizer once every two weeks during the growing period. Repot annually. Never allow the plant to become completely dry, even in winter. In summer, water generously.

When the plant becomes too large, one of the tails may be cut off, dried for two days and potted up. Early summer is the best time for rooting cuttings. Mealy bug can be a serious pest. It is easy to overlook them on a large plant. Treat the plant with a systemic insecticide.

Left:
Aphelandra squarrosa 'Louisae'
A colourful, compact plant. Prune in spring to prevent legginess. Avoid dry soil, which causes leaf drop.

Above and right:
Aporocactus flagelliformis
The popular Rat's-tail cactus, with its long hanging stems and colourful flowers, is a 'must' for a basket.

A practical hint
Azalea indica needs lots of water throughout the year; plunge the pot in water and hold it submerged until all the air bubbles have escaped.

Aporocactus mallisonii

- **Diffuse sunlight**
- **Temp: 5-30°C (41-86°F)**
- **Keep damp all year**

An excellent plant for a hanging basket, this cactus will thrive in a warm living-room but does need plenty of light. The stout stems reach a length of about 1m (39in); they are deeply ribbed and covered in short spines. In early summer, large numbers of brilliant red flowers are carried along the stems.

A good loam- or peat-based mixture is needed. Repot annually. During the summer growing period, water generously and use a liquid tomato fertilizer every two weeks.

A. mallisonii (now known as x *Heliaporus smithii*) is a hybrid and can only be propagated vegetatively. When the plant has outgrown its accommodation, cut off one of the stems. Dry for two days and pot up. Propagation is most successful in early summer. Mealy bug is the chief pest that attacks this cactus. Inspect the stems regularly. Spray with a proprietary insecticide if an infestation is found.

Aralia elegantissima

- **Light shade**
- **Temp: 18-21°C (65-70°F)**
- **Keep moist**

Also known as *Dizygotheca elegantissima*, this is one of the most attractive of the purely foliage plants, having dark green, almost black, colouring to its leaves. Graceful leaves radiate from stiff, upright stems that will attain a height of about 3m (10ft). As the plant ages it loses its delicate foliage and produces leaves that are much larger and coarser in appearance. One can remove the upper section of stem, and new growth will revert to the original delicate appearance.

Warm conditions with no drop in temperature are important; water thoroughly, soaking the soil, and allow it to dry reasonably before repeating. Feed in spring and summer, less in winter.

Mealy bug can be treated with a liquid insecticide; affected areas should be thoroughly saturated with the spray. Root mealy bugs can be seen as a whitish powder around the roots; to clear these, liquid insecticide should be watered in.

Above right:
Aporocactus mallisonii
Another ideal subject for a hanging basket, this cactus has masses of trailing stems and large flowers.

Right: **Aralia elegantissima**
A striking plant with very dark green, almost black, foliage that is delicate on young plants but becomes coarse with age. Needs warmth.

Aralia sieboldii

- **Light shade**
- **Temp: 7-13°C (45-55°F)**
- **Water and feed well**

Also known as *Fatsia japonica*. Besides being an excellent indoor plant it is hardy out of doors, and will develop into a large shrub.

The large fingered leaves have a deceptively tough appearance, as this plant can very easily be damaged by chemicals for the cleaning of foliage plants. They will also be scorched by the sun if placed too close to clear glass. In the first two or three years plants will require annual potting on until they are in 20 or 25cm (8 or 10in) pots. It then becomes impractical in the average home to advance them to larger containers, and it is important to ensure that they are regularly and adequately fed. New plants can be raised from seed sown in peaty mixture in a warm propagator in the spring.

Red spider can be troublesome in hot, dry conditions; a sign of their presence is pale brown patches on leaves. Use insecticide to treat reverse side of leaves thoroughly.

Aralia veitchii

- **Light shade**
- **Temp: 16-21°C (60-70°F)**
- **Keep moist and fed**

Not unlike *A. elegantissima* in appearance, *A. veitchii* is, however, much easier to cultivate indoors. The leaves are almost black in colour, and radiate from a stout central stem that will in time achieve a height of 1.2-1.8m (4-6ft), depending on growing conditions.

A combination of cold and wet conditions can cause death, so it is of great importance to water with care during the winter months of the year. Established plants will benefit from regular feeding, but this should be based on the practice of 'little and often' rather than giving heavy applications occasionally. Cold, draughty locations will also be harmful, and will result in the plant shedding leaves.

New plants can be raised from seed sown in spring and kept in a heated propagator, but this is not really practicable for the average indoor gardener. It is much better to buy new young plants from commercial growers.

Above: **Aralia sieboldii variegata**
A truly splendid plant with broad, palmate leaves radiating from a stout central stem. Splendidly coloured in pale green and cream.

Left: **Aralia veitchii**
Place several of these single-stemmed plants together in one pot to give an attractive display. Repot only once every two years in spring.

A practical hint
Put azaleas out of doors in summer in a lightly shaded place, but ensure that watering is not neglected. Clean and bring in before frosts occur.

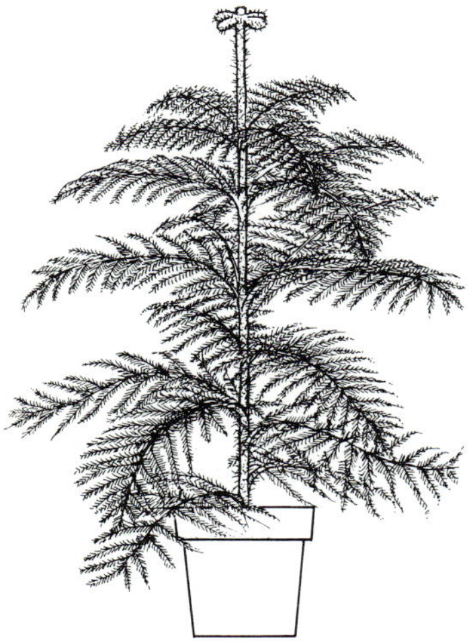

Araucaria excelsa

- **Light shade**
- **Temp: 13-18°C (55-65°F)**
- **Provide ample space**

A majestic tropical tree that originates from New Zealand. It is a marvellous foliage plant when carefully treated and not subjected to very high temperatures, which can be debilitating. Hot conditions cause normally turgid foliage to droop and become very thin. These elegant plants are best suited to important and spacious locations that will allow full development.

During early development plants should be allowed to fill their pots with roots before being potted on into slightly larger containers, using a loam-based potting mixture. When going into their final pots of 20-25cm (8-10in) diameter, the amount of loam should be increased to encourage slower but firmer growth. New plants can be raised from seed, but it is better to purchase small plants and grow them on.

Few pests trouble these pines, but excessive watering, especially in poor light, will cause browning and eventual loss of needles.

Above right: **Araucaria excelsa**
This elegant, slow-growing tree produces bright green growth each spring which gradually darkens through the year. Needs space.

Ardisia crispa/ crenata

- **Light shade**
- **Temp: 16-21°C (60-70°F)**
- **Keep moist and fed**

Although flowers are produced, the main attractions of this plant are the glossy green crenellated leaves and the long-lasting berries. It grows very slowly, and plants take several years to attain the maximum height of around 90cm (3ft). A stiff, upright central stem carries the woody branches, which will always be neat.

Offer a lightly shaded location for best results, and at no time be tempted to water excessively. Slow-growing plants of this kind are best kept on the dry side, particularly in winter. It is also important not to be too heavy-handed when feeding, and it should be discontinued altogether in winter. Plants with a slow growth rate are better grown in pots that are on the small side, and soil with a good percentage of loam must be used, as plants will quickly deteriorate in peat mixtures. Cuttings of firm young shoots can be taken in spring and rooted in peat at a temperature of not less than 21°C (70°F) to produce new plants.

Above and left:
Ardisia crispa/crenata
Dark green foliage, pink or white flowers and long-lasting red berries make this an attractive houseplant.

A practical hint
When removing dead flowers from azalea plants it is important not to damage the fresh green shoots that are under the flowers.

Ariocarpus fissuratus var. lloydii

- **Full sun**
- **Temp: 5-30°C (41-86°F)**
- **Always water carefully**

Ariocarpuses are among the rarest and most interesting of the cacti but are suitable only for greenhouse cultivation. These plants grow in desert conditions in the blazing sun. For successful cultivation they need the maximum sunlight, a very open mixture (half loam-based medium, half sharp sand or perlite) and careful watering. Water on sunny days in summer, and keep dry in winter.

A. fissuratus bears a close resemblance to a chunk of rock. It has a thickened taproot crowned by large flattened tubercles. The tubercles are greyish in colour with creamy wool among the new growth. The large satiny pink flowers appear from the centre of the plant. They open in late autumn or early winter. A mature specimen is 15cm (6in) across, and may have taken 20 years to reach that size. Mealy bug may attack the new, tender growth. Inspect the woolly centre of the plant for signs of these pests. If found, treat with a suitable insecticide.

Right: **Ariocarpus fissuratus**
Looking more like a chunk of stone than a cactus, this plant can in fact produce a most beautiful flower. It is very slow-growing.

A practical hint
For many indoor plants light is the most important need, and this is especially important for crotons and plants with variegated foliage.

Arundinaria

- **Good light**
- **Temp: 10-18°C (50-65°F)**
- **Keep moist and fed**

There are numerous varieties, some very vigorous, such as *A. gigantea* (common name, cane reed), others, such as *A. vagans*, neat and compact. These are ideal for cooler locations where there is reasonable light. In time the plants will form into bold groups of congested stems that completely fill the pots in which they are growing.

As plants increase in size they will generally require a greater amount of water, and feeding will have to be stepped up. The time will also come when plants have to be put into larger containers, and one should use a mixture containing a good amount of loam. As an alternative to potting on the complete clump one can use a fork and spade to chop the clump up into smaller sections, which in turn can be potted up as individual plants. At all stages of growth plants will need ample watering and feeding, with winter being the only time when one should ease up on both.

Above left: **Arundinaria**
Bamboo plants are suitable for growing indoors where adequate space, water and feed can be supplied. Keep cool and light.

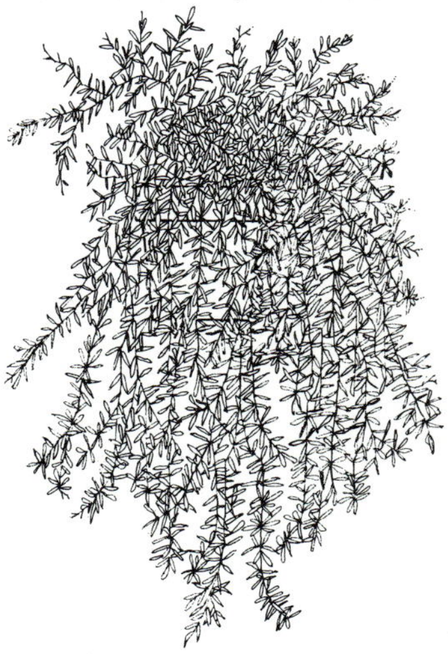

Asparagus meyerii

- **Good light, no sun**
- **Temp: 13-18°C (55-65°F)**
- **Keep moist, less in winter**

Although frequently referred to as ferns, these belong to the lily family. Not a common houseplant, *A. meyerii* is among the most elegant of indoor plants. As the common name suggests, the foliage forms pale green cylindrical plumes on stiff stems that may attain a length of 60cm (2ft). Growth forms in stout clumps and springs from soil level.

It is important when potting that the plants should be placed centrally in the new container. A loam-based potting mixture should be used to keep plants in good fettle. Once established in their pots a regular feeding schedule must be followed, especially during the spring and summer months. Plants fare better if rain water is used in preference to tap water. And when watering the soil do it thoroughly, with surplus water being clearly seen to drain through the holes in the bottom of the pot. It is then important to allow a reasonable drying-out period before further water is given. Less water is required in winter.

Asparagus sprengeri

- **Good light, no sun**
- **Temp: 13-18°C (55-65°F)**
- **Water and feed well**

Though the common name suggests a fern, this is a member of the lily family. One of the most vigorous and useful of all the many fine foliage plants, it is especially effective when grown in a hanging basket.

New plants can be raised from seed sown in spring, or one can divide mature plants at almost any time of year. Before division, ensure that the soil is thoroughly wetted. As with potting on, divided pieces should be planted in pots that give the roots space, and the potting mixture must contain a reasonable amount of loam. In order to keep the lush green colouring it is important that well-rooted plants should be fed regularly. Feeding with weak liquid fertilizer at every watering is often more satisfactory than giving plants occasional heavy doses. Although plants will appreciate good light it is important to protect them from direct sun. Also, in hot, dry conditions it will help if foliage is periodically sprayed over with water.

Above: **Asparagus meyerii**
A distinctive plant, producing long, cylindrical pale green growths. Growth emanates from soil level in the centre of the pot and sprays out in all directions.

Right: **Asparagus sprengeri**
The feathery foliage of this adaptable plant is a refreshing sight indoors and particularly effective as a foil for flowering plants. Avoid completely dry soil and spray regularly.

A practical hint
Stuffy and airless conditions suit few plants, so open windows on warmer days to offer a change of air, but avoid cold draughts.

Aspidistra elatior

- **Light shade**
- **Temp: 13-18°C (55-65°F)**
- **Keep moist**

Popular since Victorian times, when it acquired its common name of 'cast iron plant' on account of its ability to withstand trying conditions. The aspidistra has been around for a very long time and there are plants alive today with a known history that goes back for over a century. A tough plant, but – like almost all such plants – the aspidistra will be much better if reasonably agreeable conditions are provided, rather than a very spartan environment that will result in the plant surviving and little else.

Reasonable light, evenly moist conditions that avoid extremes, with occasional feeding once established, will usually produce plants that are fresh and lush and much more attractive. When potting on, use a properly prepared mixture of soil that contains a good percentage of loam. Any good fertilizer will suit well-rooted plants.

The apparently tough leaves are very sensitive to the use of cleaning chemicals, and to household cleaning chemicals in general.

Left: **Aspidistra elatior**
Famed for its ability to withstand harsh conditions, the aspidistra will grow much better if watered and fed regularly. Repot only when necessary to avoid disturbing roots.

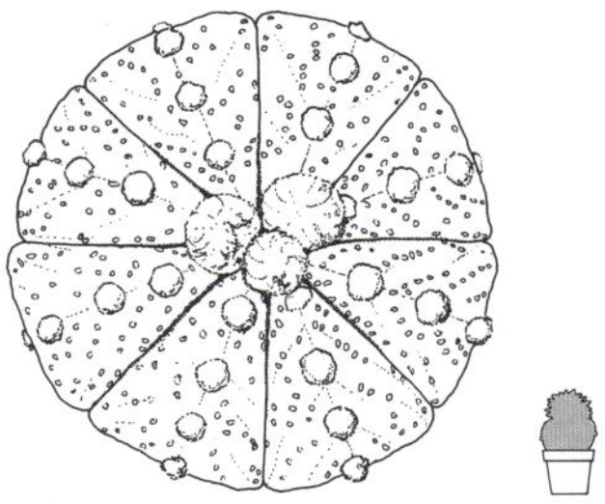

Asplenium nidus avis

- **Light shade**
- **Temp: 18-24°C (65-75°F)**
- **Moist roots and surroundings**

As small plants these are not very exciting, but once they have been advanced to pot sizes of around 18cm (7in) they have few equals. But the growing of these plants to perfection is one of the more difficult exercises in horticulture. Surrounding objects touching tender leaves will almost certainly cause irreparable damage, as will spraying foliage with unsuitable chemicals, or the presence of slugs.

Leaves can be kept in good order if a temperature of around 21°C (70°F) is maintained and plants enjoy good light but not direct sun. Open, peaty mixture is needed when potting, and water applied to the top of the soil should immediately flow through. Frequent feeding of established plants with weak fertilizer is preferred to infrequent heavier doses. Keep soil moist.

Scale insects can be seen as dark brown or flesh-coloured spots adhering to the area around the midrib of the leaf. These can be sponged off with malathion.

Right: **Asplenium nidus avis**
Smooth, pale green leaves radiate from the centre in an attractive arrangement. This plant needs moist conditions to thrive.

Astrophytum asterias

- **Full sun**
- **Temp: 5-30°C (41-86°F)**
- **Do not overwater**

Astrophytum asterias looks like a grey-green sea urchin; it could never be confused with any other cactus. Eventually it forms a flattened hemisphere about 10cm (4in) across. The stem is made up of eight spineless ribs, and the skin is covered with white spots. These vary from plant to plant: some specimens are beautifully covered in white polka dots, whereas others may have very few markings. The flowers open continuously through the summer; they are pale shiny yellow with a red throat, and sweetly scented. Seedlings about 2.5cm (1in) across will flower.

Never overwater and keep the soil completely dry during winter. A very open soil, half loam- or peat-based mixture and half sharp sand or perlite, is suitable. To ensure continuous flowering, keep the plant in the sunniest part of the greenhouse and feed every two weeks with a tomato fertilizer when the buds form.

Above: **Astrophytum asterias**
A rather unusual cactus, entirely without spines, but producing most attractive yellow flowers. Well worth the extra care it needs.

Astrophytum myriostigma

- **Full sun**
- **Temp: 5-30°C (41-86°F)**
- **Dry winter rest**

Astrophytum myriostigma is a cylindrical plant eventually reaching a diameter of 20cm (8in). The dark green skin is completely covered with silvery scales. The number of ribs varies from four to eight. They are spineless, but the prominent areoles give the plant the appearance of having been buttoned into its skin. The flowers appear on the top of the plant continuously throughout the summer. They are yellow with a reddish throat and a sweet scent.

This is the easiest of the astrophytums to grow. A loam-based or peat-based mixture plus one third extra grit is suitable. Water freely throughout the summer, giving a liquid tomato fertilizer every two weeks, but keep dry in winter. This cactus is a native of the Mexican deserts and in cultivation needs the maximum light available. Mealy bug and root mealy bug can be a nuisance. Small white mealy bugs look very much like white scales.

Above: **Astrophytum myriostigma**
A simple astrophytum to cultivate and also easy to handle, being quite spineless. The silvery hairy scales give it a rock-like appearance.

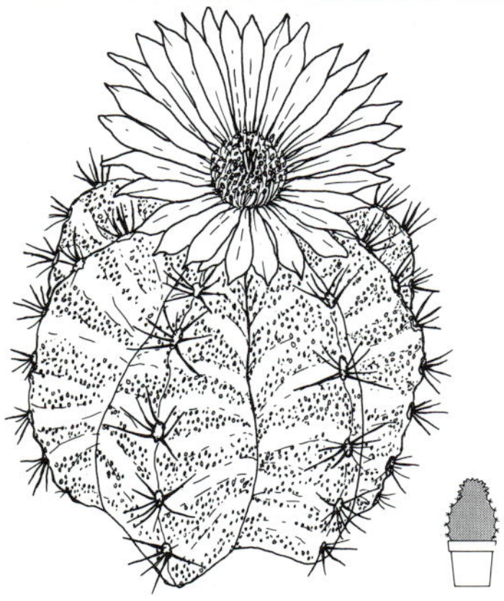

Astrophytum ornatum

- **Full sun**
- **Temp: 5-30°C (41-86°F)**
- **Water with care**

Astrophytum ornatum does not bloom until it is about 15cm (6in) high, and it will probably take about 10 years to reach flowering size. But even without flowers, this is an attractive cactus. The stem is divided by eight ribs, which carry stout amber-coloured spines. The dark green skin has bands of silvery scales running across it. The pale yellow flowers are carried on top of the plant and are sweetly scented.

To keep the vivid colouring of this cactus, it needs sun. A useful mix is two parts loam- or peat-based medium plus one part sharp sand or perlite. Water generously throughout the summer, allowing to dry out before watering again. When the buds form give a dose of tomato fertilizer every two weeks. Keep the soil dry throughout the winter. Repot the plant annually, and inspect the roots for any grey ashy deposits, a sign that root mealy bug is present; if it is, water with an insecticide.

Aucuba japonica variegata

- **Good light**
- **Temp: 7-13°C (45-55°F)**
- **Avoid summer drying out**

An old-established plant that will tolerate varied conditions, but prefers to grow in cool conditions. This is one of the few plants that do well in a draughty hallway. And it has the bonus of fairly colourful foliage.

New plants are little trouble to propagate, and one should remove the top section of the stem with about four sound leaves attached, and insert in a peaty mixture. Putting the pot with its cutting in a heated propagator will stimulate rooting, as will the use of rooting powder or liquid. Once rooted, transfer the young plant to a slightly larger pot, using a loam-based potting soil.

While plants are in active growth they should be watered freely and fed regularly; during the winter months water sparingly and discontinue feeding. Older plants that are losing their appearance can be pruned to shape in spring. During the summer, aucubas make excellent plants for the patio.

Above: **Astrophytum ornatum**
A spiny astrophytum, which needs to be fairly large before flowering but is nevertheless an interesting addition to any collection. Needs sunlight.

Above right:
Aucuba japonica variegata
The spotted laurel has pleasingly variegated foliage and is a very tough plant for cooler conditions.

A practical hint
Rather than being incidental to the room, plants can become a feature if grouped and located with care. Use a mix of flowers and foliage.

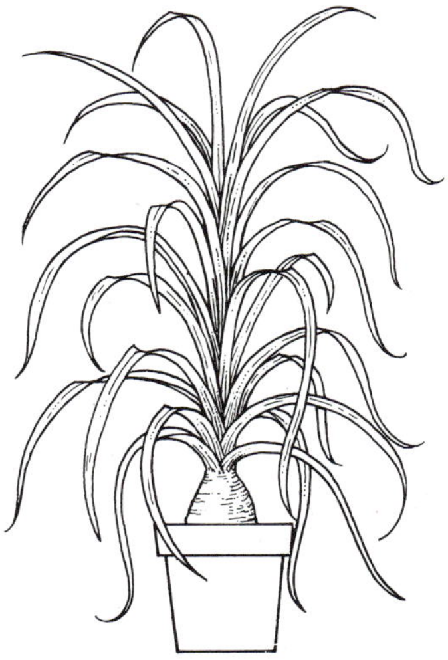

Azalea indica

- **Good light**
- **Temp: 10-16°C (50-60°F)**
- **Keep very moist**

For a colourful display there is little that can match these plants when they are well grown. With its evergreen foliage and flowers in many colours, the azalea will be more attractive and last very much longer if given cool and light conditions indoors – hot conditions definitely shorten the life of the flowers. The most sensible way of watering is to grasp the pot in both hands and plunge it in a bucket of water and leave it submerged until every vestige of air has escaped from the soil. Depending on conditions, it may be necessary to repeat this exercise two or three times weekly during the spring and summer months, with only slightly less water being given in winter.

Remove dead flowers as they occur and place plants out in the garden for the summer, being sure to bring them in before frosts occur. Use a mix of peat and well-rotted leaves when potting on.

Beaucarnea recurvata

- **Light shade**
- **Temp: 10-21°C (50-70°F)**
- **Water well in summer**

A peculiar plant that people either love or hate. Leaves are narrow, green and recurving. Small plants produce neat, firm bulbs at the base of their stems, the bulbs changing into more grotesque shapes as the plant ages. Because of its odd spreading habit of growth it is used more as an individual plant than as one of a group of plants.

New plants can be raised from seed sown in peat in warm conditions at almost any time of the year. Pot the resultant seedlings into small pots of peat initially, and into loam-based compost when they are of sufficient size. As an alternative to seed, new plants can be grown from the small bulbils that develop around the base of the parent.

The plant puts up with much ill-treatment provided the soil in its pot is not allowed to remain permanently saturated. Once established, plants respond to regular feeding while in active growth; none in winter.

Above and far left:
Azalea indica
Here is a plant that can brighten any autumn day. A compact shrub, it can be in flower for many weeks.

Left: **Beaucarnea recurvata**
An unusual species best displayed as an individual plant. It is tolerant of a wide range of conditions and is easily propagated.

Begonia boweri

- **Light shade**
- **Temp: 13-18°C (55-65°F)**
- **Keep moist**

There are a number of evergreen, fibrous-rooted begonias worth finding space for in the home, and this is one of the best of the more compact types. Flowers are white to pale pink in colour and though small in size, plentiful in number. The principal attraction, however, is the foliage, which is a mottled pale green and almost black in colour.

Growth is low and spreading, and the rhizomatous stem becomes gnarled in time, which tends to make plants less attractive as they shed their lower leaves. Rather than continue with an older and less attractive plant it is better to start fresh plants from sections of stem with a few leaves attached, or from individual leaves. Place leaves in shallow pans of fresh, moist peat at a temperature of not less than 18°C (65°F), and preferably in a closed propagator. Use peaty soil when potting on, and the plants will need moderate feeding and watering.

Begonia 'Cleopatra'

- **Light shade**
- **Temp: 16-21°C (60-70°F)**
- **Keep moist, but less in winter**

This is one of the loveliest of all the fibrous-rooted begonias, with subtle shades of green, gold and brown in its colouring. Leaf colouring will vary depending on the amount of light that the plant is given; in full sun the colouring tends to be bleached out of the plant, and in dark conditions the colouring loses much of its attractive sparkle. So this plant needs to be in a position offering good light, but not direct sunlight. Also, in poor light the leaf stalks tend to become elongated and the plant loses much of its attractive compactness. Small pink flowers are produced in spring and these can be quite attractive, but the plant is principally grown for its decorative foliage.

New plants are produced by removing firm leaves and reducing the length of the leaf stalk to about 2.5cm (1in) before inserting the stalk to its full depth in fresh peat that has been moistened but not totally saturated. Feed the plant occasionally, but not in winter.

Begonia 'Fireglow'

- **Good light**
- **Temp: 13-18°C (55-65°F)**
- **Keep moist and fed**

Developed on the European Continent, this plant has provided something of a revolution with the improvement of growing techniques and the appearance of more varied flower colouring on the scene. In the original version, there were only single red flowers but now there are single and double flowers in a wide variety of attractive shades.

In good light plants flower for many months through spring and summer, but a constant guard must be kept against mildew, which manifests itself as a white powdery patch on leaves – treat with a suitable fungicide. To combat mildew further, offer light and fresh air as opposed to stuffy and hot conditions. Dead flowers resting on lower leaves will also cause rotting of foliage.

Use peaty soil when potting and keep moist and feed moderately. Cut back in autumn after flowering and keep on the dry side over winter.

Above: **Begonia boweri**
This delightful plant has attractive mottled foliage and delicate flowers in early spring. It will thrive in moist surroundings.

Above right: **Begonia 'Cleopatra'**
The beautifully marked foliage makes this a useful addition to the houseplant scene. Avoid direct sunlight; it will bleach the leaves.

Above far right:
Begonia 'Fireglow'
This begonia needs more light than those grown for their foliage. Stunning, long-lasting flowers.

A practical hint
An even temperature will suit most plants better than fluctuating temperatures; a range of 16-21°C (60-70°F) will suit most plants.

Begonia maculata

- **Light shade**
- **Temp: 16-21°C (60-70°F)**
- **Keep moist and fed**

These are rewarding plants that will grow to 90cm (3ft) in height if given reasonable care. Leaves are an overall silver in colour with prominent and attractive spotting, and are carried on stout stems.

Plants may be propagated from sections of stem with one or more leaves attached; these should be inserted in clean, moist peat, and placed in a heated propagator. After they have rooted, put three young plants into a 13cm (5in) diameter pot, using a mixture containing a proportion of loam. When young plants are seen to be getting under way, remove the growing points; this will produce a much fuller and more attractive plant.

When watering it is advisable to water the soil well and then allow it to dry appreciably before repeating; less water is needed in winter. Feed this species in spring and summer.

Left: **Begonia maculata**
Elegant, spotted silver foliage and graceful clusters of flowers during the summer months make this a highly recommended plant.

A practical hint
Flamboyant bougainvilleas need light and cool conditions; in winter the soil should be quite dry, and the plants will shed all their foliage.

Begonia masoniana

- **Light shade**
- **Temp: 16-21°C (60-70°F)**
- **Keep dry in winter**

This fine plant grows to splendid size if given reasonable care. The rough-surfaced leaves are a brownish green in colour and have a very distinctive cross that covers the greater part of the centre of the leaf and radiates from the area where the leaf stalk is joined. This marking resembles the German Iron Cross.

During the spring and summer months it will be found that plants grow at reasonable pace if given a warm room, moist root conditions, and weak liquid fertilizer with each watering. Plants that have filled their existing pots with roots can be potted on at any time during the summer, using a loam-based potting mixture and shallow pots. Over the winter months loss of some lower leaves will be almost inevitable, but provided the soil is kept on the dry side during this time the plant will remain in better condition and will grow away with fresh leaves in the spring.

Above right: **Begonia masoniana**
Distinctive brown markings in the centre of the leaf give this plant the apt common name of 'iron cross begonia'. Plants develop into a neat, rounded shape as they age.

Left: **Begonia 'Orange Rubra'**
This is one of many tall fibrous-rooted begonias available. It grows to a height of 90-120cm (3-4ft) and is festooned with drooping flower clusters in the summer.

A practical hint
For the orchid beginner, *Bifrenaria harrisoniae* produces large creamy white flowers but requires lots of light. Complete winter rest is essential.

Begonia coccinea 'Orange Rubra'

- **Light shade**
- **Temp: 16-21°C (60-70°F)**
- **Keep moist and fed**

With glossy green leaves and lovely orange-coloured flowers this is one of the taller growing fibrous-rooted begonias (sometimes referred to as cane-type begonias). *Begonia* 'Orange Rubra' is only one example of the many cane-type begonias to be seen in florists' and nurseries, and will offer a splendid show when in flower.

As the plants age they will have a natural tendency to shed their lower leaves, which will result in less attractive, bare stems, and this is one very good reason for raising fresh plants from easily rooted cuttings at regular intervals. Cuttings with three or four firm leaves can be taken at almost any time if a heated propagating case is available. Use rooting powder on the severed end of the cutting before inserting it in peat with a little sand added. When potting cuttings on it is advisable to put several cuttings in a pot so that a fuller and more attractive display is produced. Keep the soil moist, but not sodden.

A practical hint
Shrimp plants (*Beloperone*) need lots of feeding, and potting on into loam-based soil as soon as required, to retain green colouring of foliage.

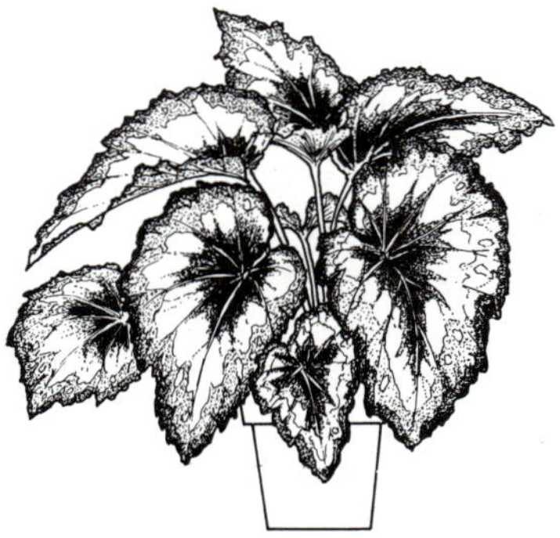

Begonia rex

- **Light shade**
- **Temp: 16-21°C (60-70°F)**
- **Keep on the dry side in winter**

These rank among the finest foliage plants, with all shades of colouring and intricate leaf patterns. Those with smaller leaves are generally easier to care for indoors.

To propagate, firm, mature leaves are removed from the plant and most of the leaf stalk is removed before a series of cuts are made through the thick veins on the underside of the leaf. The leaf is then placed underside down on moist peat (in either boxes or shallow pans) and a few pebbles are placed on top of the leaf, to keep it in contact with the moist peat. Temperatures in the region of 21°C (70°F) are required, and a propagating case. Alternatively, the leaf can be cut into squares of about 5cm (2in), and the pieces placed on moist peat.

When purchased these plants are often in pots that are much too small; repot the plant into a larger container without delay, using peaty compost.

Begonia semperflorens

- **Good light**
- **Temp: 10-16°C (50-60°F)**
- **Keep moist and fed**

Often much in evidence as a summer bedding plant, this species is also excellent for decorating windowsills indoors when grown in a pot. In fact, an interesting use for *B. semperflorens* is to grow them out of doors as bedding plants during the summer months and to dig a few up and pot them before frosts occur. The foliage can be severely cut back, and in a surprisingly short time fresh growth will develop and eventually fresh flowers will appear and last for several weeks.

Many have bronze-coloured foliage that greatly enhances the plants. All must have ample light, especially during the darker months of the year. The temperature can be quite low, providing the soil is not allowed to become excessively wet. Remember to give a weak liquid feed at every watering. For new plants, sow seed in the spring.

Above: **Begonia rex**
Wealth of colour in the foliage and intricate leaf patterns place these plants among the elite of houseplants. Leaves are borne on rhizomatous stems.

Left: **Begonia semperflorens**
This is justifiably one of the most popular begonias – it is very easy to keep and in ideal conditions can be kept constantly in bloom. Flowers may be white, pink or red.

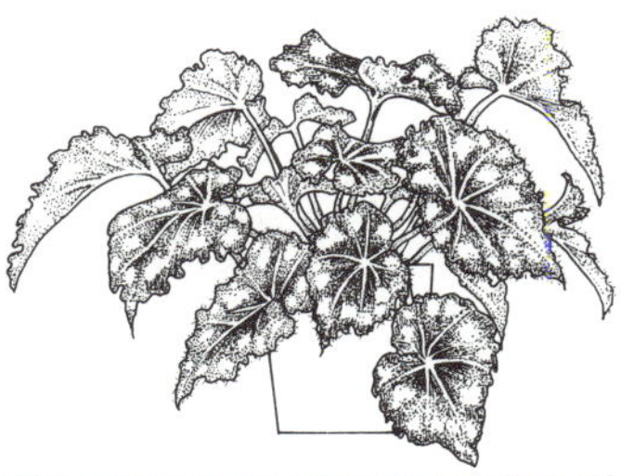

Begonia 'Tiger'

- **Good light**
- **Temp: 13-18°C (55-65°F)**
- **Keep moist**

One of the more recent begonia introductions, this plant has an attractive greenish brown base to the leaf colouring, with very prominent gold spots. The plant is fibrous-rooted, and of neat and compact habit. The neat mound of foliage will always be better set off if the plant is grown in a shallow pan rather than in a container of full depth.

If purchased plants are growing in small pots that appear too small for their growth, knock the plant gently from its pot so that the root system may be checked. If, as is often the case, there is an abundance of roots, it is advisable to pot the plant on into a slightly larger container, using a potting mixture that contains one third loam, two thirds peat. Feed established plants regularly, but not in winter. Avoid growing this plant in a dark location.

Above: **Begonia 'Tiger'**
A new introduction prized for its beautifully marked foliage. Grow in bright light but avoid strong sun.

Beloperone guttata

- **Light shade**
- **Temp: 16-21°C (60-70°F)**
- **Keep moist and fed**

The common name of 'shrimp plant' derives from the shrimp-like bracts that are freely produced on vigorous plants. On the more common 'shrimp plant' bracts are a dullish red in colour, but there is also *B. g. lutea,* which has interesting greenish yellow bracts.

Purchased plants should have their roots inspected immediately, and if a mass of roots is in evidence the plants must be potted without delay into a loam-based mixture. Failure to do so will mean leaf discolouration and a general decline of the plant. Regular feeding is also of the utmost importance, and avoid dank, airless conditions. Growing tips of young plants should be removed to encourage a more bushy appearance. And if one has the courage to do so it will strengthen young plants if all the early bracts that develop are removed.

Left: **Beloperone g. lutea**
A yellow version of this familiar houseplant. The showy bracts are produced for several months.

Bifrenaria harrisoniae

- **Cool: 11°C (52°F)**
- **Easy to grow, shy to flower**
- **Early summer flowering**
- **Evergreen/dry rest**

This is the most familiar species of the *Bifrenaria* genus. It produces creamy-white flowers, one or two to a stem, with thick waxy sepals and petals and a lip covered with short, reddish-purple hairs. Each flower can be up to 7.5cm (3in) in diameter.

It belongs to a small genus of about a dozen species, coming mainly from Brazil. They are certainly among the easiest of plants to grow, and are often offered in collections for beginners.

Although they are usually grown in the intermediate house, with plenty of light, they will also do well in the cool house with a winter minimum of 11°C (52°F). Bifrenarias are epiphytic and will succeed if grown in a pot on the staging, or in wire or wooden baskets suspended from the roof; in either position they should be kept drier at the root when not in active growth. An open compost with good drainage is important.

Allow the plant a complete rest during the winter, giving no water until the new growth is seen to appear during the very early spring. Propagation is a slow process.

Above: **Bifrenaria harrisoniae**
An easily grown species for the cool house. It requires good light and flowers during the summer.

Billbergia nutans

- **Good light**
- **Temp: 13-18°C (55-65°F)**
- **Keep on the dry side**

Two of the most popular billbergias are *B. nutans* with narrow leaves and *B. × windii* with slightly broader leaves and flower bracts. In other respects there is not much to choose between them.

One of the bromeliad family, the billbergia is a very tolerant houseplant that will thrive more on neglect than on constant, fussing care. If placed in a hanging container of some kind the pendulous bracts will be shown off to much better effect when they appear. The bracts are a galaxy of colour including a most unusual shade of green. Individual bracts last for only a week or so, but these are produced in some quantity and at almost any time of the year. Unlike most other bromeliads, *B. nutans* and *B. × windii* will do well in a loam-based potting mix. For propagation, simply divide the old clumps.

Above: **Billbergia nutans**
This is an easy-care member of the bromeliad family; it will thrive in a normal brightly lit room.

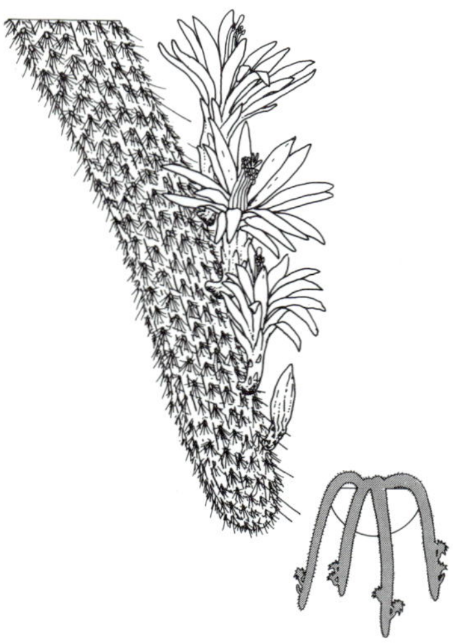

Borzicactus aureispinus

- **Full sun**
- **Temp: 5-30°C (41-86°F)**
- **Keep dry in winter**

The long elegant stems of this unusual cactus make it a fascinating addition to any collection. *Borzicactus* was previously called *Hildewintera aureispina* and *Winterocereus aureispinus*, being a victim to the name changes that take place all too frequently among cacti (and other plants!). With stems up to 50cm (20in) long and 4-5cm (1.6-2.0in) wide, it is somewhat of a challenge to manage. Branches come freely from the base, so that a cluster of stems is eventually formed. Either tie them to a stout cane pushed into the pot or use a half-pot, letting the stems trail over the edge and along the greenhouse staging or a shelf. The stems glisten with bright golden spines, and beautiful salmon-pink flowers can be expected on older specimens.

Grow borzicactus in a good standard loam- or peat-based potting mixture, to which has been added a third sharp sand or perlite.

Above: **Borzicactus aureispinus**
This somewhat unusual cactus needs careful positioning to allow for the beautiful long stems with their golden spines. Pink flowers a bonus.

Bougainvillea

- **Sunny location**
- **Temp: 13-18°C (55-65°F)**
- **Keep dry in winter**

Few flowering plants are capable of giving a display that equals that of the paper-thin bracts of the bougainvillea, particularly when seen in its natural tropical habitat.

In pots they can be more difficult to manage if the owner is someone who is forever watering. These plants should be well watered and allowed to dry reasonably before repeating, and when the foliage turns colour and drops in the autumn it is a sign that water should be withheld until the following early spring when new growth appears and watering can begin again. Pruning – it tolerates quite severe cutting back – can be done in the autumn. Repotting can be undertaken in spring, and is best done by removing some of the old soil and potting the plant into the same container with a fresh loam-based mixture. During the summer months fresh air and full sunlight are essential.

Right: **Bougainvillea**
Ideal for a sunny window or a conservatory, bougainvillea will reward a careful owner with brilliant colour all summer long.

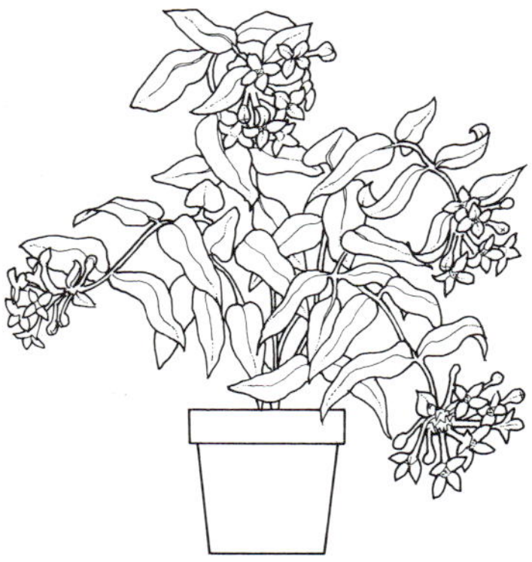

Bouvardia domestica

- Light shade
- Temp: 13-18°C (55-65°F)
- Keep moist and fed

These compact, shrubby plants produce flowers of many colours on the end of slightly drooping stems. They are ideal for a window location that offers good light and a modicum of fresh air, but not necessarily cold conditions. An added bonus with the bouvardia is that it is autumn flowering, so providing a display when there are fewer flowering pot plants around.

During the summer months established plants will be better for being placed out of doors in a sheltered position – in colder areas they will need the protection of an unheated greenhouse.

Plants should be watered freely and fed regularly during the summer months, less water and no feeding being required during winter. Plants are best potted in the spring, and a loam-based mixture will suit them better than an all-peat preparation. Spring is also the time to take cuttings or divide roots of established plants.

Left: **Bouvardia domestica**
This autumn-flowering, evergreen shrub grows to a height of about 60cm (2ft). Pruning will improve shape and stimulate flowering.

Brassavola digbyana

- Intermediate: 13°C (55°F)
- Challenge to grow and flower
- Summer flowering
- Evergreen/dry rest

This is the largest of the genus which, though still horticulturally known as *Brassavola,* is botanically more correctly *Rhyncholaelia digbyana.* In commercial catalogues it can be found under either name.

The lemon-scented flower is incredibly beautiful and contains a deep fringe to the lip, which is a rare occurrence in orchids. The reason for this deeply fimbriated lip is not fully understood, although it is thought to guide or assist the pollinating insect in some way. Usually single flowers are produced which last for up to three weeks.

The plant has been used very extensively in hybridization to produce the large-lipped brassocattleyas etc, although the distinctive shape of the fringe, so characteristic of the species, has never been reproduced to the same extent in its offspring.

The apex of the intermediate greenhouse is an ideal position for this sun-worshipping plant, where it will thrive in the air movement at the roof of the house.

Above: **Brassavola digbyana**
Does best in the intermediate section. Likes sun but can be shy flowering. Large, single booms are produced in the summer.

A practical hint
The majority of orchids are epiphytes, which means that they grow in tree branches with their roots in crevices providing anchorage.

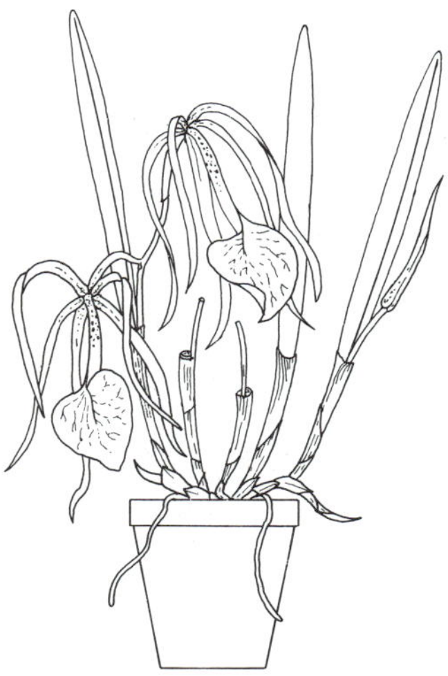

Brassavola nodosa

- **Intermediate: 13°C (55°F)**
- **Moderately easy to grow**
- **Variable flowering season**
- **Evergreen/dry rest**

Brassavolas are very popular with amateur growers, partly because they are easy to cultivate and also for the strange shapes of some of the flowers. The 15 species known are either epiphytic or lithophytic and come from Central and South America.

In this species the pseudobulbs and leaves are very slender and appear as one, both being cylindrical in shape. The plants are best grown on tree-fern fibre, with just a little compost, and suspended from the greenhouse roof. Brassavolas object to excessive moisture and should be kept quite dry during their lengthy period of rest. They do well in the conditions suitable for cattleyas.

Brassavola nodosa is very fragrant, especially in the cool of the evening or at night. It can be found in flower at any time of the year. The flowers, often four to five on a stem, are creamy-green and up to 7.5cm (3in) across when fully open. The lip is broad, and white with a few purple spots in the throat.

Above right: **Brassavola nodosa**
This is an intermediate house species that likes the sun. Flowers are freely produced at various times of the year. Beautifully fragrant.

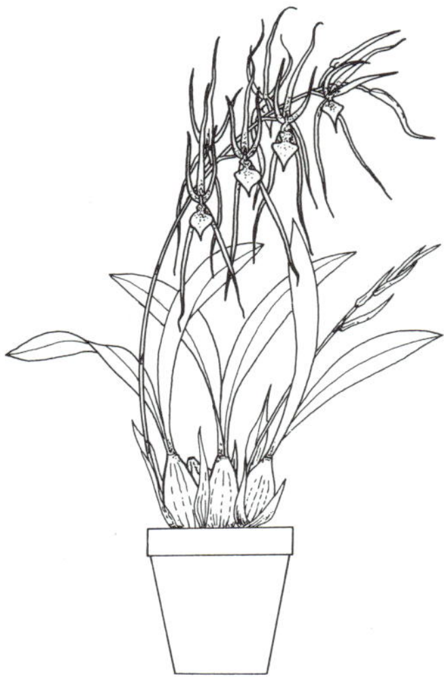

Brassia verrucosa

- **Cool: 10°C (50°F)**
- **Easy to grow and flower**
- **Early summer flowering**
- **Evergreen/semi-rest**

This is one of the most popular of the brassias, a genus of epiphytic orchids from South America. They are allied to, and will interbreed with, plants from the odontoglossum group. *B. verrucosa* is a neat, compact grower that will do well indoors or in a cool greenhouse. During the winter it requires slightly less water than in the summer months, but it should not be allowed to dry out so that the pseudobulbs shrivel. The sweetly fragrant flowers are carried on graceful sprays of up to a dozen blooms during the early summer. The sepals and petals are curiously long and narrow, which gives rise to the plant's common name of 'spider orchid'. This characteristic gives the flowers a lovely light and wispy appearance. The colour is light green with darker green spotting.

This plant will often 'climb' out of its pot and is a good subject for mounting on wood, when long aerial roots are produced. An ideal orchid for beginners.

Left: **Brassia verrucosa**
This cool-house species is a good beginner's orchid. Long sprays of fragrant flowers are produced in the early summer months.

A practical hint
Plants of the orchid *Calanthe vestita* should be fed and watered well while in growth, but gradually dried off when foliage dies down naturally.

Brassolaeliocattleya Crusader

- **Intermediate: 13°C (55°F)**
- **Easy to grow and flower**
- **Winter flowering**
- **Evergreen/some rest**

This robust hybrid is the result of a cross between *Brassolaeliocattleya* Queen Elizabeth and *Laeliocattleya* Trivanhoe, and requires intermediate temperature conditions. The large pink flowers, produced in winter, are 20-23cm (8-9in) across. The heavy, round lip is purple with a yellow patch inside the lobes.

First raised in 1941, this plant has been a very popular hybrid ever since. It has also produced some excellent offspring that continue the line of rich pink-purple colouring. It is typical of modern hybrids with three separate genera in its pedigree. These are *Brassavola, Laelia* and *Cattleya.* The qualities of all three have combined to give size and colour to the flower. These hybrids can be grown indoors provided they are given extremely good light.

In addition they require some rest after they have flowered in the winter, or until the new growth begins to show. During this rest the pseudobulbs should not be allowed to shrivel extensively.

Above right:
Brassolaeliocattleya Crusader
This beautiful intermediate-house hybrid and others like it produce fragrant flowers in winter.

Brassolaeliocattleya Norman's Bay 'Lows'

(FCC/RHS)

- **Intermediate: 13°C (55°F)**
- **Easy to grow and flower**
- **Autumn flowering**
- **Evergreen/some rest**

Probably one of the finest rose-magenta flowered hybrids, this plant is a cross of *Brassocattleya* Hartland and *Laeliocattleya* Ishtar. The flowers, which are 20-23cm (8-9in) across, have a splendid frilled lip and a lovely fragrance.

Like all intergeneric cattleyas this plant should be grown in good light and rested for part of the year. This resting period usually follows flowering and so will vary from plant to plant. Some time after flowering the new growths will show signs of activity and at this stage normal watering can be resumed.

Propagation is achieved by severing the rhizome in between the older, leafless bulbs and potting singly, or they may be left in the pot until the propagated bulbs have started independent growths a few weeks later.

These young propagations will require growing on for at least three or four years to attain flowering size. By this time the original bulb will have withered away completely.

Left: **Brassolaeliocattleya Norman's Bay 'Lows'**
This and similar hybrids are large growers suited to the intermediate greenhouse or warm sunny room.

Browallia speciosa

- **Good light**
- **Temp: 13-18°C (55-65°F)**
- **Keep moist and fed**

The flower colouring of *B. speciosa* ranges from blue to violet-blue, but there are white varieties available. It should be reasonably easy to raise new plants from seed on the windowsill for the person who is moderately competent with indoor plants. Sow seed in spring in peat to which a little sharp sand has been added, and after sowing just cover the seed with a fine layer of sand. Place a sheet of glass over the container holding the seed, and over the glass place a sheet of newspaper until the seed has germinated. When large enough to handle, the seedlings can be pricked off into a very peaty mixture with reasonable space for seedlings to develop. Subsequently, transfer the tiny plants to small pots filled with loam-based mixture and allow to grow on.

From then on keep them moist, fed, and in good light. Discard the plants after they have flowered.

Above: **Browallia speciosa**
For a colourful display in the autumn and winter months, browallia is hard to beat. Makes a stunning show in a hanging basket. Keep moist.

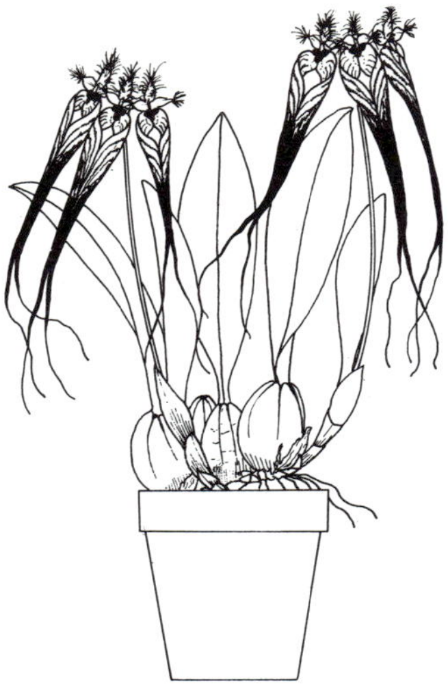

Bulbophyllum collettii

- **Intermediate: 13°C (55°F)**
- **Easy to grow and flower**
- **Spring flowering**
- **Evergreen/semi-rest**

Coming from Burma, this is a plant for the intermediate house; it flowers during the spring. It has roundish, angular pseudobulbs spaced well apart on a creeping rhizome. The four to six flowers, produced on a flower spike that appears when the new growth is only partly completed, have lower sepals that hang down, as if joined, to a length of 13cm (5in). The top sepal and petals carry tufts of short, fine hairs that flutter in even a slight air movement. The overall flower colour is maroon-red with yellow stripes.

This plant is not deeply rooted, and does best in shallow pots or on tree fern or cork bark. Good drainage is essential.

Not only are bulbophyllums widely distributed throughout the subtropical and tropical areas of the world, but their vegetative growth habit and flower size and shape are also equally varied.

They comprise the largest genus in the orchid family, containing about 2000 species.

Caladium hybrids

- **Light shade**
- **Temp: 18-24°C (65-75°F)**
- **Keep moist when in leaf**

There is a wide variety of these hybrids, all in need of some cosseting if they are to succeed. Adequate temperature is essential, and they are sensitive to the effects of bright sun through clear glass.

When potting it is important to use a high proportion of peat that will drain freely. Repot over-wintered tubers soon after they have produced their first new growth. Old soil should be teased gently away, care being taken not to damage any new roots that may be forming. Rather than transfer plants to very large pots it is better, having removed much of the old soil, to repot the plant into the same container using fresh mixture.

Leaves of these plants will not tolerate any cleaning. When buying plants, get them from a reliable retailer with heated premises, as cold conditions for only a short time can be fatal. Although arum-type flowers are produced, these are unattractive and should be removed.

Above: **Bulbophyllum collettii**
This extraordinary species can be grown in an intermediate greenhouse. Spring flowering. Must have good drainage to succeed.

Left: **Caladium hybrid**
Supreme foliage plants that have leaves thin enough to be translucent in some varieties. Growth dies down in the autumn. Provide warmth.

A practical hint
The trailing heart-shaped puffy leaves of *Ceropegia woodii* do well in hanging pots – lots of cuttings in each pot are best.

Calanthe vestita

- **Warm: 18°C (65°F)**
- **Easy to grow and flower**
- **Winter flowering**
- **Deciduous/dry rest**

With tall, upright flower spikes and many long-lasting flowers, *Calanthe* is deservedly a special favourite with orchid growers. Given warm-house conditions, it grows easily and is thus a good plant for beginners. Of the 150 species known, most are terrestrials; they come from a wide area, including South Africa, Asia and Central America.

The flowers of *Calanthe vestita* range in colour from white to deep pink, the lip often being stronger in colour than the rest of the flower.

A warm greenhouse with good light suits this plant best. This deciduous species produces rather large, angular pseudobulbs with wide, ribbed leaves. During the growing season the plant should be liberally watered and fed until the leaves turn yellow and fall during the early winter months. At this stage watering should be gradually reduced. After flowering the pseudobulbs should be repotted in a well-drained compost with the addition of a little dried cow manure in the base.

Calathea makoyana

- **Shade**
- **Temp: 18-24°C (65-75°F)**
- **Keep moist and fed**

Oval-shaped, paper-thin leaves are carried on petioles that may be as much as 60cm (2ft) long, and are intricately patterned. The peacock plant is of a delicate nature; it will rapidly succumb if the temperature is not to its liking. And it must at no time be exposed to direct sunlight, or shrivelling of leaves will occur.

Small plants are seldom offered for sale. It is usual for the specialist grower to raise plants in very warm beds of peat in the greenhouse; when plants are well established they are potted up into 18cm (7in) pots. For all potting operations a very peaty and open mixture containing some coarse leaf mould will be essential. And following potting it will be necessary to ensure that the soil remains just moist, but never becomes saturated for long periods.

Pests are seldom a problem, but established plants have to be fed with weak liquid fertilizer weekly from spring to autumn.

Centre top: **Calanthe vestita**
A very fine winter-flowering species for the warm greenhouse. Deciduous; blooms while at rest. An ideal orchid for beginners.

Above: **Calathea makoyana**
The peacock plant has large, oval-shaped leaves that are intricately patterned and paper thin. Stout leaf stalks spring from soil level.

Calathea oppenheimiana tricolor

- **Light shade**
- **Temp: 16-21°C (60-70°F)**
- **Water/feed mainly in summer**

This is much easier to manage than almost any of the other calatheas. The leaves, on long stalks, are produced at soil level and radiate from the centre of the pot, forming compact and low-growing plants. Background colouring is a very dark green with streaks of white and pink attractively dispersed around the centre of the leaves.

Plants have to be divided in order to be increased. Although the commercial grower may find it slow to build up large stocks of these plants, they are very simple for the average indoor plantsman to cope with. Water the soil well and remove the plant from its pot before proceeding to split the clump of roots as one would divide a clump of herbaceous plants in the garden. At all potting stages use a proprietary houseplant potting mixture with a little loam added. Offer plants reasonable light and protection from direct sunlight, and always avoid excessive watering.

Calathea picturata

- **Shade**
- **Temp: 18-24°C (65-75°F)**
- **Keep moist**

Oval-shaped leaves some 15cm (6in) long are carried on short stalks that are closely grouped at soil level, producing a plant of neat and compact appearance. The margin of each leaf is green and the centre is a striking silver-grey in colour; the reverse is maroon. As with all calatheas, bright direct sunlight will quickly kill them as leaves begin to shrivel up. Calatheas are happier growing in the shade of bolder plants such as the more spreading types of philodendron, such as *P. bipinnatifidum.*

Cold draughts – and cold conditions generally – must be avoided, and if possible one should provide a moist atmosphere around the plant; this is often best achieved by placing plants in a container that includes a selection of other plants. Large containers are now freely available for making plant arrangements in. Fill a container with moist peat into which the plant pot is plunged to its rim.

Above:
Calathea oppenheimiana tricolor
Perhaps the easiest of the calatheas to care for. Colouring varies; some examples have more pink.

Left: **Calathea picturata**
A compact foliage plant that will thrive in warm, humid conditions. Overcrowded clumps can be divided in late spring and potted separately.

Calathea zebrina

- **Shade**
- **Temp: 18-24°C (65-75°F)**
- **Keep moist and fed**

This incredibly beautiful foliage plant will test the skills of anyone. The bold leaves are a deep velvety green with prominent patches of deeper colouring. Maximum height of around 90cm (3ft) may be attained in a well-heated greenhouse where plants are tended with professional care.

It will be fatal to allow this plant to stand in a position exposed to full sunlight for even the shortest space of time. It is remarkable that this plant with its highly coloured exotic appearance should produce such beautiful leaves while growing in shaded locations. But *C. zebrina* always does very much better when placed under and in the shade of taller plants such as ficus and philodendrons, which offer a dark canopy of leaves. When watering, use tepid water and be sure that the soil is thoroughly soaked each time; but allow a drying-out period between waterings. Feed while new leaves are growing.

Above: **Calathea zebrina**
The leaves of this plant have a velvety texture, and are among the most beautiful of all foliage plants. Warmth and shade are essential.

Calceolaria hybrids

- **Good light**
- **Temp: 10-16°C (50-60°F)**
- **Keep moist and fed**

These pouch-like flowers are available in a bewildering range of colours. Many different strains are available and all will give a splendid display if a few standard rules are followed. First and foremost is that these plants must have good light, a loam-based mixture in which to grow, and regular feeding once they have filled their pots with roots.

When buying a mature plant from a retailer it is important to check the roots in the pot on getting the plant home; an overcrowded root system means the plant should be potted on straight away. It is also wise to give plants a general inspection before buying, particularly on the undersides of leaves, and to reject any that have pests present.

These are temporary plants and should be discarded after flowering.

Right: **Calceolaria hybrids**
Calceolarias provide a bright splash of colour in the spring. The colour combinations available are almost limitless. Keep cool.

A practical hint
The trailing *Campanula isophylla* produces very lengthy growth and is best pruned hard back in the autumn, and kept dryish till spring.

Callistemon citrinus

- **Good light**
- **Temp: 13-16°C (55-60°F)**
- **Keep moist and fed**

An Australian plant, the callistemon gets its common name of 'bottlebrush plant' from the formation of the unusual flower, which is in the shape of the brush used for cleaning out bottles.

It is a green-leaved woody shrub that will, in time, reach a height of about 150cm (5ft) if growing conditions are agreeable. Position it in a light, although not necessarily sunny, location, and it will be better if the growing temperature is around 16°C (60°F), as warmer temperatures tend to produce softer and less attractive plants.

The soil should be kept moist, but not saturated for long periods, though much will depend on the growing position; in sunnier spots it will obviously be necessary to water more often. Use free-draining loam-based mixture when potting on. When established, the plants need frequent feeding.

Camellia japonica

- **Good light**
- **Temp: 10-16°C (50-60°F)**
- **Keep moist with rain water**

These make fine garden plants in sheltered areas if the soil in which they are growing is acid rather than alkaline.

Perhaps not so good for the indoor location, they are nevertheless excellent plants for porches and conservatories that offer a little shelter from the elements. Plants that are grown from seed sown in the spring, or from cuttings rooted in the autumn, can be purchased in small pots from good retailers.

With careful handling these small plants can be gradually potted on until they are in containers of 25cm (10in) in diameter – use the acid soil recommended for camellias at each potting stage, and collect rain water for watering.

In time plants of about 150cm (5ft) in height will have developed, and in early spring there can surely be nothing more appealing than camellia blooms in white, pink or red.

Above left: **Callistemon citrinus**
This summer-flowering shrub will grow readily indoors. It can be pruned after flowering and propagated by shoot cuttings.

Above: **Camellia japonica**
Many varieties of this flowering shrub are available. All will bloom best in a cool conservatory. Home propagation is difficult.

A practical hint
The orchid *Cattleya bowringiana* flowers profusely and needs lots of water to do well, but potting mixture must be well drained and not soggy.

Campanula isophylla

- **Good light**
- **Temp: 10-16°C (50-60°F)**
- **Keep moist, but dry in winter**

This exquisite plant is available in both pale blue and white colouring. The species is quite tough, but will be happier in lower temperatures, around 10°C (50°F), than it will be if grown in hot, stuffy rooms.

The leaves are small and pale green in colour and flowers are bell-shaped and produced continuously over a very long period from spring through into autumn. To encourage the maximum number of flowers, it is advisable to remove all dead flowers as soon as they appear.

Set off to best effect when grown in hanging baskets or containers, these plants will need frequent watering and ample feeding during spring and summer.

In the autumn when they are becoming more miserable in appearance they can be severely cut back, kept on the dry side, then repotted in the spring to start life all over again.

Right: **Campanula isophylla 'Star of Italy'**
Stunning in a hanging basket, this plant thrives in cool, airy conditions. Propagate by tip cuttings taken in early spring. Prune in autumn.

Capsicum annuum

- **Good light**
- **Temp: 10-16°C (50-60°F)**
- **Keep moist and fed**

These bright red-fruited plants are raised from seed sown in the spring in temperatures of not less than 21°C (70°F). When large enough to handle, the tiny seedlings are transferred from their initial boxes or pans to small pots filled with loam-based mixture, and subsequently go on into 13-18cm (5-7in) pots depending on the size of the plants required.

When in their final pots, it is much better to place the plants out of doors in full sun for the summer months, plunging pots in peat to reduce the amount of watering needed.

At all times full light is essential, and this is of particular importance once the fruits have formed, as they fall alarmingly when light is poor – during fog for example. Discard these plants at the end of the growing season.

Above: **Capsicum annuum**
The decorative fruits ripen and remain through the winter. Depending on the plant and season they may be white, yellow, orange, red or purple. Keep in good light.

A practical hint
The old man cactus, *Cephalocereus senilis*, produces an upright cylinder of growth that will in time develop what appears to be fine grey hair.

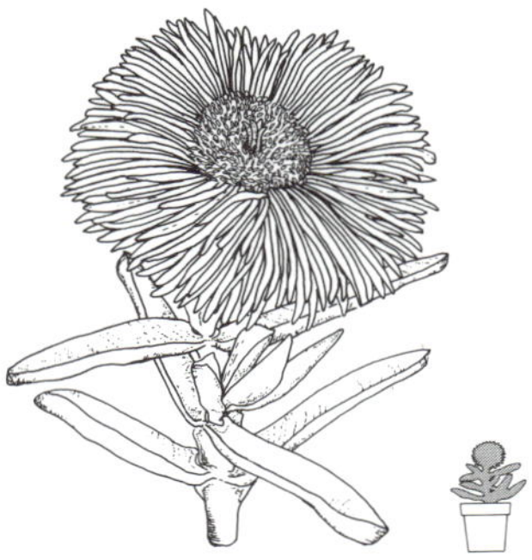

Carpobrotus edulis

- **Full sun**
- **Frost-free conditions**
- **Water generously in hot weather**

Like many shrubby succulents, *C. edulis* does better if planted outdoors during warm weather. It can either be lifted in the autumn, or cuttings can be taken in late summer and wintered indoors. In mild regions it can remain outside.

The plant is a strongly growing shrub with prostrate branches 1m (39in) long. It can be grown against a small wall and the branches allowed to trail over it. The large triangular leaves are grass-green in colour. Although this is not a prolific flowerer, the blooms are large, about 10cm (4in) across, and a vivid magenta, yellow or orange in colour.

If grown outdoors the plant will suffer from the same pests as other garden plants, and should be given similar treatment. It should be placed in a sunny position and given an occasional watering during prolonged dry weather. Cuttings should be wintered on a light windowsill or in a frost-free greenhouse. Keep slightly moist.

Above: **Carpobrotus edulis**
This succulent can be grown out of doors in mild regions of temperate countries, ideally in a sunny rock garden, where its sprawling stems and colourful flowers are a delight.

Catharanthus roseus

(Vinca rosea)

- **Sunny location**
- **Temp: 13-18°C (55-65°F)**
- **Keep moist and fed**

This is a charming, trouble-free little plant that may be easily grown from seed sown in the spring or from tip cuttings taken at the same time of year. Cuttings of about 7.5cm (3in) in length should be taken from plants of the previous year and inserted in peat and sand mixture at a temperature of about 21°C (70°F).

Leaves are a bright glossy green and flowers may be either white or pink. It is really best to treat these as annuals so that fresh plants are raised in the spring each year and older plants discarded. A loam-based potting mixture will suit them best and once they have got under way it is advisable to remove the growing tips to encourage a more compact shape. They should be kept on a bright windowsill; while in active growth keep moist and feed with a weak liquid fertilizer at each watering.

Left: **Catharanthus roseus**
Delicate pink or white flowers (depending on variety) adorn this plant during the summer months. Best raised anew each year from seed or stem cuttings.

A practical hint
Many being tree dwellers in their natural habitat, most orchids must have light and air surrounding them to thrive.

A practical hint
To propagate, most clump-forming succulents can be teased apart and planted separately; allow any cut stems to dry before planting.

A practical hint
Any rotting detected in close groups of succulents should be cut out and the area treated with benomyl to prevent spread and possible botrytis attack.

Cattleya aurantiaca

- **Cool: 11°C (52°F)**
- **Easy to grow and flower**
- **Summer flowering**
- **Evergreen/slight rest**

This small bifoliate species comes from Guatemala and neighbouring countries. It has drooping clusters of red-orange flowers, 7.5-10cm (3-4in) across, produced in summer. The plant is peculiar in that it produces seedpods by self-pollination, which means that often the flowers do not open properly and the prettiness of the flowers is lost. Today plants are raised from selected nursery stock that produces fully opening flowers.

This species is one of the smallest growing and flowering varieties of *Cattleya* in cultivation. The plant will flower when only 15cm (6in) tall and is therefore easily accommodated in a small greenhouse or indoor growing case. Because of its diminutive pseudobulbs, *Cattleya aurantiaca* should not be allowed to remain in a dry state for any prolonged period. It is at its best when grown on into a large mature plant without being divided.

Above right: **Cattleya aurantiaca**
One of the smallest of the cattleya species. Cool growing, summer flowering. Very pretty.

A practical hint
For the beginner with cacti, the upright and reasonably fast-growing *Cereus peruvianus* will provide both height and interest to plant groups.

Cattleya Bow Bells

- **Intermediate: 13°C (55°F)**
- **Easy to grow and flower**
- **Spring flowering**
- **Evergreen/some rest**

One of the world's most famous cattleyas, this beautiful hybrid has been bred from the cross of *C.* Edithae and *C.* Suzanne Hye. It produces large heavy flowers, 15cm (6in) across, with pure white overlapping petals and a sulphur-yellow mark in the back of the throat. It is a plant for the intermediate house and requires a rest during the winter after the new growth has matured. The flowers are produced in the spring.

Where this and other *Cattleya* hybrids are grown together the flowering season can be extended through the autumn and winter months well into the spring and early summer. The colours available vary from deep lavenders and pinks through to pure white. The glistening sepals and petals of the white cattleyas are among the purest colour to be found in orchids. To encourage the blooms to last longer in perfection the plants should be kept dry while in flower.

Cattleyas such as this provide the largest of flowers cultivated.

Left: **Cattleya Bow Bells**
One of the finest of the white-flowered cattleyas. Large fragrant blooms are produced in the spring.

Cattleya bowringiana

- **Intermediate: 11-13°C (52-55°F)**
- **Easy to grow and flower**
- **Autumn flowering**
- **Evergreen/winter rest**

This highly productive plant can produce as many as 20 rose-purple blooms, 7.5cm (3in) across, with a deep purple lip, marked with golden yellow in the throat. It requires more water than most to support the long pseudobulbs, which are slightly bulbous at the base. The flowers open during late autumn, and the plant benefits from a short mid-winter rest after flowering, during which time watering should be withheld.

This is an excellent plant for a beginner, although it is now becoming increasingly difficult to obtain. The plant is slow growing from seed, and is not therefore readily available as nursery-raised stock. However, it can be grown and propagated with ease, so it is worth looking out for. Like all cattleyas it prefers a well-drained compost and is intolerant of soggy conditions.

This species originates from Guatemala and grows epiphytically in the wild. Some very interesting hybrids have been raised from it since its introduction in 1884.

Above left: **Cattleya bowringiana**
Grows in the intermediate house and flowers in the autumn. Produces large heads of attractive flowers.

Cattleya forbesii

- **Intermediate: 13°C (55°F)**
- **Easy to grow and flower**
- **Late summer flowering**
- **Evergreen/semi-rest**

Discovered in Brazil in 1823, this plant is a bifoliate of dainty growth, with pencil-thin pseudobulbs. Its yellow or tan-coloured flowers, produced in summer, are 7.5-10cm (3-4in) across, and have a tubular lip with side lobes of pale pink on the outside, and a deep yellow throat marked with wavy red lines.

This is an easy plant for the beginner and is also suitable for culture in an indoor growing case. It should not be overpotted, but kept in as small a pot as possible; unlike many cattleyas it rarely becomes top heavy. It should be grown in a position of good light all the year round and during the summer months can be lightly sprayed with water, taking care to avoid the flowers while in bloom. At one time this plant was considered a rather insignificant member of the genus, but today its smaller, pastel flowers are welcomed as charming and delicate.

This species has been little used for hybridizing. The plant can be propagated by careful division when large enough.

Above: **Cattleya forbesil**
One of the smaller cattleya species. It blooms in late summer and is an ideal orchid for beginners.

A practical hint
Potted chrysanthemums are treated with a chemical that restricts upward growth, but the effects wear off when they are planted outdoors.

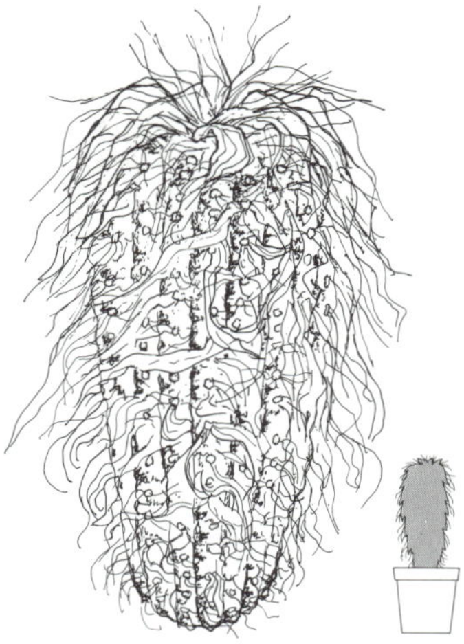

Celosia argentea

- **Good light**
- **Temp: 10-16°C (50-60°F)**
- **Keep moist and fed**

The variety *C. argentea* 'Cristata' is generally referred to as the 'cockscomb' because the bract it produces resembles the comb of the cockerel. The variety 'Pyramidalis' has plumed flowers in red or yellow. In any event, these are annual plants that are produced in large quantities both for indoor decoration in pots and for use as a bedding plant in the garden.

Over the years there have been many new varieties of this plant, but most have a somewhat grotesque appearance and leave much to be desired, but they clearly have attraction for some indoor-plant growers. Cheapness has some bearing on *C. argentea*'s popularity. Although it is discarded after flowering, the plant is very easily raised from seed sown in the spring. Seedlings are subsequently pricked off, and grown on in larger pots – the eventual size of pot dictating to some extent the dimensions of the mature plant.

Right:
Celosia argentea 'Pyramidalis'
This is the plumed variety, perhaps the more attractive of the two available. Easily raised from seed, the celosias provide vivid colour.

Cephalocereus senilis

- **Full sun**
- **Temp: 7-30°C (45-86°F)**
- **Water very carefully**

In its native Mexico, this cactus forms a column 12m (40ft) high and 45cm (18in) across. These plants are said to be 200 years old, so there is little fear of a seedling outgrowing its accommodation. The white flowers are not produced until the plant is 6m (20ft) high, so this cactus must be grown for the beauty of its form.

The pale green stem with its yellow spines is completely hidden by long, white hairs. These will pick up dust, so to keep the plant gleaming white, shampoo it with a dilute detergent solution and rinse thoroughly; choose a hot sunny day. With advancing age, the lower hairs will inevitably become permanently discoloured. The upper part of the stem may be cut, dried for three days, and potted up. Take cuttings in late spring.

A very open soil – half loam-based mixture and half grit – and a dry winter rest are essential. Keep this cactus in the warmest, sunniest position available.

Above left:
Cephalocereus senilis
'Old man cactus' aptly describes this plant, with its mass of twisted white hairs and almost no spines. It makes an ideal pot specimen.

A practical hint
Perhaps the easiest of all the cacti is *Chamaecereus silvestrii,* with silver-coloured small cylinders of growth, easy to root.

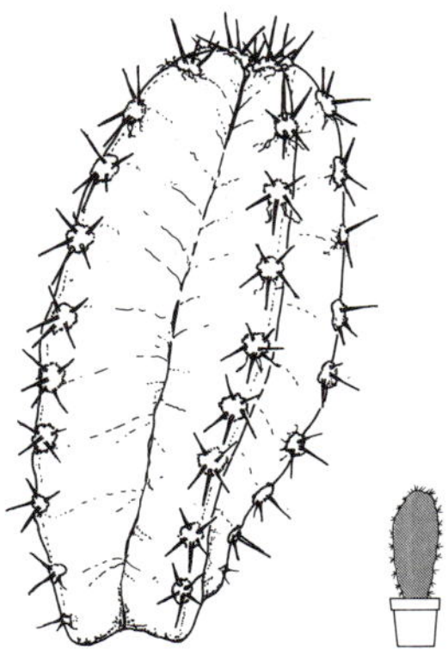

Cereus peruvianus

- **Full sun**
- **Temp: 5-30°C (41-86°F)**
- **Water generously in summer**

This columnar plant forms a handsome addition to any cactus collection. It is a vigorous plant and in a matter of a few years will form a blue-green column about 2m (6.5ft) high. The stem is ribbed, and the ribs carry stout spines. It is possible to flower this cereus in cultivation; the large white flowers open at night. In the wild, this plant will reach a height of 9m (30ft). When it reaches the roof of the greenhouse, cut the cereus about 1m (39in) from the top, dry for three days, and then pot up the top. The base will send out branches, which can be used for propagation.

Grow in a loam-based mixture and repot annually. Water generously during summer, and feed about once a month with a liquid fertilizer with a high potassium content (tomato fertilizer). Keep dry in winter. *C. peruvianus* is tough and vigorous, and unlikely to be bothered by pests.

Above right: **Cereus peruvianus**
Although it can be a giant in the wild, the attractively spined, slender stems of this cactus make an ideal contrast with the more globular plants in the collection.

Ceropegia woodii

- **Suspend in good light**
- **Temp: 13-18°C (55-65°F)**
- **Moist, but dry in winter**

With the current fashion for hanging plants of all kinds this is the ideal plant to try, as it is so different from almost all other potted plants. Small, fleshy heart-shaped leaves are attached to wiry stems that hang perpendicularly from the plant. *C. woodii* is a hanging plant with no desire whatsoever to climb or do anything different. The leaves are mottled and grey-green in colour and the flowers are pink and tubular.

The common name of 'hearts entangled' comes from the manner in which the foliage twines around itself when the plants are growing actively. There is also the additional fascination of the gnarled bulbous growths that appear at soil level and along the stems of the plant, from which new growth sprouts. Indeed, the bulbils with growth attached can be used to propagate fresh plants, or they can be raised from cuttings.

When planting hanging containers it is advisable to propagate a batch of plants and to put five or so into each.

Left and above: **Ceropegia woodii**
This naturally trailing plant has grey-coloured, heart-shaped leaves with a succulent, puffed up look. Exquisite, tubular pink flowers appear during the autumn months of the year.

Chamaecereus silvestrii

- **Full sun**
- **Temp: 0-30°C (32-86°F)**
- **Keep dry in winter**

Sometimes recently listed as *Lobivia silvestrii* (another victim of botanical name changes), it seems more appropriate here to use the name of so many years standing. The spreading stems are somewhat finger-like in shape and size, bright green in colour and covered with short spines. Offsets, somewhat resembling green peanuts, appear along the length of the stems, hence the popular name. They detach themselves at the slightest touch, and can be potted up at once – surely the easiest cactus to propagate! But the great joy of this plant is the brilliant scarlet flowers, 4cm (1.6in) across; produced in profusion, they almost cover the stems during spring and summer.

This is not a fussy plant, so grow it in any good potting mixture. Water freely in spring and summer. One of the hardiest cacti, it will survive in a cold frame if quite dry.

Top and centre:
Chamaecereus silvestrii
Very popular and easy to grow. Finger-like stems are covered with flowers in spring and summer.

Chamaecereus silvestrii, yellow hybrid

- **Full sun**
- **Temp: 0-30°C (32-86°F)**
- **Keep dry in winter**

Taking advantage of the close relationship between *Chamaecereus* and *Lobivia*, plant breeders have produced hybrids between these two groups of cacti. The result is a compact plant with short, stubby, upright, branching stems. Offsets are still formed and do not fall off so readily as with *C. silvestrii* itself, but propagation by means of these is still very easy. Flowers, in this case bright yellow and about 4cm (1.6in) in diameter, are freely produced in spring and summer. Other similar hybrids exist with red and also orange blooms.

Water this cactus freely in spring and summer and feed every two weeks with a high-potassium fertilizer, from when the buds form. This will encourage flowering, as will a cold winter rest; use an unheated room in the house. Grow in a good standard loam- or peat-based potting mixture. Extra grit is needed only if there is doubt about drainage.

Left:
Chamaecereus yellow hybrid
One of the many attractive hybrids of the cactus. A more compact plant than the top one.

A practical hint
Radiators and heating appliances can be death to plants if placed too close to them. Plants will invariably succumb if over radiators.

Chlorophytum comosum variegatum

- **Airy, good light**
- **Temp: 10-16°C (50-60°F)**
- **Frequent feeding**

Like privet hedges in the garden the chlorophytums of the houseplant world appear to be everywhere. Yet they are not always as bright and healthy as their ease of culture would suggest they should be – in fact, many are extremely poor specimens. This may be due to the fact that owners feel that they are so easy to grow that they don't have to bother at all.

Give the chlorophytum good light to prevent it becoming thin and straggly, and keep it moist at all times, especially during summer.

The most important need of all, and the one most neglected, is that of feeding, and feeding the spider plant means giving it very much more than the average indoor plant. Frequent potting on is also essential, and this could be necessary twice a year for vigorous plants. Spider plants produce large fleshy roots and quickly become starved if not supplied with sufficient nourishment. Use a loam-based potting mixture.

Above: **Chlorophytum comosum variegatum**
The familiar spider plant develops natural plantlets that can be used for propagating new plants.

Chrysanthemum

- **Good light**
- **Temp: 13-18°C (55-65°F)**
- **Keep moist**

This has become one of the world's most popular flowering pot plants, mainly because it can be produced at any time of the year by commercial growers with the right sort of equipment and facilities.

The natural flowering time of this plant is from late summer through the autumn when about two thirds of the day is dark. It is these conditions that cause chrysanthemum flower buds to initiate and subsequently come into flower. However, by using black polythene to cover plants over and reduce the amount of daylight, the grower can simulate autumn light conditions and induce plants to flower at an unnatural time. Additional artificial lighting can be used to extend the day length if required.

Trouble-free indoors, these plants need good light, moisture, and weak feeding. Plant in the garden after flowering; they will survive where winter conditions allow but artificially dwarfed forms will revert to their regular height.

Right: **Chrysanthemum**
For temporary colour in the home at any time of the year these plants reign supreme. Keep cool and moist for maximum bloom.

A practical hint
With bristling spines along its stately grey columns of growth, *Cleistocactus strausii* will be better balanced in clay pots.

Chysis bractescens

- **Cool/Intermediate: 10-13°C (50-55°F)**
- **Fairly easy to grow**
- **Early summer flowering**
- **Semi-deciduous/dry rest**

The flowers of this species, up to 7.5cm (3in) in diameter, grow rather close together on a single but comparatively short stem produced from new growth. They are white, turning to cream with age; the lip is white on the outer surface and tinged with yellow inside.

The six species of *Chysis* recorded, which come mainly from Mexico, are all epiphytic and semi-deciduous under cultivation. When in growth the plants require a liberal supply of heat and moisture; when they have shed their leaves they should be transferred to the cool house for a period of rest. During this time they should be kept much drier at the root until growth restarts in the spring.

Growth and form are similar in all the species. A few, often large, leaves grow from the upper half of the spindle-shaped pseudobulbs, which may be up to 46cm (18in) long. These either grow horizontally or hang down, so that the plants are best grown in baskets.

Repot every other year using a well-draining compost.

Above: **Chysis bractescens**
A fairly easy orchid for the cool or intermediate greenhouse. White flowers are produced in early summer. Needs a dry rest period.

Cineraria cruenta

(Senecio cruentus)

- **Good light**
- **Temp: 13-18°C (55-65°F)**
- **Keep moist and fed**

The compact, coarse green leaves and bright daisy flowers of this plant make it one of the most popular pot plants among the cheaper range. Ideally, seed should be sown in early spring and plantlets pricked off and potted on as they establish themselves.

Seed should be chosen wisely, and where growing space is limited the more miniature varieties should be selected. Seed of larger-growing types will develop into plants of splendid size in time if potted on and given regular feeding. A loam-based mixture is important as these are greedy plants that thrive on ample nourishment, both from the soil in which they are growing and from the subsequent feeding that they receive.

When raised in a greenhouse the cineraria can become the host for every pest that has ever been thought of, so inspect plants regularly for greenfly, leafminers, and other pests. Discard after flowering.

Right: **Cineraria cruenta**
These one-season plants are sold in a beautiful range of colours to brighten the sombre days of winter and early spring. Keep cool.

Cissus discolor

- **Light shade**
- **Temp: 18-24°C (65-75°F)**
- **Keep moist and fed**

This most beautiful climbing foliage plant has maroon undersides, and an upper leaf surface with a mixture of silver, red, green and other colours. Plants climb by means of clinging tendrils if given some support; to prevent gaps appearing as plants extend, pin some of the straying shoots down the stem.

A dry atmosphere can result in shrivelling of the leaves, as will exposure to bright sun; and very dry soil conditions also cause leaf problems. It seems necessary to renew older plants periodically rather than allow them to become straggly. Cuttings prepared from mature, firm leaves with stem attached will root in a temperature of 21°C (70°F) if put into small pots filled with moist peat. A closed propagating case and treating cuttings with rooting powder will also speed the process. Once rooted, cuttings should be potted into slightly larger pots using peaty mixture, and the soil thereafter kept moist but not waterlogged.

Above: **Cissus discolor**
The aristocrat of the decorative pot-grown vines. It has a natural climbing habit and does best in warm, shaded and moist conditions.

Citrus mitis

(Citrofortunella mitis)

- **Sunny location**
- **Temp: 13-18°C (55-65°F)**
- **Keep moist and fed**

Citrus mitis is one of the most decorative of potted plants when its branches are festooned with perfectly shaped miniature oranges. The glossy green foliage will become yellow if underfed, particularly from magnesium deficiency – to combat this deficiency treat with sequestered iron.

Full light is essential, but foliage may become scorched if plants are placed too close to window panes on very sunny days. During the summer months plants will do better if placed out of doors in full sun. While in the garden it is important not to neglect feeding and watering. Failure to keep the soil moist will result in shrivelling of leaves.

White, heavily scented flowers appear in late summer. To help with pollination draw your hands through the flowers periodically. Flowers are followed by small green fruits that will in time develop into miniature oranges – dozens of them on the better plants. Incidentally, the oranges can be made into marmalade!

Above: **Citrus mitis**
This little orange tree can produce a profusion of fruit if conditions are right. It needs plenty of sun and generous watering.

A practical hint
To do well, the orchid *Coelogyne cristata* should be potted into a container of reasonable size, then allowed to remain and develop undisturbed.

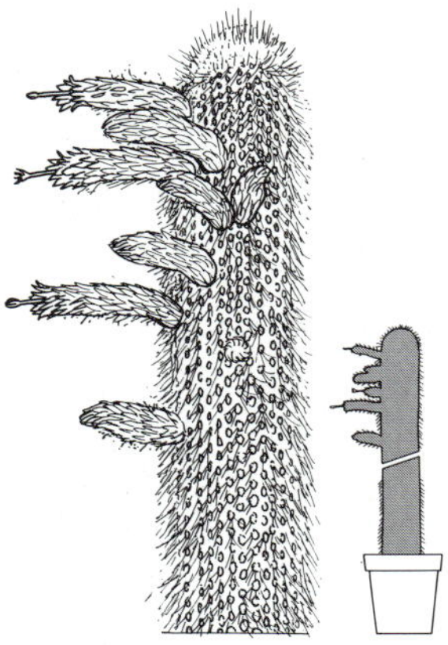

Cleistocactus strausii

- **Full sun**
- **Temp: 5-30°C (41-86°F)**
- **Water generously in summer**

Cleistocactus straussii is a slender column that will reach a height of 2m (6.5ft); the stem branches from the base. The plant is densely covered in short white spines, which give the plant a silvery gleam in the sunlight. Mature specimens flower freely in cultivation. The carmine flowers are carried on the sides of the columns and have a very characteristic shape: they consist of a long narrow tube with an opening only large enough for the stamens to protrude.

This is a vigorous cactus and to keep healthy it needs a good loam-based mixture and an annual repotting. Water generously during summer, give an occasional high-potassium liquid feed, and keep it dry in winter. To encourage flowering, put it in the sunniest position available. Some of the stems may be removed and used as cuttings if the plant is becoming too crowded.

Above right:
Cleistocactus strausii
This beautiful silvery column can reach a height of over 100cm (39in) but is unlikely to out-grow its welcome in the average collection.

A practical hint
Trailing columnea plants come in several varieties, and generally flower better if soil is kept on the dry side in winter.

Clerodendron thomsoniae

- **Good light**
- **Temp: 16-21°C (60-70°F)**
- **Keep moist and fed**

This is a useful plant for spacious surroundings, or for training against the wall of a heated greenhouse or conservatory. It is a natural climbing plant, the stems of which will entwine themselves around any sort of climbing framework that may be provided.

New plants are started from cuttings taken from any firm shoots that are not producing flowers – a temperature of about 21°C (70°F) is needed to encourage rooting. When a reasonable amount of root is evident the young plants can be potted into small pots filled with loam-based potting soil.

In the early stages of growth a temperature minimum of 18°C (65°F) should be the aim, with a slightly lower level for plants that are established in larger containers. The plant has coarse green leaves attached to woody stems, but the red and white flowers that develop in clusters are the main attraction. Prune to shape after flowering.

Left: **Clerodendron thomsoniae**
Where space permits this splendid climber will provide a colourful display in spring and summer with striking red and white flowers. To thrive it needs warmth and humidity.

Clivia miniata

- **Shade**
- **Temp: 16-21°C (60-70°F)**
- **Keep moist**

To encourage these plants to flower freely, keep their roots in pot-bound condition – not a very difficult task as they very quickly make sufficient root to fill existing containers. Getting these plants to produce their exotic orange bell-flowers is always a problem, but older plants will usually reward the patience expended on them in the end.

Leaves are thick, broad, and strap-like and are produced from very large bulbous stems at soil level. Clean leaves with a damp cloth to keep them looking their best. Inevitably, plants will require quite large pots as they mature, and when potting on it is advisable to use a loam-based mixture that will sustain the plant over a longer period of time.

Having outgrown their pots and perhaps their allotted space indoors, the bulbous clumps can be divided to make new plants.

Right: **Clivia miniata**
Clivia produces superb flowers in early spring, but only if the plant has been given a dormant period of several weeks at about 10°C (50°F) during the late autumn.

Cocos weddelliana

- **Light shade**
- **Temp: 16-21°C (60-70°F)**
- **Keep moist and fed**

Possibly the most beautiful and delicate of all the many palms offered for sale. However, being slow growing it is seen less often these days, as the commercial grower concentrates his efforts on palms that attain saleable size in a shorter time. One choice specimen of *C. weddelliana* is over 60 years old, with many fine stems reaching a height of some 3m (10ft).

A position out of direct sunlight is advised but one should not put the plant in the darkest corner, as reasonable light is essential to its well-being. Established plants can be fed at every watering with weak liquid fertilizer, with less being given – perhaps none at all – in winter. Some chemicals are harmful, so one should check suitability with the supplier before applying.

Its principal enemy is red spider mite. These mites cause pale discolouration of the foliage and are mostly found on the undersides of leaves.

Above: **Cocos weddelliana**
The best of the finer foliaged palms, and a slow growing plant that will seldom outgrow its allotted space. With age a basal trunk will form.

Codiaeum hybrids

- **Good light**
- **Temp: 16-21°C (60-70°F)**
- **Feed and water well**

Also known as crotons, these plants are among the most colourful of all foliage plants, as the common name suggests.

Full light, with protection from the strongest sunlight, is essential if plants are to retain their bright colouring. In poor light, new growth becomes thin and poor, and colouring is less brilliant. Besides light there is a need for reasonable temperature, without which shedding of lower leaves will be inevitable. Healthy plants that are producing new leaves will require to be kept moist with regular watering, but it is important that the soil should be well drained. Frequent feeding is necessary, though less is needed in winter. On account of vigorous top growth, there will be a mass of roots in the pots of healthy plants. Large plants that seem out of proportion to their pots should be inspected in spring and summer. If well rooted they should be potted into larger pots using loam-based compost.

Above: **Codiaeum hybrids**
Codiaeums in general are among the most highly coloured of all foliage plants, but must have ample light if they are not to revert to green.

A practical hint
Small and easily accommodated, the orchid *Colax jugosus* flourishes in cool conditions and produces creamy white flowers during spring and summer.

Codiaeum 'Eugene Drapps'

- **Good light**
- **Temp: 16-21°C (60-70°F)**
- **Feed and water well**

One of the queens of potted plants. The leaves are lance-shaped and almost entirely yellow in colour; only on closer inspection is it seen that there is also some green present.

New plants are grown from cuttings taken from the top section of the stem. Cuttings will have four or five leaves, and will be 15cm (6in) or more in length. A temperature in excess of 21°C (70°F) is needed to encourage rooting, and conditions should be close and moist. Once rooted in their peat propagating mixture, plants must be potted into loam-based compost as soon as they have made a reasonable amount of root. Once plants have got under way the top of the stem should be pinched out, to encourage the plant to branch.

In common with all codiaeums, this one will almost certainly attract red spider mites. These are difficult to detect on yellow foliage and a magnifying glass is usually necessary.

Above left:
Codiaeum 'Eugene Drapps'
By far the best yellow-coloured of the commonly named Joseph's coat plants. Grow in good light.

Coelogyne cristata

- **Cool: 10°C (50°F)**
- **Challenge to flower**
- **Winter flowering**
- **Evergreen/dry rest**

Perhaps the most familiar of the genus, this species likes to grow on undisturbed into a specimen plant. The flower spike appears from the centre of the new growth and its snowy-white flowers, broken only by a blotch of golden yellow at the centre of the lip, appear in mid-winter and last for four or five weeks.

Although the genus contains well over 100 species, few coelogynes are found in collections today. This is a pity, for they are orchids of great merit. They are, in the main, easy to grow and many species thrive in cool conditions, requiring a warmer environment only during their active growing season. Rest well in winter to achieve flowering.

Many coelogynes are suitable for growing on into specimen plants. However, be warned: a specimen plant of one of the larger-growing species can take up a considerable amount of space in the greenhouse. Fortunately, it is possible to choose from a wide range of smaller-growing species, and even a single-growth plant in flower is a valuable addition to any orchid collection.

Left: **Coelogyne cristata**
A delightful cool-house species that must be rested well to flower regularly. Blooming starts in mid-winter and continues until spring.

A practical hint
Growing orchids on tree branches to simulate natural conditions is not practical indoors, but is possible in a conservatory or greenhouse.

Coelogyne ochracea

- **Cool: 10°C (50°F)**
- **Easy to grow and flower**
- **Early summer flowering**
- **Evergreen/dry rest**

This popular species from India has shiny green pseudobulbs topped by a pair of leaves. The flower spikes are produced freely from the new growth while it is very young. Like all coelogynes, it prefers to be grown on into a specimen plant with as little disturbance as possible, although this species is unlikely to become unmanageable in size. The flowers are extremely pretty and full of fragrance.

After flowering grow the plant on well into the autumn, by which time the season's growth will have matured and the plant will rest. Place in full light for the winter and withhold all water until the new growths appear in early spring. The pseudobulbs will shrivel during this time but they will quickly plump up again when normal watering is resumed.

Ideal for beginners, it is equally at home indoors or in a cool greenhouse. The most frequent mistake made is watering while the plant is resting in the winter, when it must be kept dry at the roots. Repot when necessary after flowering.

Coelogyne pandurata

- **Intermediate/warm: 16°C (60°F)**
- **Fairly easy to grow**
- **Summer flowering**
- **Evergreen/dry rest**

The fragrant flowers of this species can be up to 10cm (4in) across and are among the largest of all coelogynes. They are green with jet black hairs partly covering the lip and are borne in beautiful arching sprays that appear from the centre of the new growth.

The species originates from Borneo and therefore likes warmer conditions than the cool growing Indian species. It should only be attempted where sufficient room can be provided for it. The large pseudobulbs are spaced well apart along a creeping rhizome and for this reason the plant can be more easily accommodated in a boat-shaped basket or box rather than a round pot. A complete rest during the winter is vital for successful flowering.

The old pseudobulbs may be used for propagation provided their removal does not weaken the main plant. This orchid is not widely available.

Repot every other year, using a compost of coarse bark. Repot when the new growth appears.

Above right: **Coelogyne ochracea**
One of the prettiest and easiest orchids to grow. Ideal for a beginner, in a cool greenhouse or indoors.

Right: **Coelogyne pandurata**
This lovely, summer-flowering, fragrant species likes conditions in the warm greenhouse.

A practical hint
Developing into a large plant in time, *Cymbidium* Angelica 'Advent' needs cool night temperatures to produce spectacular orchid flowers.

Colax jugosus

- **Intermediate: 13°C (55°F)**
- **Fairly easy to grow and flower**
- **Spring flowering**
- **Evergreen/semi-dry rest**

Native to Brazil, this species grows well in intermediate conditions with plenty of fresh air. The plant can easily be accommodated in a small greenhouse, for it seldom grows above 30cm (12in) in height. It seems to do best when kept fairly potbound, but the compost must be of an open nature to give good drainage.

The plant develops small oval pseudobulbs, 2.5-5cm (1-2in) in height, narrowing towards the top, and two dark green leaves 15-23cm (6-9in) long. The flowers, often two but sometimes three to a spike, are about 5cm (2in) in diameter. The sepals and petals are creamy-white, the sepals being clear and the petals heavily blotched with deep purple; the lip is similarly marked. The plant flowers in spring and early summer.

The three species of *Colax* have in the past been included in the genera *Lycaste, Maxillaria* and *Zygopetalum,* but are now accepted as a separate genus, *Pabista.* However, the accepted name remains *Colax.*

Above left: **Colax jugosus**
This beautiful species will grow well in a small greenhouse kept at intermediate temperatures.

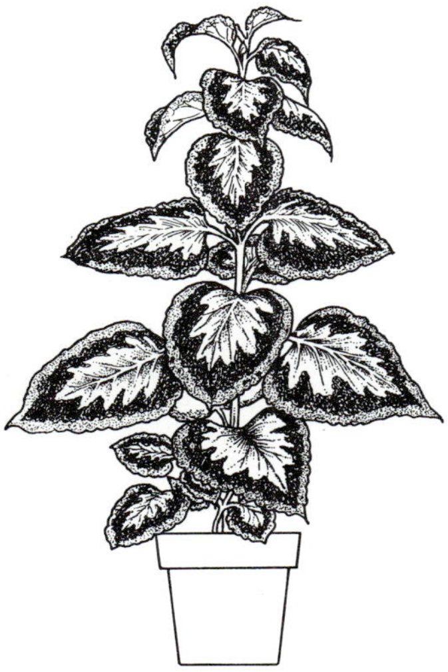

Coleus

- **Good light**
- **Temp: 10-16°C (50-60°F)**
- **Keep moist and fed**

For little outlay the coleus offers more foliage colour than almost any other potted plant. Small plants can be purchased almost anywhere during the spring.

On getting plants home, if they are growing in small pots, advance them to pots a little larger in size. All the coleuses are hungry plants and any neglect with potting – or subsequently with feeding – will result in plants of much poorer quality. Full sun streaming through unprotected glass will usually be harmful, but these plants need plenty of light if they are to retain their colouring. Due to their light position it will be necessary to water plants frequently (every day, in some instances), and to ensure that the soil is thoroughly soaked each time. Better coloured plants can be retained from one year to the next; but it is better to take cuttings from these in late summer and to dispose of the often overgrown larger plant.

Columnea banksii

- **Light shade**
- **Temp: 16-21°C (60-70°F)**
- **Keep moist, but drier in winter**

This much-neglected plant has many fine qualities, not least the fact that it is not at all difficult to rear and is almost totally free of pests. Evergreen, oval-shaped leaves are a dull green in colour and are attached to woody stems. Initially, the stems are supple and will hang naturally over the container in which the plant is growing, but in time they become rigid.

Besides the distinct advantage of being a natural hanging plant, this columnea will also oblige with a wealth of reddish-orange flowers in early spring when flowering houseplants are not so plentiful.

However, getting plants to produce their flowers can be a problem, but one way is to keep the soil very much on the dry side during winter and at the same time lower the growing temperature by several degrees. New plants are easily started from cuttings.

Columnea banksii variegata

- **Light shade**
- **Temp: 16-21°C (60-70°F)**
- **Keep moist in summer**

The columneas are generally free-flowering plants, but the variegated form of *C. banksii* can be included among foliage plants, as it rarely produces flowers. The foliage is highly variegated, slow growing, and pendulous. The leaves are plump and fleshy, and attached to slender dropping stems; plants are seen at their best when suspended in a basket or hanging pot.

Cuttings are more difficult to root than the green forms of columnea. Short sections of stem with the lower leaves removed are best for propagating; treat with rooting powder before the cuttings, five to seven in small pots, are inserted in a peat and sand mixture. A temperature of at least 21°C (70°F) is necessary and a propagator will be a great advantage. Due to the very slow rate of growth, it is necessary to allow the soil to dry reasonably between waterings. Feed with weak fertilizer, but never overdo it.

Left: **Coleus**
Easily cared for and in many brilliant colours that are seen at their best when grown in good light. Start fresh young plants each year.

Above: **Columnea banksii**
This naturally hanging plant will bloom readily if grown in high humidity when active and given a cool rest from early to mid-winter.

Above:
Columnea banksii variegata
A fine trailing plant with small, plump, green-and-white leaves. Propagation can be a slow process.

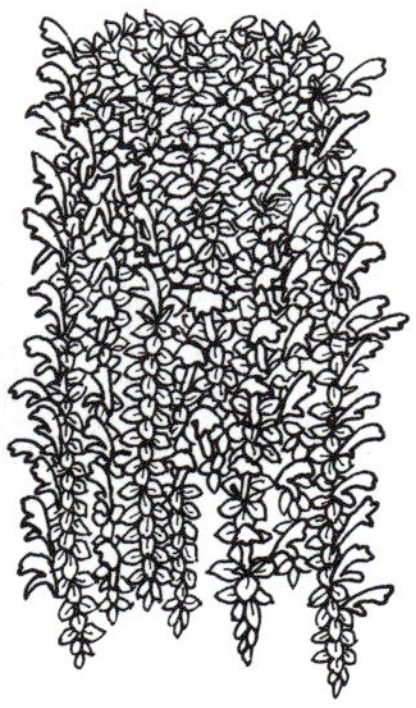

Columnea microphylla

- **Shade**
- **Temp: 18-21°C (65-70°F)**
- **Keep moist, drier in winter**

This is one of the more difficult columneas to grow successfully. The difficulty lies in the fact that it requires a constant temperature in the region of 18-21°C (65-70°F). Nevertheless, once the challenge is accepted, the results can be very rewarding. The small, oval-shaped, pale-green leaves are attached to wiry stems that hang perpendicularly from the container in which the plant is growing. Essentially, it is a hanging plant and can only be seen at its best when provided with a hanging pot or basket in which to grow.

Flowers, generally produced during the summer months, are rich orange and red in colour and on mature plants are produced in great abundance. Something that adds to their attraction is that mature plants in large baskets may have trails 1.8m (6ft) or more in length, and may well have flowers from the top to almost the bottom of the strands.

It is important to keep the soil moist and to feed regularly with weak liquid fertilizer.

Above: **Columnea microphylla**
Like all columneas, this one needs warm, humid conditions to flourish and produce those lovely tubular flowers. A winter rest is important.

Conophytum bilobum

- **Full sun**
- **Temp: 5-30°C (41-86°F)**
- **Give completely dry rest**

Conophytums are ideal plants for the small greenhouse but they need full sun. *C. bilobum* is one of the easiest species to grow. The two stemless leaves are fused to form a heart-shaped plant body, which is smooth and pale green in colour. The shining yellow flowers appear from the cleft between the leaves in late summer.

When to water can be a problem. Conophytums grow in late summer and autumn; but conditions in the greenhouse and the climatic conditions outside can influence growth, and watering is best based on observation. When watering stops, the plant body will slowly shrivel. Eventually two or three new heads emerge from the old plant. When the previous year's growth has shrivelled to a paper-thin skin, regular watering can start. It is advisable to give conophytums one good soaking in spring. Pot in very open mixture.

Above: **Conophytum bilobum**
This conophytum readily forms compact little clumps with masses of quite large yellow flowers. An ideal succulent for limited space.

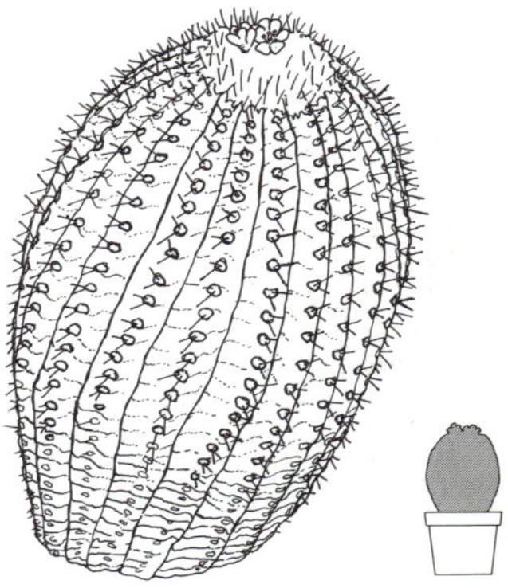

Conophytum frutescens

- **Full sun**
- **Temp: 5-30°C (41-86°F)**
- **Give completely dry rest**

Conophytum frutescens is sometimes listed under its old name of *C. salmonicolor*, which well describes the beautiful orange-pink flowers. The single pair of leaves is fused into a heart-shaped body about 3cm (1.2in) high. The leaves are green with light dots, and the flower emerges from the cleft in mid-summer. With age this plant develops stems, and ends up as a small shrub about 15cm (6in) high. If the plant seems to be deteriorating, remove the heads, leaving a short piece of stem attached to each head, and treat these as cuttings. Cuttings should be taken at the beginning of the growing period.

The soil should be very open: half loam-based mixture and half sharp sand or perlite. Repot every four or five years. During the resting period keep the plant completely dry; when the old plant body has completely shrivelled and the new heads have emerged (mid-summer), start watering, and continue until late autumn.

Copiapoa cinerea

- **Full sun**
- **Temp: 5-30°C (41-86°F)**
- **Water cautiously**

Copiapoa cinerea is one of the most beautiful cacti to come out of South America. It is grown for the beauty of its form; it rarely flowers in cultivation, probably because it is difficult to give it sufficient light to stimulate bud formation away from the burning sun of its native desert. Most plants seen in cultivation are the size of a grapefruit. It is chalky-white in colour, and the ribs carry glossy black spines that contrast beautifully with the white skin.

Copiapoas need very good drainage; use an open soil, of half loam-based mixture and half sharp sand or perlite. In the winter keep it dry, but during the summer water freely, allowing it to dry out between waterings. Keep this cactus in the sunniest part of the greenhouse; this will keep the plant brightly coloured.

With age, the plant will form offsets along the ribs. These may be used for propagation. *C. cinerea* looks more attractive when grown as a solitary plant.

Left: **Conophytum frutescens**
Possibly the most attractive of a delightful group of miniature succulents. The plant consists of two very fleshy leaves to each head.

Above: **Copiapoa cinerea**
Flowers are not readily produced in temperature climates, but the contrast between plant and spine colour recommends this species.

A practical hint
Raise cacti from seed thinly sown on surface of well-drained, sandy soil in spring at temperatures around 18-24°C (65-75°F).

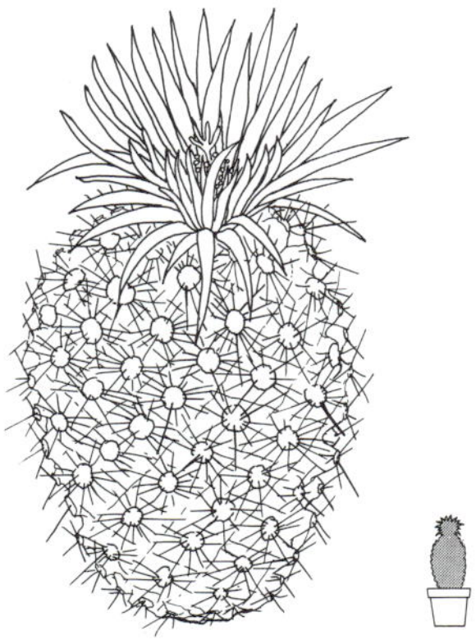

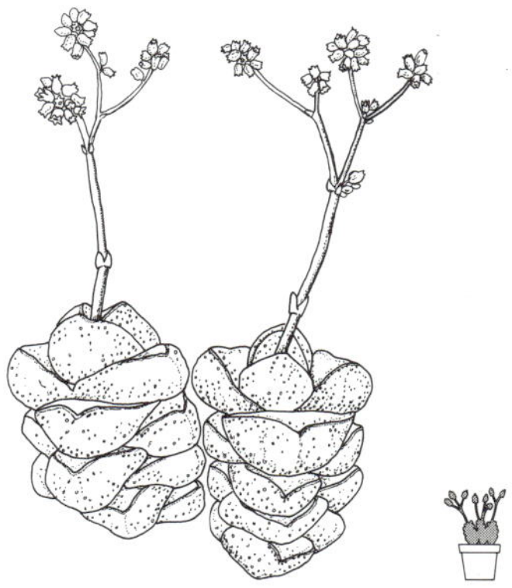

Coryphantha vivipara

- **Full sun**
- **Temp: 5-30°C (41-86°F)**
- **Water carefully**

Coryphanthas are small, globular cacti, very suitable for collectors with limited space. *C. vivipara* is a freely clustering plant; it is grey in colour and the stem is divided into tubercles. The tips of the tubercles carry white spines. The reddish flowers are borne on the top of the plant during the summer. The plant may be left as a cluster or some offsets used for propagation.

Any good potting mixture, either loam- or peat-based, may be used, with about one third of extra grit. During the late spring and summer, water freely, allowing the soil to dry out between waterings. Feed every two weeks with a high-potassium fertilizer when the buds form. Keep it dry in the winter. A sunny position is needed, because strong light stimulates bud formation and keeps the spines a good colour.

Mealy bug and root mealy bug are the pests most likely to be found; if so, water with a proprietary insecticide. If root mealy bugs are discovered, wash all the old soil off the roots and scrub the pot.

Crassula arborescens

- **Full sun**
- **Temp: 5-30°C (41-86°F)**
- **Keep moist all the year**

Crassula arborescens is one of the largest of the crassulas, forming a shrub over 2m (6.5ft) high. It is an impressive background plant for a large greenhouse or may be used to decorate a paved area of the garden during the summer months. It has stout, woody stems, and the broad leaves are grey-green. The flowers are pink, but it is not an easy plant to flower; it is best regarded as a foliage plant.

A porous soil, consisting of two parts loam- or peat-based mixture and one part sharp sand or perlite, will ensure that the roots do not become waterlogged. This plant does not have a definite resting period and should be kept moist all the year. Crassulas require good light, but if the leaves start to look a little shrivelled, move the plant to a slightly shadier spot.

This plant is not greatly bothered by pests but scale insects can be a nuisance. They should be picked off by hand. If possible, avoid spraying, as this may mark the leaves.

Crassula deceptrix

- **Full sun**
- **Temp: 7-30°C (45-86°F)**
- **Keep slightly moist all year**

This is a beautiful miniature plant, ideal for a small greenhouse or a sunny windowsill. The stems are 5cm (2in) high and are completely hidden by the closely packed leaves. The succulent leaves are covered with a white coating and the plant looks as if it were carved from white stone. The stems branch from the base. This is a slow-growing plant and may be kept in a 7.5cm (3in) pot for a number of years. The white bell-shaped flowers are carried on slender stems. It flowers freely in cultivation.

C. deceptrix is easily propagated. Cut one of the stems, dry it for two days, and pot up. Although this species does not have a dry resting period, it should never be overwatered. A very porous mixture – one part loam-based potting medium and one part grit – is suitable; always allow it to dry out before watering again.

White mealy bugs on a white plant can often remain unnoticed. Inspect regularly, and pick off any mealy bugs with forceps.

Left: **Coryphantha vivipara**
A free-flowering small cactus, which usually forms a clump of globular stems. With a good, well-drained soil it can survive low temperatures.

Above: **Crassula arborescens**
This can make a large shrub but it is also a good houseplant. It is best to take cuttings and restart when it becomes too large. Keep moist.

Above: **Crassula deceptrix**
This miniature succulent has a mass of branched stems closely clad with unusually shaped leaves. Very pretty, but the flowers are tiny.

Crassula falcata

- **Full sun**
- **Temp: 7-30°C (45-86°F)**
- **Keep moist all year**

Crassula falcata has such colourful flowers that it is a popular 'florist's plant' and is the parent of many beautiful hybrids. It is a small shrub, 30cm (12in) high. The large bluish-grey leaves are sickle-shaped. The stout flower stem carries a mass of tiny scarlet flowers; each individual flower is bell-shaped and they are arranged in a large, flat inflorescence. If the plant is grown in a greenhouse border, it will branch.

The crassulas may be propagated from leaf or stem cuttings. Shrubby crassulas tend to become untidy with age and should be restarted in the early summer. Grow in a well-drained soil, two parts loam-based mixture to one part sharp sand or perlite. Keep moist all the year but allow to dry out between waterings and keep a little drier immediately after flowering. When the buds begin to form, feed with a liquid tomato fertilizer once every two weeks.

This succulent makes quite a satisfactory houseplant if it can be given a window in full sun.

Above: **Crassula falcata**
Here is an overlooked beauty, with firm clusters of brilliant red flowers that are excellent for cutting. A good succulent and easy to grow.

Crocus

- **Good light with sunshine**
- **Temp: 7-16°C (45-60°F)**
- **Keep moist while growing**

Flowering crocuses on the windowsill give a clear indication that spring is on the way, but one has to think of them in early autumn, when the corms are planted. Bold groups in shallow pans filled with houseplant soil are better than small pots with a few wispy leaves and flowers. They must be planted in early autumn and put in a dark, cool place outdoors to develop the essential roots before shoot growth begins.

A simple way of creating dark conditions is to place a black flower-pot over the pot holding the bulbs. Once growth begins, the corms can be exposed to the light and taken indoors, where they will quite quickly start to bloom. Flowers will last for a longer period in cool and airy conditions than in warmer, stuffy rooms. After flowering, the corms should be planted out in the garden, or stored to flower in new soil the following season.

Above right and right: **Crocus**
These early spring flowering plants can be raised easily indoors if they are kept cool and dark at first. The Dutch hybrids (right) are stunning.

A practical hint
For a bold display with bulbs it is better to put lots of bulbs in the same container; for maximum effect, groups of pots are best.

Crossandra infundibuliformis

- **Good light**
- **Temp: 16-21°C (60-70°F)**
- **Keep moist**

These are neat plants for the windowsill, needing light and airy conditions, with some protection from strong sunlight. The soil needs to be kept moist at all times, with less water being required in winter. In winter there will also be no need to feed plants, but while in active growth they will respond to feeding with weak liquid fertilizer. Vigorous plants will tolerate and benefit from feeding at every watering. An alternative to liquid feeding would be the use of tablet or stick-form fertilizers that are pressed into the soil and made available to the plant over a period of several weeks.

Naturally glossy green leaves are topped by bright orange flowers in the spring, with the possibility of further flowers later in the year. New plants can be started from seed or cuttings.

Above left:
Crossandra infundibuliformis
This plant thrives in warm, humid conditions. Check for red spider mites in hot, dry surroundings.

A practical hint
For appearance's sake and to check disease, remove dead flowers regularly. Flowers such as cyclamen must be removed complete with the stalk.

Cryptanthus bromelioides 'It'

- **Light shade**
- **Temp: 16-21°C (60-70°F)**
- **Keep on dry side**

A comparatively recent introduction that resembles *C. tricolor,* but is of much bolder pink and is more attractive, although individual plants vary in brightness of colour. The new variety also grows closer to the pot. The leaves are stiffer in appearance, begin with a thick base attached to a short main stem, and taper to a point.

Cryptanthuses, like all bromeliads, require to be potted into a very open, free-draining mixture. One suggestion is to prepare a mixture of coarse leaf mould and a peaty houseplant potting mixture and to pot the plants in this, using small containers. Treated tree bark that is not too coarse may be used as a substitute for leaf mould. Place a few pieces of broken pot in the bottom of the container before introducing the soil. When watering these plants it is important that they have a thorough soak and then be allowed to dry reasonably before more is given. Clean rain water will be ideal.

Right:
Cryptanthus bromelioides 'It'
Small, star-shaped radiating growth is neat and compact, making plants ideal for small plant gardens in bottles. Fascinating pink colour.

A practical hint
Cyclamen, azaleas and numerous other plants will do better and will flower over a longer period if high temperatures can be avoided.

Cryptanthus bromelioides tricolor

- **Light shade**
- **Temp: 16-21°C (60-70°F)**
- **Keep on dry side**

The pink, green and white colouring of this plant can be spectacular in well-grown specimens, but they are not easy plants to care for. Although grouped with the other flatter-growing cryptanthuses under the same common name of earth star, these have a slightly different habit of growth. The centre of the plant tends to extend upwards, and new plant growth sprouts from the side of the parent rosette. If these side growths are left attached to the parent a full and handsome plant will in time develop; or they can be removed when of reasonable size by pulling them sideways; it is then simple to press the pieces into peaty mixture for them to produce roots.

Almost all cryptanthuses are terrestrial and are seen at their best when nestled in the crevices of an old tree stump, or surrounded by a few stones. *C. tricolor,* with its more open habit of growing, can also be effective in a hanging pot or basket.

Above left: **Cryptanthus bromelioides tricolor**
This beautiful earth star is prone to basal rot so must be watered with care. It will thrive if the atmosphere is warm and humid.

A practical hint
With cyclamen, observe a rest period when foliage dies down naturally after flowering. Keep the pot bone dry in a cool place until new growth starts.

Cryptanthus 'Foster's Favourite'

- **Light shade**
- **Temp: 16-21°C (60-70°F)**
- **Avoid excessive watering**

Another splendid example from the fine bromeliad family from tropical South America. Named after a famous American nurseryman, this tends to be much larger than most cryptanthus plants and produces long leaves with a pheasant-feather pattern. The thick, fleshy leaves have the shape of a dagger blade and radiate from a short central stem.

In their natural habitat these plants grow on the floor of the forest among old tree stumps and boulders, so they are capable of withstanding rough treatment. But remember the old maxim – which applies to almost all indoor plants – that when low temperatures prevail or plants are likely to be exposed to trying conditions they will fare much better if kept on the dry side. In fact, no bromeliads will prosper if roots are confined to pots that are permanently saturated. An open potting mixture is essential so that water can drain through very freely.

Above: **Cryptanthus 'Foster's Favourite'**
The stiff, unbending leaves of this fine bromeliad form a star shape. Its unusual colour and markings make it perfect for mixed displays.

Cuphea ignea

- **Good light**
- **Temp: 10-16°C (50-60°F)**
- **Keep moist and fed**

This is a straggly plant with a mass of tiny leaves pin-pointed with an abundance of red tubular flowers. The ends of the tubular flowers are lipped with blackish-grey colouring not unlike cigar ash – hence the appropriate common name of 'cigar plant'.

New plants can be raised from seed sown in the spring or from stem cuttings taken in late summer. When only one or two plants are required it is usually better to purchase established plants, so saving the bother of overwintering or raising seed plants.

Cupheas are very easy to manage on a light windowsill, needing no particular attention other than the usual watering and feeding. Once established in 13cm (5in) pots no further potting is needed, as plants will tend to become too large. Discard after flowering.

Left: **Cuphea ignea**
An easy-care plant for a brightly lit place. Young plants carry the most flowers so it is best to start or buy new ones each year. A loam-based potting mixture is ideal.

A practical hint
When pollen is noticed on cyclamen flowers a soft brush can be used to transfer it from one flower to another. Seed sets and can be sown.

Cyclamen persicum

- **Good light**
- **Temp: 10-16°C (50-60°F)**
- **Keep moist, but dry after flowering**

Ever popular, the cyclamen has a cool beauty that is matched by few other plants. Centrally heated rooms kept at excessively high temperature can be its worst enemy. On a cool windowsill that offers good light the life of the cyclamen indoors will be much extended.

Water well by pouring water on to the soil surface and ensuring that surplus water is seen to drain through the holes in the bottom of the pot; repeat only when the foliage feels limp to the touch. But never allow leaves and flowers to flag excessively.

Clear out dead flowers and leaves complete with their stems to prevent rotting. Following flowering, plants die back naturally and should be stored cool and dry until new growth is evident – which is also the time to pot on.

Right: **Cyclamen persicum**
The classic gift plant, cyclamens are available in a dazzling range of colours throughout the winter.

A practical hint
Plants can be fascinating for pets, and are best placed out of their reach if plant leaves are not to be chewed or torn by claws.

Cyclamen 'Minicyclamen'

- **Good light**
- **Temp: 13-18°C (55-65°F)**
- **Keep moist, but dry after flowering**

'Minicyclamen' is a completely new strain of cyclamen with neat and compact leaf formation and flowers that are only 15-20cm (6-8in) in height. Flowers come in a wide range of colours and there is the added bonus that many of them are delicately scented.

More tolerant of warmer room conditions than the more common *C. persicum,* it will also go on in the same small pot for several years if feeding is not neglected. From these small plants flowers are often produced in great abundance, and will frequently set seed, even indoors; the seed will not be difficult to germinate.

As with all cyclamens it is essential that all dead material in the way of flowers and leaves be thoroughly cleaned from around the corm in the centre of the pot to prevent rotting. Allow the plant to rest after flowering in cool and dry conditions.

Left: **Cyclamen 'Minicyclamen'**
A brilliant new strain that flowers abundantly and withstands warmer surroundings than its larger cousin.

Cymbidiella rhodochila

- **Warm: 18°C (65°F)**
- **A challenge to grow**
- **Winter/spring flowering**
- **Evergreen/no rest**

This is an epiphytic plant that produces similar growth to that of a cymbidium, but has generally shorter leaves. The flowers – and there can be none more striking – are produced from winter to spring on a stem arising from the base of the pseudobulb. There can be as many as 20, which open in succession, three or four at any one time. Each flower measures about 7.5cm (3in) across and, being of heavy texture, they are long-lasting. The sepals and slightly hooded petals are yellowish-green, the latter thickly spotted with dark green; the lip, in contrast, is crimson, with some yellow and dark green spots in the centre.

Cymbidiellas are subjects for the warm house, provided with an abundance of moisture and good light, though not direct sunshine.

Only three species of this most attractive orchid are known, all native to Madagascar, and only *Cymbidiella rhodochila* is likely to be found in collections today. At first the genus was linked with *Cymbidium,* but it is now accepted as separate.

Above: **Cymbidiella rhodochila**
An unusual species suitable for the warm house, where it blooms during the winter and spring months.

Cymbidium Angelica 'Advent'

- **Cool: 10°C (50°F)**
- **Easy to grow and flower**
- **Autumn/winter flowering**
- **Evergreen/no rest**

This superb autumn to winter flowering yellow hybrid (*Cym.* Lucy Moor x *Cym.* Lucense) is fast becoming a very famous breeding plant and is being used by cymbidium hybridists throughout the world. Up to 14 large flowers, 13cm (5in) across, are carried on upright spikes. The petals and sepals are pale yellow and the cream-coloured lip is lightly spotted with dark red, the spotting becoming dense in the throat.

Cymbidium hybrids can become considerably large, and are best suited to a greenhouse where sufficient room can be given them. Overhead spraying is particularly beneficial during the summer growing season. If grown too warm without the cool night temperature recommended, the plants are unlikely to flower the following season. This is one of the earliest of the top class cymbidiums to bloom, and with careful selection of varieties the season can exceed six months. This very attractive cymbidium deserves a place in every collection.

Right:
Cymbidium Angelica 'Advent'
One of the finest varieties for autumn and winter flowers. Cool growing.

Cymbidium Ayres Rock 'Cooksbridge Velvet'

- **Cool: 10°C (50°F)**
- **Easy to grow and flower**
- **Winter/spring flowering**
- **Evergreen/no rest**

One of a new generation of cymbidiums in which the colour range has been extended even further towards the deeper pinks. The flowers, 11cm (4.25in) across, are crimson tinged with white and the lip is a rich dark crimson, boldly edged with white.

A supporting cane will be required by most of these *Cymbidium* hybrids to prevent the heavy flower spikes snapping or buckling under their own weight as they develop. Though these flowers will last eight or ten weeks on the plant, it is advisable (particularly with young plants) to remove the spike after the last flower has been open for about ten days. This reduces the strain on the plant at a time when new growths are appearing. The cut spike of flowers will last just as long in water in a cool room indoors.

This is one of the easiest orchids to propagate. The old leafless pseudobulbs can be removed from the plant at repotting time and potted singly.

Above: **Cymbidium Ayres Rock 'Cooksbridge Velvet'**
A fine dark-flowered hybrid. Spring flowering. Cool growing and easy.

Cymbidium Bulbarrow 'Our Midge'

- **Cool: 10°C (50°F)**
- **Easy to grow and flower**
- **Late spring flowering**
- **Evergreen/no rest**

The Bulbarrow hybrids have rightly gained a reputation throughout the world. The crossing of the standard Western Rose with the miniature species, *Cym. devonianum,* has resulted in some excellent clones, most of which have flowers with very fine lips of striking colours.

'Our Midge' bears spikes of up to 20 flowers in late spring. The 2.5-4cm (1-1.5in) flowers are soft rose-red with deep crimson lips.

The miniature hybrid cymbidiums provide an alternative for the grower with limited space. Being smaller and more easily managed plants, they can be accommodated in the home. Their more compact blooms are just as rewarding, and are often of rich colouring where the species *Cymbidium devonianum* has been used as a parent.

Cymbidiums, particularly if grown in the drier indoor atmosphere, can be prone to attacks from red spider mite. Regular sponging and wiping of the leaves with water, particularly the undersides, will keep this at bay.

Above: **Cymbidium Bulbarrow 'Our Midge'**
A superb miniature hybrid to bloom in the late spring. Easy to grow.

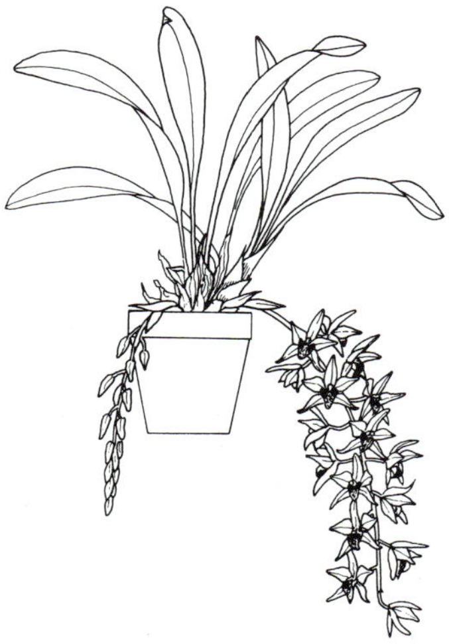

Cymbidium devonianum

- **Cool: 10°C (50°F)**
- **Easy to grow and flower**
- **Spring flowering**
- **Evergreen/semi-dry rest**

This miniature species originates from the Himalayas and has been used often in breeding miniatures. The flowers, borne on pendent spikes, normally open in late spring and early summer. They are basically green speckled with red, and the triangular lip is clouded with purple. When the flower spikes first appear they have the annoying habit of burrowing into the compost. A label should be placed under the spikes to ensure that they grow horizontally towards the rim of the pot.

This species differs in its appearance from the conventional cymbidium. The pseudobulbs are small, but the leaves are considerably wider, narrowing sharply towards the base. Unlike most cymbidiums, this species requires a semi-rest during the winter, with only occasional watering.

Above: **Cymbidium devonianum**
An ideal beginner's orchid. Cool growing and spring flowering. Flower spikes hang downwards.

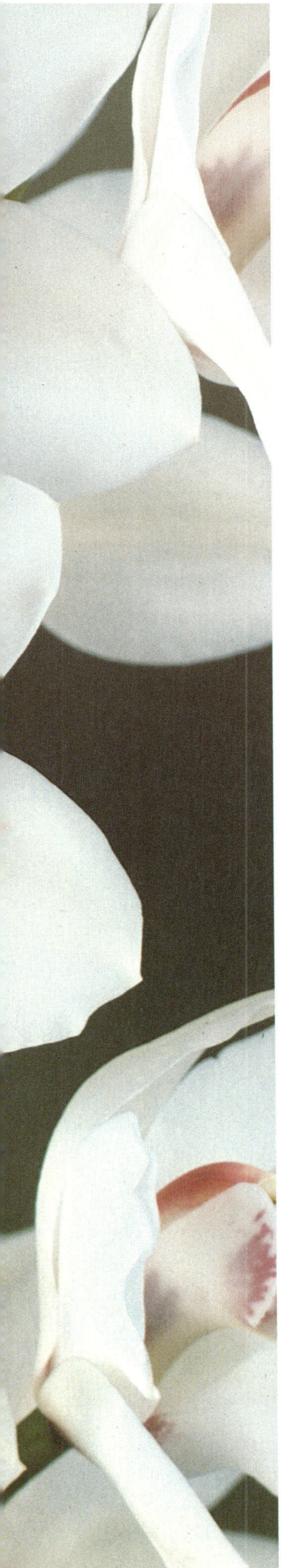

Cymbidium Dingwall 'Lewes'

- **Cool: 10°C (50°F)**
- **Easy to grow and flower**
- **Late spring flowering**
- **Evergreen/no rest**

A hybrid resulting from a cross between *Cym.* Pearl Easter and *Cym.* Merlin. Pearl Easter is a superb parent for producing flowers with clear white sepals and petals and the combination with Merlin has produced some very fine late spring flowering whites. This plant is free-flowering and bears up to 12 large 13cm (5in) flowers on an upright spike. The petals and sepals are white and the lip is marked with red.

Young plants will bloom on one flower spike from the leading growth. As the plant matures more than one new growth will be made each season. Each new growth can be capable of flowering, so the number of flower spikes on a large plant is directly related to the number of new growths. Nothing looks finer than a large plant with six or more flowering spikes, although to achieve this standard without dividing the plant, adequate room must be available. While flowering, the plants should be kept well shaded to prevent discolouration by the sun.

Cymbidium eburneum

- **Cool: 10°C (50°F)**
- **A challenge to flower**
- **Winter/spring flowering**
- **Evergreen/no rest**

Discovered in the 1830s by the botanical explorer William Griffiths, this species is native to the Khasia hills in northern India. It is a compact grower with narrow pseudobulbs, and leaves that can grow to more than 60cm (24in) in length. The erect flower spike arises higher up on the bulb than in most cymbidiums, and several spikes are often carried at the same time. The plant is often erratic in its flowering, producing from one to three 7.5cm (3in) flowers to each spike. The flowers, which open in winter and early spring, are white to ivory in colour, with a deep yellow band in the middle of the lip, flanked by two yellow keels.

Very prominent in hybridization, *Cym. eburneum* was one of the parents of the first hybrid cymbidium to be raised in cultivation – Eburneolowianum – which was registered by Veitch in 1889. Although it is an important species in breeding, the plant does not grow vigorously, and is a shy bloomer.

Cymbidium Fort George 'Lewes'

- **Cool: 10°C (50°F)**
- **Easy to grow and flower**
- **Winter/spring flowering**
- **Evergreen/no rest**

One of the finest free-flowering, green-coloured cymbidiums in the world, often giving two spikes per bulb with up to 14 flowers per spike on an upright stem. The flowers are up to 12cm (4.75in) in diameter. The bringing together of two of the most famous green-flowered parents (*Cym.* Baltic x *Cym.* York Meradith) has produced an excellent result.

To achieve regular flowering all cymbidiums should be repotted every other year, keeping them as large as can be managed. They can be fed throughout almost the whole year, reducing both feed and water to a minimum during the shortest days for three months of the year.

The blooms of cymbidiums are highly in demand as cut flowers and are certainly more popular with florists than any other orchid bloom. For this purpose they can be grown in large beds, where they grow exceedingly well, producing even more vigorous plants than those raised individually in pots in the accepted way.

Left:
Cymbidium Dingwall 'Lewes'
A fine white hybrid for late spring flowering. Cool, easy to grow.

Above: **Cymbidium eburneum**
This cool-growing species produces one to three flowers in the winter and spring months. Not easy to grow.

Above:
Cymbidium Fort George 'Lewes'
A cool-growing hybrid for winter/spring flowers. Upright spikes.

A practical hint
One essential for orchids is free-draining potting mixture. Bark chippings provide a good medium, but a beginner should purchase a specialist mixture.

Cymbidium lowianum
- **Cool: 10°C (50°F)**
- **Easy to grow and flower**
- **Late spring flowering**
- **Evergreen/no rest**

Discovered in 1887 in upper Burma, and also found in Thailand, this species has exerted its influence in almost all of our modern hybrids. The plant, which flowers in late spring, normally carries very large arching sprays of green flowers, up to 10cm (4in) across, with a V-shaped red mark on the lip. There is also the variety *concolor*, which has a yellow marking on the lip.

The plant conforms in appearance to the typical cymbidium, but it is easily identified when not in flower by the slender shape of its pseudobulbs. At one time extremely common, it lost its popularity to the numerous hybrids it helped to create. Now it is unobtainable from its native home; plants are nursery-raised in limited numbers to meet the new demand as growers rediscover this lovely species.

The plant may be quite easily propagated by the removal of the leafless pseudobulbs. To maintain a plant of flowering size, it should not be reduced to less than four or five bulbs.

Right: **Cymbidium lowianum**
Long, arching sprays are produced by this lovely, cool-growing, spring-flowering species. Easy to grow.

Cymbidium Peter Pan 'Greensleeves'
- **Cool: 10°C (50°F)**
- **Easy to grow and flower**
- **Autumn flowering**
- **Evergreen/no rest**

One of the most popular of the autumn flowering varieties, this plant will grow equally well indoors or in a greenhouse. Its compact habit enables it to be grown into a large specimen plant without division, when several flower spikes will be produced in a season. The flowers are a little over 7.5cm (3in) across. The petals and sepals are soft green, and the lip is heavily marked and edged with deep crimson. Do not allow the flowers to remain on the plant for too long. After two weeks they should be removed and placed in water.

This is a fine example of a hybrid that has inherited the best characteristics from both its parents (*Cym. ensifolium* x *Cym.* Miretta). From *Cym. ensifolium* the plant has inherited its autumn flowering habit together with a beautiful fragrance, and Miretta has greatly enhanced the quality of the flower.

Repotting, when necessary, should be done in the spring. Surplus leafless pseudobulbs can be removed and used for propagation.

Above right: **Cymbidium Peter Pan 'Greensleeves'**
A popular autumn-flowering hybrid that can be grown easily indoors.

A practical hint
A deciduous orchid that needs no water following natural leaf fall, *Dendrobium aureum* also requires good winter light to flower in the spring.

Cymbidium Stonehaven 'Cooksbridge'

- **Cool: 10°C (50°F)**
- **Easy to grow and flower**
- **Autumn/winter flowering**
- **Evergreen/no rest**

This second generation *Cym. pumilum* hybrid (*Cym.* Putana x *Cym.* Cariga) is a very good quality, medium-sized plant that produces strong spikes with up to 25 fine, 7cm (2.75in) flowers. Opening in autumn and early winter, the flowers are cream-coloured and the lip is pale yellow, edged with dark red. The plant is very free-flowering and easy to grow. Such plants are becoming increasingly popular as pot plants for the home.

While the flower spikes are developing, some support will be required. A thin bamboo cane should be inserted close to the spike and tied into position. The developing buds should not be supported until they are well developed, or the supporting ties must be adjusted almost daily as the spike grows. If the recommended night-time temperature cannot be kept down, the plant will be reluctant to bloom. During the summer such plants can be grown out of doors while temperatures permit.

Left: **Cymbidium Stonehaven 'Cooksbridge'**
A many-flowered miniature variety to bloom in the autumn and winter.

Cymbidium Touchstone 'Janis'

- **Cool: 10°C (50°F)**
- **Easy to grow and flower**
- **Winter/spring flowering**
- **Evergreen/no rest**

This miniature variety is another fine example of *Cym. devonianum* breeding (*Cym. devonianum* x Mission Bay). The plants from this crossing are small and free growing, and produce beautiful arching sprays of flowers during the winter and early spring. The flowers are bronze with contrasting deep crimson lips and are 2.5-4cm (1-1.6in) across.

An ideal beginner's plant for indoor or greenhouse culture. It should be kept watered throughout the year, never being allowed to dry out completely. During the spring, summer and autumn months the plant should be lightly fed. Cool night-time temperatures are important for successful flowering. Repotting will be necessary every other year. This should be done immediately after flowering and using a size larger pot. If there are too many leafless pseudobulbs, some should be removed to restore the balance of the plant. Water should be witheld for a few days after repotting is completed.

Above:
Cymbidium Touchstone 'Janis'
This is a beautiful miniature hybrid that carries semi-pendent spikes in the winter and spring months.

Cymbidium traceyanum

- **Cool: 10°C (50°F)**
- **Easy to grow and flower**
- **Autumn flowering**
- **Evergreen/no rest**

This very interesting and flamboyant species was exported in great quantities from Thailand at the beginning of the century. The number collected in the early years resulted in the virtual disappearance of the plant from its natural habitat.

The species is autumn to winter flowering and produces long arching sprays of 10-13cm (4-5in) flowers. The flowers are strongly scented; unfortunately, the fragrance is not altogether pleasant. The petals are green, heavily striped with dark red, and the white lip is spotted with red. It has been important as a base species for producing spring flowering types and is also in the background of some yellow hybrids.

Alone among the cultivated *Cymbidium* species, it has the habit of producing a number of short upright roots, which grow from established roots near the surface of the compost. This feature makes it instantly recognizable from other *Cymbidium* species with otherwise identical habits of growth.

Above: **Cymbidium traceyanum**
A strongly scented species that blooms in the autumn. Cool growing. Long sprays of flowers are produced. Many hybrids available.

A practical hint
The orchid *Dendrobium superbum* produces long flowering canes but is subject to attack by red spider mite during summer. Keep it dry in winter.

Cyperus alternifolius

- **Light shade**
- **Temp: 13-18°C (55-65°F)**
- **Wet conditions**

This fascinating houseplant belongs to a group of rush-like plants that in nature live at the margins of rivers and lakes. Thin, grass-like leaves surround the bases of flower stems that may reach 60-120cm (2-4ft) tall. The green or brown flowers are insignificant but leaf-like bracts radiate in all directions to produce attractive 'umbrella' canopies. The tall stems provide an interesting feature at a high level when planting indoor water gardens.

When grown indoors these water-loving plants must be given all the water they require. Although it would be death to most houseplants, place the pot in a large saucer capable of holding a reasonable amount of water, and ensure that the water level is regularly topped up.

Established plants benefit from regular feeding in liquid or tablet form. Tablets pressed into the soil at the frequency recommended by the manufacturer will provide a continual source of nutrient and is one of the best methods of feeding.

Left: **Cyperus alternifolius**
This top view shows the spreading bracts at the top of the flower stems that provide the main interest. The green flowers can also be seen.

Cyrtomium falcatum

- **Shade**
- **Temp: 16-21°C (60-70°F)**
- **Keep moist**

Ideal for a shady corner, this fern's foliage has the appearance of holly, and is dark, glossy green in colour. Individual fronds will grow to some 60cm (2ft) in length when mature.

Suitable conditions are necessary for maximum success in fern propagation. But reasonable results can be obtained in the home if a heated propagator and moist, not saturated, conditions are available. Older leaves develop spores on the back; these have the appearance of a brownish rust that could well be mistaken for disease. When spores can be seen to fall like a fine dust when the leaf is tapped, the leaf can be removed and put in a paper bag in a warm place and left for a few days. The spores can then be sown on the surface of moist peat and placed in a propagator to germinate. They should be sown sparingly, as a dense mass of young plants will appear if conditions are right. When large enough to handle, these should be potted in peaty mixture.

Above: **Cyrtomium falcatum**
With dark green, holly-like foliage (but with no spines), this plant is a long-established favourite. A robust plant for shady places.

A practical hint
Developing into a large plant, the orchid *Dendrobium* Gatton Sunray produces large trusses of flowers over a period of time, but plants are scarce.

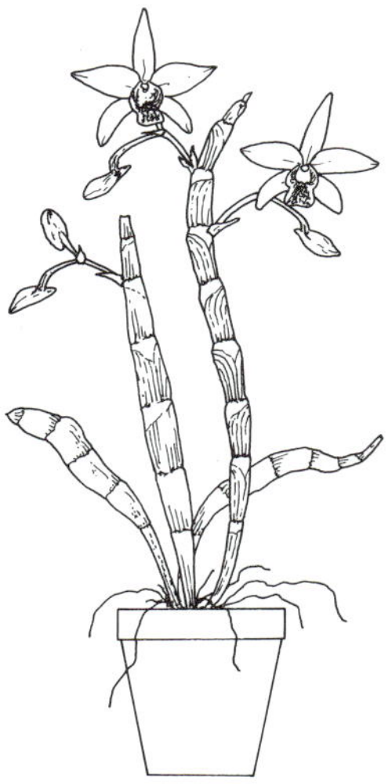

Delosperma pruinosum (D. echinatum)

- **Full sun**
- **Temp: 5-30°C (41-86°F)**
- **Keep moist all year**

Delosperma pruinosum is a small much-branched bush with plump, succulent leaves. These are covered with papillae, which have tiny bristles that give the leaves a glistening effect in the sun. The plant flowers continuously through the summer; the flowers, 1.5cm (0.6in) across, are whitish or yellow. The flowers open in the sunshine and close at night; they do not open on cloudy days or if the plant is in continuous shade.

D. pruinosum is most successfully grown in a sunny border where it can have a free root run. In climates where there is no danger of frost, it can be left outdoors permanently. Otherwise, take small cuttings during the summer, which can be wintered in a light position indoors. When it is grown outdoors the usual garden pests will be attracted and *D. pruinosum* can receive the same garden insecticides.

Above right:
Delosperma pruinosum
This unusual succulent can be kept indoors during the winter months.

Dendrobium aureum

- **Cool: 10°C (50°F)**
- **Easy to grow and flower**
- **Early spring flowering**
- **Deciduous/dry winter rest**

A widely distributed species found throughout India and in the Philippine Islands. The Indian variety is in general cultivation: the Philippine variety may be offered under the name of *D. heterocarpum.* The type produces stoutish bulbs of medium length and is deciduous in winter, when it needs a definite rest. Water should be discontinued when the leaves turn yellow and drop off naturally. A position of good light is essential during the winter to encourage flowering in the spring. The flowers appear during the early spring months, making it one of the first dendrobiums to flower. The blooms, up to 5cm (2in) across, are creamy-yellow with a buff brown lip covered in short hairs. They are pleasantly fragrant.

During the growing season keep a lookout for red spider mite, which can attack this plant. It is easily propagated from old canes cut into sections, or new plants can be raised from adventitious growths on old canes. Repot after flowering.

Right: **Dendrobium aureum**
An easy-to-grow, cool, compact species that is ideal for the beginner. Flowers in the early spring.

A practical hint
When contemplating the growing of orchids indoors, the beginner should consult a specialist grower, who can suggest the easier species.

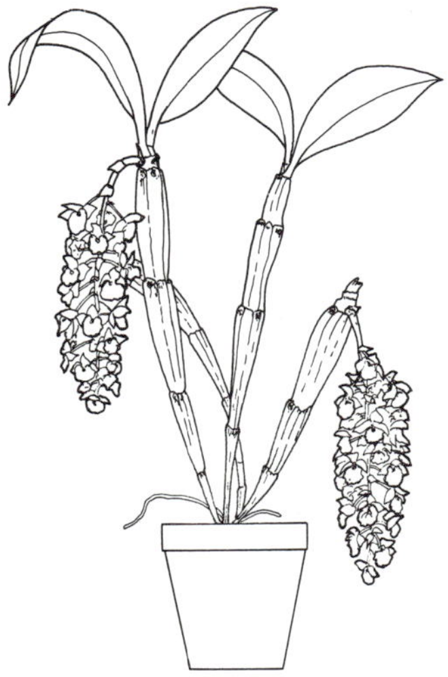

Dendrobium densiflorum

- **Cool: 10°C (50°F)**
- **Easy to grow and flower**
- **Early summer flowering**
- **Evergreen/dry winter rest**

Once plentiful, this delightful species is becoming increasingly difficult to obtain. The flowers, up to 5cm (2in) across, are carried in large pendent trusses from nodes at the top half of the club-shaped bulbs. They develop at great speed during the spring months and last for up to ten days in perfection. Their colour is a brilliant golden yellow, the lip similarly coloured and very striking. The plant likes to be grown in the cool greenhouse with a decided rest in the winter.

The rest period should be commenced as soon as the season's canes have matured and produced new terminal leaf. The plant will flower from the older canes, which may or may not be in leaf. Full light during the autumn and winter is important for regular flowering. Keep the plant dry while in flower to extend flowering.

Not easy to propagate; grow on to a large plant and divide if required. Repot when new growth is seen. This species is evergreen and loses only a few leaves each year.

Left: **Dendrobium densiflorum**
One of the most beautiful of the spring-flowering species. Dense, golden yellow trusses in spring.

A practical hint
Rather than in pots, some orchids will do better and look better if planted in slatted rafts that will offer maximum air circulation.

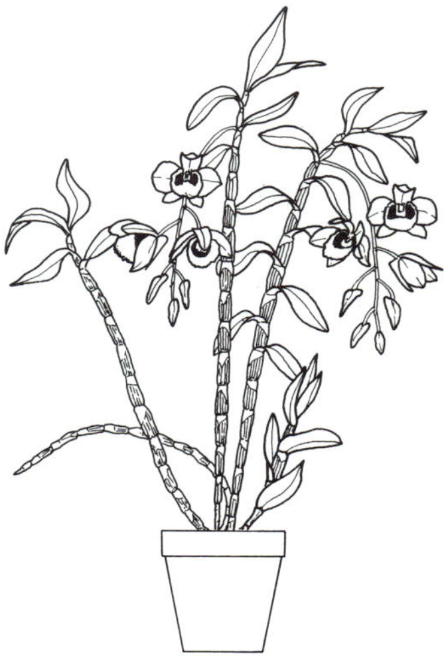

Denbrobium Fiftieth State

- **Warm: 16-18°C (60-65°F)**
- **Moderately easy to grow**
- **Summer flowering**
- **Evergreen/semi-dry rest**

This fine hybrid illustrates a completely different type of dendrobium, which has been bred from species of Australasian origin. The 6cm (2.4in) flowers of *D.* Fiftieth State are similar in shape to those of *D. phalaenopsis,* although the rich magenta colour of the species appears as overlying veins of soft red in the hybrid. Raised in Hawaii, the plant is warm growing and will succeed in high temperatures and almost full sunlight. It should be watered freely while growing but allowed a complete rest after flowering. The flowers are extremely long-lasting and appear on lengthy sprays from the top of the completed bulb.

Propagation from the old canes is not easy to achieve and the plant should be grown on without division. Do not overpot, or allow undue shrivelling of canes while at rest. Water as required. Repot when new growth has started.

The beautiful flowers may be used for florist's work, and last well when cut and displayed.

Above: **Dendrobium Fiftieth State**
A warm-growing hybrid that blooms in the summer sunshine. Very long-lasting, beautifully marked flowers.

Dendrobium Gatton Sunray

(FCC/RHS)

- **Intermediate: 13°C (55°F)**
- **Moderately easy to grow**
- **Summer flowering**
- **Evergreen/dry winter rest**

A magnificent hybrid, this is the largest of the cultivated dendrobiums, and requires plenty of growing space. It is an extremely robust plant, the canes growing to a height of 2m (6.5ft) or more. The extremely large and showy flowers, which appear in trusses during the early summer, are more than 10cm (4in) across and last in perfection for about ten days. A large plant will produce numerous trusses, each carrying several flowers. This will extend the flowering period, as not all the trusses come into flower at the same time.

The plant succeeds best in an intermediate greenhouse where it can be given good light and a decided rest during the winter months.

This plant is quite rare in cultivation and may take some finding. In view of its large size it should not be attempted where adequate space and light cannot be given. Propagation is very slow. Repot every other year in the spring when the new growth is seen.

Right:
Dendrobium Gatton Sunray
This is a massive grower that needs plenty of room in the greenhouse.

A practical hint
Shade and fresh air suit the orchid *Dracula chimaera*; it must never dry out, as there are no pseudobulbs for water storage. It does well on a raft.

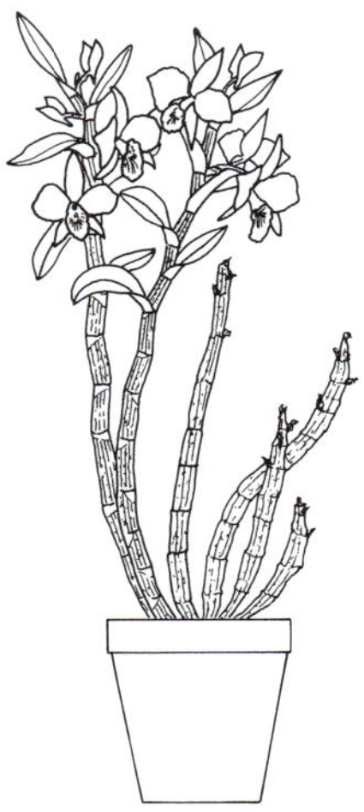

Dendrobium infundibulum

- **Cool: 10°C (50°F)**
- **Easy to grow and flower**
- **Spring flowering**
- **Evergreen/semi-dry rest**

A very fine and distinct species producing large, white flowers, 10cm (4in) across, of a soft papery texture. One to three flowers are produced from each node at the apex of the completed bulb. Well-grown plants produce huge heads of long-lasting flowers, the lip stained with bright yellow in the throat.

D. infundibulum is an evergreen variety and enjoys cool house conditions. In its native India it grows at considerable altitudes. The stems and the sheaths around the young buds are covered in short, protective black hairs.

This plant shrivels easily if kept completely dry for too long during its resting period. Therefore, water sparingly to keep the canes plump at all times. Old leafless canes may appear useless, but should not be removed unless brown and completely shrivelled. Propagation is sometimes possible with older canes. Keep in a small pot and repot after flowering.

The plant will grow well out of doors during the summer months.

Above far left:
Dendrobium infundibulum
One of the showiest dendrobiums. Cool growing; spring flowering.

Dendrobium Louisae

- **Warm 16-18°C (60-65°F)**
- **A challenge to grow**
- **Autumn/winter flowering**
- **Evergreen/semi-dry rest**

A very popular plant, this evergreen hybrid is widely grown and is readily available on both sides of the Atlantic. The plant was raised in Indonesia and resulted from the crossing of two showy species native to New Guinea, *D. phalaenopsis* var. *schroederanum* and *D. veratrifolium,* both of which bear long sprays of rose-mauve flowers. *D.* Louisae combines the characteristics of both parents and produces long arching sprays of flowers from the top of the bulbs. The 6cm (2.5in) flowers, which are a rich rose-purple, are extremely long lived and appear during the autumn and winter. The showy flowers can be used in floral arrangements to good effect. The plant can be grown in a warm sun room or greenhouse where it enjoys an abundance of light. Generous growing conditions will produce excellent results.

Propagation is very slow, and not easily achieved from the old canes. The plant should be grown on without division, unless considerably large. Do not overpot. Repot as soon as new growth is seen.

Left: **Dendrobium Louisae**
A warm-growing, sun-loving hybrid for autumn/winter blooming. Long-lasting sprays of flowers.

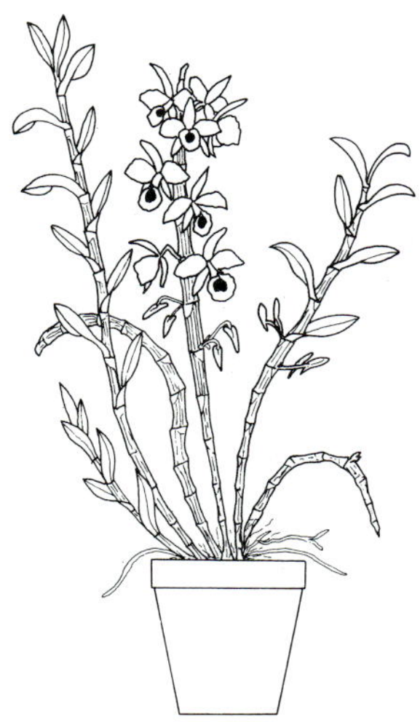

Dendrobium nobile

- **Cool: 10°C (50°F)**
- **Easy to grow and flower**
- **Spring flowering**
- **Semi-deciduous/dry rest**

Perhaps the most popular of all the cool-growing dendrobiums, this superb plant from India blooms during the spring. The flowers appear in ones and twos along the complete length of the previous year's bulbs, which are fairly tall and stoutish. The flowers, 5cm (2in) across, are rosy purple at the petal tips, shading to white towards the centre of the bloom. The lip carries a rich maroon blotch in the throat.

During the winter rest water should be withheld until the flower buds have clearly started their development in the spring. If watering is started too early embryo flower buds will develop into adventitious growths. Water well all summer, and keep cool. Too high temperatures will restrict flowering.

Propagates easily from leafless canes, or new plants can be raised from adventitious growths. Do not overpot. If the plant becomes top heavy put the pot into a larger weighted container. Repot when new growth appears.

Right: **Dendrobium nobile**
A very popular, cool-growing species that blooms in the spring. It flowers the entire length of the bulb. Requires good light to thrive.

Dendrobium pierardii

- **Intermediate: 13°C (55°F)**
- **Easy to grow and flower**
- **Spring flowering**
- **Deciduous/dry winter rest**

A very handsome species from India that produces extremely long, cane-like pseudobulbs that assume a pendent habit unless trained upright in a pot. The plant becomes deciduous during the winter months, when it is important to allow full light to ensure successful flowering the following spring. The 5cm (2in) blooms are produced on the entire length of the previous year's canes and are extremely pretty. They are beautifully coloured a rosy pastel pink, and the rounded lip is creamy yellow, streaked with purple at the base.

This species is at its best when grown into a large plant. Start watering after flowering; adventitious growths are produced if the plant is watered too early in the year. High summer temperatures are necessary to encourage complete growth of the extra long canes. Watch out for red spider mite during the growing season. Regular overhead spraying will help to keep this pest at bay. Do not overpot; does best mounted on bark. Remove old canes only when shrivelled.

Above: **Dendrobium pierardii**
An extremely tall-growing species for the intermediate house, best grown downwards. Flowers the length of the bulb. Deciduous.

Dendrobium secundum

- **Intermediate: 13°C (55°F)**
- **Easy to grow and flower**
- **Spring/summer flowering**
- **Evergreen/semi-dry rest**

An extremely pretty and distinctive species with a wide distribution down the Malaysian peninsula and into the Philippine Islands. The unusual flowers are individually very small, clustered tightly together into compact sprays 8-10cm (3.5-4in) long. The rosy pink flowers, with an orange blotch on the lip, appear for an extended period through the spring and summer months. The flower clusters appear from the topmost section of the previous year's canes, which may or may not be in leaf. The same cane can flower for more than one season.

It is a neat and attractive-looking plant with slender well-leafed canes that hold their foliage for several years before shedding a few leaves at a time. It does not propagate readily from old canes; it should be grown on into a large plant and divided only when large enough. Keep in as small a pot as possible. Repot when new growth is seen.

No hybridizing has been done with this species, which may be difficult to find in some areas of the world.

Above: **Dendrobium secundum**
Dense clusters of small, attractive flowers in spring and summer. An evergreen variety suitable for the intermediate house.

A practical hint
Needing careful watering that errs on the dry side, the orchid *Encyclia mariae* also prefers shade to bright sun. Its leaves are susceptible to water spray.

Dendrobium speciosum

- **Intermediate/warm: 13-18°C (55-65°F)**
- **A challenge to flower**
- **Spring flowering**
- **Evergreen/extended dry rest**

A most attractive species from Australia, this plant enjoys warmth and humidity during its growing season, with a decided rest during the winter. It is not unusual for this rest period to last for many months. No water should be given while the plant is at rest.

If ripened sufficiently the plant will bloom profusely in the spring, producing a shower of flower spikes bearing many rather small, densely packed flowers, off white in colour with the lip lightly spotted in purple. The flowers have a particularly delightful fragrance.

Not often seen in cultivation, this is a rewarding plant to grow where generous conditions permit. It can attain considerable size and is one of the largest of the genus, although slower growing than most. It does not propagate from old bulbs and should be grown on to a large plant and eventually divided. Repot when new growth is seen.

No hybrids have been produced from this particular species.

Right: **Dendrobium speciosum**
This beautiful species produces fragrant flowers in the spring. Needs a definite rest period.

Dendrobium superbum

- **Warm: 16-18°C (60-65°F)**
- **Easy to grow and flower**
- **Early summer flowering**
- **Deciduous/dry winter rest**

One of the finest dendrobiums from the Philippine Islands, this is a deciduous species that produces extremely long canes. The fragrant flowers appear during the early summer, along the entire length of the previous year's canes; they are 5-6cm (2-2.4in) across, and a rich magenta-purple, the lip a deeper shade. There is also a variety *album*, which produces pure white flowers. Although rarer in cultivation it can sometimes be found. The very long canes make this species ideal for growing upside-down on a wooden raft.

This species will occasionally propagate from old canes, but it is best when grown into a large plant. Be wary of attack from red spider mite during the growing season. When the leaves turn yellow withhold water until flowering starts in the following spring. If grown in a pot, careful staking will be required. Remove old canes only when brown and shrivelled. Repot when the new growth is clearly seen.

Above: **Dendrobium superbum**
A large-flowered, highly fragrant species for the warm greenhouse. Early summer flowering, deciduous.

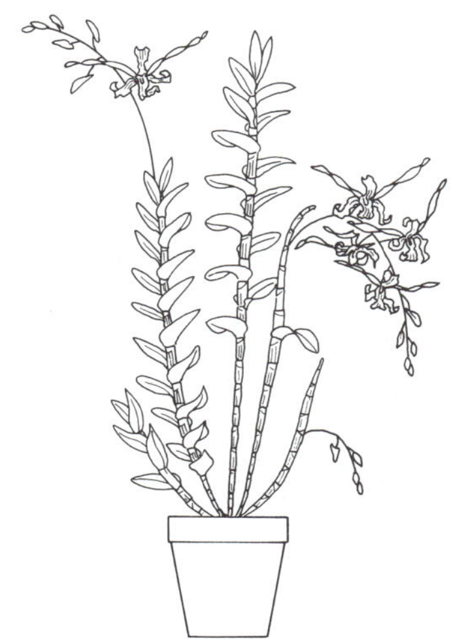

Dendrobium Tangerine 'Tillgates'

- **Intermediate: 13°C (55°F)**
- **Moderately easy to grow**
- **Spring/summer flowering**
- **Semi-deciduous/semi-rest**

Rather different from the 'traditional' cultivated dendrobium, this outstanding hybrid was raised from a little known but beautiful species, *D. strebloceras,* which comes from western New Guinea. Its name means 'crumpled horn' and refers to the long twisting petals. In the hybrid these petals stand erect, closely resembling the horns of an antelope. The plant is more colourful than its parent species, the 7.5cm (3in) flowers having bright orange petals and mustard yellow sepals and lip. Although the plant is little grown outside the tropics, its unusual and delightful flowers make it a desirable addition to any collection. A subject for the intermediate greenhouse, it would not do well in the house, as it requires full light throughout the year.

The plant is of neat habit, producing elegant canes that are leafed at the top. Flowering is from the top of the canes. It does not propagate readily and should not be hastily divided.

Above:
Dendrobium Tangerine 'Tillgates'
An unusual and elegant hybrid suitable for the intermediate house.

A practical hint
Many orchid species produce large pseudobulbs on rhizomatous stems, and these will act as food and water stores for the plant.

Dendrobium transparens

- **Intermediate: 13°C (55°F)**
- **Easy to grow and flower**
- **Spring flowering**
- **Deciduous/dry winter rest**

An extremely pretty and free-flowering species from India that grows well on bark in a pendent position. Its flowers, produced early in the year along the length of the previous season's canes, are 4cm (1.6in) across and pale rosy mauve, the colour heightening towards the tips of the petals; the lip carries two distinctive purple stains. It is a deciduous species which should be well rested before the next spring flowering season. After the leaves have turned yellow do not water until the flowers appear. Where generous summer conditions are provided ample flowering will follow. Watch out for red spider mite during the growing season.

If pot culture is preferred this plant can be beautifully trained into a fan shape. Do not overpot. Adventitious growths are easily produced and can be used for propagation. Otherwise grow into a large plant before dividing. Remove old canes only when brown and shrivelled. Repot after flowering.

Top left:
Dendrobium transparens
A fragrant species for intermediate conditions. Flowers the length of the tall, slender bulbs in the spring.

Dendrobium wardianum

- **Cool: 10°C (50°F)**
- **Easy to grow and flower**
- **Winter flowering**
- **Deciduous/dry winter rest**

One of the most handsome of the cool-growing species, this too comes from India. The 5-6cm (2-2.4in) flowers, produced along the length of the previous year's canes, are white, with the petals, sepals and lip tipped with amethyst purple; the lip is also brightly stained with yellow and two maroon blotches at the base. The canes can become tall on a large plant, and it grows well on wooden rafts.

This is another plant that can be affected by red spider mite because of its soft, short-lived foliage. Do not overpot. Water well during the growing season and provide good winter light for successful flowering. Some staking will be necessary if the plant is grown upright in a pot; to prevent it becoming top heavy place the pot in a weighted container. Remove old canes only when brown and shrivelled. It is occasionally possible to propagate the plant from old canes. Repot immediately after flowering, by which time the new growth will be clearly showing.

Top centre:
Dendrobium wardianum
A cool-growing species that blooms early in the year. Flowers the length of the bulb. Easy to grow.

Dendrobium williamsonii

- **Cool: 10°C (50°F)**
- **Easy to grow and flower**
- **Spring/summer flowering**
- **Evergreen/semi-dry rest**

This is a stout species whose bulbs do not form very tall canes. Being fairly small in size this is a most adaptable plant that never becomes unmanageable; it grows wider rather than taller. The numerous flowers appear in early summer from the top of the newly completed bulbs and are ivory white, the lip handsomely marked with brick red. They are 4cm (1.6in) across, fragrant and long-lasting.

This species does not propagate easily and is best grown on into a specimen plant, when its full beauty can be appreciated. It will flower with less light than most dendrobiums, and is therefore more suited for indoor culture. Do not overpot. Old canes will often produce a second flowering another year. Do not allow canes to shrivel durings its semi-dry winter rest. Repot immediately new growth is seen.

The plant grows equally well mounted on bark, when it will quickly grow into a large plant, producing several new growths each year.

Right: **Dendrobium williamsonii**
A compact-growing, fragrant species for the cool house or for growing indoors. Flowers in early summer. Not very easy to propagate.

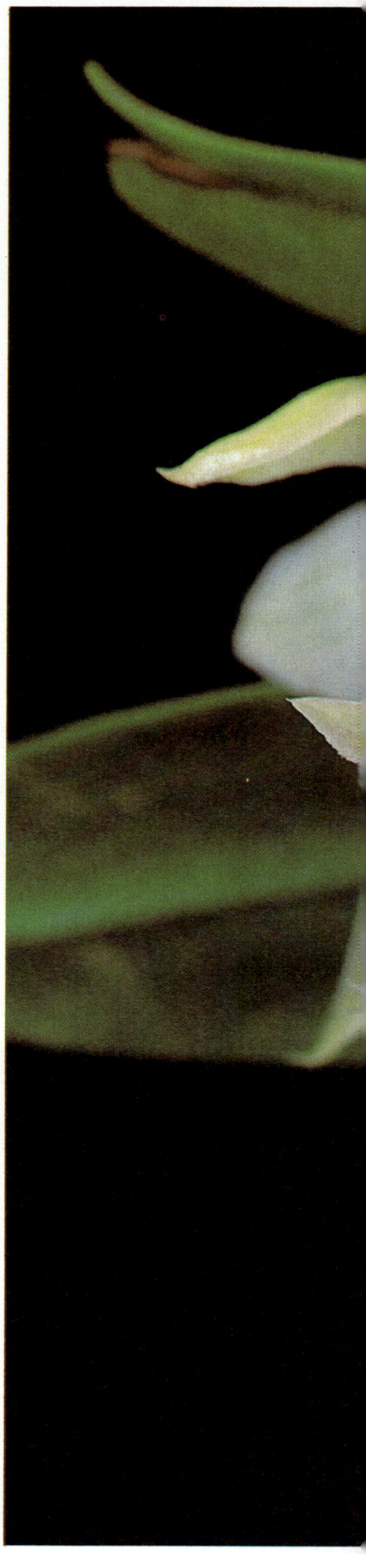

Dichorisandra albo-lineata

- **Light shade**
- **Temp: 16-21°C (60-70°F)**
- **Keep moist and fed**

This member of the tradescantia family is also known as *Campelia zanonia albo-marginata.* Growing to a height of some 120cm (4ft) when confined to a pot, it produces lance-shaped leaves that are green and white in colour, edged with red. Stems are woody and plants are attractive enough, but they shed their lower leaves as they increase in height, which produces leafless stalks with rosettes of foliage at the top. Put them with other plants, so that they occupy the rear position with shorter plants in front.

Alternatively, the top section can be removed and rooted in warm conditions; when growing well it can be planted at the base of the parent plant to grow up and partly cover the bare stem. New growth will appear below where the cuttings were removed. Plants should be kept moist and warm, and when potting, loam-based mixture should be used. Plants can be fed while growing new leaves, but not in winter.

Above:
Dichorisandra albo-lineata
A tall-growing plant of the tradescantia tribe with lovely green-and-white variegated leaves.

A practical hint
When locating plants it is advisable to place them out of reach of an inquisitive toddler until the child realizes that plants are not for eating.

Dieffenbachia amoena

- **Light shade**
- **Temp: 18-24°C (65-75°F)**
- **Keep moist and fed**

This is possibly the largest of the dieffenbachias. The large, striking grey-green leaves with central colouring of speckled white and green will add much to any collection of indoor plants, but mature plants attain a height of 1.2-1.5m (4-5ft) with equal spread. However, stout stems can be cut out with a small saw. When carrying out any sort of work on dieffenbachias, though, gloves should be worn to prevent any sap getting onto one's skin. Even moving plants that have wet foliage may result in skin disorders. Also keep plants out of reach of children and pets. The common name of dumb cane derives from the fact that if the sap of the plant gets into one's mouth it will have unpleasant effects. Fortunately, such an occurrence is unlikely, as the sap has a very nasty odour.

Dieffenbachias belong to the same family of plants as the philodendrons, and respond to the same sort of conditions.

Above: **Dieffenbachia amoena**
One of the most majestic of the dumb canes, growing to a height of 150cm (5ft) and 120cm (4ft) across. Green leaves with a tracery of white.

Dieffenbachia camilla

- **Light shade**
- **Temp: 16-21°C (60-70°F)**
- **Keep moist and fed**

The beauty of this plant lies in the incredible colouring of the leaves, which have a green margin and a central area that is almost entirely creamy white. And anyone who knows their plants will be aware that areas of white in any leaf constitute a weakness that renders the plant vulnerable to leaf rot. But the thin marginal band of green seems to offer some form of protection, and this is in fact a reasonably easy plant.

With a maximum height around 60cm (2ft), it is much better suited to indoor conditions of today than most of the dieffenbachias available. Even as a small plant this one will have a natural tendency to produce basal shoots around the main plant stem, which gives a fuller and more attractive appearance. This plant is one of the indispensables when it comes to arranging plant displays. In groups indoors many moisture-loving plants will do much better if they are placed together in arrangements.

Right: **Dieffenbachia camilla**
Introduced in the late 1970s and one of the finest of all the many dieffenbachias. The green-margined leaf is almost entirely cream.

A practical hint
Most plants that are located as individuals will be the better for a decorative container, but take care the pot does not become a water sump.

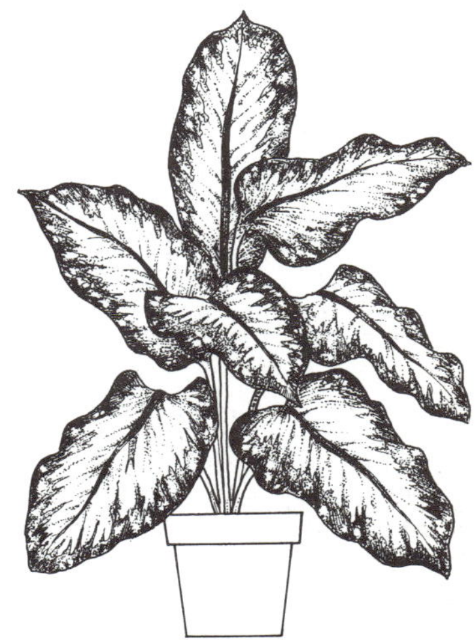

Dieffenbachia exotica

- **Light shade**
- **Temp: 16-21°C (60-70°F)**
- **Keep moist and fed**

The introduction of *D. exotica* within the past decade was something of a revolution as far as dieffenbachias were concerned. Previous plants of this kind were decidedly difficult subjects to grow at the nurseries, to transport, and to keep once they arrived at the home of the purchaser; they were also inclined to be too large for the average room of today.

D. exotica is a neat plant growing to a maximum of 60cm (2ft) – much more suitable for indoors – and with a much tougher constitution. It tolerates lower temperatures, and if not too wet does not seem to suffer. It produces clusters of young plants at the base of the parent stem, and can be propagated easily by removing the basal shoots and planting them separately in small pots filled with peat. Once rooted they should be potted in a peaty houseplant compost. Shoots can often be removed with roots attached, but gloves should be worn.

Dieffenbachia picta

- **Light shade**
- **Temp: 18-24°C (65-75°F)**
- **Keep moist and fed**

This is one of the traditional warm greenhouse plants that may have been found in many a Victorian conservatory at the turn of the century when exotic plants were all the rage. Not seen so frequently today, *D. picta* has speckled yellowish-green colouring and grows to a height of 90cm (3ft) when given proper care. If the top of the plant is removed when young, the plant will produce numerous side growths that will make it a more attractive shape. An effective display plant when carefully grown.

In common with all the many fine dieffenbachias these plants require warm and humid conditions. Permanently saturated soil must be avoided, but it is important that the pot is well watered with each application, and surplus water is seen to drain through the bottom of the pot. It is equally important that the soil should dry reasonably before further water is given.

Above left: **Dieffenbachia exotica**
The forerunner of the more compact dumb canes. It produces young growth at the base of the parent stem to give the plant a full appearance.

Left: **Dieffenbachia picta**
A well-established plant of graceful appearance with attractive pale green speckled foliage. Remove the top for a bushier plant.

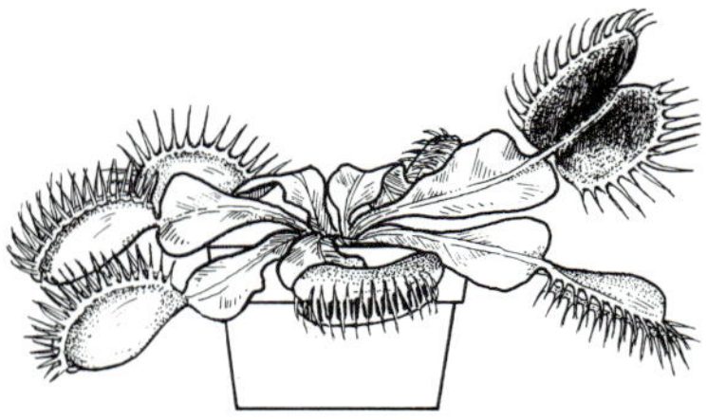

Dieffenbachia 'Tropic Snow'

- **Light shade**
- **Temp: 18-24°C (65-75°F)**
- **Keep moist and fed**

This is a close relative of *D. amoena*, the difference being that the leaves of this plant are stiffer in appearance and have a greater area of white.

New plants are raised from cuttings, and these may be prepared either from the top section of the stem with two or more leaves attached, or from sections of thick stem that have no leaves whatsoever. Top sections are put into pots of peat at a temperature of 21°C (70°F). The stems are cut into sections 10cm (4in) long and laid on their sides in boxes of peat; it is important that the stem cutting should have a growth bud from which growth may in time develop.

Leaves of this plant are inclined to be brittle and are easily damaged if carelessly handled. There is also need for care when plant leaves are being cleaned: a supporting hand should be placed underneath the leaf as the upper area is wiped clean with a soft cloth or sponge. Do not use chemical cleaners too often.

Above:
Dieffenbachia 'Tropic Snow'
Bold foliage plants with stout green-and-white leaves. Needs warm, moist, shady conditions to thrive.

Dionaea muscipula

- **Light shade**
- **Temp: 18-27°C (65-80°F)**
- **Moist atmosphere**

The Venus's fly trap is one of the most difficult of potted plants to care for indoors, but the appealing common name will ensure that it retains continued popularity.

Plants may be bought in pots in dormant stage or be acquired in leaf and growing in small pots covered by a plastic dome. The dome offers the plant some protection and helps to retain essential humidity around the plant while it is in transit, so making the dome-covered plant a much better buy. When caring for these plants adequate warmth and high humidity are essential.

When the leaves are touched, a mechanism within the plant induces the oval-shaped leaves to fold together. There are also long stiff hairs along the margins of the leaves; a fly, alighting on the leaf, will activate the mechanism and become trapped. The plant can digest the fly, and feeding flies and minute pieces of meat to the leaves is one way of nourishing the plant.

Above: **Dionaea muscipula**
The well-known Venus's fly trap is very difficult to care for, but has the fascinating ability of being able to catch flies in its sensitive leaves.

Dipladenia splendens 'Rosea'

- **Good light**
- **Temp: 16-21°C (60-70°F)**
- **Keep moist and fed**

This is a natural climbing plant best suited to the heated conservatory or greenhouse, but a challenging plant that will be good for the ego of the houseplant-grower who cultivates it successfully. Indoors, it is best to confine the roots to pots of modest size so that growth is restricted. However, very small pots are often difficult to manage, so pots of 13cm (5in) diameter will be best.

For potting, use a loam-based mixture as opposed to a very peaty mix, which will tend to produce soft growth.

During the summer months healthy plants are festooned with attractive soft pink flowers, and these are the principal feature of the dipladenia. After flowering the plant can be pruned to shape, if necessary.

The soil should be kept moist without being totally saturated for long periods, and regular feeding will be beneficial when growth is active; feeding is seldom needed during the winter months.

Right:
Dipladenia splendens 'Rosea'
An elegant climbing plant that needs warmth and humidity to flourish. Plants will flower at 25cm (10in).

Dolichothele (Mammillaria) longimamma

- **Full sun**
- **Temp: 5-30°C (41-86°F)**
- **Keep dry in winter**

Dolichothele longimamma is a free-flowering small plant, ideal where space is limited. The bright, glossy yellow flowers are 6cm (2.4in) across and are produced on and off all summer. The cactus itself is bright green with very pronounced tubercles, which have weak spines on their tips. The plant grows from a pronounced thickened tap root. With age, a few offsets are formed: these may be removed and used for propagation. *D. longimamma* can also be propagated from tubercles: remove a tubercle, dry it for two days, and pot up separately.

A good open mixture for this plant consists of two parts loam-based potting medium and one part sharp sand or perlite. During the spring and summer growing period water freely, but keep it dry during the winter. Sunlight is necessary to stimulate flower bud formation. Once the buds appear, water every two weeks with a high-potassium fertilizer.

Above:
Dolichothele longimamma
The extra-long tubercles make this free-flowering cactus rather different from most mammillarias.

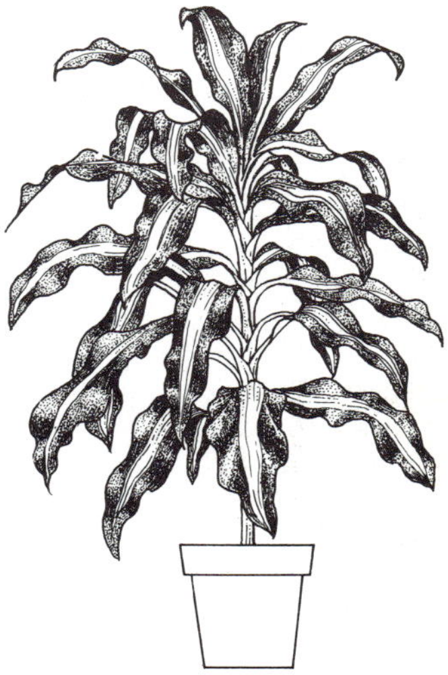

Doritis pulcherrima

- **Warm: 18°C (65°F)**
- **Fairly easy to grow**
- **Varied flowering season**
- **Evergreen/no rest**

A native of Southeast Asia, this species is much prized in modern collections and grows well in warm house conditions suitable for *Phalaenopsis*.

In plant habit and appearance it is much like *Phalaenopsis*, but is inclined to grow taller. It has three to four pairs of stiff grey-green leaves, spotted with dark purple on the upper surface.

The flower spikes are held upright and grow to a height of 60cm (24in) or more, producing ten to 25 flowers which open, a few at a time, on the upper half of the spike. Flowers appear at any season and often more than once in the same year. As individual flowers last for many weeks, a single spike can bloom for four or five months. The flowers vary widely in size (2-4cm; 0.75-1.6in) and colour; the sepals and petals range from pale rose-purple to deep magenta, with parts of the lip often of a deeper hue.

This species has been used extensively in hybridization, particularly with *Phalaenopsis.*

Dracaena deremensis

- **Light shade**
- **Temp: 16-21°C (60-70°F)**
- **Keep on the dry side**

There are numerous improved forms of this dracaena, all erect with broad, pointed leaves up to 60cm (2ft) long. The variations are mostly in leaf colour: *D. deremensis* Bausei has a dark green margin and glistening white centre; in *D. deremensis* Souvenir de Schriever the top-most rosette of leaves is bright yellow, but the leaves revert to the grey-green with white stripes of the parent plant as they age.

An unfortunate aspect of this type of dracaena is that they shed lower leaves as they increase in height, so that they take on a palm-like appearance with tufts of leaves at the top of otherwise bare stems. Although loss of lower leaves is a natural process, the incidence of dying and falling leaves will be aggravated by excessive watering. Water thoroughly, and then allow the soil to dry reasonably before repeating. These are hungry plants and will be in need of regular feeding, with loam-based soil recommended for potting on.

Dracaena fragrans

- **Light shade**
- **Temp: 18-24°C (65-75°F)**
- **Keep moist and fed**

The green-foliaged type is seldom offered for sale, but there are two important cultivars. The easiest to care for is *D. fragrans* 'Massangeana', which has broad mustard-coloured leaves attached to stout central stems; and presenting a little more difficulty there is *D. fragrans* 'Victoria' with brighter creamy-gold colouring.

As with most dracaenas there will be loss of lower leaves as plants increase in height, but plants eventually take on a stately, palm-like appearance.

Fortunately, few pests trouble these plants, but there is the occasional possibility of mealy bugs finding their way into the less accessible parts that lie between the base of the leaf and the stem of the plant. Prepare malathion solution and with the aid of a hand sprayer inject the insecticide down among the base of the leaves. As with all activities involving insecticides, wear rubber gloves and take all recommended precautions.

Left: **Doritis pulcherrima**
An attractive warm-house species with tall, upright flower spikes. May bloom more than once a year. Treat as Phalaenopsis for success.

Above left: **Dracaena deremensis 'Souvenir de Schriever'**
A stately plant with grey-green and white or yellow striped foliage that grows to a height of 2.4-3m (8-10ft).

Above: **Dracaena fragrans 'Massangeana'**
A strong, upright stem carries broad, gracefully curved leaves. Keep warm and humid for best results.

A practical hint
Placing plants under artificial light in the evening enhances appearance, but avoid close contact, or strong light may scorch foliage.

Dracaena marginata tricolor

- **Good light**
- **Temp: 16-21°C (60-70°F)**
- **Avoid wet conditions**

This plant has a natural tendency to shed lower leaves as it increases in height. Nevertheless, it can be an elegant plant if carefully grown, having attractive light and darker colouring running along the entire length of the slender, pointed leaves.

The main stem of the plant will need a supporting cane to remain upright. Plants sometimes produce young shoots naturally along the main stem so that multiheaded plants result. Alternatively, one can remove the growing tip of the main stem when the plant is about 60cm (2ft) tall, so that branching is encouraged. If plants are grown in soil that is constantly saturated, the incidence of leaf damage will be much increased. The soil for these plants should always be on the dry side, especially so during winter.

Feeding is not desperately important, but weak liquid fertilizer during the spring and summer months will do no harm; winter feeding is not advised.

Right:
Dracaena marginata tricolor
The striking colours of the narrow leaves will develop well in good light. Soil should be kept on the dry side.

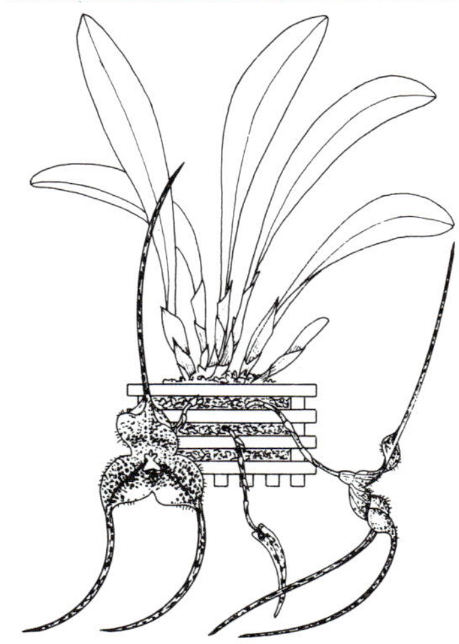

Dracaena terminalis 'Firebrand'

- **Good light**
- **Temp: 18-24°C (65-75°F)**
- **Keep moist and fed**

Few foliage plants can match the rich red colouring of this dracaena though it is not the easiest of potted plants to care for. The colourful leaves are erect and spear-shaped.

Plants are grown by the nurseryman in a very open mixture composed mainly of pine leaf mould; this ensures that when water is poured onto the soil it drains freely through. It is preferable to use rain water, and to ensure that the soil is saturated each time. Avoid bone-dry conditions, but endeavour to allow some drying out of the soil between each soaking.

Good light is needed for *D. terminalis* to retain its bright colouring, but full sun through glass window-panes may cause scorching of foliage, so plants should be protected from such exposure. While new leaves are growing it will be important to feed plants at regular intervals, but it is not normally necessary to feed during the winter months.

Above: **Dracaena 'Firebrand'**
This brilliantly coloured plant grows to a height of 60-90cm (2-3ft) and needs light and warm conditions. Good drainage is essential.

Dracula chimaera

- **Cool: 10°C (50°F)**
- **Moderately easy to grow**
- **Winter/spring flowering**
- **Evergreen/no rest**

Because of the high-altitude conditions of its natural habitat, the cool house with plenty of shade and fresh air during the summer months provides the ideal environment for this plant. As this orchid does not produce pseudobulbs – the thick leaves spring directly from a creeping rhizome – the plant should never be allowed to become dry. Good drainage at the root is also important.

Because this species is inclined to grow in pendent form and down into the compost, it is a good idea to grow the plant in a basket, where the flower spike can come through the sides.

The flowers open one at a time, in succession, on a single spike. Each flower can be from 15-30cm (6-12in) measured vertically, sepals terminating in long tails. They are cream-coloured, lightly or heavily spotted with a deep reddish purple and covered with short purple hairs. The lip is larger in this species, orange-pink in colour, and hinged so that it rocks when the flower moves.

Above: **Dracula chimaera**
Formerly classified as Masdevallia, this unusual, cool-house species produces distinctive flowers from winter until spring. Keep moist.

A practical hint
For a range of fascinating colouring there are few plants that can compare with the attractive rosette-forming echeverias. Flowers are a plus.

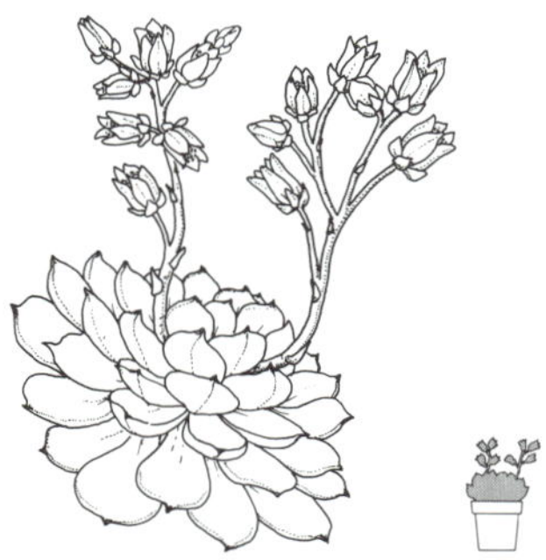

Echeveria derenbergii

- **Full sun**
- **Temp: 5-30°C (41-86°F)**
- **Keep moist all year**

Echeveria derenbergii is a charming small plant that does equally well in the greenhouse or on a sunny windowsill. It is a small, tightly leaved rosette, which forms offsets to make a small cushion. The bluish-grey leaves end in a red tip. The plant flowers freely during summer; the petals of the small bell-shaped flowers are yellow inside and orange outside.

Echeverias are easy to cultivate, in a loam- or peat-based medium, with moderate watering in summer, plus a dose of high-potassium fertilizer every two weeks. In winter, keep slightly moist. In the wild, echeverias shed their lower leaves during the winter dry period, as a way of conserving moisture. In cultivation, even though the plant is not short of water, the lower leaves still shrivel, leaving a rather untidy plant in the spring. Remove the offsets and re-start the plants in early spring.

Echeveria 'Doris Taylor'

- **Full sun**
- **Temp: 5-30°C (41-86°F)**
- **Never allow to dry out**

Echeverias are such charming small pot plants that a number of hybrids have been developed. 'Doris Taylor' is a cross between *E. setosa* and *E. pulvinata.* It is a freely branching plant that looks its best in a half-pot. The pale green leaves are densely covered with white hairs and are carried on reddish-brown stems to form neat rosettes. The reddish-orange flowers are bell-shaped, and open in the spring.

'Doris Taylor' should be grown in loam-based potting mixture in a light position – either in a greenhouse or on a windowsill. Water generously during spring and summer, and feed every two weeks with a high-potassium fertilizer. Keep slightly moist in winter. During the winter, the lower leaves shrivel: they should be removed or fungus will grow on them, which can cause the death of the plant. In spring, the plant will be leggy. Behead the main rosette and remove the smaller ones for potting.

Above right:
Echeveria derenbergii
Being one of the most beautiful of the echeverias and also one of the easiest to grow makes this plant perhaps the ideal succulent.

Right: **Echeveria 'Doris Taylor'**
A cultivated hybrid echeveria with beautiful velvety leaves and multicoloured flowers. Offsets often have roots while still on the parent plant, making propagation easy.

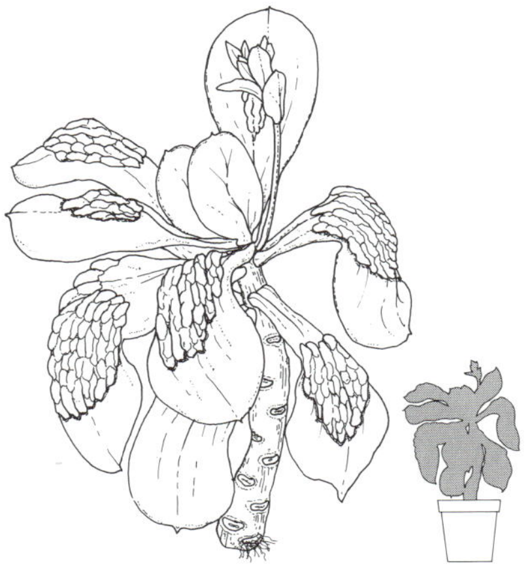

Echeveria gibbiflora var. **caruncúlata**

- **Full sun**
- **Temp: 5-30°C (41-86°F)**
- **Keep slightly moist in winter**

Echeveria gibbiflora is one of the tall echeverias and seldom branches. The large leaves, 25cm (10in) long, are a lovely lavender-pink, and covered with large protuberances that are bluish to green. The protuberances are formed in autumn, so young plants may have completely plain leaves, but they will get their markings when autumn comes. The light red flowers open during the winter.

This plant tends to become leggy, and in the spring it should be beheaded. The base should be kept and with luck one or two offsets will form at the old leaf scars. These can be removed when about 2.5cm (1in) across and potted up. The top of the plant is, or course, also potted up. This is the only way to propagate this plant. Any good loam-based potting mixture may be used. Water generously during spring and summer. Keep just moist during the winter.

Echeveria harmsii

- **Full sun**
- **Temp: 5-30°C (41-86°F)**
- **Keep moist all year**

Echeveria harmsii is the one echeveria that is grown for the beauty of its flowers rather than for its highly coloured leaves. The plant forms a small branching shrub with rosettes at the ends of the stems. These are made up of long, soft leaves covered in downy hair. The flowers are bell-shaped, 2.5cm (1in) long, and scarlet with a yellow tip.

Grow this plant in a loam- or peat-based potting mixture and keep it on a sunny windowsill. During summer, feed every two weeks with a high-potassium fertilizer and water generously, but give less water in the winter. If the plant looks untidy in spring, cut the rosettes off and treat as cuttings.

Echeverias are prone to harbour mealy bug. Pick the insects off, and if badly infested water the soil with a systemic insecticide. Since the plant is re-rooted every year, root mealy bug should not occur, provided the cuttings are planted in clean pots.

Above left: **Echeveria gibbiflora** var. **caruncúlata**
A curious rather than beautiful plant grown mainly for the strange warty growths that appear on older leaves. Restart leggy stems by beheading.

Above: **Echeveria harmsii**
The large flowers are really the showpieces of this echeveria and they are freely produced. The plant itself is straggly and is best kept under control by taking cuttings.

Echeveria setosa

- **Full sun**
- **Temp: 5-30°C (41-86°F)**
- **Water with caution**

Echeveria setosa is a flat, almost stemless rosette about 15cm (6in) across. The soft, dark green leaves are covered with dense white hairs, which gives the plant an attractive furry appearance. This plant needs a sunny position. In the spring, mature specimens flower; the blooms are red and yellow.

The leaves of this echeveria are pressed very closely to the ground. Even in summer, the plant should be carefully inspected, and any shrivelled or rotting lower leaves removed. If left on, a grey mould will attack the decaying leaves.

A loam-based potting mixture will suit this plant, which should be grown in a half-pot. Water all the year round but allow it to dry out between waterings. When the flower buds start to form, feed every two weeks with a high-potassium (tomato) fertilizer. Mature specimens produce an occasional offset, which may be removed for propagation.

Echinocactus grusonii

- **Full sun**
- **Temp: 7-30°C (45-86°F)**
- **Keep dry in winter**

Young specimens of *E. grusonii* have very pronounced tubercles and look like golden mammillaria. After a few years, the tubercles re-arrange themselves into ribs, usually about 28 per plant. *E. grusonii* is very long-lived and eventually reaches a diameter of 1m (39in). But in cultivation a plant of 15cm (6in) is a good-sized specimen and will be about 10 years old. The awl-shaped spines are pale golden-yellow and there is golden wool at the top of the plant. The small yellow flowers are produced on very large plants but only if exposed to very strong sunlight. In cooler climates, this plant is grown purely for the beauty of its colouring.

It needs an open soil, a loam- or peat-based mixture plus one third sharp sand or perlite. Water generously during summer, but allow it to dry out between waterings. Keep dry in winter. The chief pests are mealy bug and root mealy bug.

Above: **Echeveria setosa**
The compact hairy rosette of this succulent is attractive in itself apart from the magnificent array of red-and-yellow flowers shown here.

Right: **Echinocactus grusonii**
Only really large speciments of this cactus will flower. Winter cold can cause brown markings, so best moved to a living-room.

Echinocactus horizonthalonius

- **Full sun**
- **Temp: 7-30°C (45-86°F)**
- **Water with care**

Echinocactus horizonthalonius is the baby of the genus, the only species that can be flowered in a pot. The flowers are pink and form a ring around the top of the plant. This cactus is a flattened plant, bluish-green in colour, with thick greyish spines. A flowering sized plant is 30cm (12in) across.

Although a very choice plant, *E. horizonthalonius* is not the easiest plant to cultivate. It is an extreme desert plant, and in its native state it bakes in the sun and has perfect drainage. The best treatment is to place the plant in the sunniest part of your greenhouse and grow it in a very open potting mixture. A loam-based mixture plus an equal quantity of sharp sand or perlite is suitable. Water on sunny days during spring and summer, but always allow the plant to dry out between waterings. Keep it dry during the winter.

Above:
Echinocactus horizonthalonius
This cactus is a challenge to cultivate but worth the effort. Lovely pink flowers open during the summer months. Needs good drainage.

Echinocereus knippelianus

- **Full sun**
- **Temp: 5-30°C (41-86°F)**
- **Keep dry in winter**

Although this cactus may consist of a single oval or globular stem, about 5cm (2in) thick, for a few years, it will eventually form branches from the base, resulting in a compact clump. The stems have five ribs with a few short, bristly spines along them. Not being fiercely spined, it is quite an easy plant to handle. The deep pink flowers, 4cm (1.6in) or so across, appear from around the sides of the stems in spring and summer, and contrast delightfully with the dark green of the stems. Propagate this cactus by carefully cutting away a branch of at least 2.5cm (1in) across in spring or summer, letting it dry for a few days, and pushing it gently into fresh potting mixture.

Good drainage is essential, so grow this cactus in a mixture of two parts good standard potting material (peat- or loam-based) and one part sharp sand or perlite. When buds form, feed every two weeks with a high-potassium fertilizer.

Echinocereus pentalophus

- **Full sun**
- **Temp: 5-30°C (41-86°F)**
- **Keep dry in winter**

The small upright stem of this cactus soon branches and the ultimate result is a mass of sprawling shoots up to about 12cm (4.7in) long and 2cm (0.8in) thick. The spines are quite short and soft. On the whole perhaps it is not a particularly striking plant, but the magnificent blooms more than compensate for any lack of beauty in the cactus itself. Quite small specimens (one stem) will produce reddish-purple flowers up to 8cm (3.2in) across.

The stems, being rather soft and fleshy, are prone to rot with any excess water, so it is particularly important to use a well-drained potting mixture with no risk of waterlogging. Make this by adding one part of sharp sand or perlite to two parts of a standard potting mixture, which can be either peat- or loam-based. Propagate it by removing a suitable branch in summer, letting it dry for a few days, and potting up.

Echinocereus perbellus

- **Full sun**
- **Temp: 5-30°C (41-86°F)**
- **Keep dry in winter**

One of the so-called 'pectinate' echinocerei, this shows a completely different type of stem from the more prostrate species. Here we have a predominantly solitary cactus, which may nevertheless form a low cluster with age. The stem is at first almost spherical and about 5cm (2in) across, but may eventually become more elongated. This stem is beautiful in itself; its many small ribs, closely decorated with short white spreading spines ('pectinate', or 'comb-like'), give a delightful, clean, neat appearance. The deep pink to purple flowers add to the attraction: about 5cm (2in) across, they open from hairy buds.

This cactus is almost completely hardy and can withstand dry freezing conditions in winter; but, to be on the safe side, keep to the recommended temperature, if possible. Grow it in a standard potting mixture to which has been added about one third of sharp sand or perlite.

Above:
Echinocereus knippelianus
This clump-forming cactus is easy to grow and flower. Check regularly for rotted branches and cut them out.

Above right:
Echinocereus pentalophus
The sprawling stems of this cactus are more than compensated for by the large reddish-purple flowers.

Right: **Echinocereus perbellus**
This small, globular cactus has a most distinctive spine formation and is worth growing for that alone. The flowers appear on young plants.

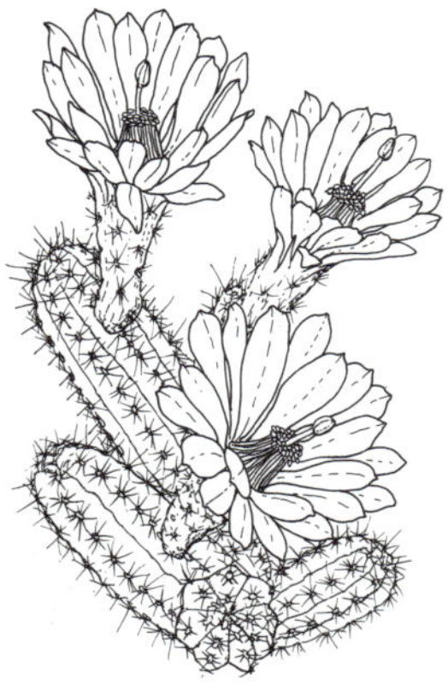

Echinocereus salm-dyckianus

- **Full sun**
- **Temp: 5-30°C (41-86°F)**
- **Keep dry in winter**

There are two types of echinocereus: those with fairly soft, mostly sprawling stems; and the pectinate (or comb-like) ones, with stiffer, elegantly spined, upright stems. This cactus belongs to the former group. Although small specimens consist of a single, upright stem, this soon branches at the base, eventually forming a clump of ribbed stems about 20cm (8in) long and 5cm (2in) thick, with short yellowish spines. It is probably the most attractive among the echinocerei, an attractiveness emphasized by the appearance of the funnel-shaped, orange flowers. These are about 7cm (2.8in) wide and can be up to 10cm (4in) long.

Grow in a mixture of one part sharp sand or perlite to two parts of any good standard material, to give the good drainage essential to this cactus. A gravel top dressing will protect the base. Feed every two weeks during the flowering season, to keep the flowers going.

Above:
Echinocereus salm-dyckianus
One of the softer-stemmed echinocerei, this has more upright stems than most. Flowers well.

Echinopsis multiplex

- **Full sun**
- **Temp: 5-30°C (41-86°F)**
- **Keep cool and dry in winter**

The delicate pink flowers of this cactus open during the night and remain open during the following day. The flowers have a long tube about 20cm (8in) long and a sweet lily-like scent.

The genuine *E. multiplex* has long thick spines, but many pink-flowered echinopsis plants sold under this name are very short-spined hybrids, probably with *E. eyriesii.*

E. multiplex produces a profusion of offsets. To enable the main plant to reach flowering size quickly and to keep the plant within bounds, most of the offsets should be removed.

Large numbers of flowers are produced in early summer, and the plant should be fed during the flowering period with a tomato fertilizer. Any good potting mixture, either loam- or peat-based, is suitable for this species. Repot annually. Water freely during spring and summer, allowing the compost to dry out between waterings.

Echinopsis Paramount hybrid 'Orange Glory'

- **Full sun**
- **Temp: 5-30°C (41-86°F)**
- **Keep cool and dry in winter**

'Orange Glory' is one of the beautiful *Echinopsis x Lobivia* hybrids that have been produced in the USA. The flowers are a deep glowing orange, a colour not found in pure echinopsis species. The cactus itself is cylindrical, with many ribs; the ribs carry short spines. A few offsets are produced on young plants; these may be left on the plant if a large specimen is desired, or removed for propagation.

This cactus may be grown in any loam- or peat-based mixture. Repot annually. Water freely during the spring and summer months, when the plant is in vigorous growth, but allow to dry out between waterings. When flower buds form feed every two weeks with a tomato fertilizer.

This is a desert plant and needs to be grown in full sunlight to stimulate bud formation and to encourage the growth of strong, well-coloured spines. This plant is tough and resistant to most pests.

Above: **Echinopsis multiplex**
The pink flowers of this easy cactus are unusual in that they are sweetly scented, but unfortunately they usually fade away after a day or two.

Right: **Echinopsis Paramount hybrid 'Orange Glory'**
This is probably the most strongly spined of the hybrid echinopsis. Radiant, large orange flowers.

Echinopsis Paramount hybrid 'Peach Monarch'

- **Full sun**
- **Temp: 5-30°C (41-86°F)**
- **Feed while flowering**

Echinopsis species have possibly the most beautiful flowers of any desert cacti, and among the most colourful are the hybrids developed in Paramount, California.

The peach-pink flowers of 'Peach Monarch' open during early summer, and there may be a dozen long-tubed flowers open at one time. Once the buds begin to form, the cactus should be kept moist and fed every two weeks. The best liquid feeds are those with a high potassium content.

'Peach Monarch' is 15cm (6in) high and 10cm (4in) across; short spines are carried on the numerous ribs. A few offsets are formed on young plants; use for propagation.

Echinopsis plants are easy to grow, in either a loam-based or a soilless compost. They are greedy plants, so repot annually. Give the plant a position where it will get maximum sunlight: strong light is necessary for bud formation.

Above: **Echinopsis Paramount hybrid 'Peach Monarch'**
A vigorously growing echinopsis hybrid. The peach-pink flowers have a beautiful satiny texture.

A practical hint
Most orchids will need to be potted into new containers every second year, but in any event it is essential to ensure that the plant is well rooted.

Encyclia cochleata

- **Cool: 10°C (50°F)**
- **Easy to grow and flower**
- **Varied flowering season**
- **Evergreen/slight rest**

A subject for the cool house, this South American species produces flattened pear-shaped pseudobulbs about 18cm (7in) tall. The flowers resemble the shape of an octopus in water, with their thin green sepals and petals which droop down below the rounded, dark purple, almost black lip.

Several flowers are produced at a time in succession on a flowering spike which, on a large mature plant, can continue flowering for up to two years. Such is the vigour of this species that this in no way impairs its new growth, with the result that two years' flower spikes can be in flower at the same time.

It is one of the few orchids that can be repotted while in bloom. This will be necessary when the new growth has started in the spring.

The old leafless pseudobulbs can be removed for propagation. When potted up singly they will readily develop new growths.

This is an excellent species for beginners; and it can also be grown successfully indoors.

Encyclia mariae

- **Cool: 9°C (48°F)**
- **Moderately easy to grow**
- **Summer flowering**
- **Semi-deciduous/dry rest**

This species is similar in appearance to *E. citrina* but is grown upright in a pot. One to five flowers are carried on a thin stem, each being about 5cm (2in) wide; the sepals and petals are lime green and the very broad lip, which is often the widest part of the flower, is pure white. *E. mariae* is considered to be one of the loveliest of all the summer-flowering orchids.

The flowers are extremely large for the size of the plant, and last well. The plant should not be heavily watered at any time and is intolerant of soggy conditions. Allow the plant to rest while not in active growth, and keep in a fairly shady aspect. Propagation from the oldest pseudobulbs is slow; it is better to leave them on the plant provided it is healthy. The plant should not be sprayed, as the leaves are susceptible to water marks.

This plant can also be grown on a piece of bark, where it should be allowed to remain undisturbed for a number of years. If too many leafless bulbs build up, these should be removed very carefully without disturbing the plant.

Above right: **Encyclia cochleata**
This is a very popular cool-house species suitable for beginners. Flowers appear in succession.

Right: **Encyclia mariae**
Large showy flowers from a small plant. This species is cool growing and blooms during the summer.

A practical hint
For spectacular flowers there are few plants that can compare with the epiphyllums, which have succulent foliage and are little trouble to care for.

Encyclia pentotis

- **Cool: 10°C (50°F)**
- **Shy to flower**
- **Early summer flowering**
- **Evergreen/semi-rest**

A beautiful Mexican species that succeeds well in a cool greenhouse or indoors in a position of good light. It has thin cylindrical pseudobulbs which are topped by a pair of slender, dark green leaves. From between the leaves come the flowers, almost stemless. Usually two are produced, back to back with the lip uppermost, resembling alighting butterflies. The lip is cream, streaked with red, and the sepals and petals are creamy white with a slight hint of light green. This very pretty species is beautifully fragrant. The plant can be seen at its best when flowering on a large specimen, when it becomes very free-flowering. Small plants are reluctant to bloom, but a year or two's patience will be amply rewarded when flowering occurs in profusion.

The species grows and propagates easily; several new growths are usually produced each season. Propagation from the old leafless bulbs is possible. The plant may be sprayed in summer and given a semi-dry rest in winter.

Left: **Encyclia pentotis**
A lovely summer-flowering species for the cool house and ideal for the beginner. Highly fragrant flowers.

Encyclia vitellina

- **Cool: 10°C (50°F)**
- **Easy to grow and flower**
- **Autumn flowering**
- **Evergreen/dry rest**

The most colourful of the South American encyclias, this plant likes to be grown under cool house conditions, and will also do well indoors, where it is more tolerant of the drier conditions. The pseudobulbs are oval and carry two blue-green leaves. The flower spike appears at the top of the bulb from between the leaves and grows to 30cm (12in) or more in length on a large plant. At least 12 star-shaped flowers of the most brilliant orange-red are produced on branching stems. The narrow lip, in balance with the rest of the flower, is orange. The blooms are long-lasting, and a colourful sight in the early autumn.

The plant can be grown in a pot or, where greenhouse culture is provided, mounted on a piece of cork bark, where it will make a fine specimen. It will prefer the slightly drier conditions afforded to this type of growing. A dry rest is required for the duration of the winter while the plant is inactive. Overhead spraying is not recommended, as the foliage easily becomes water marked.

Above: **Encyclia vitellina**
An unusually brightly coloured species suitable for the cool house or indoors. It flowers in the autumn.

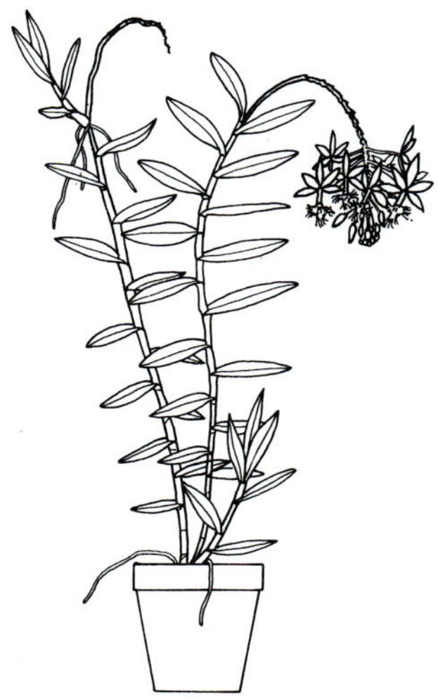

Epidendrum ibaguense

- **Cool: 9°C (48°F)**
- **Easy to grow and flower**
- **Varied flowering season**
- **Evergreen/no rest**

Often known as *E. radicans,* this is a reed-stem species. The stems vary from 60-150cm (2-5ft) in height according to environment and produce rounded leaves and many aerial roots over most of their length. The flowers (2.5cm; 1in) are orange-red or scarlet, the lip flat and very frilled. This is a plant for the cool greenhouse with good light. One successful specimen is known to have flowered continuously for four years.

The epidendrums are one of the largest genera: over 1,000 species are known, coming mainly from Central and South America. So varied are the plants accepted within the genus, in vegetation and flower size and appearance, that some groups have been accorded a genus of their own. Those that remain within the genus are epiphytic.

Epidendrums seem to divide naturally into two categories: those with oval or rounded pseudobulbs, and those that produce reed-like stems.

Above: **Epidendrum ibaguense**
Can become very tall. A cool-growing, reed-type epidendrum that flowers at various times of the year.

Epidendrum stamfordianum

- **Intermediate: 13°C (55°F)**
- **Easy to grow and flower**
- **Early summer flowering**
- **Evergreen/dry rest**

This Central American species produces tall, club-shaped pseudobulbs that carry two or three thick leaves. The branching flower spike comes from the base of the plant, a unique feature among the epidendrums. The flower spike is many flowered; the fragrant blooms are yellow, spotted with red. The plant likes to be grown fairly warm, in a position of good light, and is therefore best suited to an intermediate greenhouse. It should be well watered during the summer growing season and allowed a complete winter's rest. The plant may be grown in a pot or on bark, where it will grow an extensive aerial root system. Propagation is best achieved by division of the main plant when it is large enough.

This large-growing plant is a good example of a bulb-type epidendrum as distinct from the reed type. It is also one of the most attractive epidendrums, although it is not frequently seen in collections.

Above right:
Epidendrum stamfordianum
Attractive fragrant flowers on branching spikes from the base.

Epiphyllum 'Ackermannii'

- **Partial shade**
- **Temp: 5-27°C (41-81°F)**
- **Keep almost dry in winter**

Epiphyllums (also known as Epicacti) are among the most un-cactus-like cacti and are often grown by plant lovers who profess no interest in conventional cacti. Nevertheless, they are true cacti, but living naturally in tropical rain-forests rather than in the desert. Plants normally cultivated are hybrids between the various wild species and other cacti; such plants are hardier and have more colourful flowers. 'Ackermannii' is a typical example and is one of the oldest in cultivation, but its flowers have not been surpassed in beauty of colour. They are about 8cm (3.2in) across and brilliant red, but not perfumed. The blooms appear along the notched edges of the stems and may last for several days.

You can grow epiphyllums in a standard houseplant mixture, but if you add extra peat or leafmould to it, this is beneficial. Also, good drainage is important. Feed with high-potassium fertilizer when in bud and flower.

Right: **Epiphyllum 'Ackermannii'**
This beautiful hybrid is a long-established favourite; its blooms are stunning in shape and colour.

Epiphyllum 'Cooperi'

- **Partial shade**
- **Temp: 5-27°C (41-81°F)**
- **Keep almost dry in winter**

The white flowers of this hybrid epiphyllum are perfumed; quite unusual for a cactus! Unlike those of other similar cacti, the flowers come from the base of the plant, not along the side of the stem. When the large buds are fully formed in spring or summer, they will open in the evening, and if they are in the living-room, a strong lily-like perfume will pervade the whole room at about 10pm. One can almost watch the buds unfold, to give brilliant white blooms maybe 10cm (4in) across.

This cactus will survive at the lower temperature in winter, but will do better if rather warmer. This is easy indoors, in a shady window. Water freely in spring and summer, and keep moister indoors in winter than in a greenhouse. But it appreciates a moist atmosphere; an occasional spray with water will help. Use a good standard potting mixture and feed occasionally using a high-potassium fertilizer; too much nitrogen in the feed can cause brown spots.

Above: **Epiphyllum 'Cooperi'**
Unusual among epiphyllum hybrids in producing flowers from the base. They are sweetly scented and open during spring or summer evenings.

A practical hint
Potting of succulents is best done in late spring/early summer, but is necessary only when the existing pot is well filled with healthy roots.

Epiphyllum 'Deutsche Kaiserin'

- **Partial shade**
- **Temp: 5-27°C (41-81°F)**
- **Keep slightly moist in winter**

The parentage of many of the epiphyllum hybrids is somewhat obscure, and this one probably has no true epiphyllum ancestry at all, being a hybrid between two jungle cacti. But it is so like an epiphyllum in appearance and cultivation requirements that it is normally included with these plants. Most epiphyllums need staking when the stems reach a length of about 30cm (12in), but this one is really pendent, making it ideal for a hanging basket. In spring and summer the trailing stems, which may be up to 60cm (24in) long, are covered with masses of deep pink flowers, about 5cm (2in) across – a truly magnificent sight.

Grow this beautiful jungle cactus in a good standard potting mixture; if you add extra leafmould or peat it will be appreciated, as well as a feed every two weeks in spring and summer with a high-potassium fertilizer. Spray it occasionally and avoid full sunshine.

Epiphyllum 'Gloria'

- **Partial shade**
- **Temp: 5-27°C (41-81°F)**
- **Keep almost dry in winter**

There are literally dozens (if not hundreds) of epiphyllum hybrids available, and space prevents the mention of more than a few. But they all require much the same treatment. A good, nourishing potting mixture is important; add extra sharp sand or perlite if it looks at all compacted. Leafmould is not too readily available, but if you have any mix some with the potting mixture. Never add limestone or chalk. Never let the plant dry out completely, and water it freely in spring and summer, feeding every two weeks or so.

'Gloria' is a particularly attractive hybrid with immense orange-pink flowers up to 20cm (8in) across. But like those of most of the day-flowering types, these blooms are without scent. This hybrid is reasonably hardy, and a cool greenhouse is perfectly adequate. In the drier conditions of a living-room, an occasional spray with clean lime-free water is beneficial.

Left:
Epiphyllum 'Deutsche Kaiserin'
A particularly floriferous hybrid with masses of pink blooms along the straplike stems in spring/summer.

Above: **Epiphyllum 'Gloria'**
Epiphyllum hybrids are grown for their flowers rather than for the somewhat uninteresting stems. This one produces immense blooms.

A practical hint
In airless conditions mildew may become a problem; irregular white spotting on leaves can be caused by this fungus. Treat with benomyl fungicide.

Episcia cupreata

- **Good indirect light**
- **Temp: 16-21°C (60-70°F)**
- **Keep on the dry side**

This is an attractive plant that grows in a pendulous fashion and looks good in small hanging pots. Leaves are an attractive greyish silver and green, and flowers, though small, are of brilliant red colouring and appear for many months in the middle of the year. Where growing conditions are to their liking, these plants can be grouped in hanging baskets of reasonable size to make a splendid feature in a room.

Good light is essential, but strong, direct sunlight should be avoided. In terms of temperature there is little to worry about in the summer, but the winter temperature should not drop below 16°C (60°F). Plants need to be potted with a peaty mixture.

In winter it is important to give water sparingly and only when it is really needed by the plant. Winter feeding is not necessary, but plants will benefit from regular applications at other times.

Episcia dianthiflora

- **Light shade**
- **Temp: 13-18°C (55-65°F)**
- **Keep on the dry side**

A delightful plant, *E. dianthiflora* has small rosettes of green leaves and produces mis-shapen tubular flowers, white in colour with lace-like, ragged edges to the petals. Growth hangs perpendicularly on stems that will become firm as they age, which makes this one of the best natural trailing plants for indoors.

Avoid excessively wet conditions; aim to give the potting mixture a good watering and allow it to dry quite appreciably before repeating. If plants are growing in hanging pots with drip trays attached it is important to empty these trays an hour or so after watering to ensure that the soil does not become too saturated. Feed established plants occasionally, but do not overdo it; pot on only when the plants are very well rooted. Raise new plants from the rosettes of leaves.

Right: **Episcia cupreata**
Propagating this dazzling little plant is an easy matter: creeping stems carry plantlets that can be cut off and potted separately.

Above right: **Episcia dianthiflora**
Although appearing for only a short period during the summer, the fringed flowers of this basket plant are a delight. Check for aphids.

Eria javanica

- Warm: 18°C (65°F)
- Easy to grow and flower
- Winter/spring flowering
- Evergreen/semi-rest

This is a particularly showy species. The pseudobulbs are about 7.5cm (3in) in height, and produce two upright leaves, 30-60cm (1-2ft) in length. An erect flower spike develops to a height of 60cm (2ft) from the top of the pseudobulb, and many well-spaced flowers are produced. These are about 4cm (1.5in) across and creamy green.

Although there are some 500 species of *Eria*, most coming from India or Malaysia, not many are found in collections today. This is surprising as some are very showy and generally they are not difficult to cultivate.

A few species will grow in cool conditions but most do well in the intermediate or warm section of the greenhouse. Some require shade, but others enjoy full light. Most require a period of rest at the completion of their growing season and will flower more freely if this can be given in cooler conditions than those in which the plant has been grown. The flowers of some erias are very short lived; this species is longer lasting than most.

Erica

- Good light
- Temp: Below 16°C (60°F)
- Keep moist

There are numerous types of ericas, or heathers as they are more commonly known, but for the most part they will develop into neat mounds of needle-like foliage with colourful flowers appearing throughout the year. Individual varieties produce their blooms over a period of weeks, but from a well-chosen collection you could get flowers throughout the year, even in winter.

Almost all the ericas that grow outside will also do very well in large shallow containers. They should be periodically clipped to retain their shape and can spend most of their time on the patio out of doors, being brought in while in flower. In the home these plants require the lightest and coolest location for a long life. Following the flowering period, transfer the plants to the patio and trim any untidy growth.

Above left: **Eria javanica**
An attractive but little known species that likes to grow in the warm. The fragrant blooms appear on sprays during the early spring.

Above: **Erica hyemalis**
This winter-flowering erica can be grown successfully indoors in cool conditions. Mist-spray the leaves regularly. Discard after flowering.

A practical hint
Check purchased plants immediately and, if well rooted, pot on into pots a little larger. Delay in attending to potting can be harmful.

Eucalyptus gunnii

- **Good light**
- **Temp: 7-16°C (45-60°F)**
- **Keep moist and fed**

In the tropics the blue gums are invasive major trees, but for our purpose the smaller-leaved variety, *E. gunnii,* makes a very acceptable indoor plant, and is hardy outside in many areas. Rounded leaves have a grey-blue colouring that can be very pleasing in plant groupings.

For cooler areas that offer adequate light these are excellent plants that will overwinter without trouble if roots are not excessively wet while temperatures are at lower levels. During their more active summer months they will need regular watering and feeding. These are quite vigorous plants and should be regularly potted on during their early stages of growth. Peat-based potting mixes will be fine for plants in their early development, but as they advance beyond the 13cm (5in) pot it will be essential to use a loam-based potting mixture. Also, as plants tend to become tall and thin it is advisable to use clay pots,which will provide a more stable base than plastic ones.

Above right: **Eucalyptus gunnii**
An attractive blue gum with small leaves closely grouped on slender stems. Must have cool conditions and excellent light to thrive indoors.

Left: **Eucharis grandiflora**
Fragrant white blooms adorn this plant during the warm months. For successful flowering a dry rest is vital. About 75cm (30in) tall.

Eucharis grandiflora

- **Good indirect light**
- **Temp: 13-18°C (55-65°F)**
- **Keep dry when resting**

Grown from bulbs placed one to a 13cm (5in) pot, these are indeed exciting plants to grow, both indoors and in a frost-protected greenhouse, where they should be placed in good light but not full sunlight. The plant's broad green leaves are pleasing enough in themselves, but it is not until the creamy white flowers appear that the full beauty of this easy-care plant is appreciated.

Following flowering and natural dying down of the foliage it is essential that the plant be kept very dry and allowed to rest in a cool, dry place until new growth is evident, when watering can begin again in the normal way. Ideally, resting plants should be placed on their sides under the greenhouse staging. If treated in this way plants will be more inclined to produce their exotic flowers. Feed occasionally with liquid fertilizer when in leaf.

A practical hint
Poinsettias need maximum light at all times, but to flower they must have only natural daylight during the autumn months.

Eulophia guinensis

- **Warm: 18°C (65°F)**
- **Fairly easy to grow**
- **Summer flowering**
- **Deciduous/dry rest**

Most of the 200 known species of *Eulophia* come from tropical and sub-tropical Africa, and almost all are terrestrial. The genus can be divided roughly into two groups according to vegetation and flower form.

In the first, the plants have a broad, pear-shaped pseudobulb that produces fairly long deciduous leaves that fall when the growing period is completed. The sepals and petals of the flowers are small in comparison with the lip, which is the main attraction.

This species belongs to the first group and is probably the most familiar. After a cool, dry rest throughout the winter the plant should be brought into the warm house and encouraged into growth by light and watering. When growth is still in progress, the flower spike appears and grows to a height of 60-90cm (2-3ft), producing six to 15 flowers. The lip is 2.5-4cm (1-1.6in) in diameter, spade-shaped and rose-pink with darker veins. The sepals and petals are recurving, short and narrow, dullish-purple in colour with green veins.

Right: **Eulophia guinensis**
Elegant pink blooms appear on this warmth-loving orchid during the summer. The plant is leafless in the winter, when it should be kept dry.

Euonymus japonicus medio-pictus

- **Good light**
- **Temp: 7-18°C (45-65°F)**
- **Keep moist and fed**

This is another of the hardy outdoor plants that can be put to good use as subjects for indoor decoration. The leaves of this one are bright yellow in the centre with a green margin. With proper care it will grow to a height of 120cm (4ft). The woody stems can, however, be trimmed to a more manageable size at any time. There are other members of the euonymus family, such as the silver-foliaged *E. radicans*, which are more prostrate, and these will be the better for an annual clip into shape.

Good light is essential so plants need a fairly bright windowsill, but full sun will be harmful. Excessive watering will be damaging, particularly during the winter months when growth is less active. Feeding can be undertaken while plants are growing but should be discontinued in winter. When potting on a loam-based mixture is ideal.

Some branches will have a tendency to revert to green colouring, and it is best to cut these out.

Above: **Euonymus japonicus**
Hardy out of doors, but also a fine bushy plant for cooler areas in the home. Good light will keep foliage colours bright. Check for mildew.

Euphorbia bupleurifolia

- Full sun
- Temp: 10-30°C (50-86°F)
- Keep dry in winter

A choice, less common euphorbia, and although not one of the easiest to grow, it should not be too difficult for the careful collector. It is a small, spineless succulent, usually reaching a height of about 10cm (4in). The thick stem, which rarely branches, is covered with warty tubercles, and a tuft of leaves appears on the top during spring, and usually falls off at the approach of winter. The plant is grown more for its appearance than for the small flowers, which are produced in spring.

If greenhouse heating is kept low in winter, it is best to bring this plant indoors to an unheated room before any really cold weather, but put it in your lightest window.

Good drainage is essential for this plant, so add about one third of extra drainage material (sharp sand or perlite) to the potting mixture, which can be either loam- or peat-based. Water in spring and summer, but only when the soil is almost dry.

Above: **Euphorbia bupleurifolia**
A particularly choice succulent euphorbia. The flowers are small but attractive, and the warty stems most unusual. The male and female flowers are on separate plants.

Euphorbia fulgens

- Good light
- Temp: 16-21°C (60-70°F)
- Keep on the dry side

This is an untidy sort of plant that produces small but brilliantly coloured scarlet flowers in early spring – a good time for indoor flowering plants when there is so little colour around. Like the more common *E. pulcherrima* (poinsettia) the bright scarlet flower is in fact a bract that surrounds the smaller and insignificant central flowers.

New plants can be grown from tip cuttings about 10cm (4in) in length, which should be inserted in clean peat moss and kept at a temperature not less than 21°C (70°F). The sap of this euphorbia can cause skin irritation, so gloves must be worn when the stem of the plant is being cut. Feed occasionally. Avoid both wet and cold conditions.

Plants will grow to a height of about 120cm (4ft) in ideal conditions. Check regularly for mealy bugs which may infest this plant if it is grown in too dry an atmosphere.

Above right: **Euphorbia fulgens**
This flowering shrub needs bright light indoors but never too much water. Take stem cuttings in spring for new plants. The sap is poisonous. Check regularly for mealy bugs.

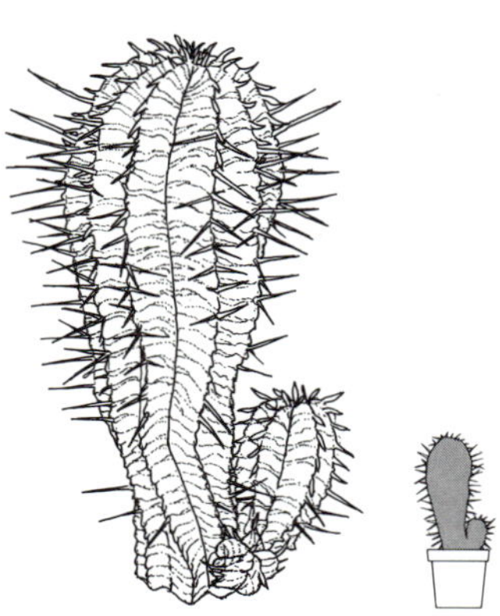

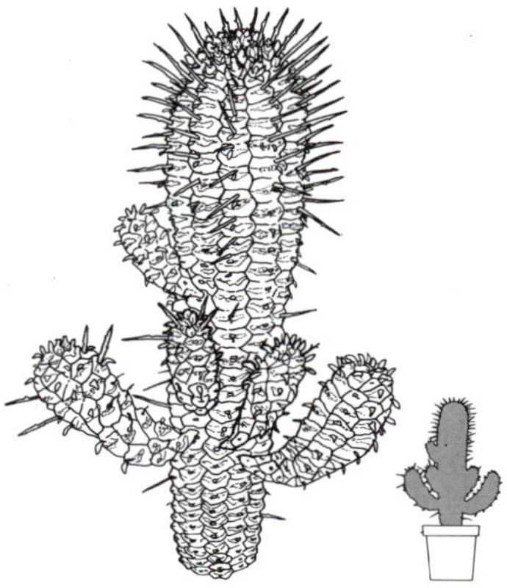

Euphorbia horrida

- **Full sun**
- **Temp: 5-30°C (41-86°F)**
- **Keep dry in winter**

Although a very cactus-like plant, this is one of the 'other succulents'. The very small flowers and stout spines (not needle-like) give it away. It is not a 'horrid' plant; the name *horrida* means 'spiny'. In its native South Africa it can reach quite a large size, but a good cultivated specimen is not likely to be more than about 20cm (8in) high and 5cm (2in) thick. The attraction of this succulent is more in its shape than in its tiny flowers, although when clustered at the top these can be quite pretty. Plants are male or female.

E. horrida can be propagated from seed (but remember you need a pair) or from the branches that sometimes form at the base. If you remove the branches, wash off the oozing latex and let the cutting dry for a week before potting up. For this plant use a mixture of three parts standard soil and one part sharp sand or perlite.

Left: **Euphorbia horrida**
Euphorbia flowers are mostly small and somewhat insignificant, but if examined closely they are really beautiful. Well worth using a magnifier to study them.

Euphorbia mammillaris var. variegata

- **Full sun**
- **Temp: 5-30°C (41-86°F)**
- **Keep dry in winter**

A beautifully variegated form of *E. mammillaris* (itself an attractive little succulent), this plant attains a height of around 20cm (8in) and a thickness of 5cm (2in). Grow it for its form and colour rather than its insignificant flowers. The freely produced branches soon give rise to a small bush of deeply ribbed stems, variegated with white, on which the blunt spines appear in bands.

If you want to propagate this euphorbia, remove a branch, wash off the sappy latex, and let it dry for a week before planting. A pity to spoil the look of the plant, but sometimes an ill-positioned branch can be found. To grow this euphorbia well, use any good standard potting mixture with about one third of sharp sand or perlite added. With the consequent good drainage, watering can be quite liberal during spring and summer.

Above: **Euphorbia mammillaris** var. **variegata**
The daintily variegated stems and compact growth of this succulent make it a most attractive plant, though it has small flowers.

Euphorbia milii var. splendens

- **Full sun**
- **Temp: 10-30°C (50-86°F)**
- **Keep slightly moist in winter**

This delightful little shrub, only slightly succulent, is very popular as a houseplant, and deservedly so, as it is more suited to a well-lit living-room window in winter than to the average colder greenhouse, where it will certainly lose its long leaves, and probably its life also!

The plant's great attraction is its brilliant scarlet flower-like bracts, about 1.5cm (0.6in) across, produced freely in spring and summer. There is also a yellow version.

If the stems become too long, encourage more bushy growth by cutting them down to size; this also provides ample cuttings for spare plants. Keep any sap away from your eyes or mouth. Let the pieces dry for a few days and pot up; they should root fairly easily in spring and summer. Grow this euphorbia in any good loam- or peat-based potting mixture, and water freely in spring and summer.

Above and above right:
Euphorbia milii
The stems of this small shrub are covered in sharp prickles. Bright red bracts give the plant great appeal. Avoid cold draughts in winter.

A practical hint
To ensure free drainage for succulents, place pieces of broken clay pot in the bottom of the pots before adding soil.

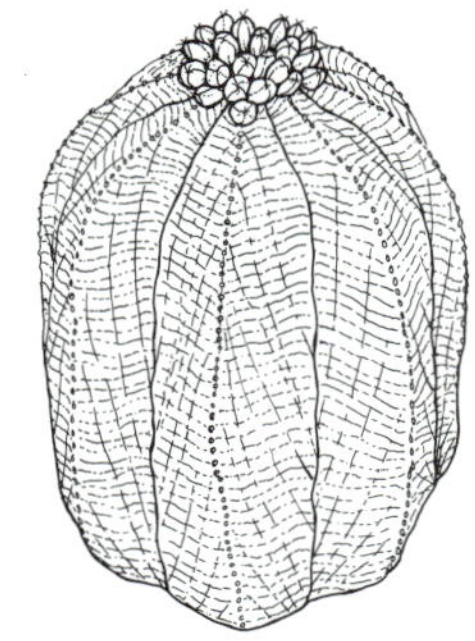

Euphorbia obesa

- **Full sun**
- **Temp: 5-30°C (41-86°F)**
- **Keep dry in winter**

A true succulent in every sense of the word; there could hardly be a greater difference between this euphorbia and the preceding one. It has a most distinctive spineless, leafless greyish-green stem with a pale purple pattern. At first almost spherical and up to about 7cm (2.8in) across, it usually becomes taller with age. Having neither offsets nor branches, propagation is only from seed, which requires both male and female plants, as the sexes are separate. Tiny flowers with a delightful, delicate perfume are formed at the top of the plant, and followed by seed pods in the case of a female plant that has been pollinated.

Grow this attractive novelty in a well-drained medium consisting of two thirds of a standard potting mixture and one third sharp sand or perlite. This euphorbia tends to have a long tap root, so use a fairly deep pot for it.

Left: **Euphorbia obesa**
An extreme succulent. This is a female plant with seed pods at the top of the single stem. Be sure to water during the spring and summer months only. Propagate from seed.

A practical hint
Indoors, if conditions are dark and airless, there will be a marked tendency for succulents to become pale and sickly and less attractive.

Euphorbia pulcherrima

- **Good light**
- **Temp: 16-21°C (60-70°F)**
- **Keep moist and fed**

This plant with its bright red, creamy green, or pink-coloured bracts is by far the finest of all winter-flowering indoor plants. The end of autumn to early winter is their natural flowering time and, given reasonable care, they will continue in colour for many months.

Avoid temperatures below 16°C (60°F) and be careful to water plants and allow them to dry reasonably before repeating. Feeding should never be to excess – weak liquid fertilizer can be given each week, and this should be sufficient for most plants.

To get plants to flower for a second year indoors ensure that only natural daylight is made available from early autumn until early winter. When not in flower, prune to shape.

Tip cuttings can be taken from new side-shoots after the bracts have dropped. Wash the poisonous latex from the cut end and insert in a mixture of equal parts peat and sharp sand.

Right: **Euphorbia pulcherrima**
This is one of the most popular houseplants for winter colour. This photograph shows several individual plants grouped together, each one with bracts of a single colour.

A practical hint
Only very large succulents need big pots. Pot plants on in spring, or simply remove from the pot, brush off old soil and repot in the same pot.

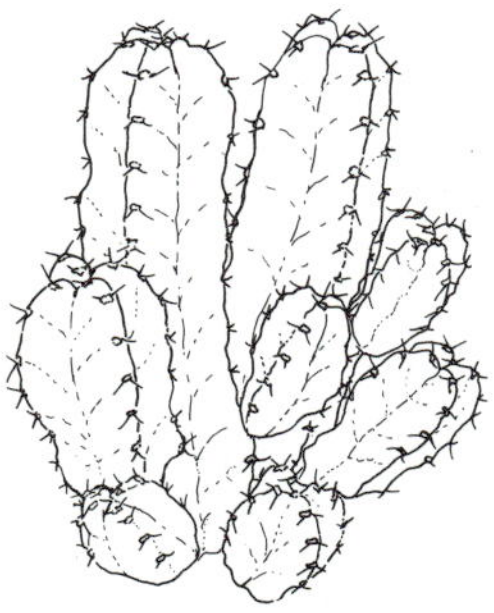

Euphorbia resinifera

- **Full sun**
- **Temp: 5-30°C (41-86°F)**
- **Keep dry in winter**

This is probably the oldest known succulent plant of all, having been discovered by an eastern king about 25BC! In cultivation it is a low, much-branched shrub, with four-angled bright green stems up to 30cm (12in) high. There are short spines in pairs along the edges of the branches. Flowers are seldom or never produced on cultivated plants, but if they were, they would be tiny and rather insignificant. Branches can be cut away and used for propagation, but the cut ends 'bleed' profusely with a white milky sap; this should be washed off with water and the branch allowed to dry for a week. Do this only during spring and summer.

Grow this euphorbia in a good, well-drained potting mixture of three parts standard peat- or loam-based material with one part of sharp sand or perlite. Water it quite freely in spring and summer but then gradually reduce for its winter rest.

Right: **Euphorbia resinifera**
One of the rather cactus-like succulents, which eventually forms quite a large clump. It is an easy plant to cultivate, provided it has a well-drained potting mixture and is kept dry in winter. The sap is irritant.

A practical hint
The majority of plants will benefit from tepid water, as opposed to cold tap water, but water must not be in any way hot. Cold tea is fine!

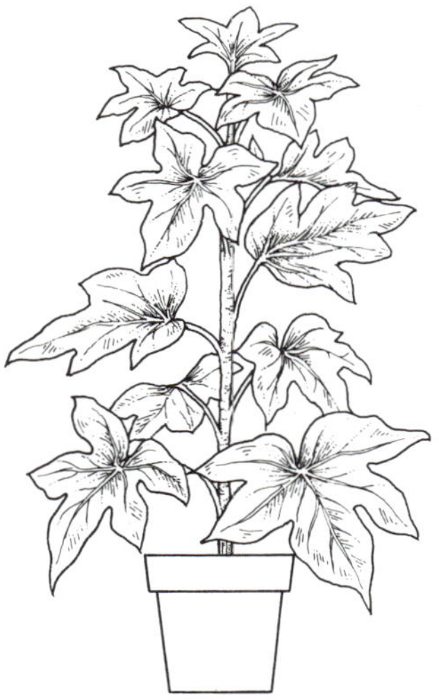

Exacum affine

- **Good light**
- **Temp: 13-18°C (55-65°F)**
- **Keep moist and fed**

In small pots on the windowsill there can be few prettier plants than *E. affine,* which has glossy green foliage and scented lavender-blue flowers. An added bonus is that, if old flowerheads are removed, the plant will continue in flower for many months from midsummer onwards.

In common with almost all flowering plants this one should have a very light location in which to grow. But very strong sunlight must be avoided, particularly when it is being magnified by window panes. Besides being a good individual plant *E. affine* is an excellent subject for including in mixed plant arrangements. Keep established plants moist and fed. New plants should be raised annually from seed.

New varieties with bright blue and with white flowers are available, so extending the colour range of this delightful plant.

Fatshedera lizei

- **Light shade**
- **Temp: 4-16°C (40-60°F)**
- **Keep moist and fed**

This plant does not have the flexibility of the stems of *Hedera* (ivy), which is one of its parents, but is more in keeping with the stems of *Fatsia*, which is the other parent. Leaves have the shape of the ivy leaf and are glossy green in colour. For cooler locations the ivy tree is ideal, as it prefers low rather than high temperatures and is hardy in sheltered areas. Plants have a tendency to lose lower leaves, especially in hot, dry conditions.

New plants may be propagated either from the topmost section of the plant with three firm leaves attached or from sections of stem with a single leaf attached. In both cases they will do well in a temperature of around 18°C (65°F) if inserted in peat and sand mixture. In order to provide plants of full appearance, it is best to put three or four rooted cuttings in the growing pot rather than a single piece. The soil for potting up cuttings should be on the peaty side.

Above left: **Exacum affine**
These charming, one-season plants are covered with fragrant flowers for several months. A moist atmosphere will benefit their growth and picking off the dead flowers will keep them blooming for a longer period.

Left: **Fatshedera lizei**
The naturally glossy green leaves are attached to strong stems that should be supported so that the foliage can be seen to best advantage. Plants will grow to a height of about 90-120cm (3-4ft).

Fatshedera lizei variegata

- **Light shade**
- **Temp: 4-16°C (40-60°F)**
- **Keep moist and fed**

Most variegated plants are that little bit more difficult to care for than their green counterparts, and the variegated fatshedera is no exception. But provided it is not subjected to very high temperatures for long periods it will not prove too much of a problem.

Plants should be kept moist and well fed during the growing season and on the dry side with little or no feeding in winter. In agreeable conditions they will grow quite quickly on long single stems. However, the tip of the plant can be removed to encourage side shoots to grow and give the plant a more attractive appearance.

Besides the white variegated form there is now a cultivar with more golden foliage often labelled as *F. lizei aurea.* In my experience of growing the latter it would seem to be a marginally more difficult plant to care for, but none of the fatshederas can be classed as difficult.

Above: **Fatshedera lizei variegata**
Yellow and white variegated forms are available, both of which need cool conditions. Give them a little more light than green forms.

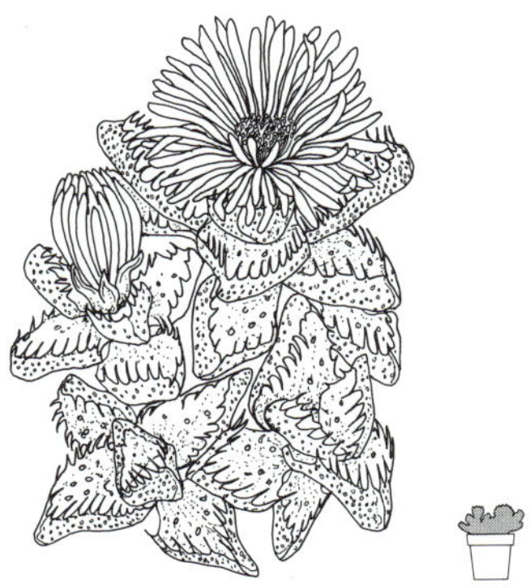

Faucaria tigrina

- **Full sun**
- **Temp: 5-30°C (41-86°F)**
- **Keep almost dry in winter**

Faucarias are not only pretty, but also easy to grow. These small succulents will grow on a sunny windowsill or in a sunny greenhouse. *F. tigrina* is a low-growing plant consisting of rather crowded succulent leaves, each of which has an edging of 'teeth'. The leaves are grey-green in colour, and covered with tiny white dots. The large golden-yellow flowers appear in autumn; they open in the afternoon if it is sunny, and close at night.

If overwatered, faucarias tend to become too large. Grow them in a soil consisting of half loam-based material and half sharp sand or perlite. Water freely in summer, but allow them to dry out in between. Give only an occasional watering in winter. With age, faucarias develop pronounced woody stems. In late spring, cut the heads off, with about 0.5cm (0.2in) of stem, and dry for a day before potting up.

Above: **Faucaria tigrina**
An almost stemless succulent with pairs of leaves looking like tiny jaws. An easy plant that needs repotting only once every three years.

Fenestraria rhopalophylla

- **Full sun**
- **Temp: 5-30°C (41-86°F)**
- **Completely dry in winter**

Fenestraria rhopalophylla has grey-green cylindrical leaves that end in a transparent 'window'. In the desert regions of south-west Africa, the leaves are buried in the ground up to their tips and the light is filtered down to the chlorophyll through the 'window'. In cultivation the plant is grown completely above ground, partly because of the poorer light and also to prevent rotting.

The leaves, about 2.5cm (1in) long, grow in little clusters. The plant is vigorous and will soon fill a pan. The growing period starts early in spring and continues through the summer. White flowers appear in summer; they open in the sunshine and close again at night.

Grow in a sandy soil. It does not need repotting annually; when potting on, be careful not to disturb the roots. Water freely during spring and summer but keep completely dry during autumn and winter. Propagate by removing the heads during early summer.

Right: **Fenestraria rhopalophylla**
A most unusual succulent with fascinating window-tip leaves and white flowers during the summer. Allow to dry out between waterings.

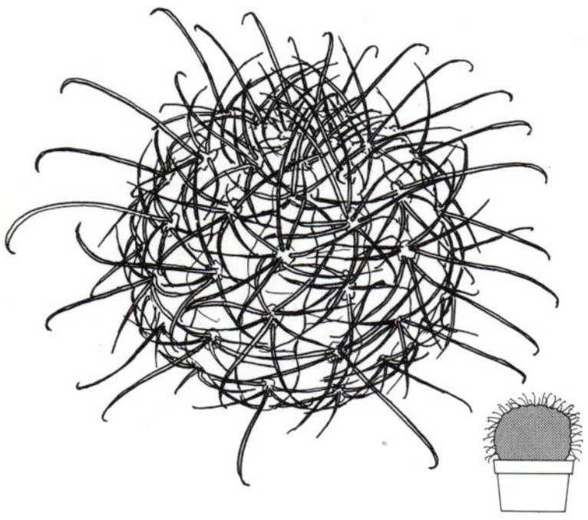

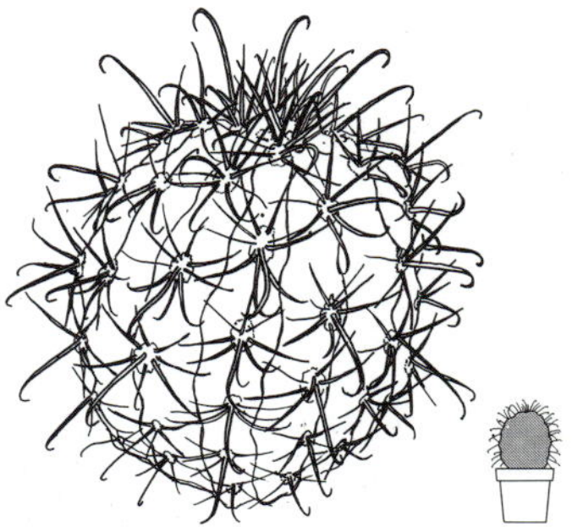

Ferocactus acanthodes

- **Full sun**
- **Temp: 5-30°C (41-86°F)**
- **Keep dry in winter**

'Ferocactus' means 'ferocious cactus' and this aptly describes these plants, with their array of sharp, tough spines. *F. acanthodes* is a particularly attractive member of the group. It is spherical, becoming more elongated with age, and the many ribs are furnished with reddish spines up to 4cm (1.6in) long, some of them curved. A giant cactus in nature, it is slow-growing and perfectly suitable as a pot specimen; in a pot it can attain a diameter of 15cm (6in) or more, but takes years to do so. However, small plants do not usually flower.

Ferocacti are particularly sensitive to insufficient light and overwatering, so give this one all the direct sunshine you can, and add extra drainage material to a standard peat- or loam-based potting mixture (one part to two parts mixture). It is best to water only when the mixture has almost dried out. A top dressing of grit or gravel will keep the base dry.

Ferocactus horridus

- **Full sun**
- **Temp: 5-30°C (41-86°F)**
- **Keep dry in winter**

A fiercely armed cactus with an almost globular stem – which in cultivation is unlikely to exceed a diameter of 10cm (4in) – divided into about 12 ribs. Very strong, reddish spines occur in groups along the ribs, up to 5cm (2in) long; the longest spine in each group is flattened and hooked at the tip. Ideally designed to catch in the clothing and pull the plant off the staging! Although yellow flowers can be produced, they are unlikely on smaller plants, so it is best not to hope for them, but to be content with the plant itself.

Grow this ferocactus in a porous potting mixture, which you can make up by adding one part of sharp sand or perlite to two parts of a standard material, and mixing it thoroughly. It is best to water only on sunny days in summer, to avoid any risk of the potting mixture becoming too wet. If the plant should lose its roots, cut it back to clean tissue and allow to dry out for a few days before replanting.

Above: **Ferocactus acanthodes**
Normally only large specimens of this cactus will flower, but the colourful spines are beautiful. Keep in the sunniest place.

Above right: **Ferocactus horridus**
'Horridus' *here means spiny, and this cactus is very spiny indeed. Only larger plants are likely to come into flower as here. Never overwater.*

A practical hint
When locating cactus plants indoors ensure a full sun position that also offers fresh air as opposed to stuffy conditions.

Ferocactus latispinus

- **Full sun**
- **Temp: 5-30°C (41-86°F)**
- **Keep dry in winter**

Probably the best-known of the ferocacti, and if you want only one from this group, this is the one to choose. Unlike most of the others, which usually need to reach massive proportions before flowering, this is a species that should burst into bloom when it reaches a diameter of about 10cm (4in). The flowers, 4cm (1.6in) across, are a beautiful purple-red in colour, and open in succession from autumn until early winter. But here lies the snag: unless the autumn is warm and sunny, the buds will probably not open at all! The deeply indented ribs of the bright green stem bear rows of strong, deep yellow spines, some flattened and tipped with red; the whole plant when in flower is a magnificent sight.

As with other ferocacti, a well-drained potting mixture is essential; one part of sharp sand or perlite mixed into two parts of a standard material will prevent any risk of waterlogging, often fatal.

Left: **Ferocactus latispinus**
This ferocactus is quite likely to flower, but usually only if the weather is warm and sunny. The strong spines make a striking display.

Ficus benjamina

- **Good light, no direct sun**
- **Temp: 16-21°C (60-70°F)**
- **Keep moist and fed**

Of very graceful weeping habit, *F. benjamina* will develop into tree size if provided with the right conditions. However, excess growth can be trimmed out at any time. To maintain plants in good condition with their glossy leaves gleaming it is important to feed them well while in active growth, and to pot them on into loam-based mixture as required. Little feeding and no potting should be done in winter, and it is also wise during this period to water more sparingly unless the plants are drying out in hot rooms. The weeping fig has a tendency to shed leaves in poorly lit situations.

Not many pests affect ficus plants, but scale insects seem to favour *F. benjamina*. These are either dark or light brown in colour and cling to stems and the undersides of leaves. Another sign of their presence will be dark sooty deposits on leaves below where the pests are clinging. It is best to wash them off with malathion.

Above: **Ficus benjamina**
The elegant weeping fig has glossy green foliage and naturally cascading branches – a combination that produces one of the finest plants.

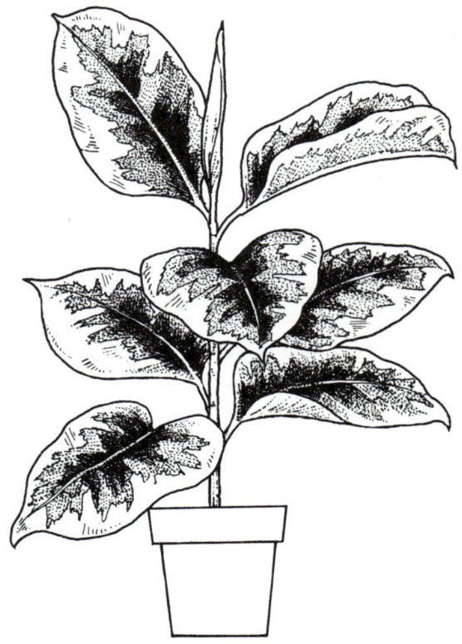

Ficus benjamina 'Hawaii'

- **Light shade**
- **Temp: 16-21°C (60-70°F)**
- **Keep moist and fed**

A recent introduction with white-and-green variegated leaves that seems likely to become a very successful indoor subject.

To get the best from these plants they need good light without bright sun, and the temperature should not fall below 16°C (60°F). Watering should follow the standard procedure for larger indoor plants, ie well watered from the top with surplus water clearly seen to drain out of the bottom of the container. The plant should then be left until the soil has dried out to a reasonable degree before watering again.

Younger plants should be provided with a supporting stake and the plant tied to the stake as new growth develops. However, a few strands should be allowed to hang over so that a plant with weeping growth all the way up results.

Like the green *F. benjamina*, this will tend to shed leaves at a rather alarming rate if it is placed in too dark a location.

Ficus europa

- **Good light**
- **Temp: 16-21°C (60-70°F)**
- **Keep moist and fed**

Far and away the best variegated broad-leaved rubber plant ever to be produced. Leaf colouring is a bright cream and green and the stems are bold and upright. Unlike previous variegated rubber plants this one does not have the usual tendency to develop brown discolouration along its leaf margins, and it is altogether more vigorous.

Taller plants will require supporting stakes, and ample watering and feeding while new leaves are being produced. This should be all year except during the winter months. However, some plants are slow to get on the move and such plants should be watered with care until it is seen that new leaves are on the way at the top of the stem.

All the broad-leaved rubber plants will be the better for cleaning with a damp cloth or sponge periodically, but one should not be too enthusiastic when it comes to use of chemical cleaners.

Above: **Ficus benjamina 'Hawaii'**
Similar in appearance to the weeping fig, but of more erect habit and with brightly variegated leaves that are seen at their best in good light.

Above right: **Ficus europa**
Easily the best variegated form of broad-leaved rubber plants, with remarkably fine colouring and relatively easy to care for.

A practical hint
Feeding is essential for all plants and ought to begin from the time of purchase as suppliers recommend. Winter feeding is seldom needed.

Ficus lyrata

- **Light shade**
- **Temp: 16-21°C (60-70°F)**
- **Keep moist and fed**

One of the more majestic members of the fig family, *F. lyrata* develops into a small branching tree. Leaves are glossy green with prominent veins and are shaped like the body of a violin. The original single stem of the plant will naturally shed lower leaves and the plant will produce leaf buds in the axils of the topmost four to six leaves, and in time these will become the branches of the tree.

It is important to seek out plants that have fresh, dark green leaves rather than those that may be marked or discoloured. Indoors they should be offered reasonable light and warmth, and in their early stages of development they will need careful watering; the plants are best kept on the dry side rather than too wet. More mature plants in larger pots will require more watering and more frequent feeding, with less of both being given in winter. The plant can be pruned at any time to improve its shape.

Left: **Ficus lyrata**
Leaf shape gives the common name of fiddle leaf fig to one of the boldest and most vigorous indoor plants. Veined leaves are naturally glossy.

A practical hint
Potting on should be done in gradual stages, with the plant going into the next pot size up, and not from small to very large pots in one go.

Ficus pumila

- **Light shade**
- **Temp: 16-21°C (60-70°F)**
- **Keep moist**

A simple plant, yet one of my personal favourites. Leaves are quite small as ficus plants go and are oval in shape. The plant may climb if provided with a support, or be allowed to trail in a natural manner. A good plant for mixed displays.

These plants must have reasonable temperature, and it is imperative that they be kept moist at all times; drying out of the soil will almost inevitably result in the loss of the plant. However, plants should not become sodden through standing permanently in water. They will tolerate drying out a little between waterings, but it must not be excessive. Feed them while they are growing, giving little or none in winter, and when potting on use a peaty mixture.

Cleaning individual leaves can be tedious, and I would suggest that a quick and adequate job can be done by inverting the plant in a bucket filled with soapy water and giving it a good swish around.

Left: **Ficus pumila**
Commonly named the creeping fig, it will also climb a damp wall or can be trained to a moss-covered support. The oval leaves are pale green.

A practical hint
The worst possible combination of conditions for indoor plants is that of wet and cold. In low temperatures most should be dry at their roots.

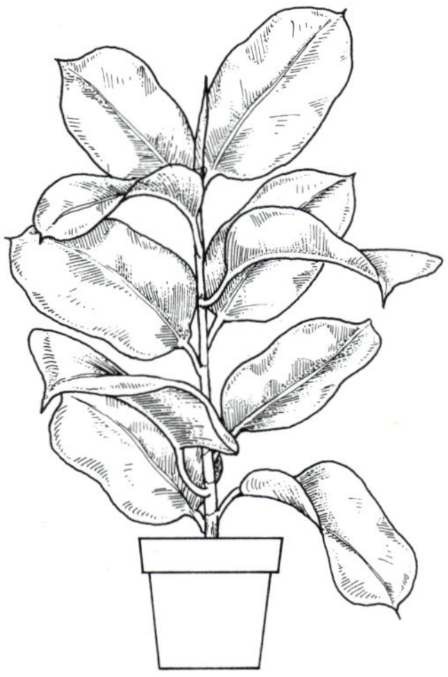

Ficus robusta

- **Light shade**
- **Temp: 10-18°C (50-65°F)**
- **Avoid very wet conditions**

Almost the symbol of the modern-day houseplant business, the rubber plant is still grown and sold in large quantities. *Ficus robusta* now seems firmly established as the favourite rubber plant, and we seldom see its predecessors these days. The original variety was *F. elastica*, which in time was replaced by *F. decora*. The new plant is superior in almost every way, particularly in its ability to stand up to indoor conditions.

Failure with these plants usually arises from overwatering. Permanently wet soil results in roots rotting away, which will mean loss of leaves. It is especially important to prevent plants becoming too wet during the winter months. During the winter it is also wise to discontinue feeding. Potting should be undertaken during late spring or early summer, using loam-based mixture. Leaves will be brighter if occasionally cleaned with a damp sponge.

Above right: **Ficus robusta**
One of the symbols of the houseplant business, the rubber plant has broad glossy green leaves attached to stout upright stems. Clean the leaves with a sponge.

A practical hint
An autumn or winter 'spring clean' suits many foliage plants, when they can be pruned to shape and dead or dying pieces can be removed.

Fittonia argyroneura nana

- **Shade**
- **Temp: 18-24°C (65-75°F)**
- **Keep moist and humid**

The smaller-leaved version of the silver snakeskin plant is much less demanding than its big brother. The leaves are oval in shape and produced in great quantity by healthy plants. Neat growth and prostrate habit makes them ideal for growing in bottle gardens or disused fish tanks.

Cuttings roots with little difficulty in warm, moist and shaded conditions. Several cuttings should go into small pots filled with peaty mixture, and it is often better to overwinter these small plants rather than try to persevere with larger plants. At all stages of potting on a peaty mixture will be essential, and it is better to use shallow containers that will suit the plant's prostrate growth.

Not much troubled by pests; the worst enemy by far is low temperature allied to wet root conditions. Recommended temperature levels must be maintained, and this is especially important during cold weather.

Left: **Fittonia argyroneura nana**
The silvery-grey colouring is heavily veined with a tracery of darker green that gives the oval leaves appeal. Plants have a creeping habit and need warmth and moisture.

A practical hint
Fuchsias shed flowers and buds alarmingly if placed in poor light; a position outside will suit them better, if indoor light is poor.

Fittonia verschaffeltii

Fittonia (large-leaved)

- **Shade**
- **Temp: 18-24°C (65-75°F)**
- **Keep moist and humid**

There are two of these that one will be likely to come across, neither of them very easy to care for. With large reddish-green leaves there is *F. verschaffeltii*, and with attractively veined silver leaves there is *F. argyroneura*. Both are of prostrate habit, with leaves tending to curl downwards over their containers. In my experience these plants rarely do well on the windowsill. They fare much better in miniature greenhouses, disused fish tanks or bottle gardens. In such situations the plants are free of draughts.

Bright sunlight will play havoc with the tender foliage so these plants must be in the shade, but not necessarily in very dark locations. When applying water it is best to warm it slightly and to dampen the area surrounding the pot as well as the soil in which the plants are growing. Frequent but small feeds will be better than occasional heavy doses – a little with each watering.

Right: **Fittonia verschaffeltii**
Paper-thin leaves are of dull red colouring and are heavily veined, providing an exotic appearance. Difficult to care for, the plant needs warm, moist, shady conditions.

Freesia

- **Good light**
- **Temp: 10-16°C (50-60°F)**
- **Moist; dry in winter**

Among the most fragrant of all flowers the freesias are available in many wonderful colours, and will fill the entire room with their scent. The small bulbs belong to the iris family, and should be planted in loam-based houseplant soil in the autumn. Plant just below the soil surface and place bulbs almost touching in a shallow pot about 18cm (7in) in diameter. Pots are then placed in a cool, sheltered place (an unheated greenhouse, for example) in good light to establish. Once under way they can be transferred to a warmer location to develop their flowers, and placed on a light and cool windowsill indoors when blooms are present. Freesias are excellent as cut flowers, too.

Keep moist while in leaf; feeding is not normally necessary as bulbs are planted in fresh soil each autumn. Dry off and store bulbs after flowering.

Fuchsia

- **Sunny location**
- **Temp: 13-18°C (55-65°F)**
- **Keep moist, and feed well**

Given proper care this is possibly the best of all the potted plants as far as flower production and length of season goes. They can produce blooms from spring until early autumn with a seemingly never-ending display. But they can also be extremely disappointing for the indoor plant grower, as fuchsias must have maximum light if they are to flower as well as they might. It will often mean that plants are happier and produce more flowers if grown on the windowsill outside the window rather than the sill in the room. In poor light indoors it will be impossible for plants to produce flowers.

A loam-based potting mix is essential for healthy plants. Keep them moist and well fed while in active growth, and prune back severely in the autumn when they begin to lose their summer sparkle.

Right: **Freesia**
These beautifully fragrant plants can be grown in a cool greenhouse. They are available in a wide range of colours and are excellent for cutting and displaying in a vase.

Above: **Fuchsia 'Snowcap'**
It is possible to grow these lovely plants in a cool bright location indoors. It is vital to keep them moist and regularly fed while they are actively growing. Take cuttings.

A practical hint
Black coloured pots are becoming common and are better for plant roots, as no light is allowed through, so less algae form around the roots.

Gardenia jasminoides

- **Light shade, no sun**
- **Temp: 18-21°C (65-70°F)**
- **Keep moist**

These are shrubby plants with small oval-shaped green leaves that will have a marked tendency to take on chlorotic yellow colouring if conditions are not to the liking of the plant. They are difficult plants to care for, needing a temperature of not less than 18°C (65°F), a lightly shaded location, and careful watering and feeding. Rain water is preferable to tap water and it will benefit plants if the foliage is misted over with water when the atmosphere tends to be dry. Frequent weak feeding will be better than giving occasional heavy doses. Use an acid-type fertilizer and pot the plants in an acid or peat-based mixture.

But, in spite of the problems, the gardenia is well worth trying to raise, as there are few flowers that can match its heavy, almost overpowering scent. Flowers are creamy white and up to 10cm (4in) across. They appear in summer mainly, but some varieties can be flowered in early winter. In pots gardenias reach a height of about 45cm (18in).

Left: **Gardenia jasminoides**
These magnificent plants need care to ensure that they flower indoors. Sudden temperature changes when the flower buds are forming will cause them to drop. Keep potbound.

Gasteria maculata

- **Partial shade**
- **Temp: 5-30°C (41-86°F)**
- **Keep slightly moist in winter**

Probably the most popular of the gasterias, this succulent is often to be seen in home and office windows, where its very existence is a tribute to its ability to survive adverse conditions! It is one of the easiest of succulents to grow, but so frequently ill-treated. Just water it freely in spring and summer and give it something nourishing to live in, and it will reward you with an appearance quite different from its ill-treated relatives. The flattened leaves are about 15cm (6in) long and 4cm (1.6in) wide, glossy green with white spots or bands. They form two rows, rather than a rosette, at least in younger plants. Offsets are freely produced, soon forming a clump, which will probably have to be split up eventually, unless it can be grown in a wide pan.

This gasteria will survive at 5°C (41°F) in winter if it is quite dry, but it is happier at a rather higher temperature and moister, in a living-room or kitchen. It may be outdoors in summer.

Above right: **Gasteria maculata**
An ideal plant for the house or office if given reasonable light, without full sun, and not allowed to become desiccated. Propagate it by detaching rooted offsets and potting.

A practical hint
All flowering plants should be checked for aphids, especially in spring and summer; they are mostly found in the area of soft top growth.

Gloriosa rothschildiana

- **Good light**
- **Temp: 13-18°C (55-65°F)**
- **Keep moist, but dry when dormant**

These showy plants have glossy leaves and upright habit. They produce a wealth of exotic flowers during the summer months in orange and yellow with a crimson edge.

Plants should be started from tubers; these should go one to an 11.5cm (4.5in) pot in peaty soil and later be transferred to pots of about 18cm (7in) in diameter when the smaller pots are well filled with roots. Use a loam-based mixture at this stage and put at least three of the contents of the smaller pots into the larger one, so that a good show is provided when the plant comes into flower.

It is also wise to place three or four 150cm (5ft) canes around the edge of the pot to which plants can be tied as they develop. Rest tubers during winter in a cool dry place.

Left: **Gloriosa rothschildiana**
Where space permits, this vine offers a summer spectacle of richly coloured blooms. It needs plenty of water and feed when active but none when dormant. Divide tubers.

A practical hint
Gymnocalycium mihanovichii 'Hibotan' is an interesting plant with orange colouring and barrel-type growth; it is seen grafted to other stock.

Glottiphyllum linguiforme

- **Full sun**
- **Temp: 5-30°C (41-86°F)**
- **Water with great caution**

Glottiphyllum linguiforme is an attractive plant, provided it is not overwatered. It will mop up any amount of water, becoming more and more distorted in the process. This glottiphyllum has two rows of thick tongue-like leaves, which are 5cm (2in) long, and bright shiny green in colour. The plant blooms on sunny days in late autumn or early winter. Like many South African succulents, its shining yellow flowers open on sunny days and close at night. The plant will form side shoots, which may be removed for propagation during the latter half of the summer.

A good potting mixture is half loam-based medium and half sharp sand or perlite. The plant should be repotted every third or fourth year. During late summer and autumn, water on sunny days, allowing it to dry out between waterings. Watch for mealy bugs, which are the main pest. Spraying with a proprietary insecticide will eliminate them.

Above right:
Glottiphyllum linguiforme
These are attractive plants with fleshy leaves and lovely flowers.

Gomeza crispa

- **Cool: 10°C (50°F)**
- **Easy to grow and flower**
- **Summer/autumn flowering**
- **Evergreen/no rest**

Although there are about ten species of this epiphytic orchid available to growers, only one, *Gomeza crispa,* from Brazil is grown.

It is a plant for the cool house, requiring some protection from full light during the summer months. Free drainage for the root system is of great importance and for this reason it is a good subject to grow on a raft or piece of cork bark. If grown in a pot, a coarse material, such as fir bark, should be used. As the plant grows upwards, away from the pot, the roots should be allowed to grow outside, where they should gain sufficient nourishment from the atmosphere. Spraying during the summer is helpful.

The plant produces pseudobulbs and leaves similar to those of odontoglossums, only paler in colour. The flowers are carried on arching sprays, up to 23cm (9in) long, and there are often two sprays to a pseudobulb. The sweetly scented, lime-green flowers, about 1.25cm (0.5in) across, are densely clustered on the spike and appear during the summer and autumn.

Right: **Gomeza crispa**
A small grower for the cool house. Dainty sprays of flowers appear in the summer. An easy orchid.

A practical hint
Some orchids produce natural aerial roots from their stems, and it is important to allow these roots to hang over the pot.

Gongora galeata

- **Cool/intermediate: 10-13°C (50-55°F)**
- **Easy to grow and flower**
- **Summer flowering**
- **Evergreen/semi-rest**

These plants are to be found throughout South America from Mexico to Brazil, where they grow as epiphytes. About 12 species are known. Of these, a very few are occasionally found in cultivation. *Gongora galeata* is both interesting and showy as well as being highly fragrant. The fragrance is of oranges.

The plant has a neat habit with oval-shaped, ribbed pseudobulbs, each carrying two slender leaves and a fine rooting system. The flower spikes are extremely thin and can pass unnoticed in their early stage of development or be mistaken for a new root. They develop downwards, so the plant should always be placed in an open basket to allow the spikes freedom to grow. They extend to about 15cm (6in) below the plant and produce up to six or eight flowers. The curiously shaped flowers are about 5cm (2in) long and are usually tawny yellow to buff orange in colour.

The plant should be well watered during its summer growing season, and lightly fed. A position of good light will suit it at all times, especially during the winter.

Left: **Gongora galeata**
This curiously attractive species is cool growing. It flowers freely in the summer on pendent sprays

A practical hint
While they are resting it is important that orchids are positioned where they will obtain the maximum amount of available light.

Grammangis ellisii

- **Warm: 18°C (65°F)**
- **Moderately easy to grow**
- **Summer flowering**
- **Evergreen/semi-rest**

This species is a member of a small genus of remarkably handsome epiphytic orchids of which five species are known. It is a large robust plant that requires plenty of room in which to grow. The pseudobulbs are tall, spindle-shaped and four-sided, which is an unusual feature. Several long, leathery leaves are set towards the top half of the bulb. The flower spikes emerge from the half-completed new growth during the summer. These are naturally arching and many flowered. The slightly fragrant flowers are 9cm (3.5in) across and similar in shape to a *Lycaste* flower. The prominent sepals are basically yellow, this colour partially obscured by dense, reddish brown bars. The petals and lip are smaller.

The plant is suitable for a warm greenhouse and while growing should be watered and fed liberally. During the winter less water but extra light should be given. The plants do not like disturbance and should only be repotted when absolutely necessary. The plant is a native of Madagascar.

Above right: **Grammangis ellisii**
A large, robust-growing species for warm-house culture. It blooms in the summer on long arching sprays. Slightly fragrant flowers.

Grevillea robusta

- **Light shade**
- **Temp: 4-21°C (40-70°F)**
- **Feed and water well**

An Australian plant, the silk oak makes a splendid tree in its native land, and is a fairly fast-growing pot plant in many other parts of the world. It is tough, has attractive, green silky foliage and is one of the easiest plants to care for. It can be readily raised from seed.

The grevillea will quickly grow into a large plant if it is kept moist and well fed, and if it is potted into a larger container when the existing one is well filled with roots. A loam-based soil is best. If plants become too tall for their allotted space it is no trouble to remove the more invasive branches with a pair of secateurs – almost any time of the year will do for this exercise.

During the summer months when the plant is in full vigour it will be important to ensure that it is obtaining sufficient water, and this will mean filling the top of the pot and ensuring that the surplus runs right through and out at the bottom drainage holes.

Left: **Grevillea robusta**
When well grown the leaves of the silk oak have a silvery sheen that is most attractive. These vigorous plants need frequent feeding.

A practical hint
Plant fertilizers come in many forms and one should follow directions for use. Avoid feeding plants that are dry at their roots or newly potted.

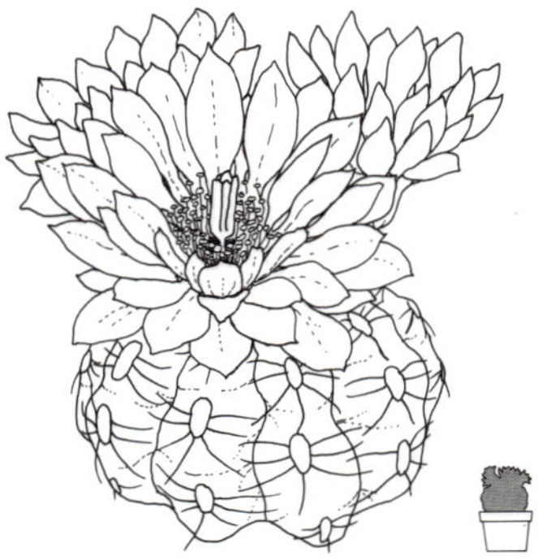

Guzmania lingulata

- **Good light**
- **Temp: 13-18°C (55-65°F)**
- **Keep on the dry side**

Belonging to the fine bromeliad family, there are a number of guzmanias that can be found in the quest for new plants to add to the houseplant collection, and all of them will be very easy to manage indoors.

The growing habit is that of most bromeliads – the plant forms a stiff rosette of leaves that protrude from a short and stout central trunk. Overlapping leaves make a natural watertight urn, which must be kept filled with water. However, it is advisable to empty the urn and refill with fresh water periodically. Rain water is preferred but try to avoid getting the soil in the pot too wet. Impressive orange-scarlet bracts develop on short stems from the centre of the urn during winter. New plants can be started from offsets.

Bromeliads should be grown in a free-draining mixture; equal parts of a loam-based medium and peat will be ideal. Alternatively, a commercially prepared bromeliad mix can be used.

Above right and right: **Guzmania lingulata 'Minor Orange'**
The stunning display of colour lasts for several months during the winter. Keep the humidity high.

Gymnocalycium andreae

- **Full sun**
- **Temp: 5-30°C (41-86°F)**
- **Keep dry in winter**

Most gymnocalyciums are fairly small, compact cacti, very suitable for the average collection, but this one is particularly desirable as it only reaches a diameter of about 5cm (2in), although a small clump is eventually formed. The spines, some of which are curved, are quite short. This little plant is very free-flowering, producing its bright yellow blooms, about 3cm (1.2in) across, in spring and summer. The colour is unusual for a gymnocalycium, which mostly have white or greenish-white flowers. Offsets soon appear on the main plant; they can be removed for propagation, or left on to produce eventually a rounded mass of beautifully flowering heads.

Full sun is needed, and any good potting mixture may be used, either loam-based or loamless. But good drainage is essential and about one third of extra sharp sand or perlite should be added. During late spring and summer water freely but let the plant become almost dry first.

Above:
Gymnocalycium andreae
The bright yellow flowers make this an unusual gymnocalycium. Single heads soon form into a clump.

Gymnocalycium bruchii

- **Full sun**
- **Temp: 5-30°C (41-86°F)**
- **Keep dry in winter**

Another small-growing cactus, and if one had to choose a single beauty, easily obtainable, from among a lovely group, this could well be it. But it has a confusing alias; it is sometimes called *G. lafaldense*, so take care not to buy the same plant twice! A small compact clump of neatly spined, rounded heads is soon formed, which produces pinkish blooms very freely. Far better to leave this cactus as a clump, but often the heads become so crowded that a few can be removed to make room for the others. Carefully cut them away with a thin knife, allow them to dry off for a few days and just press them into fresh potting mix in late spring and summer.

Either loam- or peat-based potting mixture may be used, but increase the drainage by mixing in about one third of sharp sand or perlite. Watering can be quite free in spring and summer, and every two weeks or so give a dose of fertilizer.

Above: **Gymnocalycium bruchii**
A small, compact cactus, soon forming a freely flowering clump. This plant is sometimes listed in catalogues as G. lafaldense. *Easily divided for new plants.*

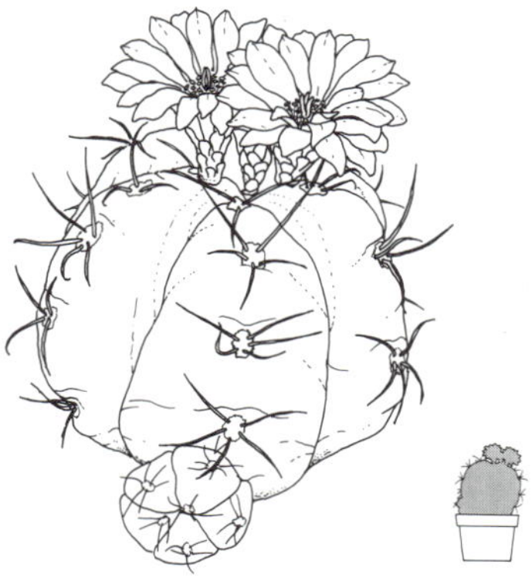

Gymnocalycium denudatum

- **Full sun**
- **Temp: 5-30°C (41-86°F)**
- **Keep dry in winter**

This is perhaps the best-known gymnocalycium and more or less typical of the whole group. It is an almost globular cactus reaching the size of about 15cm (6in) across and 10cm (4in) high. The deep green plant body or stem is furnished with broad ribs and the notches along them give the typical 'chin' effect, although this is less pronounced than in other similar plants. The popular name of 'Spider cactus' refers to the short spreading spines, somewhat resembling small spiders crawling over the plant. Beautiful greenish-white or pinkish flowers add to the attractiveness of this cactus during spring and summer. They are about 5cm (2in) across.

Grow this cactus in a potting mixture of about two thirds standard growing medium and one third sharp sand or perlite and feed occasionally with a high-potassium fertilizer during the bud and flower stage.

Gymnocalycium horridispinum

- **Full sun**
- **Temp: 5-30°C (41-86°F)**
- **Keep dry in winter**

One of the attractions of gymnocalyciums is their great variety of shape, spines and flowers, and this one is indeed a beauty among them. It is rather less typical of the group as a whole, being more elongated than globular; an average-sized plant is about 13cm (5in) tall and 8cm (3.2in) broad. Also it has delightful pink flowers up to 6cm (2.4in) across. In spite of their size, three or four flowers can be produced at a time, and they may last for up to a week. Unfortunately, they have no perfume! There are well-formed 'chins' along the ribs of the bright green stem and these bear stout, spreading spines, about 3cm (1.2in) long. Incidentally, its Latin name does not mean 'horrid', but 'prickly' or 'spiny'.

Grow this lovely plant in the usual well-drained standard potting mixture with extra sharp sand or perlite, and feed occasionally in spring and summer.

Left: **Gymnocalycium denudatum**
The magnificent flowers are produced freely during spring and summer; they usually last for several days, and may be followed by seed pods. The seeds can be sown.

Above:
Gymnocalycium horridispinum
The unusually coloured flowers of this cactus make it outstanding even in this group of beautiful plants. This gymnocalycium needs a dry rest.

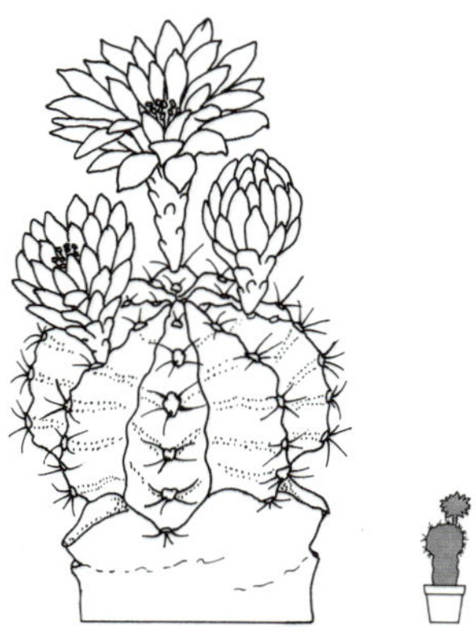

Gymnocalycium mihanovichii 'Hibotan'

- **Partial shade**
- **Temp: 10-30°C (50-86°F)**
- **Keep dryish in winter**

Looking something like a tomato on a stick, this cactus, sometimes also called 'Ruby Ball', is certainly unusual. It was first developed in Japan. Some cacti suppliers incorrectly call it the 'everlasting flower'. But the top is no flower, simply an abnormal version of *G. mihanovichii*, lacking chlorophyll. Consequently this novel cactus must always be grown grafted.

A tender jungle cactus, hylocereus, identified by its three-cornered stem, is most often used as a grafting stock; unless you can keep a winter temperature of at least 10°C (50°F), it is better to re-graft onto something tougher, such as a trichocereus. Otherwise treat 'Hibotan' as a houseplant, for which it is ideally suited. You may be rewarded with attractive white or pink flowers. Use a potting mixture of three parts of a standard material and one part of sharp sand or perlite, and be careful never to overwater.

Above: **Gymnocalycium mihanovichii 'Hibotan'**
A novelty cactus that must always be grown on a graft, as it contains no food-making chlorophyll.

Gynura sarmentosa

- **Good light**
- **Temp: 13-18°C (55-65°F)**
- **Keep moist and fed**

Scented flowers are a bonus with almost all plants, but the gynuras have been blessed with a scent that is obnoxious enough to be almost damaging to the senses. Weedy flowers appear in summer and should be removed before they have a chance to open. However, there are almost always compensations in nature and the gynuras are favoured with violet-tinged foliage that is hairy and very striking when seen in sunlight. They will grow at a rampant pace in light conditions if they are being watered carefully and fed regularly. Given a supporting cane plants can be encouraged to climb, but they are seen at their best when trailing from a pot or basket.

Untidy growth can be trimmed back at almost any time, and firm pieces may be used for propagating new plants. This should be done regularly as older plants tend to become untidy and lose their bright colouring. It is best to put several cuttings in each pot and to pinch out tips for bushy plants.

Above right: **Gynura sarmentosa**
A member of the nettle family. The leaves are a vivid purple with a generous covering of tiny hairs that give the plant a rich glow of colour.

Haemanthus katharinae

- **Good light**
- **Temp: 16-21°C (60-70°F)**
- **Keep moist, dry when dormant**

Haemanthus are grown from bulbs planted to a little over half their depth in a free-draining, loam-based potting mixture. To help with the drainage incorporate a good amount of sand and ensure that some drainage material – pot shards, for instance – is placed in the bottom of the pot before adding the mixture.

Water sparingly until green leathery leaves appear, then more freely, but never to excess. On stems about 30cm (12in) in length the plant bears globes of small orange-red flowers in late spring. Place single bulbs in pots of 13cm (5in) diameter and continue growing the plants in the same potting mixture for several years to get the best results. When foliage naturally colours at the end of the summer allow the soil to dry completely and store the bulb in a warm dry place.

Right: **Haemanthus katharinae**
A brilliant flower head of starry blooms is produced in late spring. This beautiful bulbous plant resents disturbance; repot only occasionally.

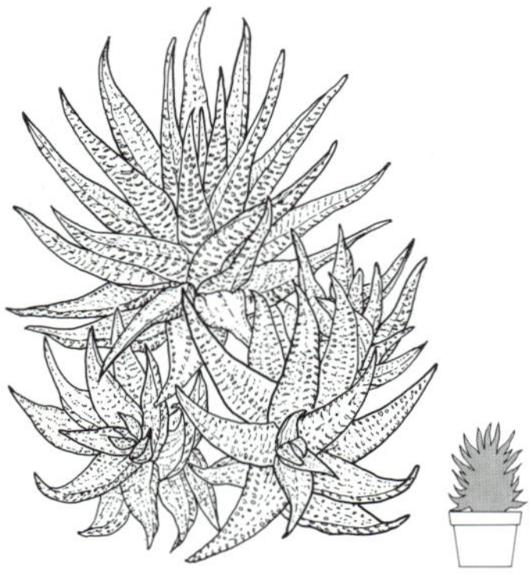

Haworthia attenuata

- **Partial shade**
- **Temp: 5-30°C (41-86°F)**
- **Keep slightly moist in winter**

In their native Africa, haworthias receive shade from the larger plants among which they are growing. If exposed to very strong light, the leaves become unattractively bronzed. In a greenhouse they thrive in shady corners or under the staging – places where most succulent plants become distorted because of the poor light. They also do very well as room plants; their tolerance of partial shade and their small size make them ideal.

Haworthia attenuata forms a stemless rosette of tough, dark green leaves. These have bands of white tubercles, which glisten attractively. Haworthias are all grown for the beauty of their form, not for their flowers; the tiny white bells are carried on the end of long straggly stems.

Grow this species in half-pots, in a loam-based potting mixture, and repot annually. With age *H. attenuata* will form offsets, which can be removed and used for propagation.

Above: **Haworthia attenuata**
Haworthias make good houseplants as they enjoy reasonably shady conditions. Best grown under the staging in a greenhouse.

Haworthia maughanii

- **Diffuse sunlight**
- **Temp: 5-30°C (41-86°F)**
- **Water with caution**

This is one of the choicest haworthias. The semi-cylindrical leaves are arranged in rosettes. The leaves are about 2.5cm (1in) long, and look as if someone had sliced the tip of the leaf off. The leaves have 'windows' at the ends. In their native desert the leaves are buried with only the tips showing, and light is filtered into the plant through the exposed 'windows'. However, in cultivation the plant is grown completely above the soil, to prevent rotting. The leaves are dark green, and the plant flowers during early winter, producing small white bells.

A growing medium consisting of one half loam-based potting mixture and one half sharp sand or perlite will ensure that the plant does not become too wet. Always allow it to dry out between waterings. This is a very slow-growing plant and will live in a 7.5cm (3in) pot for many years. During the resting period, the thick contractile roots will shrivel and be replaced by new ones.

Above: **Haworthia maughanii**
One of the more unusual haworthias; it has flattened leaf tips, with transparent 'windows' to allow light to reach the inner tissues.

Hedera canariensis

- **Good light**
- **Temp: 4-16°C (40-60°F)**
- **Keep moist and fed in summer**

This is one of the most rewarding indoor plants of them all, having bright green-and-white variegation and being reasonably undemanding to grow. The principal need is for light, cool conditions and a watering programme that allows for some drying out of the soil between each good soaking.

Plants can be encouraged to climb or trail, and they are excellent for those difficult cooler places such as hallways. In hot, dry conditions the plants are likely to become infested with red spider mite. These are minute insects that increase at an alarming rate if left to their own devices. In time the mites will make tiny webs from one part of the plant to another, but initially they are difficult to detect and are almost invariably found on the undersides of leaves. When infested with mite the leaves tend to curl inwards and appear hard and dry. Thorough and frequent drenching with insecticide is the best cure and should be done carefully out of doors on a still day.

Right: **Hedera canariensis**
In poor light the colourfully variegated foliage will revert to green. Offer good light. Check regularly for red spider mites.

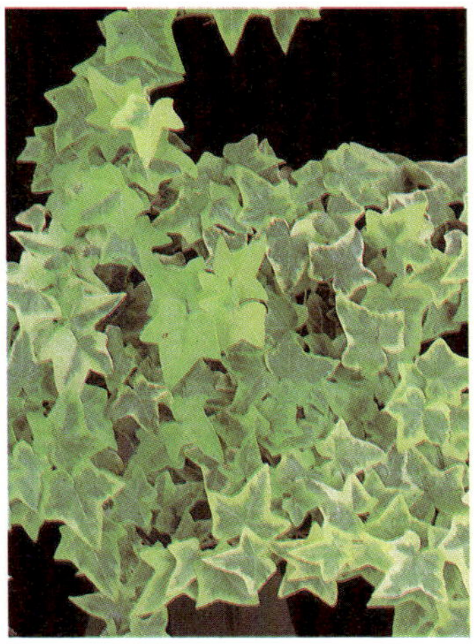

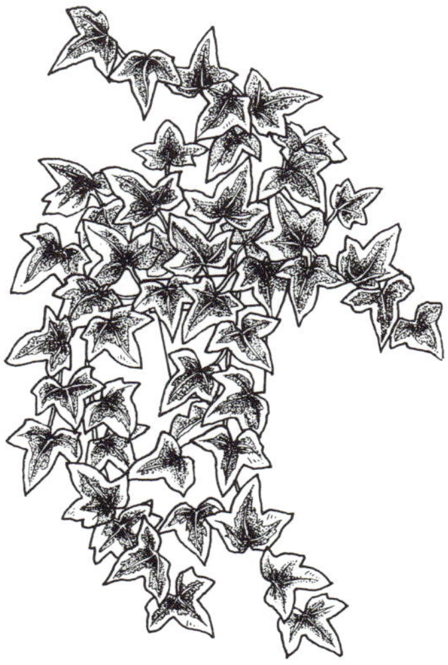

Hedera helix 'Goldchild'

- **Good light**
- **Temp: 7-16°C (45-60°F)**
- **Keep moist and fed**

One of the loveliest ivies of them all, having green-and-gold foliage with the latter being much the more predominant. Shallow plastic saucers for larger flower pots are excellent for displaying them in. Saucers should have holes made in their base, and several young plants are then planted in the containers. The result will be a flat mass of golden greenery that I once heard described as 'a bowl of sunshine'. When incorporating ivies in indoor displays, however, it is important to ensure that the position is not too hot and dry.

Cool, light conditions are best, and will help considerably in reducing the incidence of red spider mite. Smaller-leaved ivies develop a black rot among their stems and foliage if they are allowed to become too wet and the conditions are dank and airless. When watering, give a thorough application and then allow to dry reasonably before repeating. Feed in spring and summer.

Above: **Hedera helix 'Goldchild'**
Warm golden-yellow colouring places this ivy ahead of most foliage plants – it was once described as 'a bowl of sunshine'. Feed well.

A practical hint
Flowers of hibiscus plants last for only 24 hours, but they come in profusion if good light is offered and the plants are kept moist and fed.

Hedera maculata

Hedera (large-leaved)

- **Light shade**
- **Temp: 4-16°C (40-60°F)**
- **Keep moist and fed**

There are several larger-leaved ivies, other than *H. canariensis*, that are good for use as backing plants in arrangements either indoors or out.

Possibly the best-known of these is *H. maculata*, with dull gold and green mottled foliage, which makes a fine plant when trained to a support. With larger, very dark green leaves, each with a dull yellow splash in the centre, there is *H.* 'Goldleaf', one of the quickest growing of all the ivies. Also with very dark leaves, but unrelieved by other colouring, there is *H.* 'Ravenholst'. Perhaps the best of the larger-leaved forms, albeit seldom available, is *H. marmorata*, which has stiff, twisting stems and firm, well-variegated leaves.

As with almost all the other hederas, these plants will do better in cooler conditions, and should be well fed and watered during the more active summer months of the year. They will also attract red spider mites, which can be very harmful to the plant if allowed to go unchecked.

Hedychium gardnerianum

- **Good light**
- **Temp: 16-21°C (60-70°F)**
- **Keep moist, and feed well**

These plants of the ginger family (Zingiberaceae) can be grown by dividing the rhizomes in the spring and planting them independently. Once under way plants will grow apace and in time will require containers of about 25cm (10in) diameter. Once established, these plants need regular feeding. Lemon-yellow flowers are produced in summer on stems that may be 120cm (4ft) or more in length. Immediately after flowering, these stems should be cut down.

Where the climate permits, the plants in their pots can be placed out of doors during the summer months. They make excellent terrace plants when in decorative containers. Water freely in summer, but plants must be brought indoors before the weather turns cold and wet.

Right: **Hedera maculata**
With mottled greenish-gold foliage this is one of the larger-leaved ivies. It must have a supporting stake. Very effective in mixed displays.

Above right:
Hedychium gardnerianum
Beautiful yellow flowers with bright red stamens are produced during the summer months. Needs warmth.

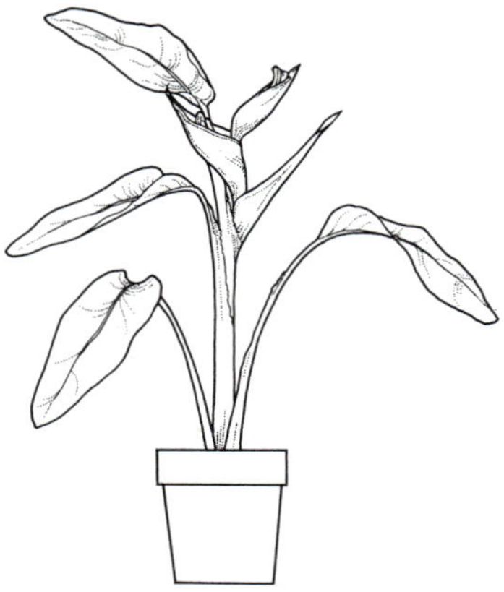

Heliconia angustifolia

- **Good light**
- **Temp: 13-18°C (55-65°F)**
- **Keep moist; dry winter rest**

A native of Brazil and belonging to the same family of plants as the banana, *H. angustifolia* flowers during the summer months. Flowers are white and green in colour with scarlet spathes and can be quite dramatic against glossy green foliage.

New plants can be started by dividing roots in early spring and planting them in 13cm (5in) pots filled with a loam-based potting mixture. These are hungry plants and will quickly exhaust the goodness contained in an all-peat growing medium.

Plants should be freely watered during the summer months and will benefit from having the foliage misted with water at regular intervals each day. Feed well during these active months. No water is required during the winter months when the plants are resting.

Heliotropium hybrids

- **Sunny location**
- **Temp: 13-18°C (55-65°F)**
- **Keep moist and fed**

An old-fashioned plant that is as popular as ever, being easy to care for and free-flowering both in the garden and on the windowsill indoors.

New plants may be grown from seed sown in the spring, or from stem cuttings inserted in a peaty houseplant mixture. Cuttings of non-flowering pieces about 10cm (4in) in length can be taken at any time during the summer months. Once under way it is advisable to remove the growing tips of the young plants to encourage branching. Standard plants can be grown, but this will take some time and entails growing a single stem that should be stripped of all foliage except for the topmost cluster of branches. These plants must be protected from winter cold.

The attractive flowers appear in the summer and, depending on the variety, are violet, lavender or white in colour. The plants are generally disease-free but when grown in a greenhouse may be susceptible to attack by whitefly.

Left: **Heliconia angustifolia**
The green-and-white flowers can be seen emerging from the striking scarlet bracts. This tropical plant needs a moist atmosphere to thrive.

Above: **Heliotropium hybrid**
Although basically garden plants, these can be grown indoors or in a greenhouse in light but fairly cool conditions. Flowers in summer.

A practical hint
Nurserymen treat hibiscus plants with a chemical to keep them short, but the effects wear off indoors. Winter pruning will help to reduce height.

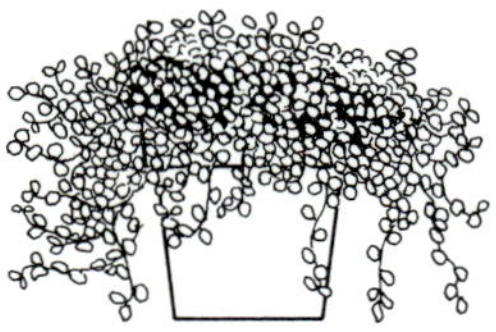

Helxine soleirolii

- **Light shade**
- **Temp: 4-18°C (40-65°F)**
- **Keep moist**

There are green- and golden-foliaged kinds, with the latter being the better choice. Although they will become straggly and untidy in time, the helxines are generally seen as neat mounds of minute leaves that make a pleasant change from the usual run of houseplants. Almost any pieces that may be snipped off when tidying up will make new plants if placed in peaty compost.

Shallow pans suit their low growth best and they will do well on almost any light windowsill. Plants should be watered carefully by pouring water into the pot under the leaves; water poured over the leaves will disarrange the neat mounds of growth and mar the plants' appearance. Less water is needed in winter, and no feeding, although a weak feed regularly given in summer will be appreciated.

A loam-based compost will be best when it comes to potting on, and regular trimming around with scissors will maintain a neat shape.

Above right: **Helxine soleirolii**
Minute bright green leaves are tightly clustered and provide plants that are neat hummocks of growth. Easily propagated from shoot cuttings.

Heptapleurum arboricola

- **Good light, no strong sun**
- **Temp: 16-21°C (60-70°F)**
- **Keep moist and fed**

In some parts of the world this plant may be seen labelled as *Schefflera*, which it strongly resembles. However, the difference lies in the size of the leaves. Both are green and palmate, but the schefflera leaf is very much larger.

Marginally more difficult to care for than *Schefflera* the parasol plant has an alarming habit of shedding leaves for no apparent reason. My view is that they often get much colder than the temperature recommended here. If plants are very wet at their roots and are subjected to low temperatures as well they will almost certainly lose leaves. There is some compensation, however, in that plants produce fresh growth later if the conditions improve.

Individual stems will grow to a height of 3m (10ft) in a comparatively short time. However, one can cut the stem back to more manageable size at any time of the year. As a result of this pruning treatment the plant will produce many more side growths.

Left: **Heptapleurum arboricola**
Elegant, upright, green-foliaged plants with palmate leaves that offer a canopy of umbrella-like growth. Prune regularly for better shape.

A practical hint
Tidy plant supports to which foliage can be trained do much for climbing plants; so when fresh growth is evident in spring, check staking.

Heptapleurum arboricola variegata

- **Good light, no strong sun**
- **Temp: 16-21°C (60-70°F)**
- **Keep moist and fed**

The fingered leaves and habit of growth are exactly the same as the green form, but the leaves are liberally splashed with vivid yellow colouring to give the plant a glowing brightness when it is placed among others in a large display. Elegance lies in the graceful and light distribution of leaves and stems, which enables one to see through and beyond to other plants in the display. And indoors it is equally important to have graceful plants rather than a solid wall of foliage.

In common with almost all the variegated plants this one should have a light location, but exposure to bright sun close to window-panes should be avoided if the leaves are not to be scorched. This is especially important if the leaves have been treated with chemicals. Most of the leaf-cleaning chemicals are perfectly suitable for the majority of plants, but one should never expose treated plants to direct sunlight.

Right: **Heptapleurum arboricola variegata**
Having the same habit as the green form but somewhat slower growing. Excellent for mixed plant displays.

A practical hint
Bulbs of hippeastrum produce very fine flowers, but must be kept fed and watered after flowering and rested dry when the leaves are shed.

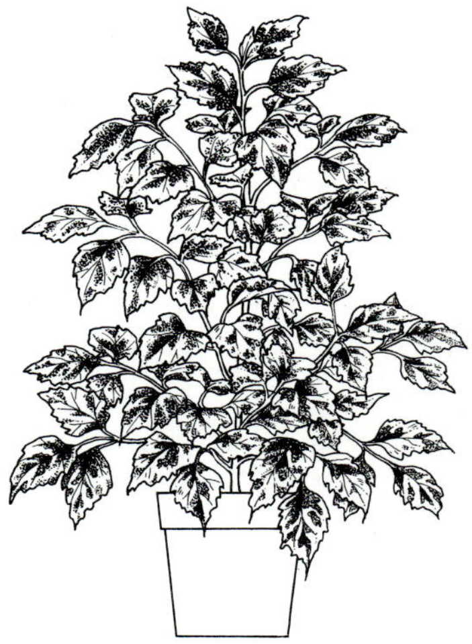

Hibiscus rosa-sinensis

- **Sunny location**
- **Temp: 13-18°C (55-65°F)**
- **Keep moist and fed**

These shrubby plants are widely dispersed throughout the tropics. They make fine indoor plants for the very light window location. Special growth-depressing chemicals are used to keep the plants short and compact, and to induce abundant blooms.

Trumpet flowers in numerous colours remain open for only a single day, but they are constantly being renewed from new buds during the summer months. It is important that plants have the best possible light and that the soil does not dry out during spring and summer; less water is required in winter.

Harsh pruning is not necessary, but in the autumn plants may be trimmed back to better shape. In the spring, when new growth is evident, pot the plants on into slightly larger containers. Use a loam-based mixture for best results.

Above right:
Hibiscus rosa-sinensis
Depending on variety, these plants produce showy flowers in red, orange, pink, yellow or white. Take tip cuttings for propagation.

Hibiscus cooperii variegata

- **Good light; some sunshine**
- **Temp: 13-21°C (55-70°F)**
- **Water well, but less in winter**

These handsome variegated plants in better specimens are almost white in colour, but will generally be a bright green and white combination. They come into their own as larger plants, and can be encouraged to produce stems 1.8m (6ft) or more in height. However, for general requirements they are probably best kept as bushy plants that form spreading clumps 90cm (3ft) or more in diameter.

New plants are started from top sections of stem about 13cm (5in) in length, with three or four leaves attached. These will require a temperature around 21°C (70°F) to be reasonably sure of getting them under way. Once rooted they can be potted into 13cm (5in) pots, using a mixture containing some loam. When they are established in their new containers it is essential to ensure that regular feeding is given, as these are greedy plants. They also need good light to preserve the variegation.

Right:
Hibiscus cooperii variegata
Grown for its striking foliage, this plant will prosper in a light location indoors. Prune it regularly to maintain an attractive shape.

Hippeastrum hybrids

- **Good light**
- **Temp: 13-18°C (55-65°F)**
- **Keep moist; dry winter rest**

Production of high-quality hippeastrum bulbs is one of the great skills of the more specialized commercial growers. But once matured, and in good light, these bulbs will produce their exotic trumpet flowers in a range of many colours. These are carried on stout stems 90cm (3ft) or more in height.

Bulbs can be purchased complete with their pots and growing soil and simply require the addition of water to start them growing. They should be kept moist but not excessively wet. However, problems can arise in subsequent years as not everyone can manage to get these plants to flower a second time. It helps to continue to feed the bulb and leaves after flowering until such time as the foliage dies down naturally, when the soil should be dried out and the plant stored cool and dry for the winter.

Hosta

- **Light shade**
- **Temp: 4-21°C (40-70°F)**
- **Keep dry in winter, wet summer**

These are marginal houseplants, and have the added disadvantage that because they are deciduous they are often lost or forgotten during the winter months.

Despite these drawbacks I find them very useful as clumps in large tubs in cooler locations around the house, and we seem to be seeing new varieties all the time. All of them are superb when used as foliage accompaniment to flowers in mixed arrangements.

During the summer plants should be kept very moist and regularly fed. As they die down naturally in late summer only the minimum amount of moisture should be maintained in the soil until new growth is seen.

New plants are very easily made by dividing larger clumps in the autumn and planting them individually in pots. A peaty mixture with some loam added will suit them fine. Older plants can be planted successfully in the garden.

Left: **Hippeastrum hybrids**
These glorious bulbs can be brought into bloom every year with a little care. Keep them slightly potbound and repot only every three or four years. Propagate from offset bulbs.

Above: **Hosta**
There are many attractive forms of these hardy plants, all developing into attractive clumps that need airy, light and moist conditions to thrive. Divide clumps for new plants.

Hoya australis

- **Good light**
- **Temp: 16-21°C (60-70°F)**
- **Keep moist and fed**

These attractive plants will climb or trail. To climb they will need a supporting frame, and to trail a hanging basket is ideal. The growing tips should be removed to encourage a bushy appearance. However, avoid unnecessary pruning as plants produce their flowers from older rather than new growth.

A loam-based, well-drained potting mixture should be used and the addition of a little charcoal when potting will prevent the mixture becoming sour. Remember to keep plants on the dry side during winter months.

New plants can be raised from stem cuttings taken from the previous year's growth and inserted in peat and sand at a temperature of about 21°C (70°F). Or, more simply, trailing pieces of stem can be pegged down during the summer and then cut from the parent plant and potted individually when they have rooted.

Above: **Hoya australis**
The clusters of dainty white blooms, waxy in texture, are produced in the summer. While actively growing, feed with a high-potassium liquid fertilizer to encourage flowering.

Hoya bella

- **Light shade**
- **Temp: 16-21°C (60-70°F)**
- **Keep on the dry side**

When well established and in full bloom there can be few more rewarding plants than *Hoya bella* growing in a hanging container. The small pale green leaves are attached to wiry stems, but it is the flowers hanging in clusters that are the main attraction. Individual flowers have the appearance of exquisitely cut jewels, white in colour flushed with a delicate shade of pink.

For best results use a loam-based potting mixture that incorporates a reasonable amount of sand to ensure good drainage. If the hanging container is provided with a built-in drip tray, then check an hour or so after watering and tip away any surplus water in the tray. Also, check regularly for signs of mealy bug on the undersides of leaves.

Right: **Hoya bella**
The smallest of the hoyas, this one is particularly suitable for growing in a hanging container. The tiny flowers are fragrant and are borne in clusters 5cm (2in) wide. Avoid wetness.

A practical hint
Cold draughts can be harmful, but most flowering plants will be the better for a change of air on warm days if rooms are very hot and stuffy.

Hoya carnosa

- **Good light**
- **Temp: 13-21°C (55-70°F)**
- **Keep moist and fed**

The twining stems and dark green leaves of this vigorous plant are quick to grow but the flowers that sprout from the leaf and stem joints are slow to appear. They are more likely to appear first on mature plants, but the clusters of pendulous pink jewels are well worth waiting for. As with all the hoyas, let the old flowers fall naturally and do not break off the flower stalks as these are the source of the following year's flowers.

This hoya makes a rather untidy basket plant, and is seen to best effect when trained to a framework of some kind. In this respect the plant is well suited to a heated conservatory, where growth can be trained overhead so that the flowers can be admired to full advantage when they appear. Well-draining, loam-based potting mixture is essential. Give frequent checks for mealy bugs in branches.

Above right: **Hoya carnosa**
This is the most commonly grown hoya. Be sure to give it sufficient room to grow; it can reach a height of 6m (20ft) and needs a support as it climbs. The flowers are fragrant.

A practical hint
Hyacinths intended for winter flowering must be *prepared bulbs,* as ordinary bulbs are not suitable and flower much later.

Huernia zebrina

- **Full sun**
- **Temp: 5-30°C (41-86°F)**
- **Keep almost dry in winter**

The name refers to the zebra-like stripes on the flowers of this miniature succulent — if a zebra could have purple-brown stripes on a yellow background! But, accurate or not, this flower is delightfully attractive and unusual. The five striped lobes surround a thick purple central ring, the whole flower being about 4cm (1.6in) across. There is almost no smell, but what little there is is unpleasant, characteristic of most of the stapelia-type succulents! The plant itself consists of sharply toothed, angled stems, bright green in colour and around 8cm (3.2in) long and 2cm (0.8in) thick.

Grow this huernia in a mixture of two parts of a standard material and one part of sharp sand or perlite. Never allow the potting mixture to become too wet, or rot or infection can set in. This is indicated by black marks, or black tips to the stems. In winter, give only enough water to prevent severe shrivelling, but in spring and summer water freely.

Left: **Huernia zebrina**
The flowers are the chief attraction of this little succulent. They are large for such a small plant and most strange in appearance, with a slight, unpleasant smell. Grow in full sun.

A practical hint
The intermediate varieties of orchids need a minimum night temperature of 13°C (55°F), and high level temperatures similar to those of the cool-house types.

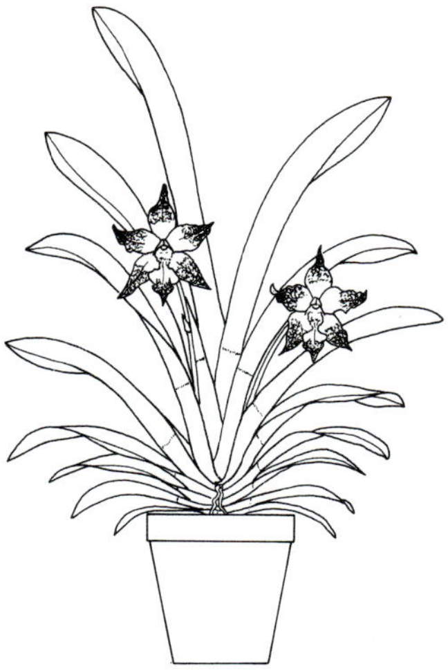

Huntleya burtii

- **Intermediate: 13°C (55°F)**
- **Can be difficult to grow**
- **Summer flowering**
- **Evergreen/no rest**

This South American plant grows without pseudobulbs. The leaves, about 30cm (12in) in length, develop from a central stem in the form of a fan. Single flowers 6.5-7.5cm (2.5-3in) across, are produced on a 15cm (6in) stem. The sepals and petals are approximately equal in size and uniform in marking; at the base they are greenish-white, changing through yellow to a reddish-brown marked with yellow. The lower half of the lip is reddish-brown, graduating to white in the upper part. These flowers are thick and waxy in texture and last well.

Huntleya burtii has a reputation for being rather difficult to maintain in good condition, but failure is often due to one of two reasons. The first is that many growers have a tendency to keep the plant in too warm and humid an environment, causing it to rot; the second is that the new growths which develop part way up the stem are often mistakenly removed and repotted. It is far better to allow the plant to grow into a clump, and to let the roots from new growths develop as aerial roots.

Above right: **Huntleya burtii**
A superb species for the intermediate house that blooms in the summer. Large single flowers.

A practical hint
Impatiens grows at prodigious pace; it needs lots of water and feeding, and should be reguarly inspected for aphids.

Hyacinthus orientalis

- **Good light**
- **Temp: 10-16°C (50-60°F)**
- **Keep moist; dry rest**

During the winter there can be few more pleasing sights than a bowl of colourful and fragrant hyacinth flowers. It is essential to purchase bulbs that have been specially prepared to flower at this time, as ordinary bulbs will not succeed. Plant three or more bulbs in a peaty, fibrous mixture during the autumn and then plunge the pot to a depth of about 13cm (5in) out of doors in peat or sand. In these cool conditions the bulbs will develop a sound root system, and plants can be taken indoors when growth is evident. Alternatively, keep the pot indoors in a cool, dark place for several weeks.

In warm rooms flowers will go through their cycle more rapidly, so it is advisable to provide a cool room and, perhaps, bring the plants into the sitting room for special occasions! After flowering, plant in the garden.

Above left: **Hyacinthus orientalis**
Available in many varieties and colours, these bulbs provide winter bloom and fragrance.

Hydrangea macrophylla

- **Good shade**
- **Temp: 10-16°C (50-60°F)**
- **Keep wet; rest in winter**

The quality of hydrangeas offered for sale as potted plants, like every other potted plant, varies enormously. So, when purchasing hydrangeas ensure that they have fresh green leaves and are not simply a few leaves at the top of a leafless stem with a few ragged flowers attached. Quality plants in many varieties are available, so choose well.

Hydrangeas in pots are offered in the spring and from the moment of acquisition they must be thoroughly watered until the autumn, when plants die back and should be rested overwinter.

Good light and cool conditions are also essential, and when plants have finished flowering indoors they may be placed on the terrace in tubs, or planted in the garden where they should be protected against spring frost. Take stem cuttings in the summer for new plants.

Left: **Hydrangea macrophylla Lacecap type**
These plants need to be kept cool and constantly moist to thrive.

Hypocyrta glabra

- **Light shade**
- **Temp: 16-21°C (60-70°F)**
- **Keep just moist; drier in winter**

With so many plants to choose from, the glossy green succulent foliage and curiously shaped orange flowers make the hypocyrta an excellent plant for rooms offering limited space. Plants can be grown conventionally in pots on the windowsill, or they may be placed in smaller hanging containers. As hanging plants the generally drier conditions that prevail will suit hypocyrtas as they are capable of storing a considerable amount of water in their attractive puffy leaves.

Temperatures in the range 16-21°C (60-70°F) will suit them fine, as will a watering programme that errs on the side of dry rather than wet. These are hungry plants, but an occasional feed will keep them in good trim and help to retain their bright green colouring. New plants can be raised from stem cuttings.

Hypoestes sanguinolenta

- **Good light**
- **Temp: 10-16°C (50-60°F)**
- **Keep moist and fed**

In the last few years the hypoestes has enjoyed a new lease of life through the introduction of a much more colourful cultivar with a greater proportion of pink in its leaves.

Plants are easy to manage, although they frequently suffer through being confined to pots too small for the amount of growth that these quick growers will normally produce. Any purchased plant that appears to be in too small a pot should be potted into a larger one without delay. Use loam-based potting soil, as peat mixtures can be fatal for this plant if they dry out excessively. Also, it is wise to remove the growing tips so that plants branch and become more attractive. Untidy or overgrown stems can be removed at any time, and firm pieces about 10cm (4in) long can be used for propagation.

Extremely dry soil will cause loss of lower leaves, so check daily to ensure that the soil is moist.

Above: **Hypocyrta glabra**
This easy-to-grow plant produces orange 'pouch' flowers in summer, when it benefits from high humidity. Prune to encourage new growth.

Right: **Hypoestes sanguinolenta 'Pink Splash'**
This new variety has more pink than the species. Keep this vigorous plant well fed and watered for success.

Impatiens wallerana

- **Good light**
- **Temp: 10-16°C (50-60°F)**
- **Keep wet and fed**

Capable of attracting a wide assortment of destructive pests, impatiens is, nevertheless, one of the most appealing of all our less costly potted plants.

Good light is essential, and the feeding of established plants is a must. Purchased plants that appear too large for their pots – and this is often the case – should be potted into larger containers without delay. The potting mixture should be loam-based, and the new pot should be only slightly larger than the existing one. In fact, impatiens is one of those odd plants that will tolerate potting more than once in a season. They can develop into splendid plants in time and are also very good in hanging baskets. Remember, though, to inspect frequently for pests and use appropriate remedies without delay.

Above: **Impatiens wallerana**
These perpetually flowering plants can provide a colourful display in the home. Grow new plants from seed or from stem cuttings. Keep moist.

A practical hint
Flowering plants seldom do well when taken from their pots and planted with foliage subjects; it is better to leave them in the pots.

Impatiens 'New Guinea hybrids'

- **Good light**
- **Temp: 10-16°C (50-60°F)**
- **Keep wet and fed**

In the past few years these hybrids have been a revelation. There are many named varieties, often with highly coloured foliage that greatly improves the appearance of the plant.

Like all of these plants they are ever-demanding when it comes to watering and feeding during their growing season, and must at no time be neglected. When dry, plants will flag alarmingly, but soon recover when well watered. Well watered usually means that the pot should be plunged into a bucket of water and held submerged until all the air has been excluded from the soil.

These new hybrids come into their own only when planted in larger containers of 18cm (7in) diameter and upwards, so potting on into loam-based compost must not be neglected. As with all impatiens plants, inspect frequently for pests.

Right: **Impatients 'New Guinea hybrids'**
These new varieties offer splendid blooms and striking foliage. Take cuttings at any time for new plants.

Ipomoea violacea

- **Good light**
- **Temp: 10-18°C (50-65°F)**
- **Keep moist and fed**

Trumpet flowers are short-lived but brilliantly coloured in shades of blue. Naturally climbing in habit, these plants are easily raised from seed sown in the spring in a temperature of 18°C (65°F) with the seed only lightly covered with soil.

Never allow plants to become starved of nourishment in their existing containers (seed trays for example), and feed frequently once established in their final pots. Failure to do so will result in leaf discolouration and plants that are much less floriferous.

For the natural climbing growth a framework of some kind is essential for the tendrils to twine around. A light location in cool conditions will ensure maximum number of flowers over the longest possible summer period.

These plants can reach a height of 2.4m (8ft) with flowers 13cm (5in) in diameter. The individual flowers open in the morning and fade in the afternoon, but picking off the dead ones will encourage continual blooming. Discard the plants after flowering and raise from seed in the spring.

Iresine herbstii

- **Good light**
- **Temp: 13-18°C (55-65°F)**
- **Keep fed and watered**

These fall among the cheap and cheerful range of plants, and have foliage of a very deep, almost unnatural red. Cuttings root very easily and plants are quick to grow; they can be propagated successfully on the windowsill if shaded from direct sun.

Mature plants, however, must have a very light place if they are to retain their colouring, and will only need protection from strong midday sun. During the spring and summer plants must be kept active by regular feeding and ensuring that the soil does not dry out excessively. When potting on becomes necessary a loam-based mixture should be used; plants will soon use the nourishment in peat mixes even if fed regularly. At all stages of growth the appearance of the plant will be improved if the tips are periodically removed.

Besides the red-coloured variety there is *I. herbstii aureoreticulata*, which has yellow colouring and needs the same attention.

Left: **Ipomoea violacea**
This colourful climber is ideal for a conservatory or sunroom, where it will grow to a height of 2.4m (8ft) or more. Grow from seed each year.

Above: **Iresine herbstii**
Keep this plant in bright light to retain its startling colour. Easy to grow and propagate, this plant is ideal for beginners. Keep humid.

A practical hint
Adequate light is essential to all flowering plants, and they will benefit if daylight is boosted by evening artificial light.

Iris pallida

- **Good light**
- **Temp: 10-16°C (50-60°F)**
- **Keep on the dry side**

There are many hardy outdoor plants that are perfectly suitable as houseplants, and this is most assuredly one of them. In a pot it seldom grows more than 30cm (1ft) high, with overlapping fans of boldly striped green-and-white leaves.

Plants do best in shallow pans of loam-based potting mixture with plenty of drainage material in the bottom of the pan. If the soil is sluggish and slow to dry out the leaves will have a droopy, tired appearance; in a well-drained, dryish mixture the leaves will remain more attractively erect. Feeding is not desperately important, but very weak fertilizer given during the summer months will aid plants that have been in the same pots for a long time.

Propagation is simply a matter of removing plants from their pots, pulling the clumps of leaves apart and potting the divided pieces into small, shallow pots of their own.

Above right: **Iris pallida**
An attractive miniature iris with pale green-and-white coloured foliage. The neat clumps of growth can be divided at any time for new plants.

A practical hint
Many plants of the araceae family – monstera, for example – produce aerial roots. These are best tied to a moist moss-covered support.

Iris reticulata

- **Good light**
- **Temp: 7-13°C (45-55°F)**
- **Keep cool**

Treated like many of the spring bulbs these miniature irises with their bright blue flowers provide a welcome splash of colour for a cool room in the late winter months.

Bulbs are generally available during autumn and three should be planted in a pot of 7.5cm (3in) diameter using a potting mixture containing some loam. For a bolder display, larger shallow containers may be used with a proportionately greater number of bulbs. After planting, the container should be placed in a cool, dry place (an unheated greenhouse, for example), no water being given until growth is evident. Avoid very wet conditions. When in bud, plants can be transferred to a light windowsill indoors, where they will give a colourful display for many weeks.

Left: **Iris reticulata 'Harmony'**
For a colourful display during the late winter months plant these bulbs in early autumn. These are available in 'kit' form, complete with pot.

A practical hint
Kalanchoes, with their many flower colours, are perhaps the most popular of the succulent plants, needing fresh air, good light and dry conditions.

Ixia hybrids

- **Good light**
- **Temp: 10-16°C (50-60°F)**
- **Keep moist; give winter rest**

The hybrids of *Ixia* come in many delightful colours that will brighten any windowsill. Flowers are fragrant and carried on slender stems.

For a full and pleasing effect try planting five bulbs in a well-draining, loam-based mixture in 13cm (5in) diameter pots in late autumn. Plant the bulbs 7.5cm (3in) deep and place the pots in a dark, cool place until growth is evident. The pots can then be transferred to a cool windowsill indoors. Feeding is not necessary, but the soil must be kept moist, with care being taken to avoid saturation over long periods.

When the foliage begins to die back naturally, cease watering and store the bulbs in a dry, frost-free place until the next season. Do not try planting in the garden: ixias are not hardy out of doors in most temperate climates.

Ixora coccinea

- **Good light**
- **Temp: 16-21°C (60-70°F)**
- **Keep moist; drier in winter**

As the name suggests, *I. coccinea* has brilliant red flowers, but there are also many other colours. All are robust plants growing to a height of about 90cm (3ft).

While in active growth these plants will need regular feeding, but none in winter. The same with watering – ample when plants are in growth, but very little over the winter period. In common with most flowering pot plants these will need a light location in order to obtain the maximum numbers of flowers.

New plants can be grown from cuttings 7.5-10cm (3-4in) long taken in spring and placed in fresh peat at a temperature of about 18°C (65°F). At all stages of potting a proprietary potting mixture is important. It is also essential to ensure that the soil is well drained. Pruning to shape can be done in early spring.

Above left: **Ixia hybrids**
Ideal for growing in a cool location indoors, these fragrant flowers will last well cut and kept in a vase. Propagate from offsets or from seed.

Left:
Ixora coccinea 'Peter Rapsley'
Warmth and humidity are essential for this tropical shrub so it is best grown in a greenhouse.

Jacobinia carnea

- **Good light**
- **Temp: 16-21°C (60-70°F)**
- **Keep moist and fed**

This attractive plant has pink flowers that bloom in late summer but there are other varieties occasionally available. Take cuttings of young shoots about 10cm (4in) in length in the spring, using fresh peat and a heated propagator to encourage rooting. Older plants should be cut down to the base after flowering and will flower in subsequent years, but it is often better, if space is limited, to produce new plants from cuttings and to discard the older plant.

While in active growth this vigorous plant will need regular feeding to retain leaf colouring, and ample watering. If an old plant is kept for the following year it will require no feed and little water during the winter. *Jacobinia carnea* is an ideal garden-room plant.

For mature plants use a loam-based potting mixture and repot regularly as the plant grows. Be sure to give a winter rest at about 13°C (55°F).

Above: **Jacobinia carnea**
Attractive pink plumes appear on this plant in late summer and last for several weeks. The plant will grow to a height of about 120cm (4ft) but is best restarted every two years.

Jasminum polyanthum

- **Good light, some sunshine**
- **Temp: 10-16°C (50-60°F)**
- **Keep moist and fed**

This climbing plant produces rampant growth in ideal conditions and must have some sort of framework for the spiralling growth to wind around. In winter, plants must be kept in the coolest possible place and will tolerate being out of doors if frosts are not expected.

New plants can be raised very easily from summer-struck cuttings, several cuttings going into a 13cm (5in) pot after they have been rooted in pans or boxes of peat. Use loam-based potting mix, putting the more robust plants in time into 18cm (7in) pots. Provide a fan-shaped framework in the pot so that foliage is well spread, which will in turn display the flowers to best effect when they appear.

The flowers are more white than pink in colour, but the unopened buds are a delicate shade of pink. Feed and water well while active.

Right: **Jasminum polyanthum**
Grow this vigorous climber in a cool greenhouse and provide support. The fragrant flowers open from midwinter until spring. Prune after flowering to keep it in shape.

A practical hint
The most troublesome foliage pest on succulents is the mealy bug, which gets into very inaccessible parts of plants; it should be treated without delay.

Kalanchoe blossfeldiana

- **Good light**
- **Temp: 10-27°C (50-81°F)**
- **Keep slightly moist in winter**

This succulent is undoubtedly a houseplant, although it can certainly be grown in a greenhouse. Many horticultural hybrids are on the market, as they are popular florists' plants, usually being available in autumn and winter in full bloom. A typical specimen would be up to 30cm (12in) high with wide, thick bright green leaves, but the plants offered for sale are usually smaller. This is predominantly a flowering plant, producing masses of bright red flowers from autumn until spring. The flowers are individually small, but they are clustered in tight heads, giving a brilliant display of colour. There is a yellow-flowered variety.

Never overwater this plant, as the stems are prone to rot off, but never let it dry out completely either. However, in a good, well-drained potting mixture it is easy to cultivate; mix some extra sharp sand or perlite with a standard material to improve the drainage. Take stem cuttings in spring; pot them straight away.

Left: **Kalanchoe blossfeldiana**
This is well-known as a houseplant. Its thickened leaves show that it is definitely a succulent. It produces masses of brilliant flowers in winter and spring. Restart it from cuttings.

Kalanchoe daigremontiana

- **Full sun**
- **Temp: 10-27°C (50-81°F)**
- **Keep slightly moist in winter**

Kalanchoes are a very varied group and this one, once known as *Bryophyllum daigremontianum*, is totally different from the previous plant, as it is grown for its attractive leaves rather than the somewhat insignificant flowers. These leaves, green marbled with brown, are arrow-shaped and may be up to 10cm (4in) long. But the great curiosity is the tiny plantlets that appear within the leaf notches. When these fall off, they will take root (actually they mostly have minute roots already!) in any patch of soil they touch, giving rise to further plants; any nearby pot will soon have a kalanchoe growing beside the rightful owner! It would not be possible to have an easier plant to propagate, since it requires no effort on the part of the grower at all. The parent plant can reach a height of 60cm (24in).

Grow this novelty in any good potting mixture, and water quite freely in spring and summer.

Above:
Kalanchoe daigremontiana
Tiny plantlets are freely produced along the edges of the leaves. The large mature leaves make this an impressive plant, but it is best to restart it when it becomes straggly.

Kalanchoe pumila

- **Full sun**
- **Temp: 5-27°C (41-81°F)**
- **Keep slightly moist in winter**

This pretty little plant is ideal for a hanging basket indoors, where it will grow and flower freely in a light window. Of course, it can also be grown in a greenhouse, where its relative hardiness will enable it to survive the lower winter temperature. The slightly thickened leaves are basically pale pinkish-green in colour, but this is almost completely masked by a grey mealy coating, giving the whole plant a delightful pearly-grey appearance. It is very free-flowering, producing masses of dark pink blooms in spring. Although these are individually only about 2cm (0.8in) across, they appear in small groups at the end of quite short stems. The plant is only about 15cm (6in) high.

To grow it in a hanging basket, line a small one with sphagnum moss or coarse peat, well damped, fill with any good potting mixture, and plant the kalanchoe in this. To propagate this succulent, cut off a few stems in spring or summer and pot them up.

Right: **Kalanchoe pumila**
A very free-flowering little succulent with pearly-grey leaves; the shade is due to their mealy coating. The thin stems eventually cause the plant to sprawl somewhat, making it very suitable for a hanging basket.

Kentia belmoreana

- **Light shade**
- **Temp: 16-21°C (60-70°F)**
- **Water and feed well in summer**

This is also seen under its other name of *Howea belmoreana*. As a young plant it will be fine for indoor decoration, but as time goes on it will outgrow all but the largest of rooms. Growth can be contained to some degree in much the same way as trees are grown by the Bonsai method in Japan and elsewhere. The roots are hard pruned every second or third year causing the plant to become shorter and more stunted, with a bulbous base to its trunk. In one of my greenhouses I have two such plants that are almost 50 years old, yet they are only just over 3m (10ft) high.

Once these plants become old and well established they seem much easier to care for than in their early years. Mine are lightly shaded from the sun and are well watered during the summer months while they are producing their usual one or two leaves. They are kept on the dry side in winter.

Above: **Kentia belmoreana**
Majestic palms that will attain a height of 3m (10ft) with roots confined to pots. Green, fingered leaves radiate from a stout central trunk that will in time develop an attractive bulbous base.

A practical hint

To counter generally drier room conditions it is wise to provide trays with a layer of moist gravel on which pots can be placed.

Kohleria amabilis

- **Good light**
- **Temp: 16-21°C (60-70°F)**
- **Keep moist and fed**

Plant *Kohleria amabilis* in hanging containers suspended at head level to appreciate fully the attractive bright green foliage and to enjoy the flowers to the full when they appear in late spring and early summer.

However, encouraging plants to produce their attractive pink blooms is not easy. Moist soil, a humid atmosphere and a light position will all help flowering. A further encouragement would be the use of a houseplant food specifically recommended for flowering plants – one that has a fairly high potash content, as opposed to nitrogen. If special fertilizers are unobtainable, try one of the many fertilizers recommended for tomato plants.

Raise new plants by taking cuttings of young shoots in late spring, or by dividing the rhizomes in early spring. Use a peaty soil for potting.

Laelia anceps

- **Cool: 10°C (50°F)**
- **Easy to grow and flower**
- **Autumn flowering**
- **Evergreen/dry winter rest**

Some 75 species of *Laelia* have been recorded, almost all from Mexico and the northern parts of South America. Though in appearance both plant and flower are similar to the cattleyas, with which many intergeneric hybrids have been made, it is a delightful genus in its own right, and is favoured by many growers. As with cattleyas, its flower spikes are produced from the apex of the pseudobulbs. The flower spike grows erect to 60cm (2ft) or more and produces two to five flowers, each about 10cm (4in) across. They are pale or deep rose-pink in colour, the lip being a darker hue than the other segments.

This is an excellent species for the beginner. It can be grown easily in a cool greenhouse or indoors, where it enjoys light conditions. If preferred, it can be grown on a block of wood or cork bark, when an extensive aerial root system will develop.

Propagation is a simple matter of separating the back bulbs and potting them up singly, when they will develop new growths.

Above right: **Kohleria amabilis**
Keep this species warm and moist while actively growing and it will produce lovely orange-pink flowers. Hybrids can bloom all year.

Right: **Laelia anceps**
This extremely popular cool-house species is ideal for the beginner. It will grow in a cool place indoors and flower in the autumn.

A practical hint
When orchid plants are in active growth you must make sure that the soil is kept well watered, and this means wetting the entire rootball thoroughly.

Laelia cinnabarina

- **Intermediate: 13°C (55°F)**
- **Moderately easy to grow**
- **Winter/spring flowering**
- **Evergreen/semi-dry rest**

This plant comes from Brazil and belongs to a group of brilliantly coloured species that are smaller in the size of their plants and flowers than the majority of laelias. This species has thin pseudobulbs, which are darker in colour than most, as is the leaf. Five to 12 star-shaped, orange-red flowers, each about 5cm (2in) across, are produced on a 23cm (9in) spike during the winter and spring. Due to importing restrictions this species is not now often seen in cultivation.

It likes intermediate conditions and is intolerant of cold and damp. The slender pseudobulbs will quickly shrivel if the plant is allowed to remain in a dry state for any length of time. It should be only semi-rested in winter, with sufficient water to ensure that the bulbs remain plump. The plant should be kept in as small a pot as possible and grown on into a good-sized plant. Propagation is by division when the plant is large enough.

This species has been used to some extent in interbreeding to increase colour in the hybrids.

Left: **Laelia cinnabarina**
A neat-growing, intermediate-house species that produces heads of flower in the winter and spring months. Avoid cold and dampness.

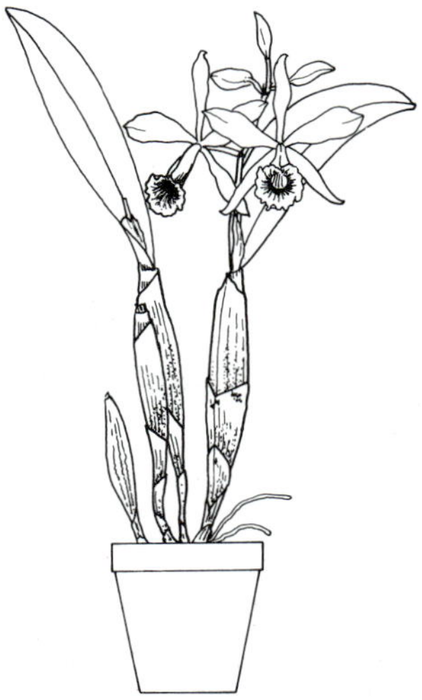

Laelia gouldiana

- **Cool/intermediate: 10-13°C (50-55°F)**
- **Easy to grow and flower**
- **Winter flowering**
- **Evergreen/dry winter rest**

One of the most popular of the epiphytic Mexican laelias. The club-shaped pseudobulbs are topped with one or — more often — two stiff, dark green leaves that are pointed at their tips. The flower spike appears from the apex of the partially completed bulb during the autumn and grows to 45cm (18in) in height carrying three to five brightly coloured 7.5cm (3in), cattleya-like flowers. Their colouring is a rich rose-purple, the lip similarly coloured. They last for several weeks during the early half of the winter.

This species is suitable for the warmest end of the cool greenhouse, or it will be equally at home in the intermediate section in a position of good light. Light is very important for successful flowering and for this reason it does not always flower well as a houseplant. Plants are at their best when grown on into large specimens; continued division can cause them to miss a flowering season. The spring growth is often slow to start and it may be summer before they really get going.

Laelia purpurata

- **Intermediate: 13°C (55°F)**
- **Easy to grow and flower**
- **Winter flowering**
- **Evergreen/dry winter rest**

This orchid is the national flower of Brazil and deserves the honour. Growing to a height of 45-60cm (1.5-2ft) including the leaf, the plant produces a short spike of two to six flowers, each 13-18cm (5-7in) in diameter. Very variable in colour, the narrow sepals and petals range from white to pale purple, with a frilled deep purple lip.

Moderate light is required and a well-drained compost is important; no laelia does well if there is an excess of water at the root. The plant requires a definite period of rest, when little or no water should be given.

This species has always been extremely popular with collectors but it is now becoming increasingly difficult to obtain. Many commercial nurseries are now raising it from seed using selected clones. Therefore, it should not die out in cultivation in the foreseeable future.

In the past this species has contributed to the production of many intergeneric hybrids with cattleyas and allied genera.

Right: **Laelia gouldiana**
Very popular cool-house species that blooms in the winter. Must have good light to flower successfully.

Above: **Laelia purpurata**
This beautiful species is easy to raise in an intermediate greenhouse. It flowers during the winter.

A practical hint
In winter many of the orchid plants will be at rest and it is essential then to ensure that the soil in the container is almost dry.

Laeliocattleya Chitchat 'Tangerine'

- **Intermediate: 13°C (55°F)**
- **Moderately easy to grow**
- **Summer flowering**
- **Evergreen/some rest**

A summer-flowering hybrid bred from a cross between *C. aurantiaca* and *Laelia* Coronet. The plant, which has clusters of delicate yellow-orange flowers 5cm (2in) across, has slender pseudobulbs and should be grown in the intermediate section of the greenhouse.

This hybrid illustrates the diversity that can be found among the bigeneric cattleya hybrids. Here we see the less flamboyant flower with simpler lines, but with the superb colouring unique to the type. Also, having one species parent, the plant shows close resemblance to that species.

This plant grows in the same conditions as other cattleya intergeneric hybrids, but will usually have a shorter resting period. The pseudobulbs are more slender and will therefore shrivel more easily if water is withheld for long periods. Light overhead spraying is an advantage during the summer.

Repotting should be carried out in the spring unless the plant is in bud, in which case it should be repotted in the autumn.

Left: **Laeliocattleya Chitchat 'Tangerine'**
This very attractive hybrid is suitable for the intermediate greenhouse.

A practical hint
The deciduous orchid *Lycaste cruenta* needs cool winter conditions, but to be rather warmer in summer when it is in active growth.

Lantana camara

- **Good light**
- **Temp: 10-18°C (50-65°F)**
- **Water and feed well**

For indoor use it is better to prune lantanas to shape annually in autumn so that a neat and compact shape is maintained. Stems are twiggy and leaves mid-green in colour. The plant will not be difficult to care for if given good light and cool conditions.

Healthy plants in the right surroundings will produce masses of globular flowers throughout the summer months; in poor light, flowers will be less plentiful. Flowers themselves are something of an enigma, as one may see flowers of varying colour on the same plant.

While they are growing more actively in summer, keep plants well watered and fed, but give less water and no feed in winter. Keep a careful check for white on the undersides of leaves, and treat as soon as noticed. This will mean the plant is infested with whitefly.

Right: **Lantana camara**
Compact flowerheads appear on this vigorous shrub from spring until the autumn. It will thrive indoors if given a light location and plenty of water while active. Prune and repot regularly. Take cuttings in summer.

A practical hint
Lithops resemble pebbles and are known as living stones. They are interesting to raise from seed, and not difficult to manage.

Lapageria rosea

- **Good light**
- **Temp: 10-18°C (50-65°F)**
- **Keep moist; drier in winter**

L. rosea can be a most rewarding plant to grow, providing all the right conditions can be met. In an ideal situation the plant will produce elegant funnel-shaped flowers that hang in the most graceful fashion. There are a number of colours available but many people feel that the original crimson form and the white-flowered variety make a stunning combination when grown together.

Grow in a lime-free potting mixture and use rain water when watering. Provide a framework either in the pot or against the wall for the foliage to climb through. Plants flower mainly in the summer and attain a height of about 4.5m (15ft). Provide good drainage and water with care, avoiding hot and dry conditions.

Left: **Lapageria rosea**
The red and the white varieties of this beautiful vining plant are shown here grown together in a greenhouse. Given room, this plant will provide a magnificent display in summer. Grow in good light for success.

Leea coccinea rubra

- Light shade
- Temp: 16-21°C (60-70°F)
- Keep moist and fed

This is a relative newcomer that may well become a very popular and trouble-free houseplant. It belongs to the Araceae family and is compact and neat, with numerous leaves closely set together on short stout stems. Leaves are open and finely cut, and are of rich russet colouring. The habit is not unlike that of its relative, *Aralia sieboldii*. Although the colouring of the foliage is a little better in good light the plant does not seem to object unduly to growing in more shaded locations.

As small plants they do well enough in peaty mixtures, but clearly approve of being potted into loam-based soils when going into 13cm (5in) pot sizes and larger. The pot should have plenty of drainage material placed in the bottom and the potting soil must be reasonably firm. Water well after potting and then keep the soil on the dry side until the plant has established in the new mixture. Once settled, plants should be fed each week when active.

Above: **Leea coccinea rubra**
A fine, relatively new plant to the houseplant range with reddish foliage that is dense and compact. Does well in light or shade. Grow in a well-draining mixture for success.

Leuchtenbergia principis

- **Full sun**
- **Temp: 5-30°C (41-86°F)**
- **Keep dry in winter**

A true cactus that bears a remarkable resemblance to an agave or aloe, this strange-looking plant is the sole representative of its group. Unlike agaves or aloes, the long tubercles are part of the stem, not leaves. These tubercles can be up to 10cm (4in) long and they are tipped with groups of soft, rather papery spines. This cactus does not appear to be very free-flowering, and to give it the best chance to produce its beautiful perfumed yellow flowers, 8cm (3.2in) across, it needs as much full sunlight as possible. It is unlikely to flower as a houseplant. Propagation is said to be possible from removed tubercles, dried for a while and potted up. This is a very easy plant to raise from seed.

Water this unique cactus freely in spring and summer; the tubercles tend to spread when the plant is moist and to close in with dryness. Use three parts of a standard potting mixture added to one part of sharp sand or perlite.

Lilium auratum

- **Good light, some sunshine**
- **Temp: 10-16°C (50-60°F)**
- **Keep moist; dry rest period**

These are not the easiest of plants to manage indoors if they are used as permanent subjects, but they are excellent as temporary plants brought indoors when in bloom.

Bulbs are ready for planting in the autumn and should be planted about half way down a 20cm (8in) pot filled with lime-free peaty mixture. After potting, place the plants in a sheltered spot outside (a cold frame, for example) and cover the pots with a 10-13cm (4-5in) layer of peat. When growth shows through, the plants can be taken into a cool room. Water moderately until the growth becomes more vigorous, then water more freely, using rain water for preference. Stems will require staking. These plants need repotting annually in fresh mixture.

Lithops aucampiae

- **Full sun**
- **Temp: 5-30°C (41-86°F)**
- **Keep dry in rest period**

These little stone-like plants are perhaps the most delightful of all the South African succulents. A large collection of them can be grown in a pan 30cm (12in) square, which makes them ideal for a small greenhouse. Lithops consist of one pair of flat-topped fleshy leaves; the stem is so short as to be invisible when the plant is potted up, and they are often described as stemless. *L. aucampiae* is one of the larger species, with leaves 2.5cm (1in) across; they are a lovely rich brown colour with darker brown dots. The golden flowers appear from between the two leaves in early autumn.

Grow this species in a mixture of half loam-based medium and half sharp sand or perlite. Keep dry all winter. Do not water until the old leaves have completely shrivelled away; this will probably be in late spring. Water on sunny days, and gradually tail off in autumn.

Left: **Leuchtenbergia principis**
This unusual plant differs from all other cacti in its triangular tubercles, which grow up to 10cm (4in) in length, and in its soft, papery white spines. Needs full sun.

Above: **Lilium auratum**
Best regarded as temporary indoor plants, these lilies produce superb flowers during the summer months. Grow from bulbs planted in autumn and be sure to support the stems.

Above: **Lithops aucampiae**
This is one of the larger species, with considerable variation in leaf colour and pattern. Yellow flowers appear from between the leaves in autumn. Water carefully.

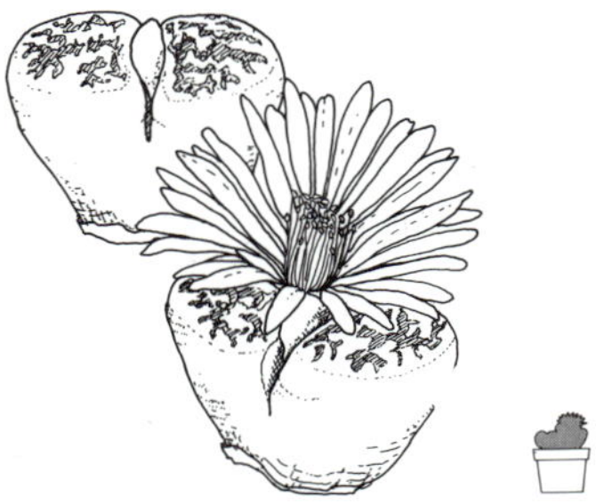

Lithops bella

- **Full sun**
- **Temp: 5-30°C (41-86°F)**
- **Keep dry in rest period**

Lithops bella has a pair of pale grey leaves with darker markings. The white flowers appear between the leaves in early autumn. This is one of the lithops that will form an attractive clump. In spring, when the old head has shrivelled away, two new heads will be found inside the old skin. The plant does not double its size every year; some years no new heads are formed, or perhaps only one head in a clump will double. Overlarge clumps can be split up. The summer growing period is the best time to do this.

No water should be given until the old leaves have completely shrivelled away, usually in late spring. Grow in a mixture of equal parts of loam-based material and grit. Do not repot annually; once every three years is sufficient. It is important to give the plant the maximum light available. The flowers open in the afternoon on sunny days, and close at night. They last for about a week.

Lithops marmorata

- **Full sun**
- **Temp: 5-30°C (41-86°F)**
- **Water only during summer**

Lithops marmorata consists of a pair of almost stemless succulent leaves. The leaves are greyish-green, marbled with grey or yellowish lines. The white flower appears from the cleft between the leaves and is large enough to hide the plant body completely. The flowering period is early autumn.

An open potting mixture consisting of half loam-based potting medium and half sharp sand or perlite will ensure that the plant does not take up too much water and become overlarge. Allow it to dry out between waterings. It is essential to grow this plant in full sun, as the flowers open only when exposed to sunlight: they open in the afternoon and close at night. Lithops look their best when grown in pans surrounded by small pebbles with similar markings to themselves. It is not necessary to repot yearly. The main pests that attack lithops are mealy bug and root mealy bug. Water with insecticide.

Above: **Lithops bella**
The flower can be seen emerging from between the leaves in this photograph. In the wild the tops of the leaves are level with the soil.

Above right: **Lithops marmorata**
Surrounded by a mass of stones, this lithops would be difficult to find when not in flower; hence the term 'living stones' or 'stone mimicry plants'.

A practical hint
In winter almost all cacti and succulents will be better in cool and dry conditions; most need only minimal watering.

Lobivia aurea

- **Full sun**
- **Temp: 5-30°C (41-86°F)**
- **Keep dry in winter**

The brilliant lemon-yellow flowers of this lobivia make it outstanding even when placed amongst a group of other beautiful cacti. Its flowers can reach a diameter of 8cm (3.2in) and appear from near the top of the stem during spring and summer. The stem itself is at first globular, later becoming more elongated, and as it reaches a height of only about 10cm (4in), it will not become too large for the collection. There are about 15 ribs along which are groups of spines from 1 to 4cm (0.4 to 1.6in) long.

Any offsets from around the base of the plant may be either left on or removed during spring or summer and, after drying for a few days, potted up for propagation. Either loam- or peat-based potting mixtures may be used for this lobivia, the most important thing being good drainage, which can be ensured by mixing in about one third of extra sharp sand or perlite.

Water may be given freely on sunny days in spring and summer and, when in bud and flower, give it a fortnightly feed with a high-potassium fertilizer.

Lobivia backebergii

- **Full sun**
- **Temp: 5-30°C (41-86°F)**
- **Keep dry in winter**

The lobivias are a large group of cacti closely related to the genus *Echinopsis*, and many hybrids exist between them. *L. backebergii* starts by being an almost globular plant and gradually becomes more oval. It will not create much of a space problem, as it reaches a diameter of only 5cm (2in). The bright green ribbed stem will sometimes form offsets from the base. Curved dark spines spread over the ribs, about 1.5cm (0.6in) long, but may be larger if the plant is grown in strong sunlight. The beautiful flowers are carmine with a bluish sheen, and are about 4cm (1.6in) across.

This cactus is quite tolerant with regard to the potting mixture. If your standard mix looks at all compacted, add some extra sharp sand or perlite. Water it freely during spring and summer, and to encourage continued flowering add a high-potassium, tomato-type fertilizer to the water about once every two weeks during this time.

Left: **Lobivia aurea**
This compact cactus thrives in full sun and low humidity. In spring and summer lovely yellow flowers are produced. Easy to propagate.

Above left: **Lobivia backebergii**
The large, brilliant flowers of this lobivia make it a showpiece in any collection. The almost globular stem is usually solitary. Easy to grow.

Lobivia famatimensis

- **Full sun**
- **Temp: 5-30°C (41-86°F)**
- **Keep dry in winter**

A small, particularly beautiful lobivia, this cactus is clump-forming, with individual 'heads' about 6cm (2.4in) long and 2.5cm (1in) thick. The yellowish spines on the 20 or so small ribs are so numerous and interlocking that they almost cover the stem. Flowers are normally yellow, around 5cm (2in) across, and occur in clusters at the top of the stems. Quite often they will open for several days in succession, closing at night. Don't be perturbed if your specimen produces flowers of another colour: there are varieties with orange, pink or red flowers.

This pretty lobivia is rather more moisture- and temperature-sensitive than many, so make sure that the potting mixture is very well drained by adding one part of sharp sand or perlite to three parts of a standard material. Water quite freely on sunny days during spring and summer. Stems can be removed for propagation in spring, but let them dry for a few days before potting.

Above: **Lobivia famatimensis**
Though it starts as a single stem, this attractive small cactus soon produces offsets around the base.

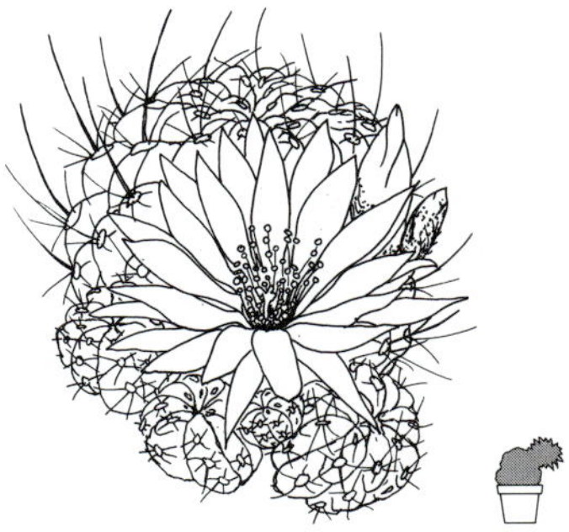

Lobivia hertrichiana

- **Full sun**
- **Temp: 5-30°C (41-86°F)**
- **Keep dry in winter**

One of the most popular and widely grown of the lobivias, this small cactus flowers very freely, even when quite young. Stems are more or less globular, ribbed, with fairly short, bristly, spreading spines. Individual heads are about 2.5-4cm (1-1.6in) thick, and the plant rapidly forms quite a large clump. But there is no need to let it become any larger than required; heads are easily removed for propagation in spring. Merely let them dry for a few days before potting up. Brilliant scarlet flowers, produced in masses in spring and summer, may be up to 5cm (2in) across.

To get the best from this attractive cactus, let it form a reasonably large clump if space permits, preferably growing it in a pan or half-pot. Use a good standard potting mixture but make sure that it is well drained. A cold winter rest is desirable to promote good flowering, as is feeding in spring and summer.

Right: **Lobivia hertrichiana**
An easy-care cactus widely prized for its freely produced scarlet flowers. Ideal for beginners.

Lycaste aromatica

- **Cool/intermediate: 10-13°C (50-55°F)**
- **Easy to grow and flower**
- **Winter/spring flowering**
- **Deciduous/dry winter rest**

As the name suggests, this species is heavily scented. The bright yellow flowers, 5cm (2in) across, often appear at the same time as the new growth, and are carried singly on a stem about 15cm (6in) long. There may be as many as ten flowers to each pseudobulb.

The plant needs moisture and warmth when in full growth, but take care not to get water on the large, broad leaves, as they tend to develop brown spots if this occurs. Cooler and drier conditions are essential when the plant is at rest and in flower.

Propagation is by removal of the older pseudobulbs, which should not remain on the plant for too many years. It is better to restrict the size of the plant to five or six bulbs, provided they remain about the same size; should the bulbs become smaller, remove all but three or four.

Between 30 and 40 *Lycaste* species are known, including both terrestrial and epiphytic plants, most of which come from Central America. Many are also deciduous, losing their leaves during the winter.

Above: **Lycaste aromatica**
A deciduous cool-house species that produces its single fragrant blooms in winter and spring.

Lycaste cruenta

- **Cool/intermediate: 10-13°C (50-55°F)**
- **Easy to grow and flower**
- **Winter/spring flowering**
- **Deciduous/dry winter rest**

A beautiful and fragrant species with the typical *Lycaste* foliage and habit of flowering. The flowers are among the largest of the cultivated species and are beautifully coloured. The sepals are yellow-green, the smaller petals and lip deep golden yellow. There is a deep red stain just visible in the throat.

In all species of *Lycaste* the sepals open wide and are longer than the petals, which are inclined to remain partly closed.

Like all lycastes, the plant enjoys higher summer temperatures while in active growth, followed by a cooler resting period. It should be given as much light as possible without burning the foliage. The leaves, which can be extremely large and spreading when mature, quickly turn yellow in the late autumn and are discarded naturally by the plant.

Annual repotting is beneficial to this species, which can quickly outgrow its pot with one season's growth. The plant is best suited to greenhouse culture, where it is a most rewarding plant to grow.

Lycaste deppei

- **Cool/intermediate: 10-13°C (50-55°F)**
- **Easy to grow and flower**
- **Winter/spring flowering**
- **Deciduous/dry winter rest**

One of the most attractive of the lycastes, this plant produces fewer but larger, longer lasting flowers than *L. aromatica* – up to 11.5cm (4.5in) in diameter. The sepals are mid-green in colour spotted with reddish-brown, and the smaller petals are pure white. The lip is yellow in colour and also spotted with reddish-brown.

The plant has a fast growing season, when it should be given slightly higher temperatures combined with ample watering and feed. When repotting, a little old dried cow manure can be included in the compost. Repotting is best done annually; because of the extended dry rest period fresh compost is essential. The leaves, which can grow quite large, should be kept dry at all times; they are susceptible to water marks, which will show as ugly black or brown patches. While in growth, the plants will take up rather more room in the greenhouse. Because they require warmer growing conditions and cooler winter quarters with high light, they are not so easy to grow indoors.

Lycaste virginalis

- **Cool/intermediate: 10-13°C (50-55°F)**
- **Easy to grow and flower**
- **Winter/spring flowering**
- **Deciduous/dry winter rest**

The flowers of *L. virginalis,* also known as *L. skinneri,* are even larger – up to 15cm (6in) across. Many colour forms are known and all are beautiful. The colour varies from all-white (which is rare) through pale to deep pink, and the lip is often spotted with crimson.

This is the most popular species of the genus and is ideal for beginners to orchid growing. It is easier to grow indoors than the other lycastes. It does not like to be overwet at any time and must be kept completely dry during the winter. The flowers of this lovely orchid bruise easily and quickly become spotted if the humidity is high. This plant usually retains its season's growth throughout the winter, resting in an evergreen state to shed its foliage immediately the new growth starts in the spring. Propagation is by removal of the back pseudobulbs. The plant is at its best when kept to about six bulbs.

There are excellent hybrids from this species, especially with the intergeneric angulocastes.

Above: **Lycaste cruenta**
This cool-growing deciduous species has lovely fragrant flowers in the winter and spring. Easy to grow.

Above: **Lycaste deppei**
A most attractive plant that produces long-lasting flowers in the winter and spring. Grow in a greenhouse.

Right: **Lycaste virginalis**
Can be grown in a cool greenhouse for winter blooming. Large, single flowers. Deciduous in winter.

Maclellanara Pagan Lovesong

- **Cool/intermediate: 10-13°C (50-55°F)**
- **Easy to grow and flower**
- **Varied flowering season**
- **Evergreen/no rest**

This is one of the latest and most impressive of the man-made intergeneric hybrids. It was raised in the USA from *Odontocidium* Tiger Butter x *Brassia verrucosa* and therefore contains three genera in its make-up – *Odontoglossum, Oncidium* and *Brassia.* The plant resembles a large *Odontoglossum* and is a vigorous and robust grower tolerant of both cool and intermediate conditions. It can be grown in almost any climate. The flower spikes can be over 90cm (3ft) tall with up to 12 large, exciting 10cm (4in) flowers that exhibit much influence from the *Brassia.* The sepals and petals are of equal size, yellow-green with large dark brown occasional spots. The handsome lip is white and spotted in a similar way.

Maclellanaras are all year round growers and should be freely watered and fed throughout the year. They should receive similar light to odontoglossums. The plants are becoming extremely popular although they are still very limited in supply in some countries.

Above:
Maclellanara Pagan Lovesong
A large, robust-growing hybrid for cool or intermediate conditions. Flowers at various times of the year.

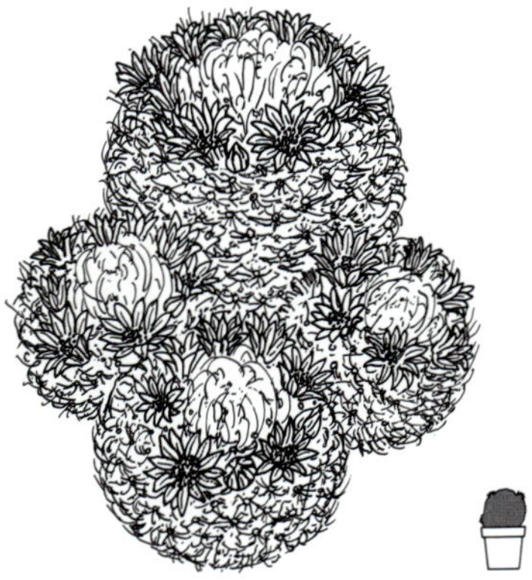

Mammillaria bocasana

- **Full sun**
- **Temp: 5-30°C (41-86°F)**
- **Keep dry in winter**

Mammillarias are the most popular of the cacti: they are small, flower freely, and have beautiful spines. *M. bocasana* is a many-headed plant that forms a cushion. The plant is blue-green and covered with silky white spines. Appearances are deceptive: underneath the soft spines are spines with hooks, which cling to the hands, clothing or anything else that touches them. The small creamy flowers form circlets around each head in spring. This is a very free-flowering plant.

This cactus needs a sunny position and ample water plus a dose of high-potassium (tomato-type) fertilizer every two weeks or so during the growing period. During winter, keep it dry. A suitable mixture is two parts of a loam-based potting medium to one part of sharp sand or perlite. Repot annually. If the plant is becoming too large, remove one of the heads, dry it for two days, and then pot it up. If the cutting is taken in spring, it will soon root.

Above: **Mammillaria bocasana**
The rounded, silky heads of this cactus and its ease of cultivation make it a popular mammillaria. But, beware! The silk conceals spines.

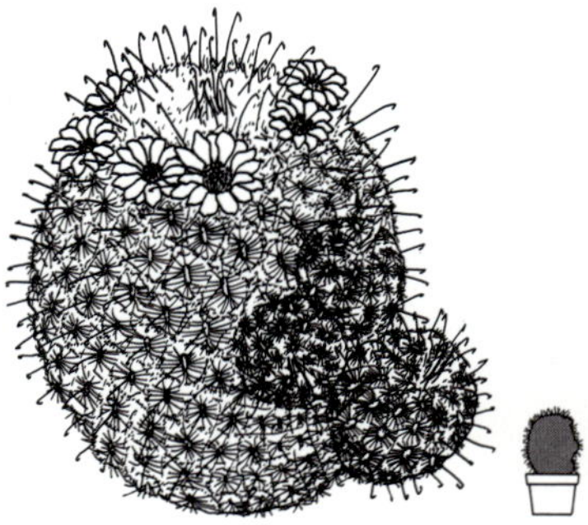

Mammillaria bombycina

- **Full sun**
- **Temp: 5-30°C (41-86°F)**
- **Keep dry in winter**

Mammillaria bombycina is one of the beautiful white-spined mammillarias. It is a cylindrical plant that clusters from the base with age. The stems are densely clad in white spines. The reddish-purple flowers form circlets around the tops of the stems in late spring to early summer. Young plants do not flower. It seems to be characteristic of mammillarias that cream-flowered species bloom easily, even as young plants, but most of the red-flowered ones bloom only as mature plants.

An open growing medium, two parts loam- or peat-based potting mixture to one part grit, is necessary for this cactus. Since it spreads outwards, it looks well grown in a half-pot. Repot annually and examine the roots for signs of root mealy bug. Water generously during summer, but allow it to dry out before watering again. Feed every two weeks with a high-potassium fertilizer when the plant is flowering. Keep dry in winter.

Right: **Mammillaria bombycina**
This species is not one of the best for flowering, at least not when young, but its delightful appearance more than compensates.

A practical hint
No collection would be complete without a selection of mammillarias with their pin cushion flowers and interesting, neat growth habit.

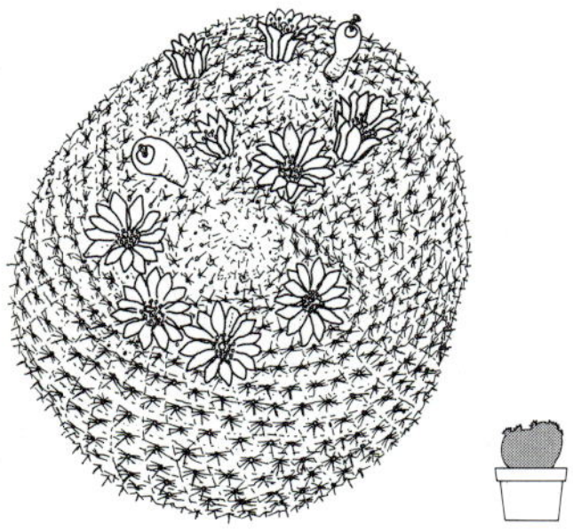

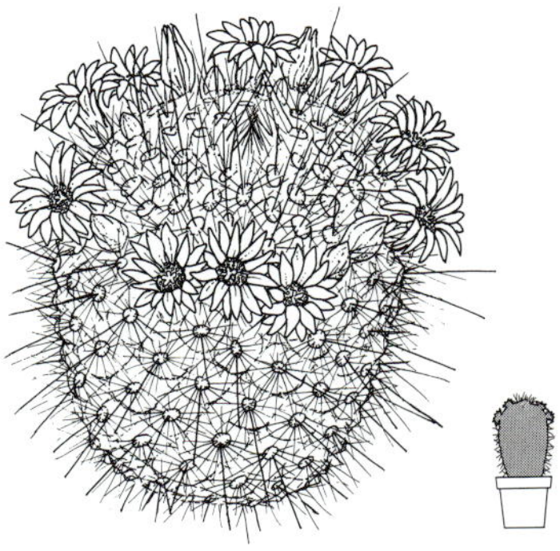

Mammillaria perbella

- **Full sun**
- **Temp: 5-30°C (41-86°F)**
- **Keep dry in winter**

Mammillaria perbella is a silvery-white cylindrical cactus, about 6cm (2.4in) in diameter, and does not usually branch. The stem is covered in short white spines. The flowering period is early summer, when a ring of flowers appears near the top of the plant. The petals are pale pink with a darker stripe down the middle.

Grow in a mixture of one part loam- or peat-based potting medium and one part sharp sand or perlite. Repot every year and examine the roots for signs of root mealy bug. During spring and summer, water on sunny days, allowing it to dry out between waterings. During the flowering period feed every two weeks with a high-potassium fertilizer. Taper off the watering in autumn and allow the plant to remain dry in winter. Keep this cactus in the sunniest part of your greenhouse; sun stimulates bud formation and spines.

Mammillaria spinosissima var. sanguinea

- **Full sun**
- **Temp: 5-30°C (41-86°F)**
- **Keep dry in winter**

Mammillaria spinosissima var. *sanguinea* has a dark green cylindrical stem and long white spines, the central spines having red tips. The purplish-red flowers are quite large for a mammillaria and form a ring in summer.

This cactus is easy to cultivate. A porous mixture consisting of two parts loam- or peat-based material to one part sharp sand or perlite is needed, and a sunny position. Repot annually. Water generously during spring and summer, but allow it to dry out between waterings. When the flower buds appear, feed every two weeks with a high-potassium (tomato) fertilizer until flowering is over. Keep it dry in late autumn and winter. When repotting, inspect the roots for any ashy deposit, which indicates the presence of root mealy bug. If found, wash the soil off the roots and replant into a clean pot; treat with a systemic insecticide.

Above right: **Mammillaria perbella**
Encourage this cactus to flower by giving it plenty of sun and a dry winter rest. Use a free-draining potting mixture and make sure that it does not become too compacted.

Right: **Mammillaria spinosissima var. sanguinea**
A double bonus of large flowers and attractive spines makes this cactus highly recommended. Ensure it stays really dry in winter.

A practical hint
Areoles of the cacti (pin cushions of prickly spines) make plants difficult to handle, so for smaller plants use tweezers.

Mammillaria zeilmanniana

- **Full sun**
- **Temp: 5-30°C (41-86°F)**
- **Keep almost dry in winter**

This is a very free-flowering mammillaria and the blooms are a beautiful reddish-violet colour; it is one of the few mammillarias of this colour to flower as a young plant. Occasionally a plant has flowers with a double row of petals, and there is also a form with white blooms. The flowering period is early summer.

The stems of this plant are cylindrical, and branch to form multi-headed clumps. Heads can be detached during summer, and used to propagate the plant. Grow in half-pots; a suitable potting mixture is two parts loam- or peat-based medium and one part grit. Water freely and feed every two weeks with a high-potassium fertilizer during spring and summer, allowing it to dry out between waterings. Let it become almost dry during winter. Keep in a sunny part of the greenhouse and inspect for mealy bug; water with insecticide.

Left: **Mammillaria zeilmanniana**
White and brick red spines decorate this cactus, and flowers are violet-red or white (variety shown at top). Very showy. Ideal for beginners; easy to propagate.

A practical hint
Garden soil is seldom suitable for tender indoor plants and a properly prepared mixture should be acquired when potting on is due.

Manettia bicolor

- **Good light**
- **Temp: 16-21°C (60-70°F)**
- **Keep moist and fed**

To keep this plant under control requires a framework of some kind through which its twining growth can be trained. Depending on the shape wanted, taller supports can be provided for plants to climb.

New plants can be raised from spring-sown seed, or from cuttings of young growth taken in midsummer and kept warm. When potting, ensure that a liberal amount of sand and charcoal is incorporated in the mixture, which should be loam-based.

Water freely and feed frequently during the growing season, and moderately when growth slows up. Delightful tubular flowers – red with a yellow tip – appear throughout the summer months. Plants can be moderately pruned after they have flowered. During the summer *Manettia* will need protection from strong sunlight.

Right: **Manettia bicolor**
This vining plant will grow well indoors and produce tubular flowers about 2cm (0.8in) long in summer. Prune severely in spring to prevent the plant becoming straggly.

A practical hint
On bright days window glass can magnify the sun's rays and scorch foliage. Also artificial light too close to plants can burn.

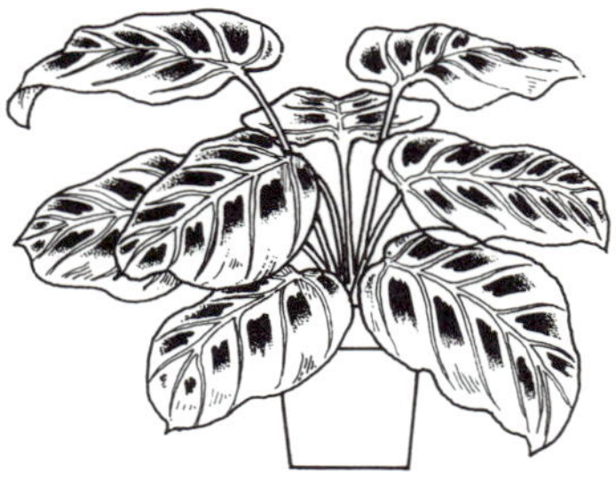

Maranta erythrophylla

- **Light shade**
- **Temp: 18-24°C (65-75°F)**
- **Moist soil and atmosphere**

With reddish-brown colouring and intricately patterned, rounded leaves, this is one of our more attractive smaller plants. Exotic colouring immediately suggests that it is difficult, but the reverse is true if sufficient warmth is maintained and reasonable care given.

These plants are best grown naturally with foliage trailing where it will. Unless the leaves are misted twice daily, hanging containers will usually prove to be too dry a location for them; it will be better to grow plants at a lower level. To improve humidity around the plant place the pot in a larger container with moist peat packed between the two pots.

Peaty mixture is essential when potting on, but one should not be too hasty in transferring plants to very large pots. Fertilizer should be very weak and given with each watering rather than in a few heavy doses.

In time the plants will become ragged and it may then be wise to start again with new cuttings.

Maranta kerchoeviana

- **Shade**
- **Temp: 16-21°C (60-70°F)**
- **Moist soil and atmosphere**

Dark spots on grey-green leaves give this plant the name 'rabbit's tracks'; the dark spots are said to resemble the tracks left by a rabbit. One of the older established houseplants, it is one of the easiest of this family to care for. It needs protection from direct sunlight and must be reasonably warm. Frequent feeding with weak liquid fertilizer is best, and one should use a peaty potting mixture.

When watering the soil should be moist but not totally saturated for very long periods, especially in winter. The danger with peat mixtures is that they will soak up very much more water than the plant is ever likely to need and will become totally waterlogged – a dangerous condition for most plants. For this reason plants should not be watered from the bottom and allowed to absorb water from the pot saucer. It is very much better to water into the top of the pot, giving sufficient to ensure that surplus drains away.

Left: **Maranta erythrophylla**
With reddish-brown and green-coloured leaves that are most intricately marked, these are very colourful foliage plants. Keep humid and avoid bright sunlight.

Above: **Maranta kerchoeviana**
With pale green, darkly spotted leaves, this is among the easiest of the marantas to care for. For best results offer moist, shaded and warm conditions. Divide clumps in spring.

A practical hint
Propagation of orchids developing pseudobulbs is not beyond the amateur. The oldest leafless bulb can be severed with a piece of rhizome, and potted.

Masdevallia coccinea

- **Cool: 10°C (50°F)**
- **Moderately easy to grow**
- **Winter/spring flowering**
- **Evergreen/no rest**

This is one of the most fascinating orchid genera, as remarkable for the uniformity of its vegetation as for the diversity of form and colour of its flowers. Three hundred species are recorded, growing mainly in the higher-altitude areas of Mexico, Brazil and Colombia. The structure of the flowers is in contrast to that of many orchids, as the sepals are very large in comparison with the other segments of the flower.

This species produces leaves 30cm (12in) in length, and the flower spikes are often much taller. These bear a single flower of 7.5-10cm (3-4in), with sepals that taper sharply towards the tips. The colour varies from lilac to deep crimson.

Because of the high-altitude conditions of its natural habitat, the cool house with plenty of shade and fresh air during the summer months provides the ideal environment. Masdevallias do not produce pseudobulbs – the thick leaves spring directly from a creeping rhizome – so the plants should never be allowed to become dry.

Above right: **Masdevallia coccinea**
A very attractive species for the cool house. The single flowers are carried on a tall stem in winter and spring.

A practical hint
Following the coloured bract display, poinsettias will die back naturally and should remain dry for several weeks until new growth is noticed.

Masdevallia tovarensis

- **Cool: 10°C (50°F)**
- **Moderately easy to grow**
- **Autumn flowering**
- **Evergreen/no rest**

A beautiful species from Colombia that produces the typical neat growth of the genus. The leaves are glossy, dark green and grow from the base of the plant from a connecting rhizome. The flowering stems come from the base of the leaves and carry two to four flowers clear of the foliage. When the flowers have died, the stem remains green and blooms again the following year, an unusual feature for an orchid. The attractive flowers are a soft powdery white and are largely composed of the three sepals, which are elongated and end with a short tail.

Odontoglossum-type culture suits these orchids well. They should be grown in cool, airy conditions and kept just moist at all times. The plants will quickly deteriorate if allowed to get too wet or too cold at any time. A well-drained compost and regular repotting are essential. Several new growths will be produced each growing season, enabling a large plant to be built up in a comparatively short time. Propagation is by division when the plant is large enough.

Left: **Masdevallia tovarensis**
A cool-growing species with neat habit. Autumn flowering. The plant blooms again on old stems.

A practical hint
The orchid *Miltonia* Peach Blossom will develop leaf blemishes if it is sprayed over with water. Never allow it to dry out, and feed when active.

Maxillaria picta

- **Cool: 10°C (50°F)**
- **Easy to grow and flower**
- **Winter flowering**
- **Evergreen/dry winter rest**

This is one of the prettiest and most popular of the genus. The plant has roundish pseudobulbs topped by two long, narrow leaves. The 5cm (2in) flowers, produced prolifically on single stems, are yellow on the inside of the sepals and petals. On the outside are reddish-brown bars that show through to the inside. The lip is creamy white and slightly spotted in red. This lovely species flowers in profusion during the middle of the winter and has a pleasant, strong fragrance.

During the summer the plant should be kept moist and lightly fed, with a decided rest in good light after the season's growth is completed. The flowering stems appear at the same time as the new growths, the stems being rounded and fatter. Several new growths can be produced in a season, resulting in a good-sized plant within a few years. Propagation is by division of the plant when large enough. This pretty orchid can be grown in a cool greenhouse or indoors.

Left: **Maxillaria picta**
This species grows in the cool house and blooms during the winter. The single blooms are extremely pretty.

Maxillaria porphyrostele

- **Cool/intermediate: 10-13°C (50-55°F)**
- **Easy to grow and flower**
- **Winter/spring flowering**
- **Evergreen/semi-rest**

This species is very easy to accommodate as it will grow into a specimen plant without needing too much space. It is best grown in a wire or wooden basket, because it grows prolifically and in time will not only cover the top of its container but also grow over the sides.

Plants produce clusters of pseudobulbs with broad leaves that develop from a horizontal rhizome. Each leading pseudobulb can produce a number of short flower spikes, which carry a yellow flower of 4cm (1.6in) diameter. The tips of both sepals and petals are incurving. The flowers are long-lasting, and appear from winter to spring.

About 300 species of this very diverse genus are known. They are widely scattered throughout tropical America and almost all are epiphytic. This genus is well-known to many growers, not only for its interesting flowers, but also for the variety of their scent.

Grow in good light and overhead spray during the summer.

Above left:
Maxillaria porphyrostele
A compact, easy-to-grow orchid that produces abundant yellow flowers.

Maxillaria tenuifolia

- **Cool: 10°C (50°F)**
- **Easy to grow and flower**
- **Summer flowering**
- **Evergreen/semi-dry rest**

In this species a creeping rhizome, which grows almost vertically, produces small oval pseudobulbs at 2.5-5cm (1-2in) intervals. The flowers, 2.5cm (1in) across, are dark or bright red speckled with yellow. The plant has a very strong scent similar to that of coconut.

Because of its creeping habit it will quickly grow out of its pot and it is therefore more easily accommodated on a slab of wood. Grown vertically in this way, the plant quickly makes itself at home. It makes new roots sparingly and usually from the older bulbs around its base. The flowers, though not numerous, cluster around the bulbs on extremely short stems. Their bright colouring makes them eye-catching.

This is a plant that thrives in light conditions and dislikes too much moisture around its base. A well-drained compost is important if the plant is grown in a pot. During the summer it can be kept just moist by overhead spraying.

Medinilla magnifica

- **Light shade**
- **Temp: 18-24°C (65-75°F)**
- **Keep moist and fed**

Native to the Philippines, this plant will be a test for all who are interested in houseplants, but the reward of seeing pink flower clusters suspended from healthy plants will make all the effort worthwhile. Warm conditions, around 21°C (70°F), and a lightly shaded location are essential. Plants must be watered well throughout the year, with slightly less needed in winter.

Pendulous flowers may appear throughout the year, with summer being the most prolific time. The plants have square-shaped stems from which the flowers sprout and develop in the most amazing fashion. Use a loam-based potting mixture to which some peat and leaf mould have been added. Feed when in active growth. To get the full effect of the pendulous flowers place the plant on a pedestal.

Above: **Maxillaria tenuifolia**
A small-growing, cool-house species that flowers in the summer. It produces short-stemmed, strongly scented flowers. Easy to grow.

Right: **Medinilla magnifica**
This luxuriant plant is best grown in a greenhouse, where warm and humid conditions can be maintained. Check regularly for red spider mites.

Mikania apiifolia

- **Good light**
- **Temp: 13-18°C (55-65°F)**
- **Keep moist and fed**

With the fashion for hanging plants we have seen the introduction of many unusual plants into the range of generally available houseplants, and the mikania is one of those. In poor light the foliage is a dullish green and not so nice, but in good light (but not full sun) there will be a marked tendency for the leaves to take on a purplish hue that can be most attractive.

New plants can be started in the spring from cuttings of firm young leaves with a piece of stem attached. Insert them in peaty mixture and keep them warm. Place several cuttings in a small pot to produce a fuller and more attractive plant. It will also improve the overall appearance of the plant if you remove the growing tip of each piece at an early stage in its development.

This plant will look its best in a small hanging container. Be sure to maintain a humid atmosphere around it and give a dose of liquid fertilizer about once a month during spring and summer.

Above: **Mikania apiifolia**
A superb plant for a hanging basket, mikania will develop its best foliage colour in bright light. Easy to propagate from cuttings.

Miltonia clowesii

- **Intermediate: 13°C (55°F)**
- **Fairly easy to grow**
- **Autumn/varied flowering**
- **Evergreen/no rest**

This is a Brazilian plant, with pseudobulbs, whose leaves reach a height of about 50cm (20in). The flower spike, which may be up to 60cm (2ft) in length, grows from the base of the pseudobulb and bears six to ten flowers, each about 6.5cm (2.5in) across. The sepals and petals are of equal size, reddish-brown and barred with yellow. The lip, in direct contrast, is white with a pinky-mauve blotch on its upper part.

Twenty species of this deservedly popular genus have been recorded. The majority are very sweet-scented and flower throughout the year, often more than once. They divide roughly into two natural groups. In the first group are plants from Brazil, which produce yellowish-green foliage and flattened pseudobulbs, well spaced on a creeping rhizome. These orchids require intermediate conditions and more light than plants in the second group, which grow in the higher regions of Colombia.

Propagation is by division when the plant is large enough.

Above: **Miltonia clowesii**
An intermediate species that is mainly autumn flowering on spikes up to 60cm (2ft) in height. Divide the rhizome for new plants.

Miltonia Peach Blossom

- **Intermediate: 13°C (55°F)**
- **Moderately easy to grow**
- **Varied flowering season**
- **Evergreen/no rest**

This is a typical *Miltonia* hybrid produced from the soft-leaved Colombian species commonly known as the 'pansy orchids'. These hybrids come in a wide variety of colours — white, yellow, pink and red. Peach Blossom is one of the most popular varieties with large, plum red flowers, the colour shading to white towards the edges of the flower.

This orchid and other similar hybrids should be grown in an intermediate greenhouse or a warm room. Their dislike of cold, damp conditions makes them ideally suited to the drier atmosphere in the home. Watering should be on a continuous basis; never allow the plants to dry out completely. The foliage should not be sprayed and feeding should be applied to the pot when watering. One weak feed every three weeks during the spring and summer should be sufficient.

Repotting should be done when the new growth is showing, which may be spring or autumn.

Left: **Miltonia Peach Blossom**
This fine hybrid can be grown easily indoors or in an intermediate greenhouse. Avoid damp and cold.

Miltonia roezlii

- **Intermediate: 13°C (55°F)**
- **Moderately easy to grow**
- **Autumn flowering**
- **Evergreen/no rest**

This extremely pretty plant is one of the soft-leaved Colombian species. It produces the typical neat oval pseudobulbs of the type and these are partially covered by soft, silver-green leaves. The flower spike appears from inside the first or second leaf on the newly completed bulb and carries two to four white flowers. The two lateral petals are painted purple at their bases and the lip has a yellow blotch that spreads out from the centre, or 'mask'. Although this plant is quite rare, supplies should be available from nursery-raised stock.

Although this species likes fairly warm conditions, it should not be allowed to suffer from too high temperatures. The intermediate section of the cool house will suit it. A beginner would find the many superb hybrids that have been raised from this species tolerant and easy to grow.

There is also a rare *alba* variety, which lacks the purple colouring at the base of the petals.

Above: **Miltonia roezlii var. alba**
A rare white form of this species, now a collector's item. Suitable for the intermediate greenhouse.

Miltonia spectabilis

- **Intermediate: 13°C (55°F)**
- **Fairly easy to grow**
- **Autumn/varied flowering**
- **Evergreen/no rest**

Another Brazilian species, this orchid resembles *M. clowesii,* but the flower spike grows to no more than 25cm (10in) in length and bears fewer, slightly larger, flowers which are white or pinky-white, with a broad, flat, purple lip.

Miltonia spectabilis var. *moreliana* is a distinct variety of this plant, and is more often seen today than the pure species. Its flower is an overall deep purple in colour with a lighter hue on the lip.

The plant has a rather untidy habit of growth and will quickly spread over the edge of its pot. It can make a grand specimen when attached to a flat piece of wood and allowed to grow on unhindered. It likes to be grown in good light and it is natural for the whole plant to take on a yellowish appearance. Given the right conditions, this is a robust grower and it passes on many of its good qualities when used for hybridization.

Propagation can be carried out by the removal of back bulbs.

Above: **Miltonia spectabilis**
Large single flowers are produced by this intermediate-house species in the autumn. Needs good light.

A practical hint
Leaf-cleaning chemicals should be applied as directed and never to excess or too often. Avoid exposure to direct sunlight after cleaning with chemicals.

Monstera deliciosa

- **Light shade**
- **Temp: 16-21°C (60-70°F)**
- **Moist roots, regular feeding**

The naturally glossy green leaves with attractive deep serrations make the monsteras among the most popular of all indoor foliage plants. The aerial roots produced from the stems of more mature plants are an interesting and often perplexing feature. Removing some excess roots will not be harmful, but in most instances it is better to tie the roots neatly to the stem of the plant and to guide them into the pot soil.

As plants mature they will naturally produce serrated leaves, but darker growing conditions can result in leaves that are smaller and complete, rather than cut out. Bright sunlight magnified by window glass can cause scorching of foliage and should be avoided, particularly while soft new leaves are maturing.

Monsteras belong to the Araceae family and in their natural jungle environment will tend to scramble along the floor before finding a tree trunk to climb.

Above right: **Monstera deliciosa**
Interesting leaves are perforated in older plants and are deeply cut along their margins. Strong aerial roots are produced from the main stem.

Left:
Narcissus tazetta 'Paper White'
In a cool bright location indoors these bulbs will put on a fine show of sweetly fragrant flowers.

A practical hint
Bulbs intended for flowering indoors in pots must have a start in a dark place outside so that a vigorous root system develops.

Narcissus tazetta 'Paper White'

- **Sunny location**
- **Temp: 10-16°C (50-60°F)**
- **Keep moist; dry rest period**

This is just one example of the many fine bulbs that can be made to flower in pots indoors in early spring, so giving a feeling of spring before its arrival. To succeed, these bulbs have to be thought of in the autumn when they are being sold by retailers. Plant them in shallow pans filled with bulb fibre so that the tips of the bulbs are just poking through the surface of the mixture. After potting, place the planted bulbs in a corner out of doors and cover the pots with about 13cm (5in) of peat or sand, then forget about them!

When the growing tips are showing through the peat or sand surface, move the pots and put them in a cool place indoors. The warmer the place the quicker the bulbs will come into flower, and the shorter will be their life once they have flowered. Avoid excesses of temperature.

Neanthe bella

- **Light shade**
- **Temp: 16-21°C (60-70°F)**
- **Keep moist but well drained**

For people with limited space who wish to acquire a palm this is the answer, as the parlour palm presents a neat and compact plant throughout its life.

This plant is often used in bottle gardens, where it takes place of honour as the taller plant to give the miniature garden some height. One might add a word here to say that when planting bottle gardens it is most essential to ensure that small, non-invasive plants are selected.

The parlour palm should not be allowed to dry out excessively, although it should be a little on the dry side during the winter months, when growth is less active. It is important to ensure that the pot is well drained, and this will mean putting a layer of broken pieces of clay pot in the bottom of the new container before adding soil. Water poured onto the surface of the soil should be seen to flow fairly rapidly down through the mixture.

Nematanthus tropicana

- **Light shade**
- **Temp: 16-21°C (60-70°F)**
- **Avoid overwatering**

This comparatively new plant has yet to make the grade as a houseplant, but early indications show considerable promise. Very similar to the better known aeschynanthus, the leaves are a very dark green and naturally glossy, and the brownish orange flowers are produced in abundance in the axils of almost every leaf.

It is ideal for small hanging containers where growth can spread and develop naturally. New plants are not difficult to raise from sections of stem with two or more leaves attached. At all stages a peaty potting mixture is required, but it is important to allow plants to establish well in their existing pots before any attempt is made to pot them on. However, very large pots are not needed, as plants can be sustained by feeding at later stages. Pinch out the tips to get a bushy effect.

Left: **Neanthe bella**
The compact parlour palm is ideal for limited space, and does well in most locations other than cold and wet. Chemicals may damage the foliage.

Above: **Nematanthus tropicana**
Ideal for a hanging basket, this easy-care plant will produce its tubular flowers in profusion. Easy to raise from stem cuttings.

A practical hint
Cactus seedlings can be allowed to become quite congested in initial pots before any attempt is made to separate and pot them individually.

Neoporteria Mammillarioides

- **Full sun**
- **Temp: 5-30°C (41-86°F)**
- **Keep dry in winter**

Although probably one of the less well-known neoporterias, this beautiful cactus, previously a pyrrocactus, is certainly one of the most attractive. The almost globular stem, perhaps up to a diameter of 8cm (3.2in), is bright green in colour, with many acute ribs furnished with tufts of straight, stiff spines. Although it is a neat, compact little plant, it is the flowers that make it out of the ordinary. They are of a deep rose-pink or red colour, yellowish towards the base of the petals, and are produced very freely at the top of the plant, usually several opening at one time and lasting for several days.

Grow this neoporteria in a good potting mixture. Mix one part of sharp sand or perlite with three parts of a standard peat- or loam-based material. A top dressing of gravel will help to reduce the risk of rotting off at the base, and with this protection you can water reasonably freely during spring and summer, but remember to reduce watering in the autumn.

Neoregelia carolinae tricolor

- **Good light**
- **Temp: 13-18°C (55-65°F)**
- **Dry at roots; keep urn filled**

Although it does produce small and inconspicuous flowers in the centre of the rosette of leaves (the 'urn' or 'vase') this is very much a foliage plant. Overlapping leaves radiate from a short central trunk and are spectacularly striped in cream and green with the added attraction, as flowers appear, of the shorter central leaves and the base of larger leaves turning a brilliant shade of red.

Following this colourful display the main rosette will naturally deteriorate and in time will have to be cut away from the small trunk to which it is attached. Take care that the small plant or plants forming around the base of the trunk are not damaged during this operation, as these will be the plants of the future. Leave the young plantlets attached to the stump to grow on or, in preference, remove them when they have developed several leaves of their own and pot them into peaty mixture.

Above right:
Neoporteria mammillarioides
Large flowers are freely produced at the top of this beautifully spined cactus and they may last for a week. Needs a cold winter rest.

Right:
Neoregelia carolinae tricolor
Spectacular plants of the bromeliad family with flat rosettes of leaves overlapping at their base to make a watertight urn best kept full.

A practical hint
Ferns are best grown in warm and shaded conditions; a moist atmosphere will suit them better than arid conditions. Avoid sun.

Nephrolepis exaltata

- **Shade**
- **Temp: 16-21°C (60-70°F)**
- **Keep moist always**

There are now many fine cultivars of this excellent plant. Any purchased plants that appear too large for their pots should be potted on without delay into a slightly larger container. A peaty mixture containing some loam will give better results than a soil that is thin and lifeless. As an alternative to putting the new plant into a conventional pot, transfer it to a decorative hanging basket.

Bright sunlight for any length of time will be fatal, as will excessive drying out of the soil. It will also be harmful should temperatures drop too low, if the soil in the pot is excessively wet. Plants will respond to feeding, but they often do better if fed with a foliar feed rather than a more conventional fertilizer taken up through the root system. New plants are normally raised from spores taken from the undersides of leaves when ripe, but may also be grown from the plantlets that develop on the runners of older plants.

Left: **Nephrolepis exaltata**
Bold ferns of which there are numerous versions, all with strong green fronds spraying out from the centre of the plant pot. Shade and warmth are needed for success.

A practical hint
Numerous foliage plants can be raised from seed. Read directions on the packet, and offer warm, moist and reasonably airy conditions.

Nephthytis 'White Butterfly'

- **Light shade**
- **Temp: 16-21°C (60-70°F)**
- **Keep moist and fed**

Also known as *Syngonium podophyllum* 'White Butterfly'; the common name of goose foot relates to the shape of the adult leaf. Pale green leaves are suffused with white, and the plant will trail or climb as required.

It will have to be kept moist at all times, with occasional misting of the foliage with tepid water. The goose foot has adapted amazingly well to hydroculture, the technique of growing plants in water with nutrient solution added. In this instance the plant has all the soil washed away from its roots before it is converted to water culture. The roots are then suspended in clay granules (a sort of artificial pebble), and a special nutrient is added to the water for the plant to feed on. If the simple directions concerning watering and feeding are followed, the goose foot will grow at three times the rate of the same plant in soil, and frequent pruning is needed.

Above right:
Nephthytis 'White Butterfly'
Free-growing plants of the Araceae family needing moisture and shade to do well. Will climb or trail.

Nerine bowdenii

- **Sunny location**
- **Temp: 10-16°C (50-60°F)**
- **Keep moist; dry in summer**

These bulbous plants are native to South Africa, and most attractive when grown as pot plants indoors or as hardy plants in the garden. Good light and cool conditions are essential needs.

The bulbs are about the same size as those of small daffodils and should be planted five to a 13cm (5in) pot during late summer. Place drainage material in the bottom of the pot then half fill it with loam-based potting mixture. Place the bulbs on this mixture then fill in the remainder of the space with more soil, firming it around the bulbs and leaving the neck of the bulbs exposed. Keep the potting mixture moist. Oddly, these bulbs rest in bone dry condition from early to late summer, when they are best placed on a sunny shelf in the greenhouse. Potting on is seldom necessary. Beautiful pink flowers appear in the autumn before the leaves.

Nerium oleander

- **Sunny location**
- **Temp: 13-21°C (55-70°F)**
- **Keep moist and fed**

Another fine plant frequently seen in the tropics, and yet equally at home in agreeable conditions indoors. A light and sunny location is essential, and plants should be well watered in summer when in active growth — less is required in winter. The same rule applies with feeding, none in winter, but once or twice each week when producing new leaves.

The semi-double rose-coloured flowers are slightly pendulous, fragrant, and a joy to have about the house. Cuttings of non-flowering shoots can be taken at any time during the summer months. Prepare the cuttings about 13cm (5in) in length and insert them in peaty mixture in modest heat. Be sure to wear gloves when taking cuttings to prevent the sap getting on to your skin. This plant is extremely poisonous if any part of it is eaten. When potting use a loam-based mixture.

Nertera depressa

(N. granadensis)

- **Good light**
- **Temp: Below 16°C (60°F)**
- **Keep moist**

These decorative little plants have become popular windowsill subjects in recent years. The leaves are very small and not unlike those of the helxine; the plants are generally seen in quite small pots, which are in keeping with their size. The slender stems are fragile and creeping in habit.

Inconspicuous greenish white flowers are produced in mid-summer and do little to enhance the appearance of the plant. The attraction of this interesting houseplant is the colourful orange berries that follow the flowers.

Plants are raised from seed sown in spring in sandy, free-draining soil – the soil suggested for sowing can be used at all stages of growth. Seed should have a thin covering of soil when sown. Very wet soil conditions should be avoided, particularly in winter. Cool conditions are essential.

Left: **Nerine bowdenii**
Easy to grow in a cool, light place, this bulbous plant produces lovely pink flowers on stems about 50cm (20in) high. Autumn flowering.

Above left: **Nerium oleander**
This colourful tropical shrub will grow to about 1.8m (6ft) high in a pot and will respond well to bright light in the home or greenhouse.

Above: **Nertera depressa**
Grown for its long-lasting berries, this little plant can be divided and kept going for several years. Keep the conditions light and cool.

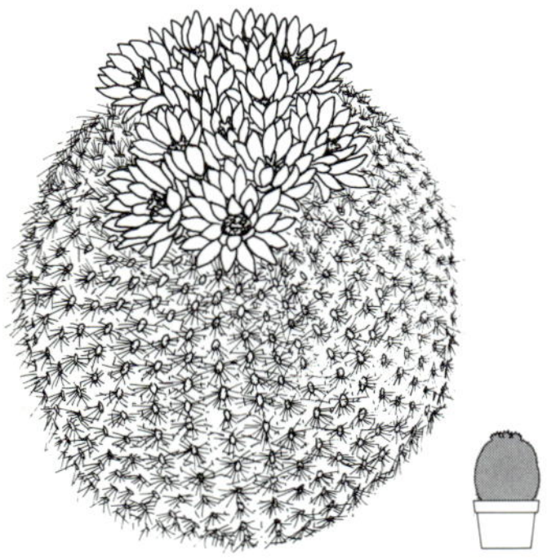

Notocactus haselbergii

- **Full sun**
- **Temp: 5-30°C (41-86°F)**
- **Water with caution**

Notocacti are found growing in the grasslands of South America, and they need full sun. *N. haselbergii* is one of the most beautiful of these cacti. It is a silver ball: the numerous ribs are densely clad in soft white spines, which gleam in the sunshine. It does not form offsets. The flowers are carried on top of the plant in late summer; they are tomato red, an unusual colour in this group of plants. Very young plants do not flower.

N. haselbergii should not be allowed to become too wet, or it may lose its roots. A mixture consisting of one part loam-based potting medium to one part sharp sand or perlite will ensure good drainage. Water freely during summer, but allow it to dry out between waterings. Feed every two weeks with a high-potassium fertilizer during the flowering period. Keep it dry during winter. The only pests likely to be found on this plant are mealy bug and root mealy bug; water with a proprietary insecticide.

Above: **Notocactus haselbergii**
Flowers are produced on a neatly spined white ball and the contrast between the plant and flower colour is most striking. This cactus does not usually flower when young.

Notocactus herteri

- **Full sun**
- **Temp: 5-30°C (41-86°F)**
- **Water with care**

All the notocacti that have been in cultivation for many years have yellow flowers, but some recently discovered species have beautiful purple flowers, and one of the best of these is *N. herteri*. It is a large globular plant with reddish-brown spines. Although seedlings do not flower, the plant grows quickly and will eventually reach a diameter of at least 15cm (6in). The deep magenta flowers are formed at the top, and open in late summer.

A porous growing mixture consisting of one part loam-based material and one part sharp sand or perlite is suitable. Water freely during the summer, allowing the plant to dry out between waterings. When the buds start to form, feed every two weeks with a high-potassium fertilizer. During winter keep the plant completely dry. It is always advisable to look plants over regularly for the presence of mealy bug: treat with a proprietary insecticide if found.

Above right: **Notocactus herteri**
The flower colour of this notocactus makes it different from the others illustrated here. The plant itself is neatly rounded and has compact spines, contrasting with its blooms.

A practical hint
Some plants of the araceae family, such as monstera and dieffenbachia, drip water from their leaf margins. This is a sign of overwatering.

A practical hint
For most succulents, sharply drained soil is essential. Cactus mixes are available; otherwise use a loam-based mix with added sand or grit.

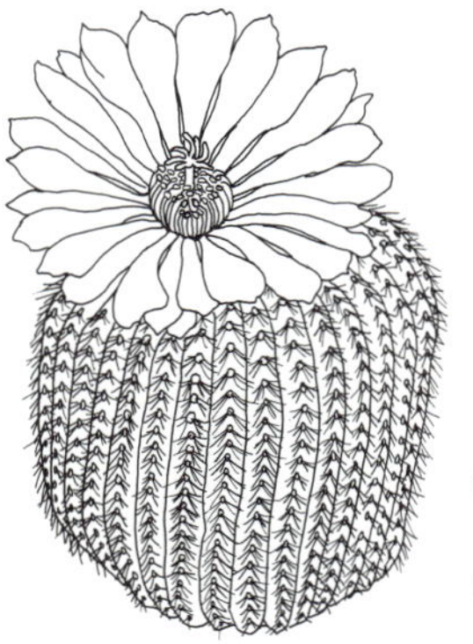

Notocactus leninghausii

- **Full sun**
- **Temp: 5-30°C (41-86°F)**
- **Keep dry in winter**

Notocactus leninghausii is a golden plant that branches and becomes columnar with age. The many close ribs carry soft yellow spines. It is characteristic that the growing centre of this plant tends to be on one side of the stem. The large yellow flowers appear on top of the plant in late summer. Young plants do not flower.

This cactus is not difficult to cultivate; a growing medium consisting of two parts peat-based potting mixture to one part grit, and a sunny position, will ensure a healthy plant. Repot annually. If the plant gets too large or the base of the stem becomes corky, branches may be removed in summer and used for propagation. Water freely during summer, allowing it to dry out between waterings. During flowering, feed every two weeks with a high-potassium fertilizer. Gradually taper the water off in autumn and keep the plant dry during the winter. Watch out for root mealy bug and mealy bug.

Left: **Notocactus leninghausii**
With golden spines and stately shape as it matures, this is an established favourite among cacti. Careful growing may be rewarded with yellow flowers on older plants.

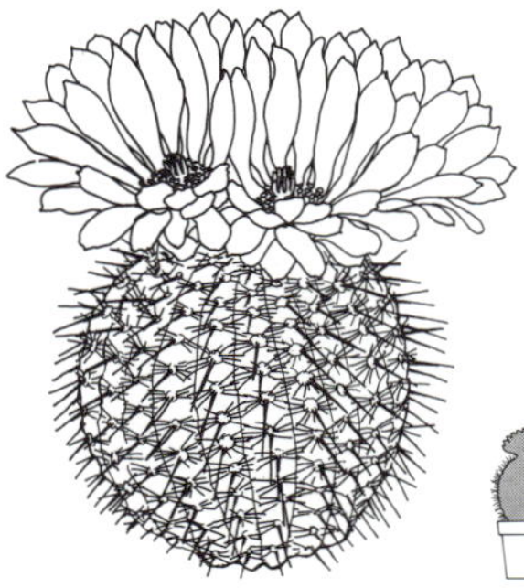

Notocactus mammulosus

- **Full sun**
- **Temp: 5-30°C (41-86°F)**
- **Keep dry in winter**

Notocactus mammulosus is a trouble-free plant that flowers freely while quite small. It is a globular cactus that remains solitary. The ribs carry long, stout spines, brownish in colour. The flowers, borne on top of the plant in late summer, are yellow with purplish stigmas. They are also self-fertile; the furry seed pods contain hundreds of seeds, which germinate easily if sown in the following spring.

Grow this notocactus in a mixture of two parts loam- or peat-based material plus one part sharp sand or perlite. Repot annually. Water freely during the spring and summer growing period, but keep it dry during the winter. When flower buds form, feed every two weeks with a high-potassium fertilizer. If really dry this cactus will withstand temperatures around freezing point. Keep in full sunlight, which ensures not only good flowering but also long, stout spines. A beautifully spined plant is attractive all year.

Above left:
Notocactus mammulosus
This is a particularly striking notocactus, with long, stout spines. This free-flowering plant will set viable seed quite readily.

A practical hint
Easy to care for, *Odontoglossum bictoniense* is a fine orchid for the beginner. Offer cool conditions, light shade, and less water in winter.

Notocactus ottonis

- **Full sun**
- **Temp: 5-30°C (41-86°F)**
- **Never overwater**

Notocactus ottonis is quite different from other notocacti; it is much smaller, and clusters freely from the base. It is deep green, and the ribs carry slender yellowish spines. Individual heads are about 7.5cm (3in) across. The yellow flowers are about 6cm (2.4in) across.

This notocactus is touchy about watering; to prevent it losing its roots, grow in an open mixture consisting of one part loam-based potting medium to one part grit. Grow it in a half-pot: the cluster looks better, and the roots are not surrounded by large quantities of cold, damp soil. Water freely during spring and summer, always allowing it to dry out between waterings. Feed every two weeks during the flowering period using a high-potassium (tomato) fertilizer. Keep it dry in winter. Place this plant where it will get plenty of light. The main pests are mealy bug and root mealy bug; treat with a proprietary insecticide.

Above right: **Notocactus ottonis**
This small, globular cactus clusters freely and produces large brilliant flowers with red centres.

Odontioda Dalmar 'Lyoth Bachus'

- **Cool: 10°C (50°F)**
- **Easy to grow and flower**
- **Varied flowering season**
- **Evergreen/no rest**

When the highly coloured odontiodas are crossed with large well-formed odontoglossum hybrids the results are a culmination of two lines of breeding, superbly illustrated by this most magnificent of plants. This hybrid has beautiful deep red flowers edged with pale mauve and 10cm (4in) across. The odontioda parent is Margia, which has been influenced by the *Cochlioda noezliana* in its background, whereas the odontoglossum parent, Mandalum, has *O. crispum* in its immediate ancestry.

This hybrid requires cool growing conditions in a position of good light. These plants do not divide or propagate very easily and should be grown on into as large a specimen as possible. Leafless pseudobulbs should not be allowed to outnumber those in leaf and are always better removed when this stage is reached. Regular repotting is essential to ensure the compost remains fresh.

Further, excellent hybrids have been produced from this one.

Right: **Odontioda Dalmar 'Lyoth Bachus'**
This lovely cool-house hybrid flowers at various times of the year.

A practical hint
Besides watering the soil it is important to keep the atmosphere around orchids moist; indoors, this will necessitate regular misting of the foliage.

Odontocidium Tigersun 'Nutmeg'

- **Cool/intermediate: 10-13°C (50-55°F)**
- **Easy to grow and flower**
- **Varied flowering season**
- **Evergreen/no rest**

The introduction of *Oncidium* species into the breeding of odontoglossum hybrids has increased in popularity over the last few years and many hybrids are becoming available. Apart from giving different types of flowers and colours, most of the odontocidiums will stand more extreme conditions than the pure odontoglossums – which is of great importance to growers in warmer climates or where a mixed collection is cultivated. *Odontocidium* Tigersun is a cross between *Oncidium tigrinum* (a popular scented species from Mexico) and *Odontoglossum* Sunmar, and produces excellent bright yellow flowers, 9cm (3.5in) across, of good substance.

In common with other intergeneric odontoglossums, this hybrid does not have a definite resting period. It should be watered throughout the year, although less so during the winter. The only time this plant is not growing is while it is in flower, which can be six or eight weeks.

Above left: **Odontocidium Tigersun 'Nutmeg'**
An easy-to-grow hybrid for a cool greenhouse or indoor culture.

Odontoglossum bictoniense

- **Cool: 10°C (50°F)**
- **Easy to grow and flower**
- **Summer flowering**
- **Evergreen/semi-rest**

This is one of the easiest and most popular species, and an ideal plant for beginners. Native to Guatemala, it is a very vigorous grower and will quickly grow into a specimen plant. Erect flower spikes appear at the end of the summer, growing quickly in warm weather to reach heights up to 120cm (48in) and bearing 20 long-lasting flowers on each spike. The flowers open in succession so that there are usually eight or nine out at once over a period of several weeks. The flowers are about 3-4cm (1.25-1.6in) across, yellowy green with brown spots and a striking white or pink lip.

O. bictoniense, which can be grown successfully as a houseplant, requires cool conditions with medium shade and does not need resting in winter, though water should be reduced when flowering has finished, until new growth appears in the spring.

This species is very variable. The plant is easily propagated from the leafless pseudobulbs.

Left: **Odontoglossum bictoniense**
Tall, upright spikes are produced by this cool-growing, late summer-flowering species. Easy to grow.

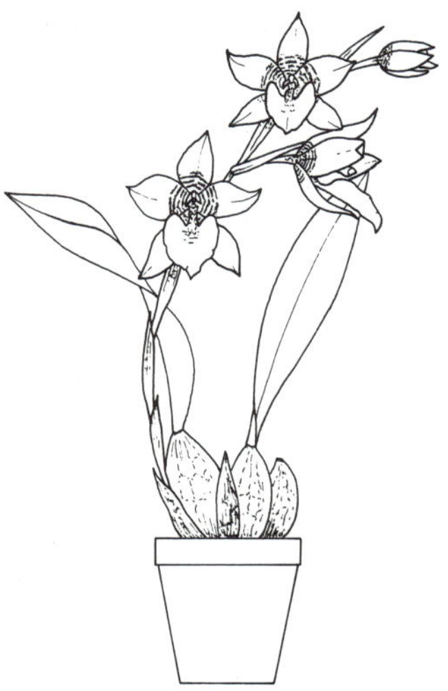

Odontoglossum cervantesii

- **Cool: 10°C (50°F)**
- **Easy to grow and flower**
- **Winter/spring flowering**
- **Evergreen/slight rest**

A delightful dwarf species from Mexico. The total height of pot, bulbs and leaves is only about 15cm (6in) and makes this an ideal subject for growers with limited space.

The flowers are produced on semi-pendent spikes, in winter and early spring, from the new growth as it starts to form a pseudobulb. In comparison to the size of the plant, the flowers are large – about 4 – 5cm (1.6 – 2in) across, beautifully white, almost round and marked with a distinctive band of chestnut rings towards the middle of the sepals and petals.

Being a species with fine roots it does not like to dry out during the growing season and thrives in a fine but free-draining compost. During the winter months water should be reduced and a small amount of shrivelling of the bulb is normal at this time. Give medium shade during the summer.

This species is at its best when allowed to grow on into a large plant. It can also be grown on bark.

Odontoglossum crispum

- **Cool: 10°C (50°F)**
- **Moderately easy to grow**
- **Varied flowering season**
- **Evergreen/slight rest**

Coming from high up in the Andes, this plant needs medium to heavy shade and cool, moist, humid conditions. The large flowers, up to 10cm (4in) across, vary considerably in presence or absence of marking. Flower spikes develop from the side of the new bulb as it is forming and, as the seasons in its native environment are not clearly defined and growth can start at any time, the flowers may open at virtually any time of year, though spring and autumn are probably the most common.

Selective breeding of varieties has been continuing for many years and this has ensured that *Odontoglossum crispum* will still be available to enthusiasts without calling on the dwindling wild stocks; moreover, these cultivated plants are of higher quality. As an ancestor, *Odontoglossum crispum* has probably contributed more towards improving the flower size and shape of *Odontoglossum* and *Odontioda* hybrids than any other species.

Odontoglossum Gold Cup 'Lemon Drop'

- **Cool: 10°C (50°F)**
- **Fairly easy to grow**
- **Autumn flowering**
- **Evergreen/no rest**

This cross between *Odontoglossum* Chamois Snowcrest and *O.* Crowbrough Sunrise is a good example of yellow odontoglossum breeding. The flowers are 6cm (2.4in) across, and a bright canary yellow with a few golden brown markings on the lip. The plant, which is proving to be a good parent in its turn, requires cool conditions with plenty of shade during the summer.

Being a pure-bred *Odontoglossum* this plant is less tolerant of varying conditions, and thus more attention must be paid to its cultural requirements. A cool, light and airy atmosphere is important at all times, conditions which are more easily obtained with the aid of a greenhouse. The flowers, which can last for a good six to eight weeks, are ideal for all florist's work, and will last for the same length of time if cut and placed in water.

An open, well-draining compost is very important. The plant should be kept watered throughout the year and never allowed to become completely dry.

Above:
Odontoglossum cervantesii
This is a small and delightful cool-growing species. Easy to flower.

Above: **Odontoglossum crispum**
An easy cool-house species that flowers at various times of the year. Long-lasting sprays of large blooms.

Right: **Odontoglossum Gold Cup 'Lemon Drop'**
This cool-growing hybrid produces sprays of large flowers in autumn.

A practical hint
For children few cacti compare in interest with *Opuntia microdasys*; the leaves resemble rabbits' ears and give the plant its common name.

Odontoglossum grande

- **Cool: 10°C (50°F)**
- **Easy to grow and flower**
- **Autumn flowering**
- **Evergreen/dry winter rest**

Known widely as the 'clown orchid' due to the clown-like figure represented by the column in the centre of the flower, this is certainly one of the most widely grown in this genus, and popular as a houseplant. The flowers are very large, up to 15cm (6in) across, yellow with bright chestnut-brown markings.

It has hard dark leaves and very tough pseudobulbs, and needs a decided rest during the winter months. During the growing season it needs plenty of moisture at the roots but excessive atmospheric moisture can result in unsightly black spotting on the foliage. As the new growth starts to make a pseudobulb towards the end of the summer the flower spike develops, and the flowers usually open in autumn. Once flowering is finished and the pseudobulbs have fully matured, watering should be withheld until spring, when the new growth appears. The plants need light shade and should be grown in a medium-grade bark compost. They should receive full light in winter.

Right: **Odontoglossum grande**
This very popular species is cool growing. The very large showy flowers appear during the autumn.

Odontoglossum pulchellum

- **Cool: 10°C (50°F)**
- **Easy to grow and flower**
- **Spring flowering**
- **Evergreen/slight rest**

An extremely popular and vigorous Guatemalan species. The waxy, white flowers, though small – 1-2cm (0.4-0.8in) across – bloom in masses and have a lovely scent, which explains why it is known as the 'lily of the valley orchid'. It flowers in spring and produces more than one shoot from each pseudobulb, making it ideal for growing into a specimen. The plants are thin-rooted and need cool conditions, a fine-grade bark mix, and medium shade in the summer.

If left unsupported the slender flower spikes will often assume a pendent position by the time they are in bloom. If an upright position is preferred, the spikes should be lightly tied to thin supporting canes, when the flowers will stand well clear of the foliage. This is an unusual species, which alone among the cultivated odontoglossums carries its flowers with the lip uppermost.

Within the genus, it has not contributed to any hybridization.

It can be easily propagated by the removal of back bulbs.

Above right:
Odontoglossum pulchellum
This attractive cool-house species is spring flowering. Lovely fragrance.

Odontoglossum rossii

- **Cool: 10°C (50°F)**
- **Easy to grow and flower**
- **Winter flowering**
- **Evergreen/no rest**

From Guatemala and Mexico, this is one of the most delightful of the miniature odontoglossums. It is very similar to *Odontoglossum cervantesii* in size of plant and size and colour of flowers, and has similar cultural requirements. The plants are thin-rooted and flourish in cool conditions and a fine bark mix or sphagnum moss that will keep them moist at all times. Medium shade is required during the summer.

A typical variety produces star-shaped flowers in winter, about 3-5cm (1.25-2in) across, white with brown markings; rarer varieties are flushed with pink, or deep pink. Probably the most popular is the Majus variety, which has a much larger flower up to 7.5cm (3in) across. However, this sought after variety is seldom seen today; the smaller forms are usually grown.

Because of their small size, the pseudobulbs should not be allowed to shrivel at any time. During the winter, when the plant is inactive for a short period, watering should be lessened slightly.

Above: **Odontoglossum rossii**
A delightful miniature species for the cool greenhouse. It produces lovely long-lasting flowers in winter.

Odontoglossum stellatum

- **Cool: 10°C (50°F)**
- **Easy to grow and flower**
- **Winter flowering**
- **Evergreen/semi-rest**

A dwarf species from Guatemala, this has attractive star-shaped flowers, yellow overlaid with brown, with a white or pink lip. These are usually borne either singly or in pairs during the winter months, but on a specimen plant they are produced in abundance, making a fine display. Each flower measures 3-4cm (1.25-1.6in) across. Found naturally among mosses on branches of trees, this species needs a fine bark mix, with medium shade during the summer; too much light will cause a yellowing of the light green foliage.

Owing to the smallness of the bright green pseudobulbs the plants should not be allowed to dry out completely at any time. During the winter, water should be reduced but not discontinued altogether. Several new growths are produced each season and the plant quickly grows into a good-sized specimen. As it gets larger it should be grown in a half pot, which will allow sufficient room for the fine root system to spread out comfortably without the danger of overwatering.

Above: **Odontoglossum stellatum**
An easy, cool-growing dwarf species that will rapidly develop into a free-flowering specimen.

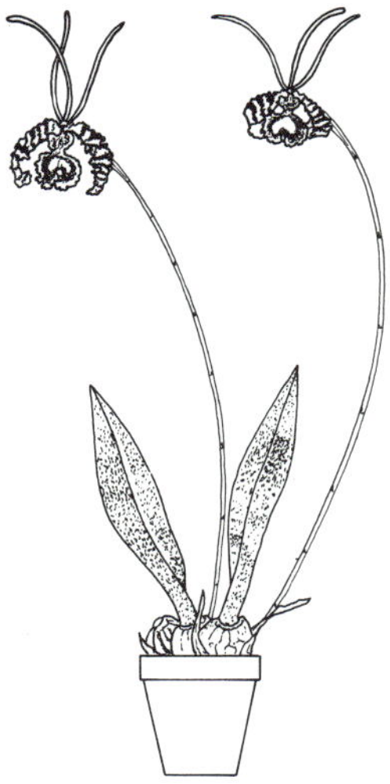

Oncidium ornithorhynchum

- **Cool: 10°C (50°F)**
- **Easy to grow and flower**
- **Autumn flowering**
- **Evergreen/semi-rest**

An extremely showy species from Mexico and Guatemala, this plant has a compact habit and light green pseudobulbs each topped with several thin leaves. The short, slender and arching flower spikes are produced very freely in the autumn and carry the individual flowers on side branches. These are about 2cm (0.8in) long, the sepals and petals curled and twisted. The colour is a soft rose-lilac with a yellow crest on the lip. They are long-lasting and beautifully fragrant. It is not unusual for two or three flower spikes to be produced by one bulb.

Propagation is by division and removal of back bulbs, although the plant is at its best when grown on into a specimen. A very fine rooting system is produced, indicating that a well-drained compost is important. The plant dislikes cold and damp and should therefore not be sprayed overhead or kept too wet at any time. Otherwise, normal cool house conditions will suit it. It is a delightful beginner's orchid of great charm that will do equally well indoors.

Above:
Oncidium ornithorynchum
A pretty miniature species for the cool house. Fragrant flowers.

Oncidium papilio

- **Warm: 18°C (65°F)**
- **Difficult to grow and flower**
- **Varied flowering season**
- **Evergreen/semi-dry rest**

Often referred to as the 'butterfly orchid' because of its resemblance to that insect, this species has flowers that open on the end of a long slender stem and sway in the slightest air movement. Only one per stem opens at any one time, but in succession, so that the plant is in flower for many months. The flowers, which can be up to 13cm (5in) across, are a mixture of chestnut brown and yellow.

The plant has squat pseudobulbs each of which supports a solitary, rigid, reddish-green leaf. The plant grows best on a raft suspended from the roof of the warm house, where it will get that little extra bit of light. It should never be kept too wet at the roots, and does best when kept continually on the dry side, relying upon the humidity in the greenhouse for most of its moisture. It should not be overhead sprayed. This is not a beginner's orchid nor a suitable plant for growing indoors.

Rare in the wild, the plants seen in cultivation have usually been grown from seed.

Right: **Oncidium papilio**
The famous 'butterfly orchid', it grows in the warm house and flowers at various times. Needs special care.

A practical hint
When properly watered orchid pseudobulbs will be maintained in plump and healthy condition, which is essential to the well-being of the plant.

Oncidium tigrinum

- **Cool: 10°C (50°F)**
- **Easy to grow and flower**
- **Autumn flowering**
- **Evergreen/dry rest**

Originating from Mexico, this is one of the most beautiful of the autumn flowering oncidiums and certainly one of the most popular. It is a neat, good-looking plant with roundish pseudobubs that each support two or three dark green leaves. The flower spikes can be up to 7.5cm (3in) tall, and branching on a large plant. Several fragrant flowers are carried on each branch as well as on the terminal part of the main stem. The petals and sepals are yellow barred with chocolate brown, and the large, spreading lip is a vivid yellow and by far the most striking part of the flower.

The plant will succeed well in the cool house, although as with many of the Mexican species it will be equally happy in intermediate conditions. The species is becoming less plentiful in cultivation but it has been used to produce some excellent intergeneric crosses within the *Odontoglossum* alliance. Generally these hybrids are tolerant of widely varying conditions and are suitable for most climates.

Left: **Oncidium tigrinum**
Adaptable and easy to grow, this oncidium produces distinctive blooms in the autumn.

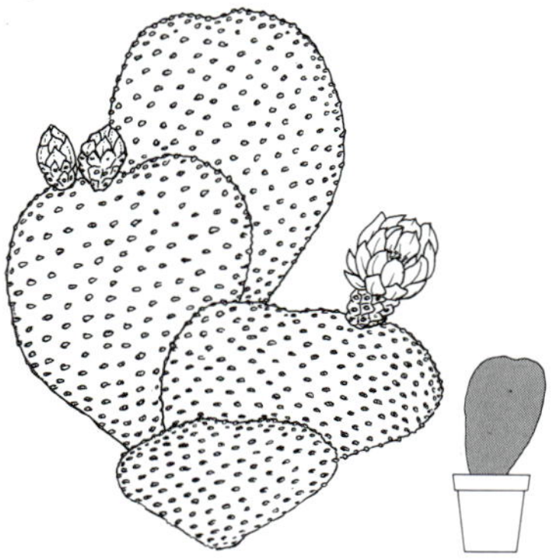

Opuntia basilaris

- **Full sun**
- **Temp: 5-30°C (41-86°F)**
- **Keep dry in winter**

If there is any typical cactus, it must surely be the opuntia, or prickly pear, although the latter name was originally applied to the spiny fruit of a desert giant. But *O. basilaris* is not a giant and is ideal for the collection as it rarely becomes more than two segments, or pads, high, sometimes branching from the base. The pads are flattened stems (beaver-tail shape), and although almost spineless, they are dotted with clusters of dark red barbed bristles (glochids), characteristic of all opuntias, spined or not. Most opuntias do not flower readily in a collection, needing to be very large before they do so. But this one, being smaller, will often produce red blooms up to 5cm (2in) across on its second segment, when about 20cm (8in) high.

Grow this opuntia in a good porous potting mixture; extra drainage material is probably not necessary. If you winter it indoors, give just enough water to prevent shrivelling. Best kept dry if in a greenhouse.

Above: **Opuntia basilaris**
Most of the opuntias, or 'prickly pears', do not flower as reasonably small pot plants, but this one will usually do so quite readily and is not too large for a collection.

Opuntia microdasys

- **Full sun**
- **Temp: 10-30°C (50-86°F)**
- **Keep slightly moist in winter**

Probably the most common cactus of all, and certainly the most popular opuntia; but also the most ill-treated cactus. Witness the poor, spotted, dried-up plants so common in windows. Although it spreads over a wide area in the wild, cultivated specimens form small branched bushes, consisting of many beautiful bright green pads, or flattened stem segments, closely dotted with clumps of yellow glochids (barbed bristles) but no other spines. There are also varieties with reddish and white glochids. All are beautiful but need careful handling, because the pads are not as innocent as they look; the glochids stick into the skin at the slightest opportunity. Rarely, yellow flowers are produced.

A well-drained potting mixture is needed, and free watering in spring and summer. Give sufficient water in winter to prevent undue shrivelling and keep this cactus rather warmer than it would be in the average cool greenhouse.

Right: **Opuntia microdasys** var. **albispina**
This variety with white glochids is particularly attractive, especially if space permits a large clump. Pads can be detached for propagation.

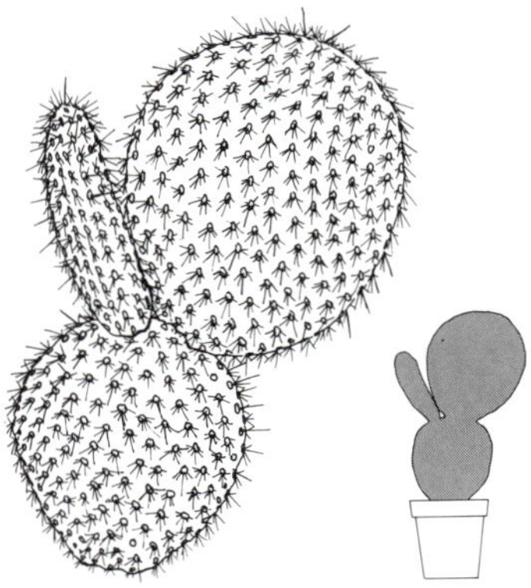

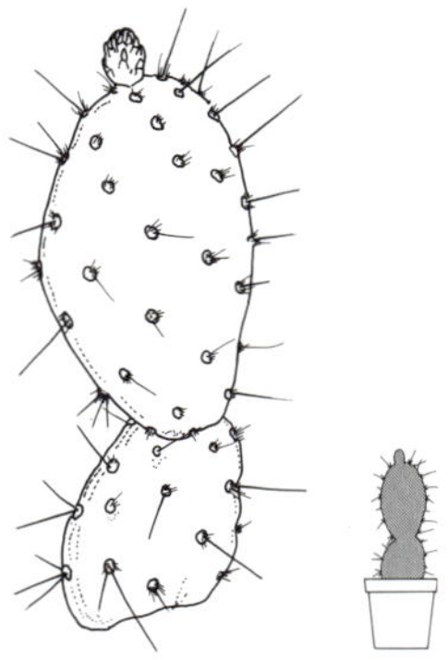

Opuntia pycnantha

- **Full sun.**
- **Temp: 5-30°C (41-86°F)**
- **Keep dry in winter**

The fact that the name is sometimes mis-spelt as *pycnacantha* detracts in no way from the beauty of this most handsome opuntia of all, with its bright green stem and contrasting groups of reddish-brown bristly spines (glochids), in addition to the lighter-coloured, longer spines. Individual flattened stem segments or pads are about 8cm (3.2in) across, each being right-angled to the one below. Fortunately this delightful cactus does not depend upon flowers for its beauty, as they are most unlikely on cultivated specimens. Tiny cylindrical leaves appear at the ends of young pads, but soon shrivel and fall off; this is quite natural.

This species is somewhat more susceptible than many opuntias to over-wet potting mixture, which results in root loss; it is best to add about one third of sharp sand or perlite to your usual good standard material. Give water generously in spring and summer; even opuntias can wilt!

Above: **Opuntia pycnantha**
Do not expect flowers on this opuntia; only large old plants are likely to produce them. But the beauty of this cactus comes from its shape and its colourful spines.

Opuntia robusta

- **Full sun**
- **Temp: 0-30°C (32-86°F)**
- **Keep dry in winter**

Although this cactus is one of the giant opuntias in its native state, where it can reach a height of 5m (16ft) with bluish-green pads the size of dinner plates, it can be tamed as a pot plant and makes a good, tough specimen for the average collection. This species grows quite quickly for a cactus, and soon makes a nice plant, but without the glorious yellow flowers of desert specimens, as you will not want it to get large enough for that!

It is easy to prevent it from becoming too big: just remove one or more pads when there is any danger of this, let them dry for a few days, and start another specimen. The old plant will send out further shoots, if you want them; otherwise, throw it away! Living up to its name, *O. robusta* is hardy enough to be grown out of doors throughout the year, if it can be protected from winter rain, but it must be dry to survive. Ordinary, good potting mixture will suffice.

Above: **Opuntia robusta**
This is a natural giant, but small specimens are attractive in a collection. However, they are not likely to flower. Easily propagated by detaching and potting the pads.

A practical hint
During the summer months of the year many of the tougher succulents will be the better for placing out of doors in the sun.

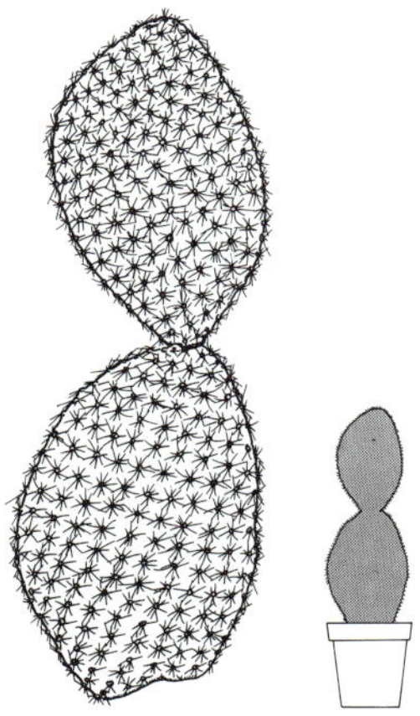

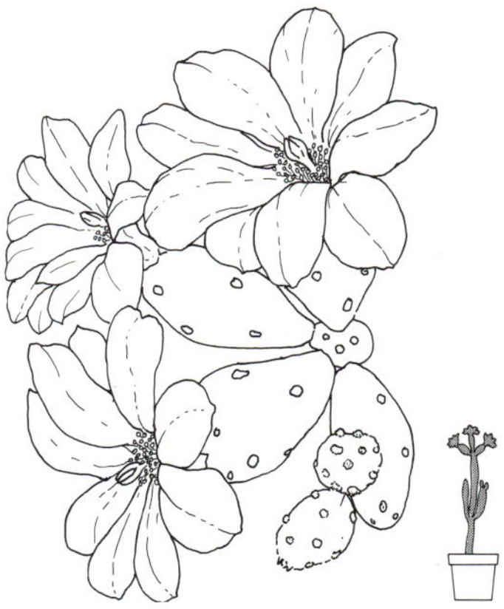

Opuntia scheeri

- **Full sun**
- **Temp: 5-30°C (41-86°F)**
- **Keep dry in winter**

By contrast with the previous opuntia, this one is ideal for the collection without any size-reducing manipulations. The flattened pads or stem segments are usually around 15cm (6in) long and 5cm (2in) broad, but older plants produce larger ones. A decorative, bushy plant results from branches off the main segment. The whole surface of each pad is covered with a network of golden spines, in addition to the inevitable barbed bristles (glochids). Flowers are yellow, but unlikely in cultivation.

Grow this cactus in a standard potting mixture, either peat- or loam-based, preferably with the addition of one third of sharp sand or perlite. Slight shrivelling of the stems may occur if the plant is quite dry in winter, as it should be if in a cool greenhouse; but in a warmer room give it just enough water to prevent this happening. You can water quite freely in spring and summer. Pads can be removed for propagation.

Above: **Opuntia scheeri**
As well as the typical glochids, or barbed bristles, this opuntia has a network of golden spines covering the joints. With its compact habit of growth and freely formed branches it is ideal for the average collection.

Opuntia spegazzinii

- **Full sun**
- **Temp: 5-30°C (41-86°F)**
- **Keep dry in winter**

There should be no trouble whatsoever in flowering this opuntia, even in a 5cm (2in) pot. It is quite different from the others mentioned: it does not have flattened 'pads' but long, slender cylindrical stems, freely branching; which in pot-grown specimens usually reach a length of about 30cm (12in) with a thickness of only 1cm (0.4in). Patches of barbed bristles (glochids) and very short spines are distributed over the stems. Large or small branches drop off at the slightest touch, usually rooting where they fall.

Grow this particularly easy opuntia in any good standard potting mixture and it should delight you every summer with its show of snow-white flowers, up to 4cm (1.6in) across, freely produced along the stems. The long, slender stems will need staking, or supporting in some way; a miniature pot plant trellis is ideal and the stems can be gently tied to this. Water freely in spring and summer; plants indoors may need a little water in winter to prevent shedding.

Right: **Opuntia spegazzinii**
This is one of the cylindrical-jointed opuntias, which are less familiar than the 'prickly pear' shape. It will flower easily in a small pot. Support the stems or grow this cactus in a hanging container.

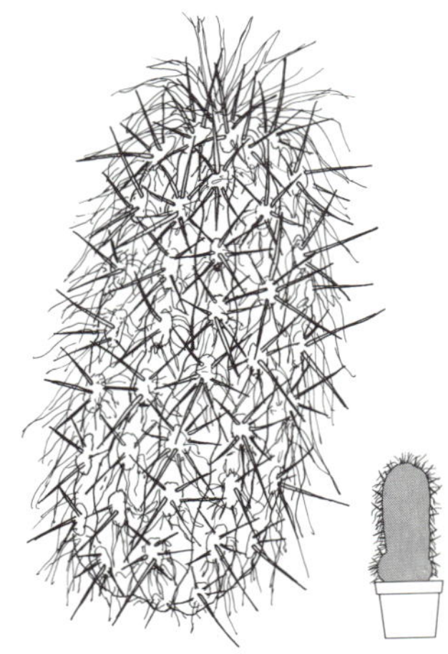

Oreocereus celsianus

- **Full sun**
- **Temp: 5-30°C (41-86°F)**
- **Keep dry in winter**

Although wild specimens of this cactus can reach a large size, it is relatively slow-growing, and in the collection it makes a majestic plant, probably eventually reaching a height of around 40cm (16in) and a diameter of 10cm (4in) but taking a number of years to do so from the usual small bought specimens. The cylindrical stem has a number of rounded ribs, and rows of stout, sharp, brownish spines up to 3cm (1.2in) long in larger specimens, and appearing through a mass of silky white hairs. In cultivation this beautiful cactus does not appear to form offsets or branches, so propagation is not practicable; nor is it likely to flower. Enjoy it for itself!

Grow in a standard potting mixture; and although this is not a demanding plant, it is advisable to mix in about one third of sharp sand or perlite, to be on the safe side. Water in spring and summer whenever the potting mixture appears to be drying out.

Above: **Oreocereus celsianus**
An impressive cactus by any standards, with its contrasting hair and sharp, stout spines. It is comparatively slow-growing; although it can eventually become very large, it will take years.

A practical hint
If grown cool and very much on the dry side in winter, then given water in the spring, many succulents will flower much more freely.

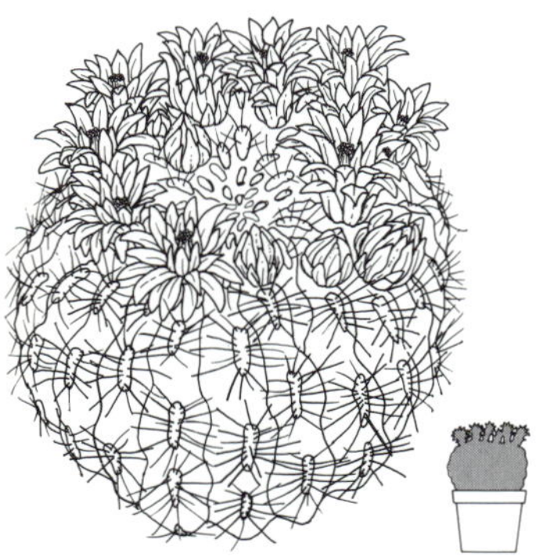

Oroya subocculta

- **Full sun**
- **Temp: 5-30°C (41-86°F)**
- **Keep dry in winter**

Oroyas are somewhat problem plants among botanists, because they do not always fit into preconceived groups. *O. subocculta* is a very neat plant and its arrangement of ribs and spines makes it a rather unusual-looking cactus. The many blunt ribs are divided into oval segments, each with a cluster of spreading spines, also arranged in an oval pattern. These are pale brown in colour, up to 1cm (0.4in) long, thin but very sharp. The roughly globular stem will probably reach a diameter of 13cm (5in). Small specimens do not usually flower readily but when the blooms do appear they are of a beautiful orange-reddish colour, yellowish underneath. Unfortunately, they are not very large, only about 2.5cm (1in) across, and unscented.

Grow this cactus in a potting mixture consisting of one part of sharp sand or perlite added to three parts of a good standard material. Water freely in summer.

Pachyphytum oviferum

- **Full sun**
- **Temp: 5-30°C (41-86°F)**
- **Keep slightly moist in winter**

Pachyphytum oviferum forms a small shrub about 20cm (8in) high. The fat leaves, arranged in rosettes on the stems, are bluish to lavender in colour and heavily covered with white 'meal'. The white bell-shaped flowers open in spring.

This succulent is not difficult to grow. During the winter months the lower leaves will shrivel; remove dead leaves regularly, or fungus will grow on them and spread to the living plant. If the plant looks leggy in spring, cut the rosettes off, dry them for two days, and repot. If the base of the plant is kept, new rosettes will form at the leaf scars.

Grow in a loam- or peat-based potting medium. Water freely during spring and summer. Be careful not to splash the white leaves. In the winter, give a little water to prevent excessive shrivelling of the plant. To keep a thick white coating of 'meal' grow in a strong light.

Above right: **Oroya subocculta**
This may not be the easiest plant to obtain but it is worth the effort. Fortunately it is most attractive in itself, because flowers are unlikely to be produced except on large plants.

Right: **Pachyphytum oviferum**
An excellent example of a leaf succulent, like sugared almonds on a stem. The leaves are covered with a whitish mealy coating, which makes them very easily marked.

Pachypodium lamerei

- **Full sun**
- **Temp: 12-30°C (54-86°F)**
- **Keep slightly moist in winter**

On the whole pachypodiums are not easy succulents and are something of a challenge, but *P. lamerei* is the least difficult and should be quite within the capability of a careful grower. The greyish succulent stem bears many thorny spines, neatly arranged in groups of three and up to 2.5cm (1in) long. Although sharp, they are not as vicious as those of many cacti. It is difficult to state an exact size, but a good cultivated specimen could be 20cm (8in) high with a thickness of about 5cm (2in). The top of the plant bears a tuft of leaves; as the stem grows they fall, to be replaced by others higher up.

Grow this pachypodium in a mix made by adding one part of sharp sand or perlite to two parts of a standard mix, and never overwater. Definitely a plant for indoors rather than the cool greenhouse in winter, but it will appreciate the extra light there in summer; indoors give maximum light and turn regularly.

Above: **Pachypodium lamerei**
Long, non-succulent leaves are formed at the top of a very succulent stem, well equipped with stiff spines. As the stem elongates, the lower leaves fall and are replaced.

Pachystachys lutea

- **Good light**
- **Temp: 16-21°C (60-70°F)**
- **Keep moist and fed**

This is a relative of the more familiar aphelandra, but has less vividly marked foliage – the pachystachys having simple mid-green, roughly lance-shaped leaves. However, where the pachystachys scores is in its much longer flowering period and in the fact that healthy plants will produce a far greater number of flowers. Flowers are erect in habit and a rich yellow in colour – or more correctly the bracts are rich yellow, the flowers produced from the bracts being white and tubular in appearance.

Success lies with light, water, and feeding. Avoid direct sun, but keep in the light, and water and feed well. No feeding and less water in winter. Repot annually in a loam-based mixture.

Above: **Pachystachys lutea**
This colourful shrub will grow to a height of about 45cm (18in) in a pot. Keep it humid and take tip cuttings in spring for new plants. It will grow best in a greenhouse.

A practical hint
Dividing clumps of plants and potting individually is the easiest and surest way of increasing plants; try it with aspidistras.

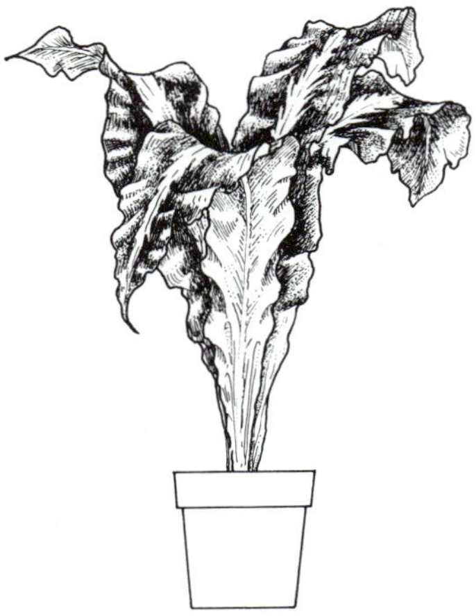

Palisota elizabetha

- **Light shade**
- **Temp: 16-21°C (60-70°F)**
- **Keep moist and fed**

Years ago at the Chelsea Flower Show I noted large clumps of this in the exhibit of one of our botanical gardens. A chat with the man in charge made it possible for me to exchange with one of my plants. The lance-shaped dense leaves are produced from soil level and have a pale yellow central colouring with darker green outside. For show purposes it is an ideal plant that can be placed almost anywhere to good effect, and is especially useful for concealing the cumbersome pots of taller specimen plants. But it does not seem to appeal much to Mr. Average when he selects plants for the home; perhaps one day there will be a change of heart.

The plant is very easy to care for, but must be kept moist and fed. To make new plants the older clumps can be divided into smaller sections and potted into loam-based mixture at almost any time. Regular feeding of established plants will be important.

Pandanus baptiste

- **Good light**
- **Temp: 16-21°C (60-70°F)**
- **Avoid too wet conditions**

This is probably the best-protected plant of them all. Vicious barbs are along the margins of the leaves, and a barbed keel runs the length of the underside of each leaf; all are capable of drawing blood if carelessly handled. However, it has the most incredible bright yellow colouring, which sets it apart from almost every other plant. The large recurving leaves are produced from a very stout trunk and will attain a length of 1.8m (6ft) and a width of 15cm (6in) or more when roots are confined to a pot. Should you be considering one of these for your home, be sure that you have a place large enough to accommodate it.

Older plants take on a further interesting dimension when they produce stout anchor roots from the main trunk; these extend in the manner of tent guy ropes around the plant to anchor it when hurricane winds hit its natural tropical island home. Maintain reasonable temperatures but treat them harshly to succeed.

Above: **Palisota elizabetha**
Forms bold clumps of mid green leaves with white midribs. The plants can be propagated by dividing clumps into smaller sections.

Right: **Pandanus baptiste**
Magnificent plants needing ample space. Leaves are striped in bright yellow with spined margins and a spined keel on their undersides.

Pandanus veitchii

- **Good light**
- **Temp: 16-21°C (60-70°F)**
- **Avoid too wet conditions**

Of the screw pines this is the most suitable for the average room, as it is reasonably compact and easier to accommodate. Leaves are green and white variegated and are produced in the shape of a large rosette, with leaves sprouting from a stout central stem. The screw pines all have vicious spines along the margins of their leaves, and a set of barbs running from the base to the tip of the leaf on the underside. Locate plants where they will be out of harm's way, perhaps by placing on a pedestal; this is also the best method of setting off these fine plants to advantage.

Being tough tropical plants that grow in exposed coastal areas, they are well adapted to harsh conditions. They will tolerate quite sunny locations and not be harmed provided they are not too close to the window-panes. Drought conditions seem to be taken in their stride, and they certainly prefer to be dry rather than too wet. Sharply draining, gritty soil is essential.

Above: **Pandanus veitchii**
This resembles a pineapple plant when young but becomes bolder with age. Leaves radiate from a short central trunk and are very spiny.

A practical hint
Paphiopedilum insigne is one of the easiest of orchids for indoors, and produces its pouch flowers for about three months in the middle of winter.

Paphiopedilum bellatulum

- **Warm: 16-18°C (60-65°F)**
- **Moderately easy to grow**
- **Spring flowering**
- **Evergreen/no rest**

One of the most beautiful of all the species, this native of Burma and Thailand has broad, fleshy leaves that are distinctly mottled and veined with lighter green. As the flower stem is very short, the lovely 6cm (2.5in) flower often nestles in the foliage. The broad, drooping petals are white or ivory, with maroon spots of varying size and density.

Extra care must be taken with its culture to prevent basal rot and other problems that can arise from too much watering or moisture around the plant. It is slow growing by comparison with others of the genus, and the beautiful foliage is easily damaged by unskilled handling. The plant must be grown in as small a pot as possible in a well-drained compost that is kept open and sweet. Water sparingly at all times and do not allow water to remain on the leaves. It will succeed best in a fairly warm greenhouse or in an indoor growing case, with good shade.

This is not an orchid suitable for beginners, who should try hybrids.

Above right:
Paphiopedilum bellatulum
A warmth-loving orchid that needs careful attention to succeed.

A practical hint
It is not always possible to move plants from an area exposed to full sun, but newspaper lightly draped over foliage will offer sufficient break.

Paphiopedilum callosum

- **Intermediate: 13°C (55°F)**
- **Easy to grow and flower**
- **Spring/summer flowering**
- **Evergreen/no rest**

This species is a vigorous grower, producing long mottled leaves. The long-lasting flower is borne on a tall stem, up to 38cm (15in) in length, which makes it very popular with the cut flower trade. The flowers are 10cm (4in) across, and coloured in varying shades of purple and green. They will last for eight or ten weeks in perfect condition.

It is a native of Thailand and is still reasonably plentiful in cultivation, no doubt because it can be easily propagated by division of the plants, which can be separated into two or three clumps every few years. The plant is suitable for windowsill culture in a warm room, where it should not be exposed to bright light. Grow in an open compost and water sufficiently to keep the plant evenly moist throughout the year. Keep the foliage dry, although indoors it will be necessary to sponge the leaves regularly to keep them free from dust. The plant may be lightly fed during the spring and summer.

This is excellent for beginners.

Left: **Paphiopedilum callosum**
This 'slipper orchid' blooms in the spring and summer. Ideal for intermediate conditions.

Paphiopedilum delenatii

- **Intermediate/warm: 13-18°C (55-65°F)**
- **Moderately easy to grow**
- **Summer flowering**
- **Evergreen/no rest**

This species from Vietnam has very dark green, heavily mottled leaves. The flowers, produced in summer and borne on a 20cm (8in) long stem, are 7.5cm (3in) across and soft rose pink in colour. This is one of the few fragrant paphiopedilums.

This plant is a fairly recent introduction and with its neat growth habit and highly attractive, unusual flowers has become justly popular. However, its requirements are rather specialized and it is not ideally suited to the beginner. It has never been very plentiful in the wild, but is easily raised from seed, and excellent young plants are becoming more readily available. It should be kept in as small a pot as possible with just sufficient water to keep it moist; it is intolerant of cold and damp conditions.

Some charming hybrids have also been raised that are proving to be more robust and easily grown. These hybrids would be a better choice for people new to orchids.

Right: **Paphiopedilum delenatii**
This attractive summer-flowering species belongs in the intermediate to warm greenhouse. Fragrant.

A practical hint
Exotic bromeliad plants produce many different types of flowering bracts; the billbergias flower well but last for days only.

Paphiopedilum hirsutissimum

- **Cool/intermediate: 10-13°C (50-55°F)**
- **Easy to grow and flower**
- **Spring flowering**
- **Evergreen/no rest**

The flowers of this Himalayan species are difficult to describe. They are basically purplish in colour, ranging from blackish-purple in the centre of the flower, to bright violet-purple at the petal tips. The pouch is brownish-purple. The plant gets its name from areas of black hair on the petals.

The plant produces neat green foliage with slender leaves. The flower bud emerges from a sheath that forms as winter approaches. The flowers open in late spring and last for eight weeks or more. The plant grows easily and will succeed in the cool or intermediate sections of the greenhouse. It is also suitable for the windowsill or for a growing case. This plant is at its best when grown on into a large clump, when it will produce several flowers in a season. However, if preferred, it may be divided when large enough; at least three growths should be retained on each plant. The plant should be kept evenly moist throughout the year and not allowed to dry out.

Left:
Paphiopedilum hirsutissimum
This species has neat foliage and a single, large, long-lasting flower.

Paphiopedilum Honey Gorse 'Sunshine'

- **Intermediate: 13°C (55°F)**
- **Easy to grow and flower**
- **Winter flowering**
- **Evergreen/no rest**

The first plant to combine the characteristics of the green and the yellow paphiopedilum groups, the 10cm (4in) flowers of this hybrid are dark yellow-green. Deeper emerald green hybrids are now being bred, but this plant will take some beating for its heavy texture – a feature usually lacking in the green colour group.

The plant contrasts beautifully with the heavier coloured and spotted flowers in the other colour ranges. It offers the grower a clear, fresh alternative to enhance any collection.

The plant should be repotted annually to ensure fresh, free-draining compost while keeping the pot size as small as possible. An intermediate greenhouse will suit this hybrid type best, where shady conditions should prevail. These hybrids are usually slower growing than many of the species and therefore splitting is not normally recommended unless or until the plant has several large growths.

Above: **Paphiopedilum Honey Gorse 'Sunshine'**
This winter-flowering hybrid bears a single, large flower per stem.

Paphiopedilum insigne

- **Cool: 10°C (50°F)**
- **Easy to grow and flower**
- **Winter flowering**
- **Evergreen/no rest**

One of the orchid 'greats', this plant has enjoyed unwavering popularity since it was first flowered in 1820. It is a native of the Himalayas and produces stocky, well-leafed growths that bloom freely in mid-winter, lasting for many weeks in perfection. The dorsal (uppermost) sepal is green with a white tip and spotted dark brown. The petals and pouch are bronze, the petals veined along their length. Among numerous varieties is the pure yellow type, *P. insigne* var. *sanderae.*

Today, though still popular, these beautiful orchids are dwindling in cultivation due to the difficulties of importing from the wild. What was, up to a few years ago, a desirable beginner's orchid is now becoming a rare collector's item. However, it will never be lost to cultivation as it will propagate easily and can be nursery raised from seed. Used extensively in hybridizing, there is hardly a modern *Paphiopedilum* hybrid that cannot trace back to this species. Beginners should try the hybrids.

Above:
Paphiopedilum insigne
This popular species is easy to grow in a cool greenhouse or indoors.

A practical hint
For most orchids fresh air is an important requirement, and plants do better in cool, airy rooms than in ones that are stuffy and airless.

Paphiopedilum Maudiae

- **Intermediate: 13°C (55°F)**
- **Easy to grow and flower**
- **Varied flowering season**
- **Evergreen/no rest**

This is probably the most consistently popular *Paphiopedilum* hybrid in the world. The plant has the grace and beauty found among a few of the species, which have been overshadowed by the heavier, rounded type of hybrids. This hybrid results from a cross of *Paph. callosum* x *Paph. lawrenceanum*, using two green varieties.

The plant is a strong, vigorous grower that can be continually divided without harm to produce further plants. The foliage is beautifully mottled in light and dark green, the leaves are short and rounded. The tall, slender stem carries a single large bloom, distinctively marked in white and deep apple green. Its coloured variety, *Paph.* Maudiae 'Coloratum', shows the same markings on a rich purple ground.

Its ease of culture and long-lasting, long-stemmed blooms, which can be produced twice in one year, have made this hybrid popular for the cut flower trade.

Right: **Paphiopedilum Maudiae**
This graceful flower is carried on a slender stem at various times of the year. For intermediate conditions.

Paphiopedilum Miller's Daughter 'Snow Maiden'

- **Intermediate: 13°C (55°F)**
- **Easy to grow and flower**
- **Winter flowering**
- **Evergreen/no rest**

This line represents the most advanced breeding for white-flowered hybrids in the world. There is nothing to compare with the perfection of the Miller's Daughter hybrids for flower size, shape and vigour. The 13cm (5in) flowers of this particular plant (*P.* Dusty Miller 'Mary' AM/RHS & GMM x *P.* Chantal 'Aloha') are white, lightly speckled all over with pinkish-brown.

The plant will succeed best in an intermediate greenhouse under moist, shady conditions. It should never be allowed to become completely dry at any time. Having no pseudobulbs in which to store water, its meagre reserves are held in the leaves; and if dryness is permitted, the foliage will become limp and dehydrated. The same symptoms will occur if overwatering has taken place; the roots drown in the sodden compost and the plant is deprived of its method of taking up water.

This lovely plant flowers during the winter months of the year.

Above: **Paphiopedilum Miller's Daughter 'Snow Maiden'**
A lovely white-flowered variety for the intermediate house.

A practical hint
The most important bromeliad is *Aechmea fasciata* with big pink bracts and startling blue flowers; the main rosette of leaves dies after flowering.

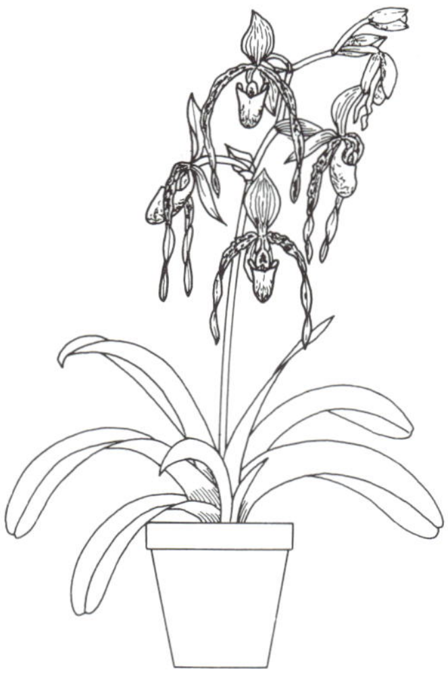

Paphiopedilum parishii

- **Intermediate: 13°C (55°F)**
- **Moderately easy to grow**
- **Winter flowering**
- **Evergreen/no rest**

A very striking species from Burma and Thailand that often grows epiphytically. The long narrow leaves are very smooth and bright glossy green. The erect flower stem, which can grow to 60cm (24in) in height, bears four to seven flowers, each about 7.5cm (3in) across, from autumn to spring. The twisted petals are long and pendulous, purplish-brown in overall colour, and spotted towards the flower centre. The pouch is greenish-brown, and the dorsal sepal greenish-yellow.

It does not require a great deal of light to flower, but will only bloom when mature. For this reason it should be grown without division. It is one of the very few paphiopedilums which produce a spray of flowers that open all at the same time on the stem. To keep the foliage clean and unmarked avoid allowing water to remain on the surface of the leaves, and be careful not to give too much light. This applies particularly to bright spring sunshine.

Above right:
Paphiopedilum parishii
Long sprays of elegant flowers are produced during the winter months.

A practical hint
Good light is essential for orchids, but plants that are placed too close to window-panes on a very sunny day may suffer scorching of foliage.

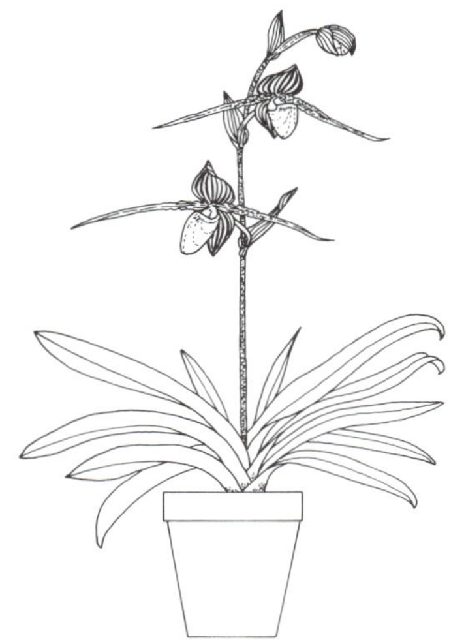

Paphiopedilum rothschildianum

- **Intermediate: 13°C (55°F)**
- **Moderately easy to grow**
- **Summer/autumn flowering**
- **Evergreen/no rest**

This species from New Guinea is one of the most striking paphiopedilums. The straight, leathery leaves are bright glossy green and can measure up to 60cm (24in) in length. The long flower stem carries two to five flowers, which can be as much as 29cm (11.5in) across. The flower markings are complicated, the overall colour being cinnamon yellow to greenish-brown, with dark brown stripes on the long petals and pointed dorsal sepal.

This plant is rarely seen today in collections. Those plants which are in cultivation are usually held as breeding stock. This ensures that it will never become extinct, and nursery raised seedlings or hybrids from it can occasionally be found. It is not really a beginner's orchid but the species or its hybrids are desirable collector's plants. Most suitable for an intermediate greenhouse, it will enjoy shady conditions in a moist atmosphere.

It should not be divided too often, but allowed to grow on.

Left:
Paphiopedilum rothschildianum
An exciting but rare species for the intermediate greenhouse.

A practical hint
The highly regarded orchid *Phalaenopsis schillerana* has attractive foliage and rose-purple flowers that are produced in quantity. It needs warmth.

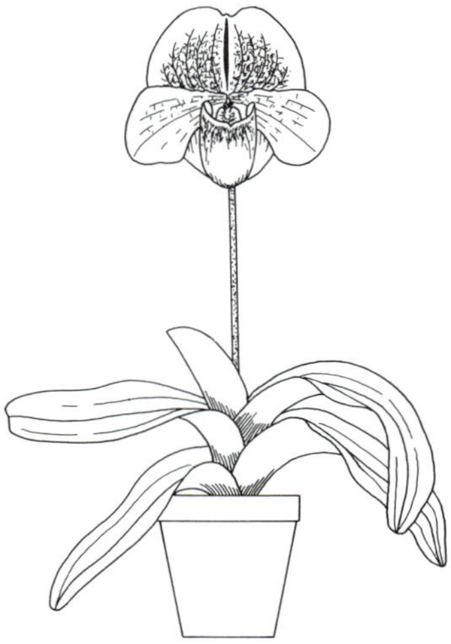

Paphiopedilum Royale 'Downland'

- **Intermediate: 13°C (55°F)**
- **Easy to grow and flower**
- **Winter flowering**
- **Evergreen/no rest**

This hybrid is a seedling from the illustrious *P.* Paeony 'Regency' (AM/RHS) line, and has very large flowers, 15cm (6in) across, borne on long flower spikes. The flowers, which are an interesting colour combination of soft rose-red shaded with green, open in the winter.

The plant should be grown in the intermediate greenhouse, under warm and shady conditions with an even moisture. Annual repotting is recommended to maintain the compost in a fresh and open condition and thus ensure a steady rate of growth. When in bloom, these heavy flowers will need the support of a thin bamboo cane and green string tie, or a thin wire stake. The blooms will last for up to ten weeks on the plant, after which the stem should be cut and the plant encouraged to make its new growth for the following season.

This plant can be recommended for beginners to orchid growing provided a warm and shady position is available for it to thrive.

Above right: **Paphiopedilum Royale 'Downland'**
This is an excellent red-flowered variety for the intermediate house.

A practical hint
The cool-house varieties of orchids require a minimum winter temperature of 10°C (50°F), a maximum of 24°C (75°F), and an average of 16°C (60°F) to succeed.

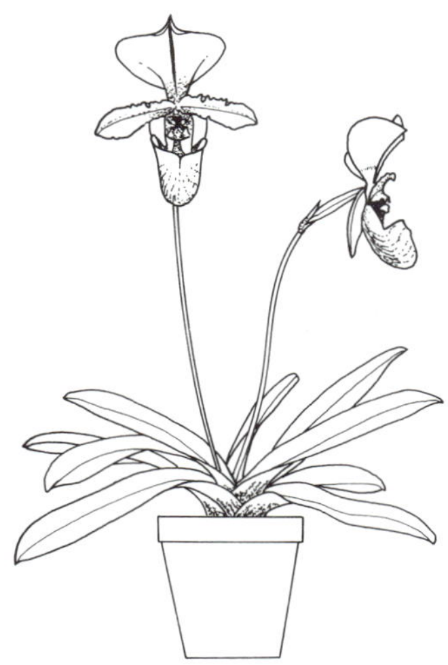

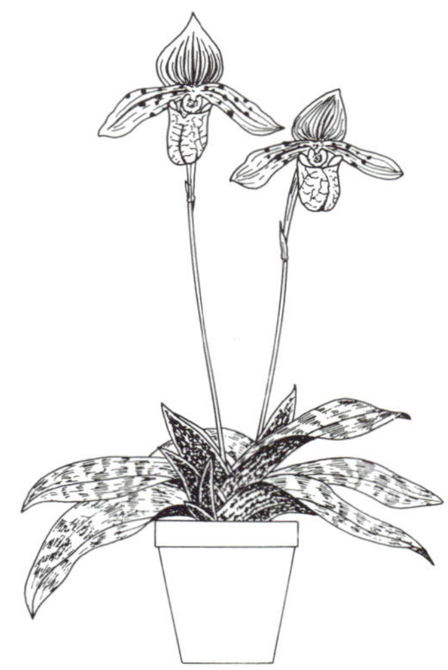

Paphiopedilum spiceranum

- **Cool/intermediate: 10-13°C (50-55°F)**
- **Moderately easy to grow**
- **Autumn/winter flowering**
- **Evergreen/no rest**

A native of Assam, this species has broad leaves with wavy margins, dark green above and spotted with purple underneath. In autumn and winter one or two 7.5cm (3in) flowers are borne on a 30cm (12in) stem. They are distinctive in markings and shape and play an important role in the breeding of hybrids. One notable feature of the otherwise bronze flower is the hooded white dorsal sepal, which carries a central purple stripe, a feature it has passed on to many of its hybrids.

An accommodating orchid, it will grow successfully in a cool or intermediate greenhouse, or in similar conditions indoors. This is a scarce species and good plants may be difficult to acquire. It is not as easy to grow as some *Paphiopedilum* species and should not be attempted by the beginner, who would do better to try a hybrid from it. The plant should be given shady conditions and kept moist all the year round with occasional light overhead spraying for good measure.

Above left:
Paphiopedilum spiceranum
This long-established species has been widely used to breed hybrids.

Paphiopedilum venustum

- **Intermediate: 13°C (55°F)**
- **Easy to grow and flower**
- **Spring flowering**
- **Evergreen/no rest**

The leaves of this species are heavily marbled with grey and green. One or, occasionally, two flowers, 7.5cm (3in) across, are borne on a 15-23cm (6-9in) stem. The petals and lip are basically yellow-green, tinged with rose-red, and the petals are slightly hairy. The dorsal sepal is white, strongly striped with green. The plant blooms in early spring.

This is an excellent choice for the intermediate greenhouse. The neat plant is attractive in and out of flower. The delightful flowers are showy and long-lasting. The species comes from the Himalayas and should be given shady conditions with a good fresh atmosphere. Regular repotting will ensure that the compost remains fresh and free-draining. This species, though still reasonably plentiful, has not been used in breeding new hybrids as extensively as a number of other paphiopedilums, and its influence is not noticeable in most of today's modern hybrids. An easy plant to grow and flower.

Left: **Paphiopedilum venustum**
An attractive compact-growing species for the intermediate house that flowers during the spring.

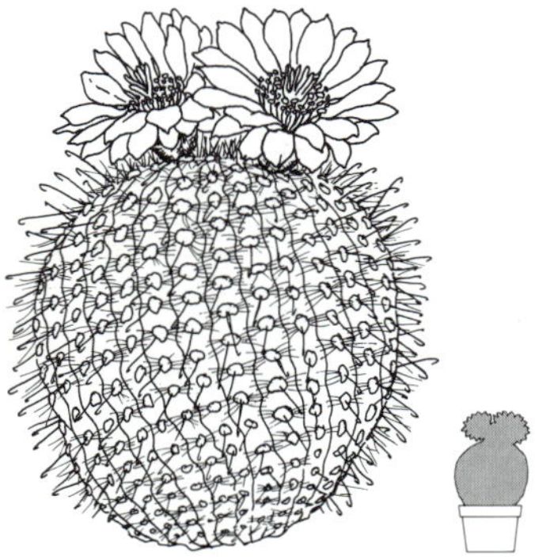

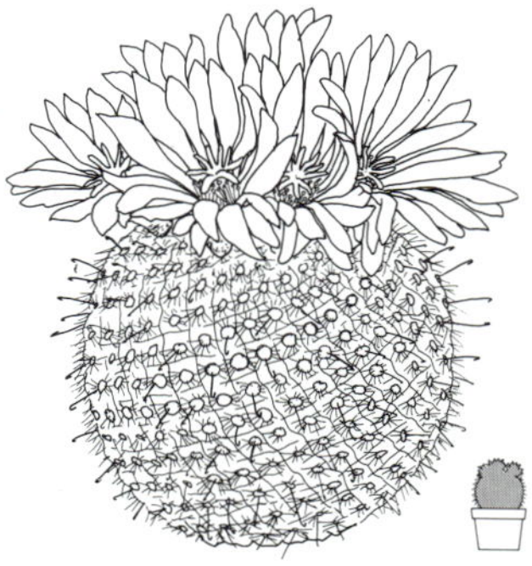

Parodia aureispina

- **Full sun**
- **Temp: 5-30°C (41-86°F)**
- **Water with great care**

Parodias are among the most beautiful of the South American cacti, but not the easiest to cultivate. They have a nasty habit of losing their roots for no apparent reason. They will regrow them but the cessation of growth can leave a scar.

Parodia aureispina is a beautiful golden ball; the spirally arranged ribs are densely covered with short yellow spines, at least one of which in each group is hooked. The large buttercup-yellow flowers are borne on top of the plant, and open during the summer. With age the plant becomes cylindrical and reaches a height of about 20cm (8in); some offsets will form.

A porous soil consisting of half loam-based potting mixture and half grit will ensure good drainage. Always allow the soil to dry out between waterings, and keep the plant dry during winter. Feed every two weeks with a high-potassium fertilizer when the buds form. Repot annually. Grow in a half-pot so that the roots are not surrounded by too much cold, wet soil.

Above: **Parodia aureispina**
This is a neat golden ball freely producing bright yellow flowers. Care with watering is necessary to avoid root loss. Summer flowering.

Parodia microsperma

- **Full sun**
- **Temp: 5-30°C (41-86°F)**
- **Water with care**

Parodia microsperma is globular when young, but with age it becomes elongated. It is a pale green plant with numerous spirally arranged ribs carrying many whitish spines. It will form some offsets, which may be used for propagating the plant. The golden-yellow flowers are about 5cm (2in) across and are carried on the top of the plant during the summer months.

Keep this plant in a sunny position and water it with care during the summer, allowing the soil to dry out before watering again. When buds form feed with a high-potassium fertilizer about every two weeks. Keep dry in winter. Grow in a half-pot in a mixture of one part loam-based mixture to one part grit. Repot annually. The only pests likely to attack parodias are mealy bug and root mealy bug. The odd mealy bug may be picked off with forceps but a bad infestation of either of these pests should be treated with a proprietary insecticide.A systemic one will deal more effectively with root mealy bug.

Above: **Parodia microsperma** var. **gigantea**
The typical form of P. microsperma *has yellow flowers. This red variety is possibly even more attractive.*

A practical hint
Feeding of cacti and succulents every 10 to 14 days is necessary in the summer, using a tomato-type fertilizer; but never feed plants in dry soil.

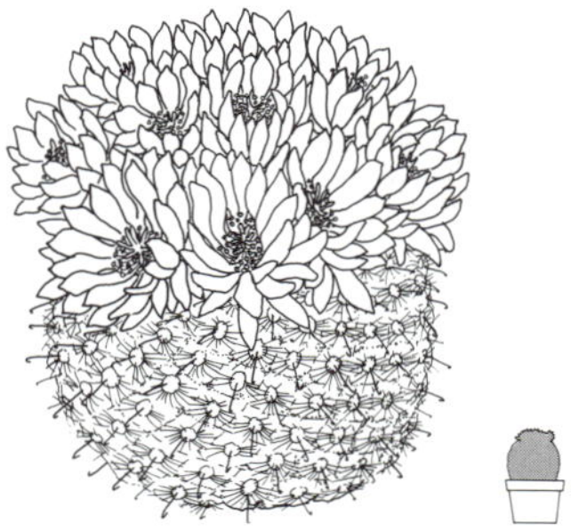

Parodia sanguiniflora

- **Full sun**
- **Temp: 5-30°C (41-86°F)**
- **Water with care**

Parodia sanguiniflora, true to its name, has large blood-red flowers. These open in summer, and make a change from the yellow flowers usual in parodias. As a young plant this cactus is globular, but it tends to become cylindrical with age. The numerous spirally arranged ribs carry many brownish spines, some of which are hooked. Some specimens form excessive numbers of offsets to the detriment of flowering. If this happens, restart the plant from an offset. For several years it will flower freely before starting to offset again.

Grow in an open potting mixture, one part loam-based medium to one part grit. Repot annually and inspect the roots for ashy deposits, which indicate root mealy bug; if found, wash off old soil and repot in a clean container. Always water parodias carefully, as they have a tendency to lose their roots if their growing medium becomes excessively wet. Feed with a high-potassium liquid fertilizer every two weeks when in flower. Keep dry during the winter.

Left: **Parodia sanguiniflora**
Brilliant red flowers up to 5cm (2in) across adorn this cactus during the summer months. Offsets can be detached and used for propagation.

A practical hint
Pelargoniums become ever more fascinating, and are now easily raised from seed, but may also be grown from cuttings.

Passiflora caerulea

- **Sunny location**
- **Temp: 10-16°C (50-60°F)**
- **Keep moist and fed**

This plant is a rampant grower that will need some form of support for the twining growth to attach itself to. Hardy out of doors in agreeable climates, but out or in the plant will give a better show of flowers if the roots are confined to a small space. If allowed a free root run it will tend to produce masses of foliage at the expense of flowers.

Sriking 7.5cm (3in) flowers intricately patterned in blue, white and purple appear in late summer and are followed by colourful orange-yellow fruits.

To do well this plant needs good light, ample watering while in active growth, and feeding with a fertilizer containing a high percentage of potash – a tomato food, for example. When potting is essential, use a loam-based mixture.

New plants can be raised from seed or cuttings in spring.

Right: **Passiflora caerulea**
This vigorous climbing plant will bloom when young and, where space permits, can be grown into a large specimen. Prune in spring to prevent the plant becoming straggly.

Above: **Pelargonium peltatum 'Rouletti'**
These trailing pelargoniums prefer more shade than the other types and are ideal for a hanging container. This is a bicoloured hybrid.

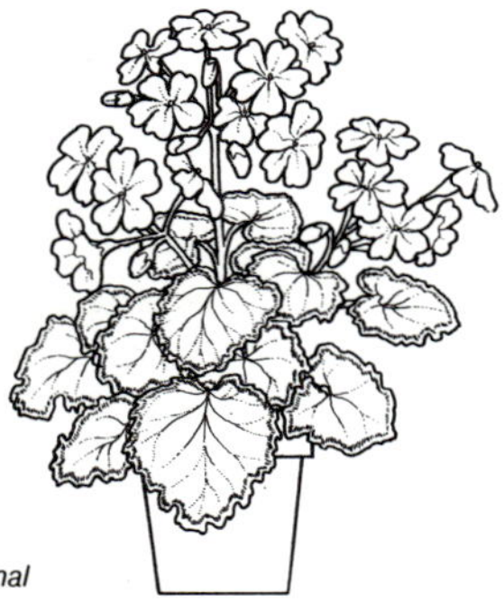

Zonal

Regal

Ivy-leaved

Below: **Pelargonium grandiflorum 'Fanny Eden'**
Abundant, multicoloured flowers up to 6.4cm (2.5in) across are produced by these popular hybrids during the summer months. Many colours.

Pelargonium

- **Sunny location**
- **Temp: 10-18°C (50-65°F)**
- **Keep moist; drier in winter**

Great favourites with many people, the pelargoniums come in three distinct types: zonals *(P. zonale)*; regals *(P. grandiflorum)*; and the ivy-leaved forms *(P. peltatum)*. Raise new plants from cuttings that have been removed from the parent plant for about twenty-four hours before being inserted in a peat-and-sand mixture. Cuttings taken in spring flower in the autumn and those taken in late summer/autumn will flower the following summer. Today, however, there is much more emphasis on raising plants from seed, and these do amazingly well.

There are pelargoniums for just about every indoor situation provided it offers ample light and the atmosphere is cool and airy. Use a loam-based mixture when potting. Never overwater.

Above: **Pelargonium zonale**
These long-established houseplants are distinguished by ring-marked leaves and compact clusters of single or double flowers borne clear of the foliage on long stems.

A practical hint

Aphids attack many potted plants and a sticky secretion on leaves is an indication of their presence; use an appropriate insecticide as recommended.

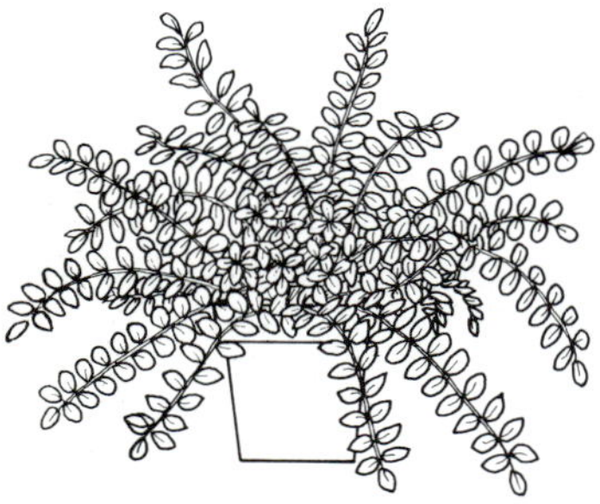

Pellaea rotundifolia

- **Shade**
- **Temp: 16-21°C (60-70°F)**
- **Keep moist**

The button fern has dark green rounded leaves attached to firm, wiry stems, and forms a dense, attractive plant.

When potting use a peaty mixture and shallow pans. Almost all ferns in small pots will quickly become root bound and will lose their vigour if not potted on. However, inspection of roots can be misleading as these are very dark brown and the colour of the peaty soil in which they are growing, so careful inspection is needed before potting on.

Potting is best done in spring or summer and the new container should be only a little larger than the last. Roots ought to be moistened before it is removed from the pot, and after potting the soil should be well enough watered for surplus to be seen draining through the holes in the base of the pot. Then keep the newly potted plant on the dry side for several weeks – careful judgement is needed, as excessive drying out of the peaty mixture can be fatal as far as ferns are concerned.

Above: **Pellaea rotundifolia**
The button fern has very dark green, rounded leaves that form into densely foliaged plants in a comparatively short time.

Pellionia daveauana

- **Light shade**
- **Temp: 13-21°C (55-70°F)**
- **Keep moist and fed**

Very easy plants to care for, and easy to propagate, yet they never seem to make the grade as indoor plants. This is rather odd, as they adapt very well as hanging plants, or do well as a creeper, in the bottle garden, or simply as an addition to the windowsill collection. Leaves are oval-shaped and produced in quantity, and they have an interesting colouring of brown and dull yellow.

To propagate new plants, remove pieces of stem, any section, about 7.5cm (3in) long, and put four or five of these in small pots of peaty houseplant soil. Cuttings can go direct into hanging pots or small baskets if desired. When they get under way, remove the tips to encourage the plant to branch out. It is essential that plants be kept moist and warm, and out of direct sunlight. When potting on becomes necessary one of the many peaty houseplant potting mixtures will suit them fine, but avoid using very large pots.

Above right: **Pellionia daveauana**
Naturally hanging or creeping plants that are easy to care for. Leaves are about 5cm (2in) in length and multicoloured. Take cuttings.

A practical hint
Watch for blackish scale insects clinging to stems and leaves of aphelandra, and wipe off with a malathion-soaked sponge.

A practical hint
Primula obconica is a very easy plant that will sometimes flower throughout the year, but can cause irritation to sensitive skin.

Pentas lanceolata

- **Good light**
- **Temp: 16-21°C (60-70°F)**
- **Keep moist and fed**

Though not often supplied by growers, this is a fine plant that can be seen in better plant collections. Plants can be started from new shoots about 10cm (4in) in length taken in the spring and placed in a peaty mixture – a warm propagating case will encourage rooting. Once rooted well, the small pots of cuttings should be transferred to slightly larger pots. Place drainage material in the bottom of the new pot before adding loam-based mixture and some grit for improved drainage.

As they develop, remove the growing tips of the young plants. This will encourage a compact habit and prevent the plants growing too tall. Keep the plants in good light and feed regularly and water well while actively growing. Keep potbound to encourage flowering.

Peperomia argyreia

- **Light shade**
- **Temp: 13-18°C (55-65°F)**
- **Keep moist and fed**

Sadly, this is one of the older houseplants that is not seen so frequently these days. The leaves are an interesting grey-green colour with darker stripes that radiate from the centre of the leaf. The darker stripes give the plant its name of Rugby football plant.

These compact plants should be grown in shallow pans of soilless potting mixture. The location must be light, with protection from direct sunlight. Watering should be done with care; err on the side of dry rather than wet conditions. Established plants can be given weak liquid fertilizer with every watering from early spring to late summer, but none in winter. Sound leaves can be removed and cut into quarters that are placed in upright position in pure peat in warm conditions. The quartered leaf will produce roots and eventually leaves along the length of the cut edge below soil level. During propagation, ensure that the cuttings do not become too wet.

Above left: **Pentas lanceolata**
Bright clusters of flowers appear on this shrub during autumn and winter. Colours available include magenta, pink, lavender and white.

Left: **Peperomia argyreia**
With dark green markings on a silvery-grey background this is one of the most attractive of peperomias. Leaves have a natural shine.

Peperomia caperata

- **Light shade**
- **Temp: 16-21°C (60-70°F)**
- **Never overwater**

This plant is neat and compact and ideally suited to growing on the windowsill, where it will not become entangled with curtains. Leaves are a blackish green in colour, and have an undulating surface. The rounded leaves are attached to long stalks that sprout directly from soil level.

Cuttings made by inserting individual leaves in peaty mixture will root with little trouble if a temperature in excess of 18°C (65°F) can be maintained. Rooted leaves produce clusters of small plants that should be potted into peaty houseplant soil when large enough to handle. Small pots should be used initially and plants ought to be gradually potted on from one size container to the next. Also, when potting low-growing plants of this kind, it is important not to select pots of full depth; shallower pans (or half pots) are now freely available. After potting, the soil should be kept on the dry side and plants should not be fed for at least three months.

Above: **Peperomia caperata**
The small leaves of this neat plant are produced in abundance and are a rich dark green in colour. A further attraction is their rough surface.

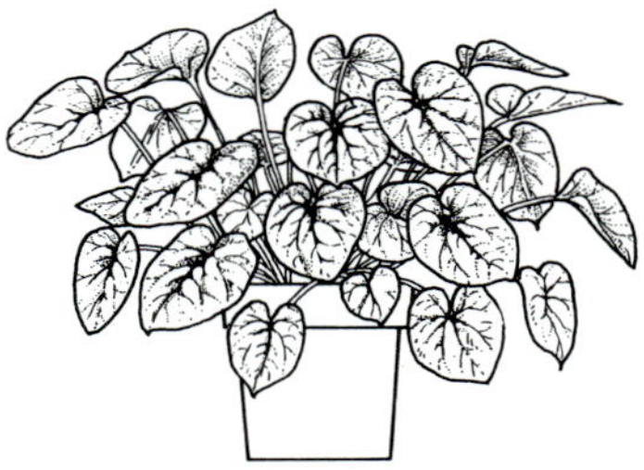

Peperomia hederaefolia

- **Light shade**
- **Temp: 16-21°C (60-70°F)**
- **Keep moist and fed**

Unusual glossy grey colouring sets *P. hederaefolia* apart from most other indoor plants. Stalked leaves are rounded in shape and emerge from soil level, there being no stem to speak of. At one time a great favourite in the houseplant league it now seems to have waned a little, probably resulting from other more interesting plants coming along to take its place. One of its main benefits lies in the fact that it occupies little space and is ideal for including in small planted arrangements of plants. Carboys are the typical example of close grouping that requires small plants that are not too invasive. Vigorous plants will quickly invade the growing space of every plant in the container.

This peperomia will enjoy a watering routine that allows the soil to dry out, but not bone dry, between each watering. It will also respond well to frequent weak feeds, but needs no feeding and less water in winter.

Above: **Peperomia hederaefolia**
Glossy, grey-coloured leaves are produced in quantity but remain small in size to form neat and compact plants that are easy care.

Peperomia magnoliaefolia

- **Good light**
- **Temp: 16-21°C (60-70°F)**
- **Keep on dry side**

The common name and the thick fleshy leaves give some clues regarding the care of this neat and colourful little plant. The succulent fleshy leaves indicate that they are capable of holding a considerable amount of water, to withstand arid conditions.

The quickest way of killing this plant is to keep it in poor light and on the cold side, and to have the soil very wet. One of the most important requirements will be to ensure that the soil dries out between each watering. Stem rot followed in all probability by the fungus disease botrytis will be the inevitable result of keeping plants too wet for too long.

Feeding is not important, but will have to be done occasionally – preferably not in winter and never in heavy doses. But in respect of nutrition there is one very important need, and that is, when potting plants on into larger containers, to use soilless potting mixture; anything else would be fatal.

Above: **Peperomia magnoliaefolia**
Most popular of the peperomias, with glossy leaves that are brightly cream and green variegated. Leaves are fleshy and retain a lot of moisture.

A practical hint
Succulents will benefit if their pots are turned when they are growing towards one sunny aspect, rather than have the same side always to the sun.

Pereskia aculeata

- **Full sun**
- **Temp: 10-30°C (50-86°F)**
- **Keep slightly moist in winter**

With this plant you will have difficulty in persuading your friends that it is a cactus at all. Pereskias are the most un-cactus-like of all cacti, but their spine formation and flower structure prove their identity. This plant is scarcely succulent at all; with its large privet-like leaves and slightly spiny long trailing stems, it somewhat resembles a wild rose. The leaves are bright green, but the variety *godseffiana* (often called *Pereskia godseffiana*) has reddish tinged leaves. The stems will need supporting in some way, with sticks or a plant trellis. In a greenhouse it can be trained up and along the roof, but the rather higher winter temperature needed makes it difficult for the cool greenhouse. Indoors, it should thrive in a light window, large enough to accommodate its stems.

Pinkish flowers, rather like those of a wild rose and about 4.5cm (1.8in) across, appear in autumn, but only on large plants. Water freely in spring and summer and feed occasionally.

Left: **Pereskia aculeata**
Almost like a wild rose, this is a strange non-succulent cactus. It definitely needs some support and protection from winter cold.

Persea gratissima

- **Good light**
- **Temp: 16-21°C (60-70°F)**
- **Keep moist and fed**

The foliage is green, coarse, and not particularly attractive, but there is the fascination of growing plants from the central stone of the fruit and no doubt a sense of achievement exists that encourages one to hang on to the plant. Very often they are left to become tall and ungainly when it would be better to pinch out the early growing tips of the plant to encourage it to branch out and adopt a better shape. Plants will also be thin and poor in appearance if they are allowed to languish in dark corners: good light is needed, but offer some protection from direct sunlight.

Raising plants from stones is relatively easy. Four cocktail sticks are pushed into the stone evenly spaced, and the stone is then suspended in a tumbler with the base submerged in about 5cm (2in) of water; in time the base of the stone will soften and roots will form in the water. When lots of roots are present the stone is potted in peaty soil.

Above: **Persea gratissima**
A novelty plant that will rapidly become leggy if it is not pruned when young. Keep warm and humid.

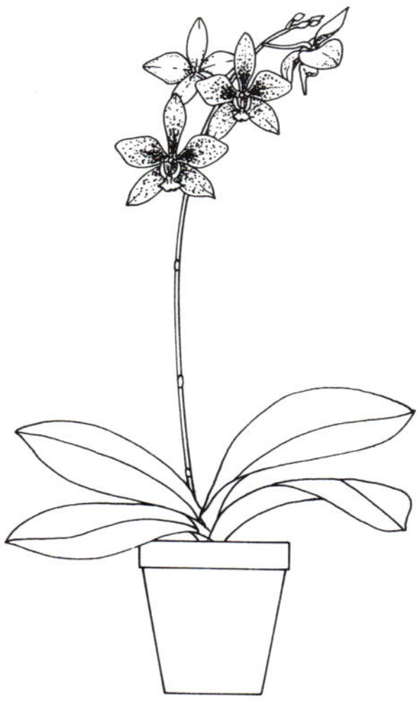

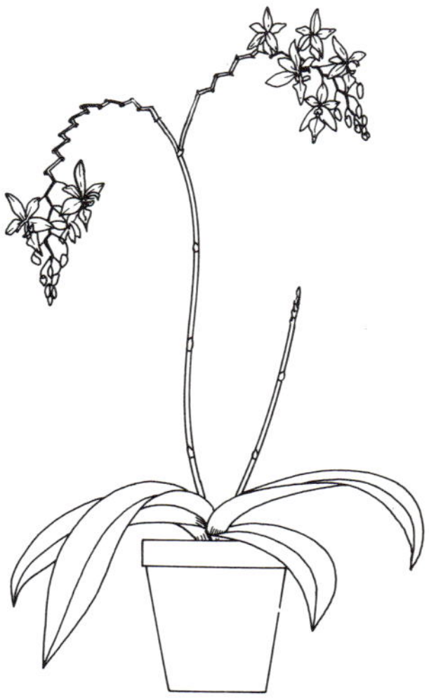

Phalaenopsis Barbara Moler

- **Warm: 18-21°C (65-70°F)**
- **Easy to grow and flower**
- **Spring/autumn flowering**
- **Evergreen/no rest**

P. Barbara Moler is a comparatively compact grower, with leaves some 30cm (12in) long and 10cm (4in) wide. The flower spikes, which are long – up to 45cm (18in) – and branched, bear flowers for many months from spring to autumn. Individually, the flowers are 7cm (2.75in) across, and of very heavy texture. There are two colour forms. The best-known is white with heavy pink spotting, giving an overall appearance of rich pink. The second form can best be described as yellow; the base colour is greenish-yellow overlaid with yellow-chestnut blotches.

P. Barbara Moler is already proving to be a very important parent in breeding for heavy texture and new colour breaks. *P.* Space Queen is an example of the type of hybrid produced from *P.* Barbara Moler breeding.

This plant thrives in warm, shady conditions and should be kept evenly moist throughout the year. It should not be grown in too large a pot for the size of the plant.

Left: **Phalaenopsis Barbara Moler**
This warm-house hybrid produces sprays of flowers in the spring. It will also grow in an indoor case.

Phalaenopsis equestris

- **Warm: 18-21°C (65-70°F)**
- **Easy to grow and flower**
- **Autumn/winter flowering**
- **Evergreen/no rest**

This species is said to be the commonest phalaenopsis of the Philippines. The plant is comparatively compact in growth and has leathery, dull green leaves some 15cm (6in) long and 7.5cm (3in) wide. The very graceful arching flower spikes bear pale rose flowers, 2.5cm (1in) across, with a darker oval lip. The flowers open in autumn and winter.

P. equestris was used as a parent to produce the first manmade hybrid phalaenopsis, *P.* Artemis, in 1892. It still plays a part in modern hybridizing where compact, small-flowered plants are in demand.

This plant is suitable for a warm greenhouse, or being a compact grower, it will be easily accommodated in an indoor growing case. It can be grown in a pot or, with equal success, in a basket, or it can be mounted on bark for hanging in a shady place. Exposure to full sun will quickly scorch the tough leathery foliage. It should be kept evenly moist throughout the year and lightly sprayed in summer.

Above: **Phalaenopsis equestris**
A miniature species for the warm house or indoor growing case. It is an extremely free-flowering variety.

A practical hint
A temperature of 18°C (65°F) will suit the warm-house orchids as a night minimum, but it is preferable to operate at a few degrees higher.

Phalaenopsis Hennessy

- **Warm: 18-21°C (65-70°F)**
- **Easy to grow and flower**
- **Varied flowering season**
- **Evergreen/no rest**

This hybrid is an example of a peppermint-striped phalaenopsis. The plant is very free-flowering, blooming throughout the year, and the branched spikes may bear up to 30 flowers at a time. The individual flowers are 9-12cm (3.5-4.75in) across, white to light pink in basic colour, with red or pink stripes or, in some forms, spots. The lip varies in colour from deep rosy pink to orange.

This hybrid type is of fairly recent breeding, and the plants are in limited supply. From a particular cross, only a percentage of the seedlings will carry the elusive candy-striped markings that are highly valued to increase the variety within the genus. *Phalaenopsis* flowers are highly susceptible to damp conditions, when premature spotting of the flowers will occur. A movement of air from an electric fan combined with a drier atmosphere while the plants are in bloom will help to prevent this common problem. The plants will also suffer if given poor light during the winter.

Above right: **Phalaenopsis Hennessy 'Candy Striped'**
An outstanding hybrid for the warm house. Flowers at various times.

Phalaenopsis lueddemanniana

- **Warm: 18-21°C (65-70°F)**
- **Easy to grow and flower**
- **Spring/summer flowering**
- **Evergreen/no rest**

This free-flowering species is easy to grow and one of the most variable of the *Phalaenopsis* genus. The leaves are usually light green, broad and long. The flower spikes, several of which may be produced at the same time, each carry 20 or so 2.5cm (1in) flowers that open in succession throughout spring and summer. The sepals and petals are white or yellow, marked with bars or spots ranging from pink to deep purple, and the small lip is usually purple. If the plant is given cooler and more shady conditions when the first buds appear, richer colours will be produced. The flower spikes readily produce plantlets at their nodes.

The species has been widely used in breeding with great success, two of the best-known hybrids from *P. lueddemanniana* being *P.* Golden Sands and *P.* Cabrillo Star. As the name suggests, *P.* Golden Sands is a fine yellow hybrid, and *P.* Cabrillo Star is a large white bloom heavily spotted with red.

It likes warm, shady conditions.

Right:
Phalaenopsis lueddemanniana
This free-flowering species will grow easily in warm surroundings.

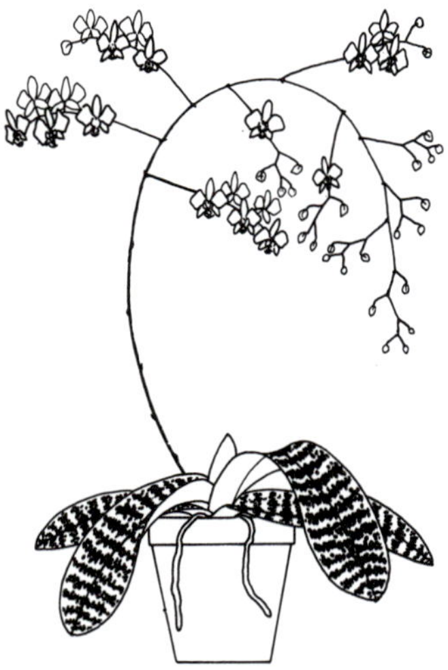

Phalaenopsis schillerana

- **Warm: 18-21°C (65-70°F)**
- **Easy to grow and flower**
- **Spring flowering**
- **Evergreen/no rest**

The best-known phalaenopsis, and held in great esteem. It was discovered in Manila in 1858 growing on trees, often very high up. The plants fix themselves to the branches and trunks by numerous flattened roots. In cultivation these roots grow to considerable lengths along any firm surface within their reach, and are almost impossible to release without breaking. As they mature they develop a beautiful silver sheen.

As a decorative plant, *P. schillerana* is hard to beat; the handsome leaves, up to 45cm (18in) or more in length, are deep green, marbled and blotched with grey and silver. The flowers, 5-7.5cm (2-3in) across, of a delicate rose purple, are often borne in great numbers during early spring on a branched arching spike, which may grow to 90cm (3ft) in length.

The plant has been used extensively in breeding and is responsible for producing many of the fine pink hybrids that are available today.

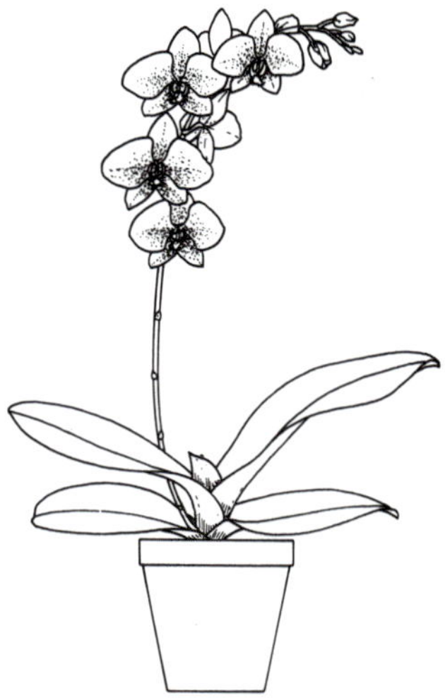

Phalaenopsis Space Queen

- **Warm: 18-21°C (65-70°F)**
- **Easy to grow and flower**
- **Varied flowering season**
- **Evergreen/no rest**

Crossing *P.* Barbara Moler with *P.* Temple Cloud has produced this hybrid with beautiful flowers of heavy substance, 9-10cm (3.5-4in) across, soft pink or white, heavily spotted with red.

This plant is a strong, robust grower which, when grown to perfection, can be expected to bloom twice a year. *Phalaenopsis* plants must not be allowed to get cold, and if the minimum recommended temperature of 18°C (65°F) or, better still, 21°C (70°F) cannot be maintained easily throughout the winter, it is better not to attempt to grow them. These beautiful orchids should be given a warm section on their own. In these conditions they are not difficult to grow, and most of the cultural problems encountered are the result of insufficient heat. Even when grown in pots, *Phalaenopsis* will make a number of long aerial roots that will meander along the staging for up to 90cm (3ft). Wherever possible these roots should be left undisturbed.

Left: **Phalaenopsis schillerana**
A superb species for the warm greenhouse. It has lovely mottled foliage and flowers in the spring.

Above:
Phalaenopsis Space Queen
Large flowers are produced on long sprays at various times. Keep warm.

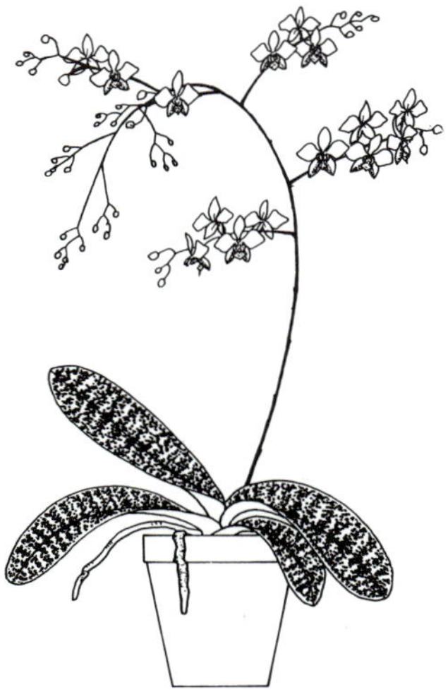

Phalaenopsis stuartiana

- **Warm: 18-21°C (65-70°F)**
- **Easy to grow and flower**
- **Spring flowering**
- **Evergreen/no rest**

This species is very similar to *P. schillerana,* and when not in flower they are virtually impossible to tell apart: the foliage is the same deep green, marbled in grey and silver, and the roots have the same flattened appearance. In the wild it is said to be found always closely associated with water, sometimes close to the shoreline, where the plants are subjected to salt-water spray.

The spike habit and quantity of flowers are also like those of *P. schillerana,* but in *P. stuartiana* the upper sepal and two side petals are white. Of the two lower sepals one half is white and the other heavily spotted with reddish-purple; the orange-yellow lip is also spotted. The overall appearance when in flower is thus distinct and striking.

Many hybrids have been registered from this species, all showing the characteristic spotting, and it is valuable for introducing orange shades to the lip when crossed with white hybrids.

Thrives in warmth and shade.

Above: **Phalaenopsis stuartiana**
Tall, branching flower sprays are produced in the spring. A lovely, easy to grow warm-house species.

Phalaenopsis Temple Cloud

- **Warm: 18°C (65°F)**
- **Easy to grow and flower**
- **Varied flowering season**
- **Evergreen/no rest**

Resulting from the crossing of two outstanding hybrids, *P.* Opaline and *P.* Keith Shaffer, this hybrid took on the finer points of both parents, producing pure white 11.5cm (4.5in) round blooms of heavy texture, and in turn proved to be a very successful parent. It can be in flower at any season.

Like all the other modern *Phalaenopsis* hybrids it is not difficult to grow and can be in bloom for months at a time provided it is given plenty of warmth. This important factor makes it ideal for growing in an indoor case, where the high temperatures required can be more easily achieved. It is a shade-loving or low light plant, which enables it to be successfully grown and flowered in artificial light conditions. The plant should be grown in as small a pot as possible, in a free-draining bark compost. It should be fed at every third watering for most of the year, and never be allowed to dry out completely.

The flowers can be cut and used for flower arrangements.

Right:
Phalaenopsis Temple Cloud
A pure white hybrid for the warm house. Varied flowering times.

Phalaenopsis violacea

- **Warm: 18-21°C (65-70°F)**
- **Moderately easy to grow**
- **Summer flowering**
- **Evergreen/no rest**

First discovered in 1859, this species has two distinct types, one from Borneo, the other from Malaya. Although it may not be the easiest species to maintain in good flowering condition, it is nevertheless very attractive, as it combines beauty with fragrance. The 7.5cm (3in) flowers of the Borneo type have the fragrance of violets and are borne in summer on a short pendulous spike, often in succession. The flowers of the Malaysian form are smaller and of a fuller shape, about 6.5cm (2.6in) across. The plant requires deep shade and high humidity.

The first hybrid, *P. violacea* x *P. amabilis,* was registered by James Veitch in 1887 as *P.* Harrietiae. In recent years, *P. violacea* has been used extensively in breeding, with great success.

Today, this plant is practically unobtainable from the wild. However, selected varieties are being raised from seed and these young plants are more easily grown than wild imports.

Thrives in warmth and shade.

Above: **Phalaenopsis violacea**
This warm-house species produces fragrant, long-lasting flowers in summer. Many hybrids available.

A practical hint
There are foliage plants that suffer if water, especially cold water, is allowed to get onto the leaves; check the needs of plants before spraying.

Philodendron bipinnatifidum

- **Shade**
- **Temp: 16-21°C (60-70°F)**
- **Keep wet and fed**

There are numerous philodendrons of similar type to this one, all requiring ample space for their radiating leaves once they reach maturity. Because of their habit of growth these are essentially individual plants to be placed on their own rather than as part of a collection. Leaves are glossy green in colour and deeply cut along their margins, and held on stout petioles attached to very solid short trunks. In time aerial roots will be produced from the trunk; direct these into the pot soil when they are long enough. With older plants it may be necessary to remove some of these aerial roots, or they can be allowed to trail into a dish of water placed alongside.

Ample watering is a must, with marginally less being given in winter; and feeding should not be neglected. When potting on use a mixture containing some loam, as these are quite greedy plants. Most of them are raised from seed and young plants are usually available.

Right:
Philodendron bipinnatifidum
Weedy plants when young but becoming most majestic with age.

Philodendron hastatum

- **Shade**
- **Temp: 16-21°C (60-70°F)**
- **Keep moist and fed**

Again we have a touch of majesty from the splendid Araceae family of plants, and the common name immediately gives the game away that this is a rather large plant. The leaves are broadly arrow-shaped, glossy green and attached to very bold, tall-growing stems; in a greenhouse it may reach a height of 6m (20ft). Normally indoor growth is thinner and less robust, but the fact that the plant has a tough constitution makes it a reasonably trouble-free plant in agreeable conditions.

As a young plant it will trail, but it is much too important for this style of growing and when purchasing one you should also acquire a moss-covered support (preferably one that can be extended) to which the plant can be tied. If the moss is kept moist by regular spraying with water from a mister it will be found that in time the natural aerial roots of the plant will grow around and into the moss. Leaves can be occasionally wiped with a damp cloth to clean them.

Above: **Philodendron hastatum**
Glossy green leaves are broadly arrow-shaped. Plants attain stately proportions and need support.

Philodendron scandens

- **Shade**
- **Temp: 16-21°C (60-70°F)**
- **Keep moist and fed**

One of the smallest-leaved of all the philodendrons and possibly the best suited to the relatively smaller rooms of today. The leaves are heart-shaped and glossy green, and it may be encouraged to either climb or trail.

Keeping the soil moist, not saturated, is important, and occasional weak feeding will suit it well. Young plants should be potted into soilless potting mixture, but older plants will respond better if potted into a mix that contains a small proportion of loam. In ideal conditions plants may be potted at almost any time, but in the average home they will do much better if the potting can be done at the start of the summer. I am often asked for plant suggestions for dark corners and the questioner invariably wants something colourful. But such plants are few and far between; it is better to select green foliage for difficult spots, and the sweetheart plant is ideal in most cases.

Above: **Philodendron scandens**
The well-known sweetheart plant has heart-shaped leaves that are deep green in colour.

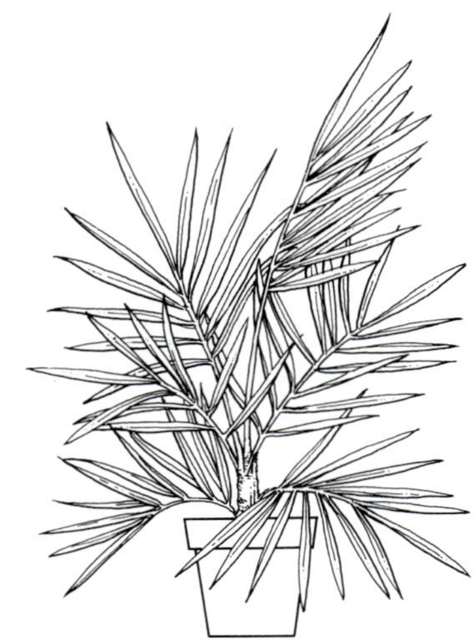

Phoenix canariensis

- **Good light**
- **Temp: 16-21°C (60-70°F)**
- **Keep moist**

In their tropical habitat these stately palms will grow to 9-12m (30-40ft) in height, but they are less vigorous when their roots are confined to pots. Leaves are coarse and open, and attached to short, stout trunks. Leaves have short petioles armed with vicious short spines, which make it necessary to handle the plant with care. Older plants are normally beyond the purse of the average person, so seek out plants of more modest size when shopping.

Smaller plants can be potted on into loam-based potting soil. Good drainage is essential, so broken flower pots or some other form of drainage material ought to be placed in the bottom of the pot before any soil is introduced. Well-drained soil is needed, but regular and thorough watering will be of the utmost importance while plants are actively growing. During growth, feed plants at regular intervals using a proprietary fertilizer and following the maker's directions.

Above: **Phoenix canariensis**
A tough tropical palm with coarse foliage and a solid, gnarled trunk that becomes a principal feature.

A practical hint
Removal of the top 2.5cm (1in) of soil and replacing with fresh will benefit all plants in spring as an alternative to repotting. This is called 'topdressing'.

Phoenix roebelinii

- **Good light**
- **Temp: 16-21°C (60-70°F)**
- **Keep moist**

Not unlike *P. canariensis* as a young plant, but later more feathery and delicate and less coarse in appearance. It is also less robust, retains its shape better, and will attain a height of around 1.5m (5ft) when grown.

Select loam-based potting mixture with some body to it. Good drainage will ensure that the soil in the pot will remain fresh and well aerated, which is essential if palm roots are not to rot and die. During the summer, plants can go out of doors in a sheltered, sunny location.

Not many pests bother this plant, but the ubiquitous red spider will usually be lurking around if the growing conditions tend to be very hot and dry. One should suspect their presence if plants become harder in appearance and develop paler colouring than usual. Some insecticides are harmful to palm plants, therefore it is wise to check suitability with your supplier before purchasing.

Right: **Phoenix roebelenii**
When mature these palms are among the most impressive of all foliage plants, with fine leaves radiating from a central stem.

Pilea cadierei nana

- Light shade
- Temp: 16-21°C (60-70°F)
- Keep moist and fed

With silvered foliage, this is by far the most popular of the pileas, but there are numerous others, all needing similar treatment.

Plants are started from cuttings taken at any time of the year if temperatures of around 18°C (65°F) and moist, close conditions can be provided. A simple propagating case on the windowsill can offer just these conditions. Top cuttings with four to six leaves are taken, the bottom pair is removed and the end of the stem is treated with rooting powder before up to seven cuttings are inserted in each small pot filled with a peaty mixture. Once cuttings have got under way the growing tips are removed and the plants are potted on into slightly larger containers in loam-based mixture.

Plants should have ample light, but not be exposed to bright sunlight. Although small, pileas need ample feeding during the growing months, if they are to retain their bright colouring.

Left: **Pilea cadierei nana**
Foliage of the aluminium plant is generously speckled with silver. Regular pinching out of the growing tips will produce neat plants.

Pilea involucrata

(P. spruceana)

- Light shade
- Temp: 16-21°C (60-70°F)
- Keep moist and fed

The friendship plant has reddish-brown colouring, and is easy to propagate; it may have acquired its common name as a result of surplus plants being distributed around the neighbourhood.

Several other pileas may be propagated with equal ease, and one or two of them will further oblige by producing an abundance of seed that will pop about in all directions when ripe, with the result that all the other pots surrounding the seeding pilea will provide a welcome bed of moist soil for the seed to germinate in. It will be wise to treat these as weeds and remove them before they take over the living room.

The friendship plant provides a neatly rounded, low-growing plant with an unusual colouring. It keeps its neat appearance for perhaps two years indoors and then begins to develop longer and more straggly stems, which spoil the plants' appearance; it could then be wise to start again with fresh cuttings.

Above: **Pilea involucrata**
Sometimes known as the friendship plant because its ease of propagation makes its distribution among friends a simple matter.

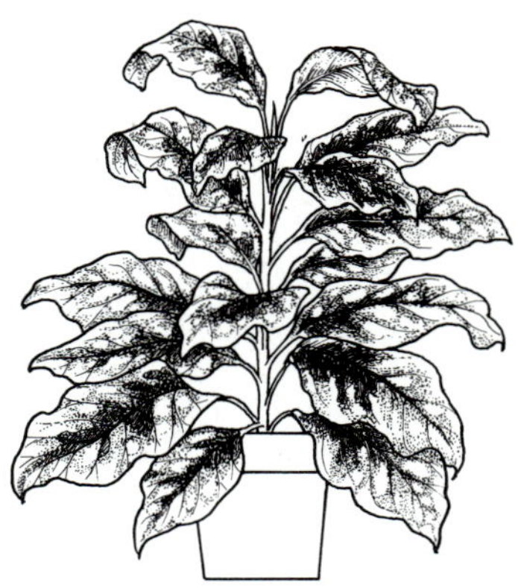

Piper ornatum

- **Good light**
- **Temp: 18-24°C (65-75°F)**
- **Keep moist**

The waxy leaves are 7.5-10cm (3-4in) long, deep green in colour and beautifully marked in silvery pink. Provide plants with a light framework onto which they can be trained so that they are seen to full effect.

Warmth is essential, and the air around the plant must not become too dry; spray leaves with tepid water from a hand mister. When potting on, avoid large pots; these plants prefer pots in proportion to the top growth. Soilless potting mixture suits them best, but it will be important to ensure that the plant is fed regularly (not in winter) and that soil never becomes too dry. Very wet conditions will be equally harmful, so allow some drying out between waterings. Plants lose much of their colouring if grown in dark corners. Provide good light but avoid direct sunlight.

Firm leaves with a piece of stem attached can be rooted in peat in warm conditions during spring in a propagating case.

Pisonia brunoniana variegata

- **Good light**
- **Temp: 16-21°C (60-70°F)**
- **Keep moist and fed**

These small tropical trees are useful plants with leaves about 30cm (12in) long, closely grouped on firm, upright stems. They have a neat habit of growth and attractively variegated leaves.

Good light with some protection from direct sunlight is necessary if plants are to retain their colourful variegation. To keep them in good fettle a reasonable, stable temperature is also needed. During the growing months plants require much more water than in winter, when care will be needed to ensure that the soil is never excessively wet; wet conditions at this time will cause roots to rot, with consequent loss of the lower leaves. Feeding is not necessary in winter, but should not be neglected for active plants.

New plants can be made from stem sections with one or two leaves attached, taken in spring; put them into small pots of peat, and place in a heated propagator. Use loam-based soil for growing on.

Above: **Piper ornatum**
This tropical vine can be grown upright or allowed to trail from a hanging container. It needs warmth and moderate humidity to thrive.

Right:
Pisonia brunoniana variegata
This striking plant for warm, humid conditions grows to about 120cm (4ft) in a pot. Good indirect light.

Pittosporum eugenioides

- **Good light**
- **Temp: 13-21°C (55-70°F)**
- **Keep moist and fed**

In the course of my duties it is almost inevitable that I should have favourite plants. For at least 20 years I have supervised the care of a pair of *P. eugenioides* plants that are now in the region of 3m (10ft) high and of full and attractive appearance. The pots in which they are growing are little more than 38cm (15in) in diameter – much too small, in the opinion of most plant growers, but my plants are superb and are sustained solely on regular feeding throughout the year, with the exception of the winter months. These plants seem to prove conclusively that plant pots of enormous size are not really necessary if the culture is correct.

The colouring of the leaves, which have attractively waved margins, is predominantly grey with a little white relief, and leaves are attached to firm, wiry stems. Good light is necessary and one must avoid excessive watering in winter to prevent browning of leaf margins.

Above: **Pittosporum eugenioides**
With grey-and-white variegated foliage, these are essentially pot plants for the cooler location indoors. Good light is an important need.

Pittosporum tenuifolium

- **Good light**
- **Temp: 7-18°C (45-65°F)**
- **Keep moist and fed**

This is much used for flower arrangements by florists. Bright green leaves have wavy margins, and the black stems provide an interesting contrast. They are quite colourful, develop a neat, bushy shape, and will tolerate cooler conditions and enjoy them rather than object by shedding leaves.

Start off small plants in peaty mixture, but from the 13cm (5in) size pot and upwards a loam-based mixture will be better. As these plants like fresh air and sunshine, pot them into decorative patio planters rather than the more conventional flower pot, and put them out of doors in summer.

On taking them in again it is fatal to place them immediately in darker areas; have them as near to a natural light source as possible where the conditions will be cool and airy.

Trimming off pieces of the plant for flower arrangments will be beneficial provided one is not too severe. Trimmed plants become bushier.

Above: **Pittosporum tenuifolium 'Irene Patterson'**
One of the many improved forms of the New Zealand pittosporums. Good for cool and light locations.

A practical hint
Ivies in many forms do well in cool, airy rooms; but out of doors is advisable in summer. Older, less attractive plants can be planted in the garden.

Platycerium alcicorne

(Platycerium bifurcatum)

- **Shade**
- **Temp: 16-21°C (60-70°F)**
- **Keep moist**

Essential requirements of all platyceriums are moist, warm and shaded conditions, and if one cannot offer all three of those then it will be difficult to grow these plants.

Plants are normally grown in pots filled with peat mixture and will seldom do well in anything that is too heavy and root-restricting. But besides the conventional pot they may be grown as mobiles, or for hanging on a wall. The plant is removed from its pot and the roots are wrapped in fresh sphagnum moss before the complete bundle is firmly secured to its support: plastic-covered wire is useful for this purpose. The plant can then be soaked thoroughly in a bucket of water and allowed to drain before it is put in position. Subsequent watering should follow the same lines.

Scale insects attaching themselves to all parts of the plant are by far the worst pest, and should be wiped off with a firm sponge that has been soaked in insecticide.

Plectranthus oertendahlii

- **Good light**
- **Temp: 16-21°C (60-70°F)**
- **Keep moist and fed**

This easy-care indoor plant is fine for hanging pots or baskets. Rounded leaves are a mottled bronze to green in colour and are crenated around their margins. Stems are square rather than round and become woody in time. Off-white flowers appear in the autumn.

As these plants age they lose much of their appearance; therefore it is wise to remove and propagate stem sections from the tip of the plant periodically; they should be 7.5-10cm (3-4in) in length and will be little trouble to root in a propagator using a standard houseplant potting mix. Five cuttings should be placed around the outer rim of each 7.5cm (3in) pot, and these should subsequently be potted on into larger hanging containers. To get a compact shape, pinch out the tips of shoots. This species is very easy to care for. Older plants should be discarded in favour of younger stock.

Above: **Platycerium alcicorne**
The foliage has a bluish-coloured bloom that adds much to the appearance of this fern. Broad fronds hold the plant in place.

Right: **Plectranthus oertendahlii**
Easy to grow and adorned with spikes of flowers in autumn, this plant needs frequent pruning to retain a neat shape. Take cuttings.

A practical hint
To propagate orchid pseudobulbs plant them firmly in small pots of potting soil, place in a heated propagator and keep surroundings moist.

Pleione formosana

- **Very cool: 4.5°C (40°F)**
- **Easy to grow and flower**
- **Spring flowering**
- **Deciduous/dry rest**

Until recently orchid growers had not taken this genus seriously, unlike the alpine growers, who cultivate pleiones with great success. The 20 known species are found growing close to the snowline of the Himalayas, and also in parts of China and Formosa. The Himalayan species are probably better suited to the conditions of an alpine house, but others do well in the cool section of an orchid house.

The plant consists of a single, squat, roundish pseudobulb, which lasts for only one year. New growth springs from the base of the pseudobulb, and in its early stages produces a flower spike from its centre. This spike bears one or two flowers, up to 10cm (4in) across. The common species has flowers ranging from pure white to pale pinky-mauve. In all variations the broad lip is frilled, and in the coloured forms it is spotted with red-purple.

In the early spring the plants should be taken from their pot, and reset about half-buried in a fine but well-draining compost.

Above right: **Pleione formosana**
Will grow very cool in an alpine house. Flowers in the spring and is deciduous during the winter.

A practical hint
With foliage colouring that ranges from pale cream to almost black, the aeoniums will branch in time and create an interesting effect.

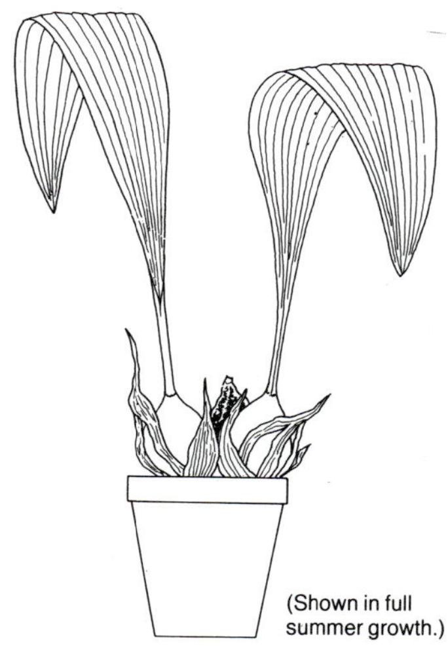

Pleione formosana variety alba 'Snow White'

- **Very cool: 4.5°C (40°F)**
- **Easy to grow and flower**
- **Spring flowering**
- **Deciduous/dry rest**

This is the white variety of the popular and very cool-growing species. Unlike the common species the single flowers on this variety have pure white, glistening petals and sepals, and the lip is lightly spotted. It is a charming orchid to grow, and one that requires the least heat of any in cultivation. During the summer, normal cool house conditions will suit. While at rest during the winter it should be kept as cool as possible. The plants make ideal windowsill orchids and are easy for beginners.

When the flower has died away, a pseudobulb develops at the base of the new growth and the parent pseudobulb shrivels. The new growth should be complete by the late autumn, when the broad but fairly short leaves turn yellow and drop. The pseudobulbs should then be stored for the winter in a cool dry place. Watering should start in the spring, sparingly at first.

Several bulbs planted in one pot will produce a good show.

Left: **Pleione formosana** var. **alba 'Snow white'**
These spring flowers will last for two to three weeks on the plant.

A practical hint
For almost guaranteed flowers in the spring it is advisable to grow a selection of compact rebutias – cacti with a brilliant range of colours.

Pleiospilos bolusii

- **Full sun**
- **Temp: 5-30°C (41-86°F)**
- **Keep dry during rest period**

Pleiospilos bolusii is one of the stone-like plants, its speckled leaves resembling a small chunk of granite. The plant consists of one pair of very succulent leaves with flattened tops; the leaves are about 2.5cm (1in) long and almost as broad. The stem is so short that the plant is often described as 'stemless'. The heads may be split off in late summer to propagate the plant. Try to include a piece of 'stem' or leaf base.

P. bolusii flowers in autumn; the flowers open in the late afternoon to early evening, but only on sunny days. They are golden-yellow in colour and 7.5cm (3in) across.

When the previous season's leaves have completely shrivelled, the current season's leaves will be well formed. This will be late summer. Start watering at this stage and continue into the autumn, when the next season's pair of leaves will be appearing. Stop watering when they are about 1cm (0.4in) high. Grow in an open mixture, half loam-based medium and half grit.

Above left: **Pleiospilos bolusii**
Looking more like a piece of rock with a flower in the cleft, this is an extreme succulent. Slightly fragrant.

A practical hint
At nightfall in winter plants should be removed from window areas, and never be left between window and drawn curtains.

Pleomele reflexa variegata

- **Good light**
- **Temp: 16-21°C (60-70°F)**
- **Keep on dry side**

These painfully slow-growing plants are not often available: anyone seeing a priced plant should stake a claim immediately! When mature and well grown, this is a fine plant. Stems are very woody, and leaves are miniature but bright yellow. Plants may be no more than 1.5-1.8m (5-6ft) tall, though at least 20 years old. Slow growth is one reason for their scarcity, and for the high price should any be on offer.

Plants enjoy good light, with shade from strong sunlight, and temperatures that fluctuate from 16 to 21°C (60 to 70°F). Water well when necessary, and allow to dry appreciably before watering again, but the surrounding area should be kept moist at all times. Feeding should be done on average once a week in summer, with none at all from the onset of winter to the early spring when new growth appears.

Few pests bother these fine plants, whose worst enemy is a combination of wetness and cold.

Right: **Pleomele reflexa variegata**
Commonly named song of India, this is an aristocrat among potted plants. Foliage is almost entirely bright yellow, with leaves 15cm (6in) long.

Podocarpus macrophyllus

- **Light shade**
- **Temp: 10-16°C (50-60°F)**
- **Keep moist, less in winter**

The open foliage of this small tropical tree provides a pleasing potful of greenery for cooler locations indoors. If grown on a single stem it may attain a height of about 1.5m (5ft); but remove the growing tip when the plant is young, and it will become more bushy.

It abhors overwatering, which can be particularly damaging during winter. Avoid the practice of placing plants in a saucer and filling it with water. With modern peaty potting mixtures there will be much more water taken into the peat by capillary action than the plant is ever likely to need, so leading to root rot. Instead, fill the space between the rim of the pot and the soil each time the plant is watered. When watering from the top, one should see the surplus draining through the holes in the bottom of the container. Before watering again, allow the soil to dry.

When growing podocarpus plants indoors they do much better in cool, light conditions, and abhor heat.

Above:
Podocarpus macrophyllus
Mature trees in their native habitat, these plants make fine bushy plants for cool places indoors.

Polyscias balfouriana

- **Light shade**
- **Temp: 16-21°C (60-70°F)**
- **Keep moist and fed**

This is another painfully slow grower that will take at least 10 years to reach 3m (10ft) in height, but in limited space this could be an advantage. Stems are woody and the leaf colouring is variegated white and green. Growth is very erect and plants seldom need to be staked. As the plant ages and increases in height, the lower stem will have a natural tendency to shed leaves.

Red spider mites seem to find this plant particularly appetizing. Although minute in size, these pests can increase at an alarming rate and completely blanket the plant to such an extent that it may well not recover. The layman often finds it difficult to believe that such minute pests can be so destructive. When they are detected, take action right away, by preparing a recommended insecticide solution and thoroughly saturating the undersides of all foliage. This task ought to be done out of doors on a warm day, and rubber gloves and a mask worn.

Above:
Polyscias balfouriana 'Pinnochio'
Leaves are rounded with pale cream and green variegation. Stems are woody and the plant slow growing.

Polystachya pubescens

- **Intermediate: 13°C (55°F)**
- **Easy to grow and flower**
- **Varied flowering season**
- **Evergreen/no rest**

The majority of the 150 known species of *Polystachya* come from tropical Africa. Though the flowers are generally small, the plants flower freely under cultivation.

These plants are subjects for the intermediate house. Being epiphytic, they require a well-drained compost, but plenty of moisture at the root while the plant is in active growth. Moderate protection from the full sun is also required. Polystachyas undoubtedly do best when left undisturbed for several years.

A notable feature is that the flowers appear upside-down on the spike, the lip being uppermost with the two sepals, normally at the base of the flower, forming a hood.

This species produces narrow, tapering pseudobulbs, which grow to a height of 5cm (2in) and have two or three short leaves. The flower spike comes from the apex of the pseudobulb and carries six to 12 bright yellow flowers, each up to 1.5cm (0.6in) across, the upper sepals and lip of which are marked delicately with red lines.

Above: **Polystachya pubescens**
A small-growing, unusual species for the intermediate house. It blooms at various times of the year.

Potinara Sunrise

- **Intermediate: 13°C (55°F)**
- **Easy to grow and flower**
- **Autumn flowering**
- **Evergreen/some rest**

With colourful magenta flowers and slightly darker lips, this hybrid is the result of a quadrigeneric cross (*Brassavola* x *Cattleya* x *Laelia* x *Sophronitis*). The flowers, which open in the autumn, are 13-15cm (5-6in) across and very showy.

Generally, the flowers of potinaras are of a slightly heavier texture, with better lasting qualities. The flowers will become prematurely spotted, however, in over-moist conditions. As with all cattleya hybrids, it is advisable to keep the plants and their surroundings on the dry side while the plants are flowering.

Repotting may be carried out after flowering in the autumn or later in the spring. The aim should be to catch the new growths when they are about 2.5cm (1in) long, just before the new roots appear. All intergeneric cattleyas do well when grown in good light and when given a rest after flowering until the new growth starts.

During the summer plants can be lightly sprayed overhead, but the foliage should be dry before nightfall.

Above: **Potinara Sunrise**
A lovely Cattleya *type hybrid for autumn flowering in the intermediate house. Large fragrant blooms.*

Primula malacoides

- **Good light**
- **Temp: 10-16°C (50-60°F)**
- **Keep moist and fed**

This is one of the most charming of all the annual flowering houseplants. *Primula malacoides* presents its lovely flowers, in many colour shades, during the winter and spring months of the year and is almost indispensable for that added touch of colour on the sunny windowsill.

Keep the plants in a cool and light place to do well, and at no time expose them to hot and dry conditions. In such conditions there is a much greater chance of the plants being attacked by red spider mites. These can be detected by careful inspection on the undersides of leaves, and should be treated with the appropriate insecticide as soon as they are noticed. Feed regularly to retain leaf colouring. New plants can be started from seed in the spring.

Right: **Primula malacoides**
Available with white, red, pink and rose-purple flowers, these are excellent plants for winter colour.

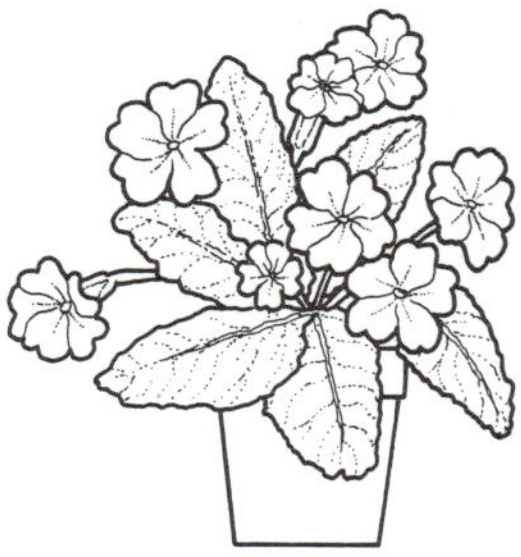

Primula obconica

- **Good light**
- **Temp: 10-16°C (50-60°F)**
- **Keep moist and fed**

These are marvellous plants that seem to flower from one year's end to the next and are very little trouble when it comes to care and attention. Flowers in a variety of colours are more plentiful in winter and spring, but they are likely to be present at almost any time on vigorous plants. Cool, light, and airy conditions are essential. Plants must be kept moist and regularly fed.

The principal drawback with this plant is that it can cause a most irritating rash. Anyone suffering any form of skin problem following the introduction of this plant to the room should immediately suspect and should not actually touch the plant.

To prolong the flowering period give a weak solution of liquid fertilizer every two weeks and pick off fading flowers. This primula can be kept for a second season provided it is kept cool and dry during the summer. In the autumn remove dead leaves and topdress with fresh soil.

Above: **Primula obconica**
Easy-care houseplants in a wide range of eye-catching colours. Individual flowers are 2.5cm (1in) across and borne in clusters on stems up to 30cm (12in) in height.

Primula vulgaris

- **Good light**
- **Temp: 10-16°C (50-60°F)**
- **Keep moist and fed**

This is now one of the most popular small plants during the winter period. Easily grown from seed sown in the spring, the plants bloom during the winter months. The leaves are pale green and rough in texture, and flowers of many colours are now available; the flowers are infinitely larger than those of a few years ago.

Excellent planted in bowls with other foliage and flowering plants, they will also provide a fine show when a number of plants of different colour are grouped together in a small container.

After flowering indoors, the plants can be put in the garden in a shaded spot to flower the following year.

Keep pot-grown plants in a humid atmosphere while indoors; hot, dry conditions may cause foliage to turn yellow and will cut down the flowering period. Use a loam-based potting mixture and feed every two weeks while the plants are in bloom.

Right: **Primula vulgaris**
Essentially a garden plant that can be easily raised indoors for winter flowers. The beautiful colours of the blooms are most effective when several plants are grouped together.

Pteris cretica albo-lineata

- Shade
- Temp: 16-21°C (60-70°F)
- Keep moist

The variegated form of *P. cretica* has a pale green outer margin to its leaves and a cream-coloured central area. There are several other variegated forms available, and all will respond well to shaded and warm conditions where a reasonable degree of humidity can be maintained. They will also benefit from regular feeding once they have become established in their pots. Many of these smaller ferns do very well if fed with a foliar feed, which is sprayed onto the leaves.

Fern plants do very much better if they can be grouped together. Large plastic trays are easily obtainable, and these are ideal for placing groups of ferns and other types of indoor plants. The tray is filled with gravel and well watered before the plants are placed on the surface; it is important that the plant pot base should not stand in water, as this would make the soil much too wet. The wet tray will provide a continual source of essential humidity.

Above: **Pteris cretica albo-lineata**
An attractive fern with pale green and off-white variegation, and one of the easiest ferns to care for. Needs moist and warm shaded conditions to thrive. Avoid bright sun and dry air.

Punica granatum 'Nana'

- Good light
- Temp: 10-18°C (50-65°F)
- Keep moist and fed

The dwarf pomegranate is a compact and shrubby plant with masses of small green leaves, and it will not be difficult to care for if given good light and cool conditions. Besides the evergreen foliage, the reddish scarlet flowers are also a feature; these are suspended from the plant in similar fashion to those of the fuchsia, but are not quite so plentiful.

If flowers are pollinated with a soft brush when pollen is present there is every chance that small pomegranate fruits will develop; these are not edible, but will be of considerable interest. To preserve a neat appearance it is advisable to periodically prune back any growth that is tending to get out of hand. Keep the soil moist, and feed occasionally, but not in winter.

Above: **Punica granatum 'Nana'**
The bell-shaped flowers, about 2.5cm (1in) long, are produced in the summer months and are followed by miniature pomegranate fruits. Propagate with heeled cuttings.

Rebutia albiflora

- **Full sun**
- **Temp: 5-30°C (41-86°F)**
- **Water with care**

Rebutia albiflora is one of the very few rebutias with white flowers. This is a very desirable plant if space is limited; it will flower when only 1cm (0.4in) across. The flowering period is spring. The plant consists of a cluster of small heads, covered in short white spines. Individual heads can be split off and used to start new plants.

This cactus has a weak root system and should be grown in a shallow pan so that the roots are not surrounded by large quantities of cold, wet soil. A loam-based mixture or a soilless medium, to which one third sharp sand or perlite has been added, is suitable for this cactus. During spring and summer water freely, allowing it to dry out between waterings. Feed every two weeks with a tomato fertilizer when the buds appear. During the winter months keep it dry.

Mealy bug and root mealy bug are the pests most likely to attack this rebutia. A proprietary insecticide spray will deal with these.

Above: **Rebutia albiflora**
One of the smallest rebutias, this has tiny clustering heads and an all-white appearance, with white spines and unusual white flowers.

Rebutia calliantha var. krainziana

- **Full sun**
- **Temp: 5-30°C (41-86°F)**
- **Avoid overwatering**

All rebutias are beautiful in the spring flowering period, but this species is outstanding. Each head is surrounded by a complete ring of orange-red flowers. The flower colour in this plant can vary from an almost true red through to a pure orange. The buds are purple.

The individual heads of this clustering cactus are cylindrical, and reach a height of about 10cm (4in). The very short white spines form a neat pattern against the green stem.

This rebutia needs a sunny position to keep it a bright colour and to ensure flowering. Any good potting mixture may be used, either loam- or peat-based. During spring and summer water freely, letting it get almost dry before watering again. When the buds form feed every two weeks with a tomato fertilizer.

Watch carefully for any signs of mealy bug, particularly around the growing point of the stems, where these woolly white pests can fade into the white wool on new growth.

Rebutia muscula

- **Full sun**
- **Temp: 5-30°C (41-86°F)**
- **Avoid overwatering**

Rebutia muscula is one of the more recently discovered rebutias, and should not be confused with the less attractive *R. minuscula.* With its clear orange flowers, *R. muscula* is a beautiful addition to any cactus collection. The flowers open in late spring. The plant body is densely covered with soft white spines. It is a clustering plant and in the sun looks like a silvery cushion. The offsets may be used for propagation.

Like most cacti, *R. muscula* needs to be grown in strong light. Any loam-based mixture may be used for this plant; to improve the drainage, add one third sharp sand or perlite. During spring and summer water freely, allowing the plant to dry out between waterings. Feed with a high-potassium (tomato) fertilizer every two weeks when buds form.

Mealy bug hide between the clustering heads and suck the sap from the plant. Their white bodies blend with the plant and make discovery difficult.

Rebutia senilis

- **Full sun**
- **Temp: 5-30°C (41-86°F)**
- **Water with care**

Rebutias are ideal cacti for the collector without a greenhouse. They are small and will flower freely every spring if kept on a sunny windowsill. One of the prettiest is *R. senilis*: the rings of red flowers show up well against the silvery white spines. The flowers are followed by seed pods, and in autumn dozens of seedling rebutias will be found nestling around the parent plant. With age *R. senilis* clusters, forming a cushion about 30cm (12in) across. Individual heads may be removed and used for propagation.

Rebutias are not fussy about their soil, and either a loam-based or a soilless mixture may be used. In spring and summer water freely, allowing the compost to dry out between waterings. When the buds form feed every two weeks with a high-potassium fertilizer.

Carefully watch for signs of mealy bug. It is easy to miss these white pests on a white-spined plant. A systemic insecticide will be ideal.

Left:
Rebutia calliantha var. **krainziana**
All rebutias are small cacti, ideal for the collection on the windowsill. This one produces magnificent flowers.

Above left: **Rebutia muscula**
Another little gem, with many offsets and beautifully coloured flowers peeping out from silky white spines. Thrives in the sunniest location.

Above: **Rebutia senilis**
This rebutia has a number of varieties with differing flower colours: pink, orange and yellow. Seed pods follow the flowers.

Rechsteineria cardinalis

(Sinningia cardinalis)
- **Light shade**
- **Temp: 18-21°C (65-70°F)**
- **Keep moist and fed**

This is a gesneriad with green velvety leaves that produces flowers of bright red colouring in the autumn. For a neat and colourful plant that is not too difficult to care for, *Rechsteineria cardinalis* (also known as *Sinningia cardinalis*) can be thoroughly recommended.

A temperature of not less than 18°C (65°F) is needed and water must be tepid rather than straight from a cold tap. Exposure to bright light will leach the colouring from foliage and mar the appearance of the plant, so place in light shade. Keep the plant out of draughts.

Water well and feed occasionally during spring and summer when plants are in leaf, but when the foliage dies back naturally withhold water and keep the rhizome bone dry and warm until fresh growth appears.

For new plants take leaf or stem cuttings, grow from seed, or plant pieces of rhizomes.

Rhipsalidopsis rosea

- **Partial shade**
- **Temp: 13-24°C (55-75°F)**
- **Keep slightly moist all year**

This is one of the jungle cacti, related to the well-known Christmas cactus, but producing its rose-pink flowers in early spring; they are about 2.5cm (1in) across. The plant itself consists of very small flattened segments, each around 2cm (0.8in) long, which, joined end to end and branching freely, eventually form a little bush. The segments carry small bushy spines along the edges and tips; they are quite harmless. Propagation is simplicity itself; just remove a small branch in spring or summer and pot it up.

Although this delightful little cactus and its many hybrids can be grown as an ordinary pot plant, it is ideal for a hanging basket. A rich growing medium is appreciated, so add about one third of peat (or leaf mould, if you can get it) to your standard potting mixture. Give a dose of high-potassium fertilizer every two weeks in spring, when buds are forming, and water freely.

Above: **Rechsteineria cardinalis**
In warm, humid surroundings this attractive plant will bear clusters of tubular red flowers. The plant grows from a rhizome.

Right: **Rhipsalidopsis rosea**
This is another cactus originating from the tropical rain forests; it needs some moisture at all times, and more winter warmth than the desert cacti.

Rhipsalis pilocarpa

- **Partial shade**
- **Temp: 13-24°C (55-75°F)**
- **Keep slightly moist in winter**

At least one rhipsalis makes an interesting addition to the collection, as these are unusual cacti with an appearance quite at variance with the popular conception of a cactus. There are many species, but *R. pilocarpa* is one of the most attractive. A mass of dark green, cylindrical trailing stems, up to 40cm (16in) long and only 3-6mm (0.125-0.25in) thick, with small bushy spines make this an ideal subject for a hanging basket. White or cream flowers, about 2cm (0.8in) across, are borne on the tips of the branches; they are not very spectacular, but they do appear in winter, and they are perfumed.

Grow this rhipsalis in a good porous potting mixture, and preferably add some extra peat (sterile leaf mould is better, if available) as it needs a rich soil. Feed from time to time and water freely in spring and summer.

Above: **Rhipsalis pilocarpa**
The trailing stems of this tropical rain forest cactus are best displayed in a hanging basket. Avoid direct sunlight in summer. Feed occasionally.

Rhoicissus rhomboidea

- **Light shade**
- **Temp: 13-18°C (55-65°F)**
- **Keep moist and fed**

Grape ivy is a tough old plant that seems to outlast all others. The three-lobed leaves are a bright glossy green. The plant should be offered some form of support through which it can entwine itself; but although generally considered to be a climber it will also do very well in a hanging container.

Plants are started from cuttings taken at any time if moist and warm conditions can be provided. When cuttings are potted put five or six into a small pot of peaty mixture.

Although tough enough to withstand harsh treatment they will fare better if kept moist and fed regularly in a location that offers reasonable light but not full sun. In bright sunlight, or if plants are starved, they become pale brown, and leaves will be generally smaller. Plants that have taken on a harder appearance may be in need of potting on, so root condition should be checked and plants potted if need be in loam-based mixture.

Above: **Rhoicissus rhomboidea**
This vigorous climbing plant will flourish in a lightly shaded spot. A good support is essential; its tendrils will search out any hold.

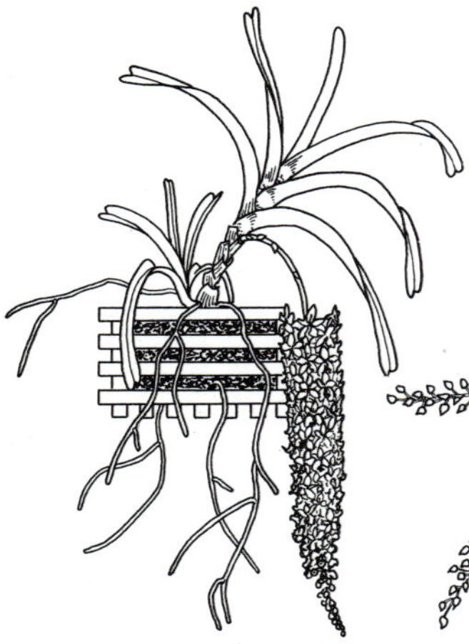

Rhynchostylis retusa

- **Intermediate: 13°C (55°F)**
- **Easy to grow and flower**
- **Winter/spring flowering**
- **Evergreen/no rest**

Four species make up this well-known and popular epiphytic genus, and all are seen in present-day collections.

Their natural habitat is Malaysia and Indonesia and, consequently, they enjoy reasonably warm conditions, similar to those of the strap-leaf vandas, which they resemble vegetatively. Because the flowers grow densely in cylindrical fashion on a pendent raceme or spike, they are commonly known as 'foxtail orchids', although this name is also given to other orchids that produce their flowers in similar fashion (eg *Aerides fieldingii*).

This species produces a plant up to 60cm (2ft) in height with a pendulous spike of 38-50cm (15-20in) which carries many thick, waxy and highly fragrant flowers, each up to 2cm (0.8in) in diameter. These are basically white but may be lightly or heavily spotted with magenta-purple. The hook-shaped lip is solid magenta. The flowers appear from winter to spring and last for only two or three weeks, but if well grown the plant will flower more often.

Above: **Rhynchostylis retusa**
Long dense sprays of small flowers adorn this intermediate species during the winter and spring.

Rivina humilis

- **Good light**
- **Temp: 16-21°C (60-70°F)**
- **Keep moist; drier in winter**

Although an evergreen, these plants will give much better results if fresh material is raised each year. This can be done by sowing seed in the spring for young and vigorous plants to be ready in the summer, or by propagating cuttings. If using the cuttings method, at least one plant must be retained from the previous year so that cuttings can be taken from it for rooting in a heated propagator in the spring.

These neat plants have thin leaves and whitish flowers in the summer to be followed by the further bonus of decorative berries of a bright red colour in the autumn. Keep moist and fed while in active growth, giving less water and no feed to plants retained over the winter period. Check plants regularly for red spider mites.

Above: **Rivina humilis**
This dependable plant offers summer flowers followed by a fine display of red berries in the autumn.

Ruellia makoyana

- **Light shade**
- **Temp: 16-21°C (60-70°F)**
- **Keep moist and fed**

Native to Brazil, these low-growing spready plants have twiggy stems; the ovate leaves of a velvety texture are olive green in colour, with attractive veins. The flowers, though small individually, are a rich carmine, and produced in quantity over a long period from late summer onwards into winter.

Although not pendulous in habit these are attractive plants for growing in small hanging containers that are positioned at head level, where both flowers and foliage can be seen to advantage.

Low temperatures combined with wet conditions will prove fatal and must be avoided; the plants are most vulnerable during the winter months. With a heated propagator it is not difficult to root new plants from cuttings a few centimetres in length. For a neat effect, pinch out the growing tips once the new plants are well established.

Right: **Ruellia makoyana**
Keep this colourful plant in a warm, humid environment for best results. The stems grow to about 60cm (2ft).

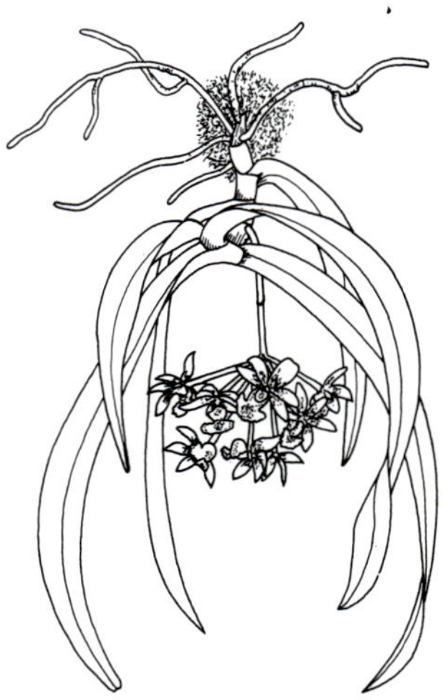

Saccolabium acutifolium

- **Intermediate: 13°C (55°F)**
- **Easy to grow and flower**
- **Autumn flowering**
- **Evergreen/no rest**

This species belongs to a small epiphytic group of about 20 species. It originates from India and is now more correctly *Gastrochilus acutifolius,* although the older name persists in horticulture. The plant produces upward growing (monopodial) stems from which grow the narrow, pointed leaves. The fragrant flowers come from between the leaves and are carried on a short, pendent stem in the form of a rosette. These are highly variable and can be pure yellow-green, shaded with brown to an almost solid red colouring. The lip is of curious shape, basically white, occasionally spotted in red with a central yellow stain, and frilled around the edge. It is the shape of the lip that gives the genus *Gastrochilus* its name: *gaster* (belly) and *cheilos* (lip).

The plant will grow happily on a piece of bark in a pendent position, when it will produce a number of dangling aerial roots. It should be kept permanently moist and prefers to be grown in fairly heavy shade. During the summer months it can be sprayed generously.

Above: **Saccolabium acutifolium**
This autumn-flowering species will grow particularly well mounted on bark in the intermediate house.

A practical hint
When watering saintpaulias it is essential to keep water off flowers and foliage; a small watering can with a thin spout is good for this job.

Saintpaulia ionantha

- **Good light**
- **Temp: 16-21°C (60-70°F)**
- **Keep moist and fed**

This is by far the most popular flowering plant. There is no particular flowering time, but bloom will be much improved if plants are grown in good light, and this means a light window – no draughts – during the day and under an artificial light in the evening. High-powered lights can scorch leaves, so care is needed.

Use tepid water and apply it to the surface of the potting mixture ensuring that it drains right through the pot – any surplus accumulating in the drip dish should be removed as it is fatal to allow plants to stand in water for any length of time. Use a standard loam-based potting mixture with some extra peat added. Feed with fertilizer every two weeks.

New plants can be grown from firm leaves taken at any time and placed in a heated propagator or a plastic bag to conserve warmth and moisture. After 6 to 10 weeks tiny plantlets appear at the base of the leaf; these can be separated and grown into mature plants.

Right: **Saintpaulia ionantha**
An established favourite the world over, the African violet blooms more readily when slightly pot-bound. Many colours are available.

A practical hint
Minute red spider mites can be fatal when present in quantity: foliage discolouration and tiny webs are signs of their presence. Treat immediately.

Sansevieria trifasciata Laurentii

- **Good light**
- **Temp: 16-21°C (60-70°F)**
- **Keep dry**

This plant is almost indestructible. The leaves are about 60cm (2ft) long, thick and fleshy, holding a lot of moisture which the plant can draw on as needed; in view of this, it is important not to overwater, nor to give any more than the plant requires.

A good watering once each month in summer should suffice, with none at all during the winter months. This may seem harsh, but if plants are to be exposed to colder winter temperatures they will get through much better if the soil in the pot is dry rather than wet. Potting ought not to be done too frequently, and one can leave the plant until it actually breaks the pot in which it is growing – the swelling bases of leaves within the pot are quite capable of breaking clay as well as plastic pots. Loam-based soil is essential when potting on, and clay pots will help to maintain the balance of these top-heavy plants.

Right:
Sansevieria trifasciata Laurentii
The true type has bright yellow margins to the leaves with mottled variegation in the central areas.

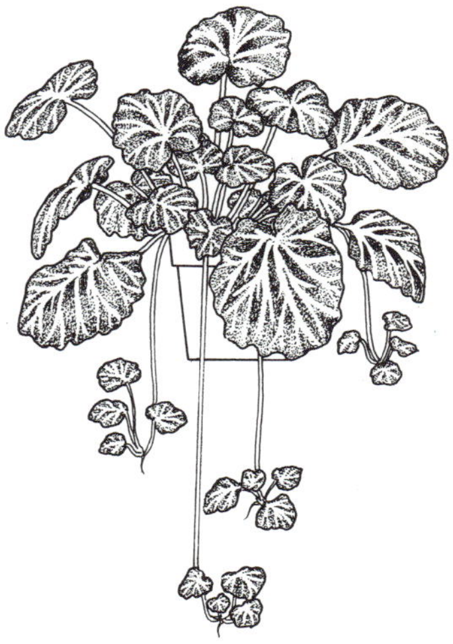

Saxifraga sarmentosa

- **Light shade**
- **Temp: 16-21°C (60-70°F)**
- **Keep moist and fed**

This is one of the simplest plants to propagate: you just detach the perfectly made plants when of reasonable size and press them into small pots filled with houseplant potting mixture. Grow the parent plant in a hanging basket with a curtain of tiny plants hanging from it and attached to threads of growth that may be 60cm (2ft) or more in length; the family of young plants will provide continual interest.

These plants are very easy to care for. Offer them reasonable light and warmth, with water and feed in moderation, bearing in mind that plants suspended from the ceiling will tend to dry out more rapidly than similar plants growing at a lower level in the same conditions. The amount of feed given will very often depend on the vigour of the plant, and during the winter months little or no feed is required.

Inspect these saxifrages regularly for pests: mealy bug, red spider or aphids might be present.

Above: **Saxifraga sarmentosa**
Aptly named the mother of thousands because of the many perfectly developed plantlets that hang naturally from the parent plant.

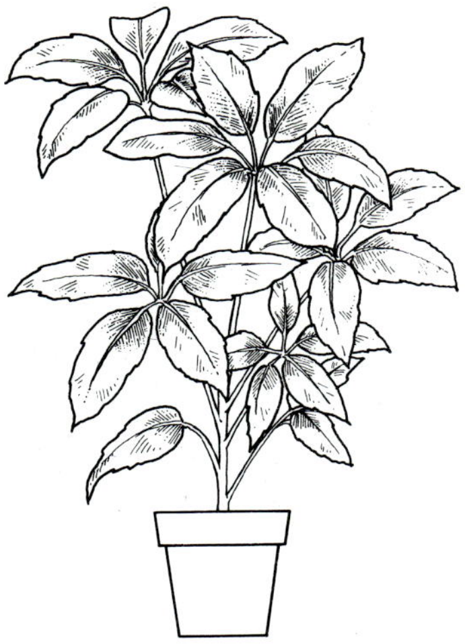

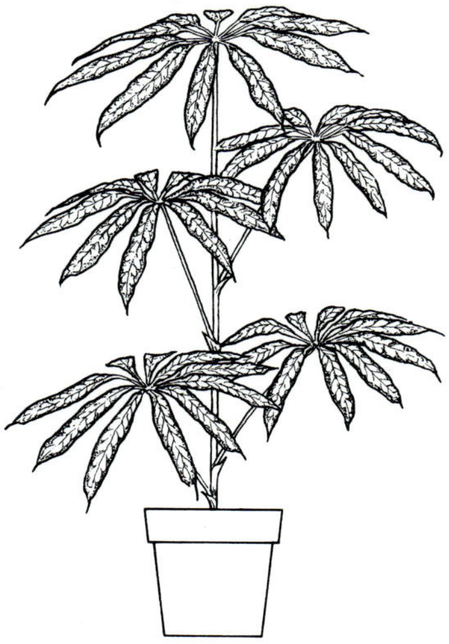

Schefflera digitata

- **Light shade**
- **Temp: 16-21°C (60-70°F)**
- **Keep moist and fed**

Even with roots confined to a pot, this majestic indoor tree may attain a height of 3m (10ft) or more. The glossy green palmate leaves radiate from the leaf petiole like the fingers of a hand. Unlike some houseplants, the schefflera does not produce more than one new shoot when the top is removed, so overgrown plants lose much of their charm when the growing top is severed. Also, as plants increase in height they tend to shed lower leaves.

New plants are raised from seed, normally sown in high temperatures in spring. When large enough, seedlings are put into small pots containing peaty mixture, later into larger pots of loam-based soil.

Indoors they respond to light, airy conditions, and the ideal temperature should be in the region of 18°C (65°F). They grow more vigorously in the warmer months, and need more water and regular feeding; in winter less water is needed and no feeding.

Above: **Schefflera digitata**
With large-fingered leaves that are attached to stout petioles, this is one of the finest indoor green plants. The leaves are naturally glossy green.

Schefflera venusta 'Starshine'

- **Light shade**
- **Temp: 18-24°C (65-75°F)**
- **Keep watered and fed**

This comparative newcomer has dark green glossy leaves, attached to the petiole like the fingers of a hand. Unlike the more common larger scheffleras, it has narrow, undulating leaves, with the result that the plant has a deal more elegance. It is also a much more compact plant, and will be better suited to the average home than the bolder schefflera types such as *S. digitata*. Avoid excessive watering and feed when active.

One problem is that the plant seems to attract mealy bugs, which will quickly spoil the appearance with their sticky, black honeydew if not dealt with. Honeydew is in fact a nice term for the excreta of the mealy bug, which drop onto the leaves below where the bugs are present, with the result that black fungus mould will form on the excreta. The latter can be wiped off with a sponge, and the mealy bugs can be removed with a swab of cotton wool soaked in methylated spirit.

Right:
Schefflera venusta 'Starshine'
A comparative newcomer, with narrow, palmate, undulating leaves. The plant is compact and upright.

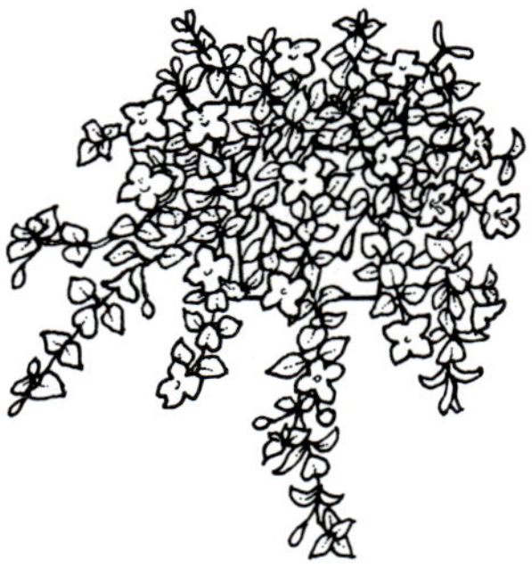

Schizocentron elegans

(Heterocentron elegans)
- **Good light**
- **Temp: 16-21°C (60-70°F)**
- **Keep moist and fed**

This compact windowsill plant is ideal for the beginner wishing to have something easy to keep in flower. Neat mounds of green foliage are topped by purplish flowers that are in evidence through the spring and into early summer.

It is best kept in a smaller pot using a loam-based potting mixture, but a keen eye must be maintained for watering and feeding, as smaller pots tend to dry out more rapidly. While actively growing, plants should be fed at every watering with a weak liquid fertilizer. Alternatively, feeding tablets may be placed in the soil as directed by the manufacturer.

New plants can be produced in the autumn by cutting back the foliage of older plants to little more than stumps, then dividing the roots. Alternatively, tip cuttings about 7.5cm (3in) long can be taken at any time and rooted in a mixture of peat and sand.

Above: **Schizocentron elegans**
This graceful flowering plant needs bright filtered light and regular feeding to thrive. Place several rooted cuttings in a hanging basket.

Schlumbergera 'Buckleyi'

- **Partial shade**
- **Temp: 13-24°C (55-75°F)**
- **Keep slightly moist all year**

There is no doubt that this is the most popular cactus of all and the one most commonly grown, in spite of the fact that many people do not consider it to be a 'true' cactus at all, whatever that means! But it *is* a cactus, a jungle type, needing more warmth and moisture than the desert cacti. The many segments, joined end to end, are true stems (there are no leaves) and the whole plant forms a densely branched bush: Unscented flowers of an unusual shape and about 3cm (1.2in) across, are freely produced in winter at the end of segments; the typical colour is carmine but varieties exist with flowers of various shades of red, pink or even white (never blue).

Use a rich potting mixture with added peat or leaf mould, and water the plant freely when in bud and flower, feeding every two weeks at this time. Reduce the water somewhat after flowering. Propagation from segments is easy.

Schlumbergera gaertneri

(Rhipsalidopsis gaertneri)

- **Partial shade**
- **Temp: 13-24°C (55-75°F)**
- **Keep slightly moist all year**

This delightful little jungle cactus resembles the better known Christmas cactus (*Schlumbergera* 'Buckleyi'). The stem segments are smaller than those of the typical Christmas cactus and are more rounded, with small bristly spines and whilst the flowers are also bright red and freely produced, they are open star-shaped and about 3.5cm (1.4in) across.

Small specimens can be grown in an ordinary pot, but soon the increasing segments will cause the stems to droop, so that eventually a hanging basket is ideal. A well-drained potting mixture is needed, so add about a third part of sharp sand or perlite to a good standard loam- or peat-based material. A fortnightly feed with a high potassium fertilizer in spring will help to ensure a good succession of flowers. Pieces of stem consisting of one or two segments will root readily if removed in spring and allowed to dry for a day before potting.

Right: **Schlumbergera 'Buckleyi'**
A fascinating houseplant for winter colour. Although watering may be reduced after flowering, this plant should never be completely dry.

Above: **Schlumbergera gaertneri**
Beautiful scarlet flowers up to 4cm (1.6in) across develop at the stem tips in winter. Feed with a high-potassium fertilizer at this time.

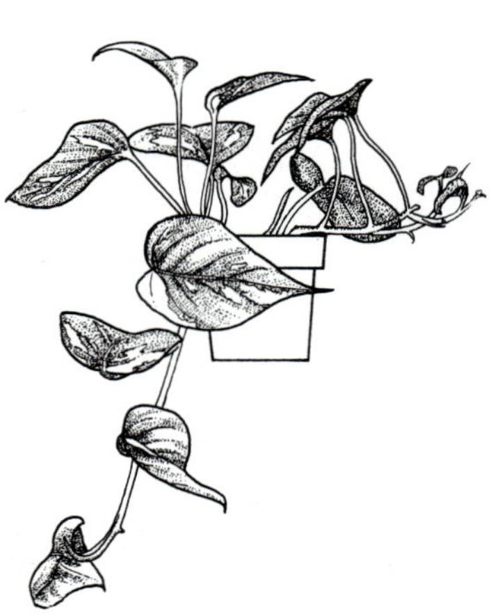

Scindapsus aureus

- **Light shade**
- **Temp: 16-21°C (60-70°F)**
- **Keep moist**

S. aureus used to be one of those varieties that were difficult to propagate and to care for indoors. Yet we now have a plant with the same name that is one of the most reliable and one of the most colourful foliage plants available. It can only be that by constant re-selection a much tougher strain of the same plant has been evolved; there is now little difficulty in propagating it, and it seems to have an almost charmed life indoors.

Belonging to the Araceae family it needs a reasonable amount of moisture in the pot and, if possible, also in the surrounding atmosphere. The variegated leaves are green and gold, and for a variegated plant it has the truly amazing capacity of being able to retain its colouring in less well lit places. Most other variegated plants deteriorate or turn completely green if placed in locations offering insufficient light. The devil's ivy will also climb or trail as desired, and does well in hydroculture.

Above: **Scindapsus aureus**
Perhaps the best of all the foliage plants, with yellow and green variegation that is retained even in poor light. Will climb or trail. Take tip cuttings 10cm (4in) long in spring.

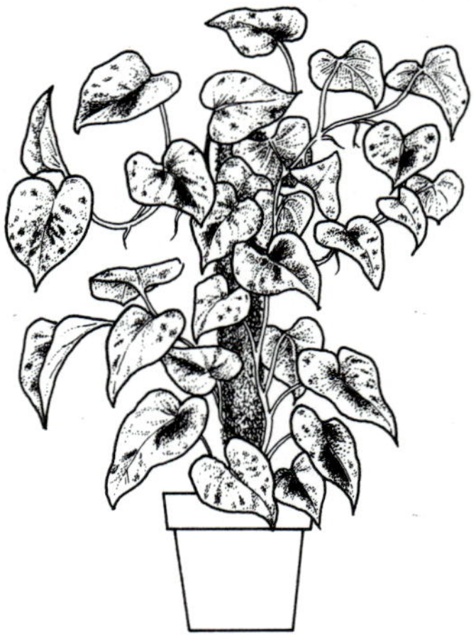

Scindapsus 'Marble Queen'

- **Light shade**
- **Temp: 18-24°C (65-75°F)**
- **Keep moist and fed**

The white variegated devil's ivy will test the skill of the most accomplished grower. Most plants with a large area of white are a problem, and this is no exception.

A temperature over 18°C (65°F) is needed, particularly in winter. Also, it will be necessary to create a humid atmosphere around the plant. (This should not be confused with watering the plant to excess.) The simplest way is to provide a large saucer or tray filled with pebbles on which the plant can stand; the saucer can be partly filled with water, but the level should never be above the surface of the pebbles, as it is important that the plant pot should not stand in water. In a warm room such a saucer will continually give off moisture around the plant. Moist peat surrounding the pot in which the plant is growing is another way of providing moisture; and there are numerous types of troughs with capillary matting for placing plants on; these are useful at holiday time.

Right:
Scindapsus 'Marble Queen'
This is one of the more difficult indoor plants because the life-sustaining pigment chlorophyll is in short supply in variegated leaves.

Sedum hintonii

- **Full sun**
- **Temp: 10-30°C (50-86°F)**
- **Keep almost dry in winter**

Many of the large number of sedums are somewhat uninteresting plants, but there are also some delightful little succulents, ideal for any collection. *Sedum hintonii* is one of the most beautiful of all. It consists of a mass of short stems bearing tiny egg-shaped leaves, densely covered with white hairs. Little white flowers appear in winter, always a welcome time. At flowering time the plant should be very sparingly watered, because it is very prone to rot if water becomes trapped within the leaves.

Grow this little gem in a well-drained potting mixture; add about one third of sharp sand or perlite to a good standard material, either loam- or peat-based. Although it will withstand quite low temperatures if kept dry, *S. hintonii* is better if kept rather warmer than in the average greenhouse in winter, and it makes a good houseplant.

Above: **Sedum hintonii**
This is a beauty, with its tiny rounded leaves clad in white hairs. It is winter-flowering, which makes a pleasant change, and must be watered sparingly at this time.

Sedum morganianum

- **Full sun**
- **Temp: 10-30°C (50-86°F)**
- **Keep slightly moist in winter**

One glance at this unusual succulent will explain its popular names of 'burro's-tail' and 'donkey's-tail', although whether the tail-like stems resemble the tail of a donkey is a matter of opinion! Stems can be up to 90cm (36in) long, branching freely from the base, and are completely clad with small succulent leaves about 2cm (0.8in) long and 1cm (0.4in) thick. Their pale green colour is masked with a whitish bloom. The only practicable way to grow this plant is in a hanging basket. Line it with sphagnum moss and pack with a good standard potting mixture.

Any pot plants beneath the basket will soon have little sedums growing in them, as *S. morganianum* sheds its leaves easily and they take root where they fall. Very attractive rose-pink flowers are borne on the ends of shoots, but only on large mature ones. Water this unusual succulent freely in spring and summer, and never let it dry out completley or leaves will be shed.

Above and right:
Sedum morganianum
A naturally trailing succulent plant with bluish-grey leaves that hang perpendicularly from the growing pot, which must be suspended.

A practical hint
Contrary to common belief, it is important that succulents are well watered while in active summer growth, but saturated conditions cause problems.

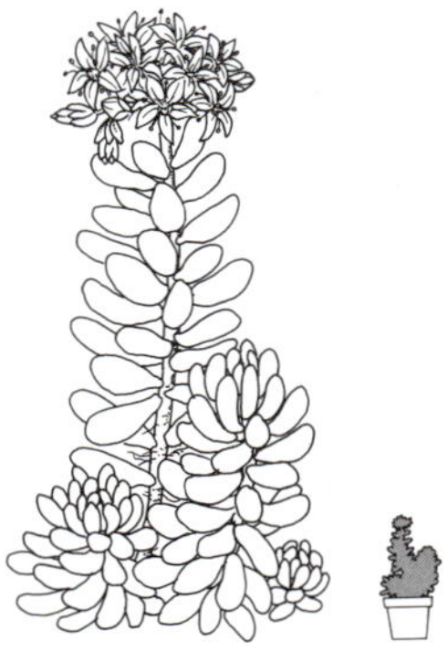

Sedum rubrotinctum

- **Full sun**
- **Temp: 5-30°C (41-86°F)**
- **Keep slightly moist in winter**

Another very attractive little sedum, this colourful succulent consists of branched stems covered with small, oval, very fleshy leaves. These are about 2cm (0.8in) long and 7mm (0.3in) thick. The basic colour is bright green but a delightful red coloration extends downwards from the tips. As the stems become longer they are likely to bend over and take root in any soil they touch. To keep a small bushy plant, remove any over-long shoots; you can always use them as cuttings. Flowers are small and yellow, but are by no means freely produced.

Any good potting mixture is satisfactory; it can be either peat- or loam-based. The plant is reasonably hardy and in winter needs only sufficient water to prevent shrivelling and leaf fall. When it is actively growing in spring and summer, you can water it quite generously, but never let the mix become soggy.

Left: **Sedum rubrotinctum**
The tiny, succulent leaves of this sedum are nicely tinted red. It is easy to propagate, as the stems tend to take root wherever they touch soil. It is usually necessary to trim the plant.

Selenicereus grandiflorus

- Diffuse sunlight
- Temp: 7-30°C (45-86°F)
- Keep moist all year

Selenicereus grandiflorus is only suitable for greenhouse cultivation; its long straggly stems are up to 5m (16ft) long and need to be trained along the roof of a greenhouse. The stems are 2.5cm (1in) thick, greyish-green in colour, and the ribs have needle-like spines.

This cactus is grown for its glorious flowers rather than the beauty of its form. The bell-shaped white flowers are about 30cm (12in) long and have a sweet scent. They open in the late evening and fade the following morning.

Grow this plant in a loam-based mixture to which bone meal has been added. Feed during the growing period with a liquid fertilizer, of the type sold for tomatoes. Repot annually. Water generously during spring and summer. Give it a little moisture during winter. When the plant becomes too large, it may be propagated by stem cuttings about 15cm (6in) long.

Senecio macroglossus variegata

- Good light
- Temp: 13-21°C (55-70°F)
- Keep moist and fed

In appearance these vigorous climbing plants strongly resemble the small-leaved ivies, and they must have some form of support for their rapid growth. During their growing season, provide moist conditions and regular feeding; less water is required in winter, and no feeding.

However well the plants may be cared for, in time the top growth extends and lower branches begin to shed their leaves. Replace older and less attractive specimens by starting afresh with a new batch of cuttings. Senecio will root like a weed during the summer if given warm and shaded conditions. Stem cuttings with two leaves attached should be prepared, and up to seven of these put into each small pot filled with peaty potting mixture.

This plant is prone to attack by aphids, which seem to find the tender succulent new growth particularly appetizing; inspect the tips for aphids, and treat with insecticide as soon as possible.

Above: **Selenicereus grandiflorus**
For those who have sufficient room this majestic cactus really deserves a place. The long trailing stems need support. Large flowers open at night.

Right:
Senecio macroglossus variegata
This vigorous plant will thrive in bright, moist conditions and is an ideal subject for a hanging basket.

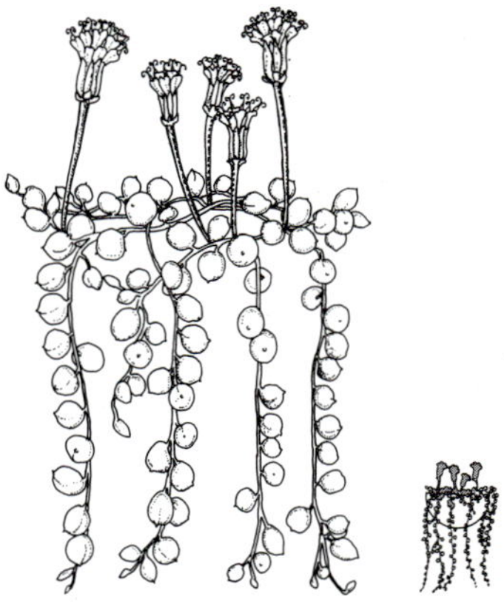

Senecio rowleyanus

- **Full sun**
- **Temp: 5-30°C (41-86°F)**
- **Keep slightly moist in winter**

Senecios are a very large group of plants; some are succulent, others are garden bushes, and they show a wide variety of shape and size. This is one of the small succulent types and a most unusual plant, with its long thin stems along which appear to be strung 'beads' in the form of spherical leaves 7mm (0.3in) in diameter. These beady stems trail and root when they make contact with the soil, so that a dense mat is eventually formed. The main interest of this little succulent is its fascinating leaf formation; the white flowers may or may not appear.

You can easily grow this senecio in a hanging basket if you persuade the stems to hang over the edge rather than rooting on the surface. To propagate, just remove a few pieces and pot them up at once. Any good potting mixture may be used; the plant is quite undemanding. Water it freely in spring and summer; feeding is not usually necessary.

Above: **Senecio rowleyianus**
Senecios show a vast difference in size; this is one of the miniature succulent ones. The stems take root easily on contact with the soil.

Setcreasea purpurea

- **Good light**
- **Temp: 10-16°C (50-60°F)**
- **Avoid wet conditions**

The humble tradescantia has many interesting relatives, including *S. purpurea*. Brilliant purple leaves are seen at their best when the plant is growing in good light with some direct sun, but very strong sun should be guarded against. They are impressive when grown in hanging pots or baskets: with all hanging plants one should endeavour to achieve a full effect, so lots of cuttings should go into each pot.

Cuttings of pieces of stem some 10cm (4in) long will not be hard to root in conventional houseplant potting mixture. Enclosing the cuttings in a small propagator, or even a sealed polythene bag, will reduce transpiration and speed up the rooting process. Several cuttings, up to five in each 7.5cm (3in) pot, will provide better plants than single pieces in the pot.

Like most of the tradescantia tribe, this one should be well watered and allowed to dry appreciably before watering again. Feed occasionally.

Sinningia speciosa

- **Good light**
- **Temp: 13-18°C (55-65°F)**
- **Keep moist; dry rest**

These plants may be acquired as tubers to be grown on, as seed to be sown and reared, or as finished plants from the retailer. Whatever the choice, splendid plants can be owned and admired; they have large, soft green leaves and their trumpet flowers up to 7.5cm (3in) across are produced throughout the summer months. A rosette of leaves develops from the tuber to be topped by almost stemless flowers.

While in leaf plants must be fed only with a high nitrogen fertilizer, but change to a high potash one when flower buds appear. Good light is maybe the most important need of this plant when in flower. Remove dead flowers to encourage new ones. When foliage dies down naturally in early autumn, allow the standard potting mixture to dry completely and store the tuber in a dry and warm place during the winter months.

Above: **Setcreasea purpurea**
A member of the tradescantia tribe. The leaves of this plant are purple all over and attached to firm succulent stems. Grow in bright light.

Right: **Sinningia speciosa**
Many fine hybrids of this plant are available, all with trumpet-shaped blooms in violet, red or white, some marked in contrasting shades.

A practical hint
Easier plants such as tradescantias are simple to propagate. Several cuttings to a small pot are better than individual pieces.

Smithiantha cinnabarina

- **Light shade**
- **Temp: 16-21°C (60-70°F)**
- **Keep moist and fed**

These interesting and colourful plants of the Gesneriaceae family can be kept in flower for many months of the year with a planned approach. Initially plants can be raised from seed or cuttings taken in the spring – keep the temperature at around 21°C (70°F) for both. Plants will grow and produce rhizomes and these can be planted at different times: spring planting for flowers in summer; early summer planting for flowers in the autumn; and mid-summer planting for flowers in winter. If a heated greenhouse is available plants can be induced to flower over this extended season to much enhance the indoor plant scene. Once indoors avoid draughts and cold.

Lush green leaves are topped by bell-shaped flowers that are available in many colours. From a packet of seed one would expect to get a good selection of different colours.

Left: **Smithiantha cinnabarina**
Grow this attractive flowering plant in warm, moist conditions and feed regularly when active. Use a loam-based potting mix with extra peat.

Sobralia macrantha

- **Cool/intermediate: 10-13°C (50-55°F)**
- **Easy to grow and flower**
- **Summer flowering**
- **Evergreen/semi-rest**

This genus contains 30 to 35 very handsome species, most of which are indigenous to tropical America. They are terrestrial plants producing long, slender, reed-like stems up to 2.4m (8ft) tall, although they are usually much shorter under cultivation. Leaves are produced along almost the full length of the stem.

The flowers, which are produced from the apex of the stems, are very similar in shape and general form to those of cattleyas. They last for only two or three days, but to compensate for this there is a quick succession of blooms from each stem, and a plant with a number of leads can be in flower for many weeks. The flowers are 13-15cm (5-6in) across, deep or pale purplish-mauve, with a yellow throat to the lip.

Sobralias like plenty of sunshine and fresh air. During the growing season they must be kept very moist at the root, whereas, when the plant is at rest, over the winter months, it should be kept drier, but never allowed to dry out. They can be overhead sprayed in summer.

Above: **Sobralia macrantha**
A tall-growing species for fairly cool conditions. Short-lived flowers in succession during the summer.

Solanum capsicastrum

- **Sunny location**
- **Temp: 10-16°C (50-60°F)**
- **Keep moist and fed**

These are cheap and cheerful shrubby plants with thin green leaves; they are normally available during the winter. Raised from seed the young plants are established in their pots then placed out of doors in full light and fresh air where they will make sturdy plants. Following the insignificant white flowers plants begin to develop green berries which will eventually turn red and become the plants' most interesting characteristic.

The orange-red berries remain colourful for many months if plants receive adequate light, but will fall at an alarming rate if the light is poor, and this need be for only a very short time. Keep plants moist and regularly fed. It is best to discard the plants after the berries have fallen.

Take care to keep these plants away from children – the attractive berries are poisonous if eaten.

Sophronitis coccinea

- **Cool/intermediate: 10-13°C (50-55°F)**
- **Moderately easy to grow**
- **Varied flowering season**
- **Evergreen/no rest**

Although only six species of this miniature epiphytic orchid are known, all of which come from Brazil, it has always been well represented in orchid collections, and its alliance with cattleyas has produced some of the most striking of the intergeneric hybrids.

In their natural habitat these plants grow mainly in areas of high humidity and shade, and therefore are subjects for the cool or intermediate house, with good shade during the summer months. They seem to grow best on a piece of cork bark, but they will also grow in a pot. Perfect drainage at the root is essential. Unfortunately, even in ideal conditions, sophronitis plants seem to have a lifespan of only a few years.

Formerly known as *S. grandiflora,* this orchid is vegetatively similar to a tiny cattleya, growing no higher than 7.5cm (3in). The single flower, 6.5cm (2.6in) across, is produced on a short stem that grows from the top of the pseudobulb. The petals are broader than the sepals and all the segments are bright scarlet, with the lip marked or lined with yellow.

Left: **Solanum capsicastrum**
Grow this decorative plant in loam-based potting mixture and keep it cool and well lit for winter berries.

Above: **Sophronitis coccinea**
Charming flowers appear on this miniature epiphytic orchid during late winter or spring. Needs care.

A practical hint
Like most succulents the stapelias produce fleshy growth, but the main interest is the intricate flowers with their repulsive smell!

Sparmannia africana

- **Light shade**
- **Temp: 16-21°C (60-70°F)**
- **Keep moist and fed**

The sparmannia may produce a few flowers but is principally a foliage plant. The leaves are very large and fresh green in colour and are produced in quantity from woody stems. Small plants have straight stems, but they will begin to branch while reasonably young, and develop into attractive small trees.

The number of leaves and vigour of growth immediately suggest that this is a hungry plant that will require adequate and frequent feeding to retain its pleasing colour and maintain its vigor without loss of leaves. Older plants can be quite severely pruned at any time of year. Firm pieces of stem with a few leaves attached can be very easily rooted in peaty mixture in a temperature around 18°C (65°F). Use peat to start them off, but pot on into loam-based potting soil as soon as they have a reasonable amount of roots.

Mealy bug can be a problem, but is easily detected and can be wiped off with methylated spirit.

Right: **Sparmannia africana**
Large, pale green leaves of coarse texture grow freely from stout stems with many branches. It will in time attain a height of about 2.4m (8ft). An easy-care plant.

A practical hint
Exotic strelitzias can be started from seed but are lamentably slow to flower and may take anything from three to ten years to mature.

Spathiphyllum 'Mauna Loa'

- **Light shade**
- **Temp: 18-21°C (65-70°F)**
- **Keep moist and fed**

Originally from the Hawaiian Islands, this is truly a very fine plant when grown in conditions that are in tune with its modest demands. The right temperature is one of its most important needs, never less than 18°C (65°F). The roots and the atmosphere surrounding the foliage should be moist, so misting will be beneficial in dry air conditions. Don't overwater, though.

In ideal conditions, plants will grow throughout the year and may produce elegant white spathe flowers at any time. Older plants can be divided to produce new ones and these should be potted into a loam-based mixture containing about 50 per cent peat. Place a layer of broken flower pot in the bottom of the container to improve drainage.

Check the undersides of leaves regularly for red spider mites which may infest the plant in too dry conditions.

Left:
Spathiphyllum 'Mauna Loa'
Constant warmth and high humidity will encourage this splendid hybrid to produce lovely white spathes up to 15cm (6in) long at any time.

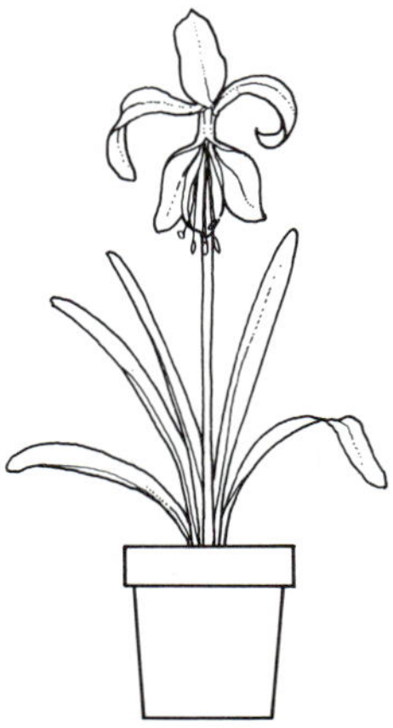

Sprekelia formosissima

- **Sunny location**
- **Temp: 10-16°C (50-60°F)**
- **Keep moist; dry in winter**

These are bulbous indoor plants with orchid-like scarlet flowers borne on stems about 50cm (20in) tall in the spring.

The bulbs, which are usually both expensive and in short supply, should be planted with their tips showing in a loam-based mixture that will sustain the plant in the same pot for several years. Following planting, keep in a light and warm place and water freely from the time growth is evident until the foliage dies naturally in the autumn. Then, the soil must remain bone dry until the following year. When flowers appear it will be a signal that feeding with weak liquid fertilizer should begin.

Although frequent potting on is not needed it will benefit the plants to topdress them with new mixture every year. Every four years the bulbs should be repotted and can be divided at the same time to produce new plants.

Above: **Sprekelia formosissima**
The striking red flower produced by this bulbous plant brings a welcome note of colour indoors during spring.

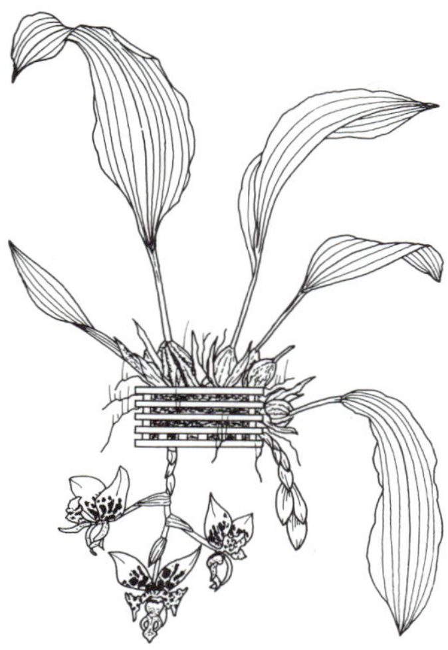

Stanhopea tigrina

- **Cool/intermediate: 10-13°C (50-55°F)**
- **Easy to grow and flower**
- **Summer flowering**
- **Evergreen/dry rest**

About 25 species of this fascinating genus have been described, although some may be variants rather than species. They are particularly remarkable for both their growth habit and their unusual flower shape. All are epiphytic and come from tropical America.

The flowering habit of stanhopeas is unusual in that the flower spike, which develops from the base of the pseudobulb, grows directly downwards through the compost to flower beneath the plant. For this reason, these orchids must be grown in wire or wooden-slatted baskets. Unfortunately, these highly fragrant flowers last for only about three days; nevertheless, the plants are of enormous interest and worthy of a place in any mixed collection of orchids.

The flowers of this species tend to be larger than those of *S. wardii*. The basic colour is ivory or pale yellow, and the sepals and petals are heavily blotched with maroon-purple. It is easily the most striking species and very fragrant. A large plant will bloom very freely in succession.

Left: **Stanhopea tigrina**
Magnificent but short-lived summer flowers in succession. A fragrant species. Grow cool in a basket.

Stanhopea wardii

- **Cool/intermediate: 10-13°C (50-55°F)**
- **Easy to grow and flower**
- **Summer flowering**
- **Evergreen/dry rest**

In common with the other species, *Stanhopea wardii* produces a 30-38cm (12-15in) broad, leathery leaf from the top of an oval pseudobulb. The flower spike, when it has emerged from the plant container, carries three to nine flowers in late summer. The buds develop very quickly and the flowers, up to 10cm (4in) across when fully open, vary from pale lemon to orange, dotted with brownish-purple, with a large blotch of the same colour on each side of the lip. The very strange shape of these flowers suggests a large insect hovering in flight.

Stanhopeas are among the easiest orchids to grow, requiring the conditions of the cool to intermediate house with moderate shade and moisture at the roots at all times. They should be grown in baskets or in purpose-made pots that have holes in the walls and base to prevent the flowers being trapped within the container. A large plant will bloom freely; the spikes open in succession, greatly extending the flowering season.

Above: **Stanhopea wardii**
This highly fragrant summer-flowering species is cool growing. Flowers last just a few days each.

Stapelia hirsuta

- **Full sun**
- **Temp: 10-30°C (50-86°F)**
- **Keep dry in winter**

This is a very succulent plant with four-angled velvety stems branching from the base. Although there are no spines, small teeth are borne along the angles of the stems; the stems can be up to about 20cm (8in) high and 2.5cm (1in) thick, but the plant may flower when only half this size. Of course, the most notable feature of any stapelia is its flower, with a supposed resemblance to carrion in appearance and colour. The flowers of *S. hirsuta* are up to 10cm (4in) across and of a starfish shape, the five 'arms' being purple-brown, striped with yellow; the whole is covered with purple hairs. The plant is less offensive to our noses than some other stapelias and you need not fear to keep it in the living-room.

Use a very well-drained potting mixture; add one part of sharp sand or perlite to two parts of a standard material, and top dress with gravel to prevent base rot.

Above: **Stapelia hirsuta**
The large flowers of this stapelia are covered with fine hairs, hence the name 'hirsuta', *or hairy.*

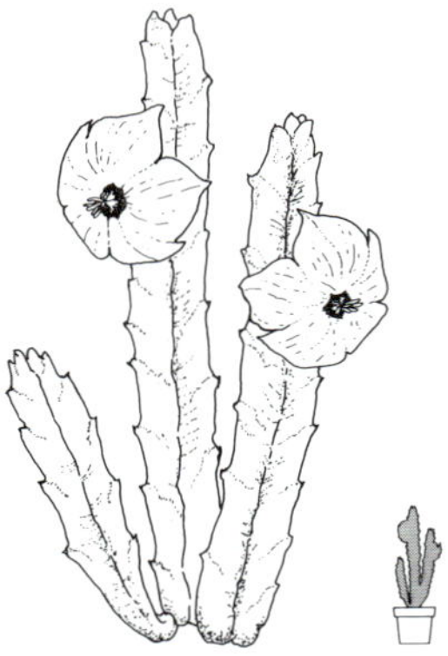

Stapelia revoluta

- **Full sun**
- **Temp: 10-30°C (50-86°F)**
- **Keep dry in winter**

The popular name of 'Carrion flower' applies to all the large-flowered stapelias, as they are pollinated in nature by flies. This unusual succulent plant has four-angled smooth stems with soft 'teeth' along the edges. The colour is bluish-green, brown towards the growing tips. Cultivated specimens reach a length of about 20cm (8in), with a stem thickness of 2cm (0.8in). Flowers of the typical starfish shape and reddish-brown in colour have the five lobes strongly reflexed backwards (hence the name 'revoluta') making the diameter of 3cm (1.2in) much less than the opened out size. Hairs on the flowers form a fringe around the edge.

Use an open potting mixture, consisting of one part sharp sand or perlite added to two parts of a standard material. Water in spring and summer, when the soil has almost completely dried out.

Stapelia (Orbea) variegata

- **Full sun**
- **Temp: 10-30°C (50-86°F)**
- **Keep dry in winter**

This is undoubtedly the commonest stapelia in cultivation and deservedly popular for the ease with which it produces its fascinating flowers. These are 5cm (2in) or more across with blunt lobes, very starfish-like, attractively patterned with chocolate blotches on a yellow background, and with a yellow central disc.

Stems are quite small; a large specimen would be only 10cm (4in) high but freely branching.

You can easily propagate this and other stapelias by removing a stem, sometimes with roots attached, in spring or summer. *S. variegata* is one of the less demanding stapelias, but nevertheless use a well-drained potting mixture; add about one third sharp sand or perlite to a good standard material. Although this stapelia will tolerate a winter temperature below 10°C (50°F), it does better if kept rather warmer. A living-room is ideal; there is no smell in winter!

Above: **Stapelia revoluta**
The fully reflexed lobes are shown in the drawing; in the photograph the position of the flower has prevented this happening completely.

Right: **Stapelia variegata**
Probably the commonest stapelia in cultivation and one of the easiest to grow and flower. Also, it seems to be the one that smells worst.

A practical hint
Glossy-leaved plants such as ficus benefit from cleaning unless cold. Use a moist sponge, but avoid excessive use of chemical cleaners.

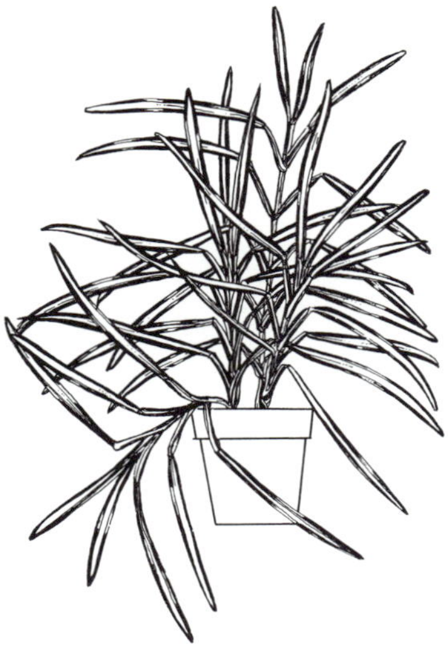

Stenotaphrum secundatum

- **Light shade**
- **Temp: 10-16°C (50-60°F)**
- **Keep very moist and fed**

This amazingly invasive grass bounds away in all directions once it has established a foothold. It is not unattractive, with cream and green variegation, the cream being predominant. Its major drawback is that as the plant produces fresh growth, so the older growth shrivels and dies, leaving dry brown leaves hanging from the lower parts of the plant. However, if one has time to remove these as they appear, the plant can be kept looking attractive.

Tufts of grassy leaves with a thicker base are produced in profusion; any removed and pushed into pots of peaty soil root almost at once. When plants appear to be past their best, root fresh cuttings and dispose of the aged parent. This is best done in the autumn, so that one will have more manageable plants to care for over the winter.

These plants will grow anywhere if there is moisture and warmth, and are very welcome as something different in the way of hanging plants.

Above far left:
Stenotaphrum secundatum
Amazingly vigorous plants that will quickly fill their allotted space. They are effective in hanging baskets.

Stephanotis floribunda

- **Good light**
- **Temp: 13-21°C (55-70°F)**
- **Keep moist; dry in winter**

Stephanotis will quickly fill its allotted space if given a free root run. Indoors, it requires a framework around which growth can be trained. Keep on the dry side in winter, and in the lightest possible location at all times, although avoiding direct summer sunshine.

The green, leathery leaves are evergreen and the flowers appear during the summer months. The white tubular flowers are produced in clusters of five or more and have the most overpowering scent.

Grow stephanotis in a loam-based mixture and repot into a slightly larger container every year. Feed with a standard liquid fertilizer every two weeks during the spring and summer and keep the soil and surroundings moist.

Pollinated flowers will occasionally result in large seedpods forming – these should be allowed to burst open before seed is removed and sown. New plants can also be grown from tip cuttings taken in spring. Examine undersides of leaves for mealy bug and scale insects.

Above left: **Stephanotis floribunda**
White waxy blooms up to 4cm (1.6in) long adorn this vigorous climbing shrub during the summer. An ideal plant for growing in a conservatory.

A practical hint
Many of the annual flowering plants can be raised from seed in modest conditions, but select only the best for growing on.

Strelitzia reginae

- **Sunny location**
- **Temp: 13-24°C (55-75°F)**
- **Keep moist; dry in winter**

This spectacular plant is suitable only where space is adequate; it grows to about 90-120cm (3-4ft) tall when confined to a pot and needs a 30cm (12in) pot when mature. It can be grown from seed but development is painfully slow; from sowing the seed to the production of flowers can be a period of five to ten years. But, if one is patient, the blue and orange flowers are quite a spectacle when they do appear, and have a very long life.

Full sunlight is essential, and plants need potting on when they have filled their existing pots with roots; use loam-based potting mixture at all stages of potting. Feeding is not desperately important and plants will tolerate long periods of draught without appearing to suffer undue harm.

Old clumps can be divided and the sections potted separately. These should flower after two to three years.

Steptocarpus 'Constant Nymph'

- **Good light**
- **Temp: 16-21°C (60-70°F)**
- **Keep moist and fed**

This is an old-fashioned yet favourite houseplant that seems to go on and on in spite of the new streptocarpus hybrids that come on the scene to challenge it. Flowers are a bright shade of blue and there rarely seems a time throughout the year when 'Constant Nymph' is not either in flower or showing signs of flowering.

Care and attention present few problems, as this plant appears to need little more than a light location, moderate watering, and the occasional feed to keep it in good order. Avoid saturating the soil.

When occasional repotting is required use a loam-based mixture and pots that are only a little larger than the one from which the plant is being removed. Raise new plants from leaves cut into sections and placed in peaty mix in a propagator.

Streptocarpus hybrids

- **Good light**
- **Temp: 16-21°C (60-70°F)**
- **Do not overwater**

In recent years, as with many other more common indoor plants, we have seen considerable improvement in the types of streptocarpus that are being offered for sale. Besides the more usual blue colouring of the variety 'Constant Nymph', there are now white, pink, red and purple shades of these plants available.

In culture they are all very similar, and require a light airy location at moderate temperatures to succeed. Place in good light with some protection from direct sunlight, and temperatures in the range 16-21°C (60-70°F). Feed every two weeks during the growing season with a high-phosphate fertilizer. Excessive watering can be damaging, so it is best to water the plant well and allow it to dry before repeating, bearing in mind that plants need much less water and no feed in winter.

New plants are raised by cutting leaves into 10cm (4in) sections and placing them in fresh peat at not less than 18°C (65°F).

Left: **Strelitzia reginae**
Striking flowers 20cm (8in) long are produced on mature plants during the spring and early summer. This plant must have very bright light.

Above:
Streptocarpus 'Constant Nymph'
Ever willing to bloom, this plant should present no problem indoors. Check for mealy bugs under leaves.

Above: **Streptocarpus hybrid**
This pink-flowered hybrid is one of the many colours made available by commercial growers. Regular feeding will prolong flowering.

A practical hint
When potting on taller cacti such as cereus it is advisable to put them into heavier clay pots that will offer stability when plants increase in size.

Streptocarpus saxorum

- **Good light**
- **Temp: 13-18°C (55-65°F)**
- **Avoid overwatering**

The sky-blue flowers are similar in shape to the more common streptocarpus, but the foliage is quite different. The individual leaves are small and succulent and produced in tight clusters on stems that become woody with age. Young growth is more pliable and will trail naturally from a suspended container, which makes the plant much more useful and interesting.

Individual flowers are small in size but are produced over a very long period – even into winter when growing conditions are favourable. Tips of growing shoots about 7.5cm (3in) in length will not be difficult to root in a propagating case heated to a minimum of 18°C (65°F). Cuttings should be placed in clean moist peat, several to each small pot, and can be taken at any time of the year.

Stromanthe amabilis

- **Shade**
- **Temp: 18-24°C (65-75°F)**
- **Keep moist**

This plant belongs to the same family as the calatheas and marantas. The oval-shaped leaves come to a point and are a bluish green in colour with bands of stronger colour running the length of the leaf. They overlap one another and are produced at soil level from a creeping rhizome. They reach a length of about 15-23cm (6-9in) and a width of 5cm (2in).

New plants are easily raised by dividing existing clumps into smaller sections and potting them up as individuals. The soil for this ought to be a good houseplant mixture containing a reasonable quantity of peat. Being squat plants they will also be better suited to shallow pans rather than full-depth pots. Shade is essential, as plants simply shrivel up when subjected to strong sunlight for any length of time. Soil should be kept moist, but it is absolutely necessary to ensure that it is moistness that is the aim and not total saturation.

Right: **Streptocarpus saxorum**
Succulent leaves and smaller blooms set this streptocarpus apart from the others but it can still provide a fine display in spring and summer.

Above right: **Stromanthe amabilis**
Similar in appearance to some of the marantas, these plants form neat low mounds of growth but need careful culture to succeed. Keep warm.

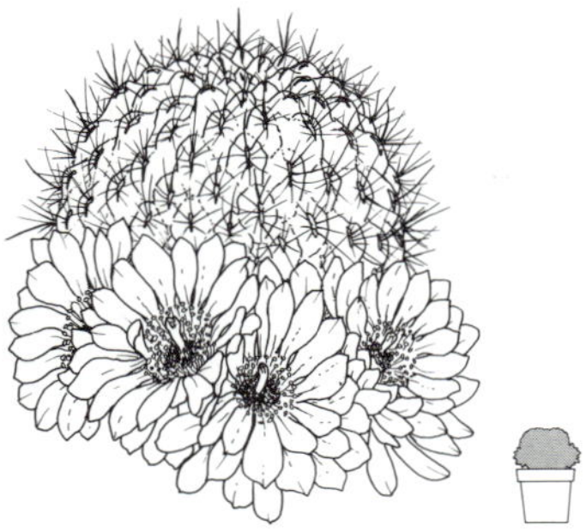

Sulcorebutia totorensis

- **Full sun**
- **Temp: 5-30°C (41-86°F)**
- **Keep dry in winter**

Sulcorebutias are small, clump-forming, low-growing cacti with large tap-roots; often there is more plant below the soil than above. They are particularly outstanding for their brightly coloured and distinctive flowers. Many have very small individual heads, but this is one of the larger growing types with heads up to 6cm (2.4in) across and almost as high. By the time the plant has reached this size there will usually be a number of offsets around the base. The deep reddish-purple flowers last for about five days, but because they open in succession, the flowering period may be four weeks.

Use a deep pot to accommodate the long root. Like all sulcorebutias, this plant needs a particularly well-drained potting mixture: up to half its volume of sharp sand or perlite.

Water quite freely in spring and summer, and when it is in full bloom feed every two weeks with a high-potassium fertilizer.

Above: **Sulcorebutia totorensis**
This is one of the larger sulcorebutias, but still quite small and forming a cluster of compact heads. Flowers open in succession.

Tetrastigma voinierianum

- **Light shade**
- **Temp: 16-21°C (60-70°F)**
- **Keep moist and well fed**

Given moist conditions in a warm greenhouse and reasonable cultural care you can almost stand and watch this plant putting on new growth! The lobed leaves are a soft green in colour and are seen at their best when the plant has freedom to climb a supporting stake or framework. As new small leaves appear, so do the fascinating hair-covered tendrils which reach out in search of an object to cling to. This is probably the quickest growing of all indoor plants, and is ideal if one needs a climber to cover a wall trellis in the minimum time.

Being vigorous plants, they have to be kept on the move with frequent feeding, doubling the fertilizer dose that the manufacturer recommends. It also means that potting on cannot be neglected: large plants of chestnut vine in small pots will never do well. The potting mixture must be a loam-based one and the potting should be done with a degree of firmness.

Above: **Tetrastigma voinierianum**
A rampant member of the vine family and perfect for covering an interior wall with its invasive, pale green growth and leaves. Clings naturally.

Thunbergia alata

- **Sunny location**
- **Temp: 13-18°C (55-65°F)**
- **Keep moist; dry in winter**

The triangular green leaves of this plant sprout from wiry stems that twine around any form of support within reach. Throughout the summer this rather plain foliage backdrop is adorned with striking bright orange flowers each with a jet black centre – hence its apt common name of Black-eyed Susan vine.

Offer a light window location and modest temperature, and feed regularly once the plants have started to grow. For the vigorous twining growth it is essential to provide a framework to which new growth can be attached or allowed to twine naturally around. When potting on use a loam-based potting mixture.

It is best to treat this plant as an annual and raise new plants from seed sown in spring.

Above: **Thunbergia alata**
Remove faded flowers to keep this climbing plant blooming. White-flowered and yellow-flowered varieties are also available.

A practical hint
Adult mealy bugs resemble woodlice with a powdery covering, and protect their young in a waxy cotton-wool substance that requires hand cleaning.

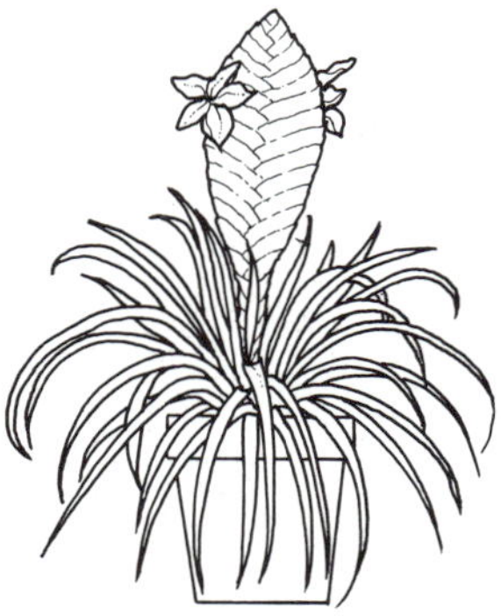

Tillandsia cyanea

- **Good light**
- **Temp: 16-21°C (60-70°F)**
- **Water moderately**

From a compact rosette of thin green leaves, *T. cyanea* will in time produce one of the most spectacular of flowering bracts, similar in shape to the cuttle fish. The bract emerges from among the leaves and eventually attains a size of about 15 by 7.5cm (6 by 3in). An added bonus is the appearance of brilliant violet-blue flowers along the margin of the bract over a period of several weeks. As one flower dies so another takes its place.

Avoid getting the soil too wet, and never be tempted to pot plants into large containers, as they will be very much happier in smaller pots in free-draining potting mixture. Use a conventional houseplant mix to which chopped pine needles have been added – the latter will keep the mixture open and prevent sodden conditions. Feeding is not important.

Above right: **Tillandsia cyanea**
Once it has flowered, the rosette of this charming bromeliad dies. New plants can be grown from offsets that form on the parent rosette. Detach when leaves are 7.5cm (3in) long.

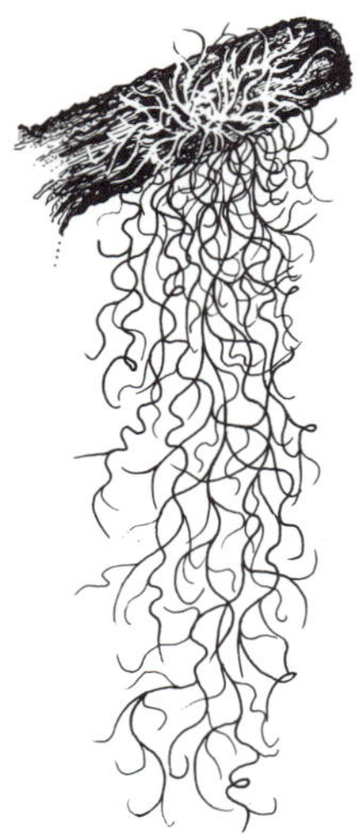

Tillandsia usneoides

- **Light shade**
- **Temp: 16-21°C (60-70°F)**
- **Spray foliage frequently**

One of the most fascinating plants of them all, in that it does not require any soil in which to grow. The plant has very slender stem-like leaves that form a tangled mass resembling a bundle of silvery-grey tangled wire. In their native Everglades of America these plants hang in dense masses from the branches of every tree.

A decorative few pieces on something like a small decorated bromeliad tree that is kept moist by frequent spraying can be a fascinating feature in the conservatory, where excess moisture will be easier to tolerate. Plants need only be hung over a branch. The clump will increase in size, and the strands in length. Ensure that the foliage is moistened regularly during the course of the day. Propagation means little more than teasing pieces away from the parent plant and hanging them up individually. Feeding is not necessary: other than water, the main need is for adequate warmth.

Above: **Tillandsia usneoides**
The thread-like growth of this unusual houseplant should be kept constantly moist by spraying. In warm surroundings the plant will grow when hung on a branch.

Titanopsis calcarea

- **Full sun**
- **Temp: 5-30°C (41-86°F)**
- **Keep dry during rest period**

'Titanopsis' means 'chalk-appearance' in Greek and describes the chalky appearance of the leaves, which closely resemble the limestone on which they grow. *T. calcarea* consists of 'stemless' rosettes 7.5cm (3in) across. Each rosette consists of two or three pairs of leaves. The grey-green leaves are wider at the tip, which is covered with whitish warts. The white and yellow flowers appear during the winter months. If it is a sunny winter the buds will open during the afternoon and close again at night. In cloudy weather the buds may abort.

The growing period of this plant is winter, when it should be watered on sunny days. Keep fairly dry in summer. Grow in a half-pot in a mixture of one part loam-based medium to one part grit. The plant may be propagated by splitting the cluster. Always include a short length of stem on the heads that are removed for propagation.

Left: **Titanopsis calcarea**
Looking just like a mound of chalky rocks, this strange succulent produces lovely flowers in winter. Grow in the sunniest part of the greenhouse, near the glass.

Tolmiea menziesii

- **Light shade**
- **Temp: 7-18°C (45-65°F)**
- **Keep moist and fed**

Interesting plants that develop into soft mounds of pale green foliage that are attractive at low level or suspended from the ceiling. Mature leaves develop perfect young plants that are carried on their backs. These can be detached when of reasonable size and potted up individually in peaty houseplant mixture. To succeed, plants should be kept in a light and airy place and be watered and fed with moderation. For mature plants use loam-based potting soil. Although they will tolerate very low temperatures and survive, they are better kept at around 16°C (60°F).

Hot and dry conditions increase the possibility of red spider mite infestation, which will in time considerably weaken plants. A sign of red spider presence will be a general hardening of the topmost leaves of the plant, which also become much paler. Check the undersides of leaves periodically with a magnifying glass; mites are very difficult to see otherwise.

Above: **Tolmiea menziesii**
The most endearing feature of this plant is the way in which perfectly shaped young plants form on the stalks of parent leaves. Needs cool conditions. Use rain water.

Tradescantia blossfeldiana

- **Good light**
- **Temp: 10-16°C (50-60°F)**
- **Keep on the dry side**

This interesting and robust plant has pale green hairy foliage and stout stems, and is capable of withstanding rough treatment. There is also a variegated form, with pale cream to yellow colouring suffused through the paler background green, and a purplish underside to the leaves. Both produce the typical three-petaled tradescantia flowers, which are purple with white tips.

One frequently sees very weedy examples of these plants about, and the trouble seems to be that the initial plants had only a single, straggly cutting put in the pot. With plants that produce lots of growth, as tradescantias do, always put several cuttings in the pot when propagating; you will then have a full and handsome final plant.

With hanging baskets of plants that become ragged in appearance, remove the tops of half a dozen shoots and insert them where there are gaps. Tradescantia cuttings root almost anywhere.

Above:
Tradescantia blossfeldiana
This is the variegated form, with attractive markings in cream, green and purple. Grow in loam-based mixture and feed during the summer.

Tradescantia 'Quicksilver'

- **Good light**
- **Temp: 10-16°C (50-60°F)**
- **Keep on the dry side**

There are numerous varieties of *T. fluminensis,* but this one is bolder and much brighter than any of the others; all, however, require very similar treatment.

Good light is important if plants are to retain their silvered variegation, but protection from bright sun will be necessary. The soil should be free to drain and at no time become waterlogged. These plants respond well to regular applications of liquid fertilizer while they are in active growth. The view that when plants are fed they tend to lose their variegation is nonsense, as variegation depends on available light and whether or not the plants are allowed to become green. In poor light leaves tend to become green; and green shoots will in time take over, if not removed.

For baskets there are no better foliage plants, and small baskets or pots can be started by placing cuttings directly into the basket potting soil.

Above: **Tradescantia 'Quicksilver'**
A vigorous variety of this popular plant and one that is ideal for growing in a hanging basket. Be sure to remove green growth to keep the plant attractively variegated.

A practical hint
Cacti produce many spiteful spines that make handling and potting difficult. A collar of paper placed around the plant offers protection.

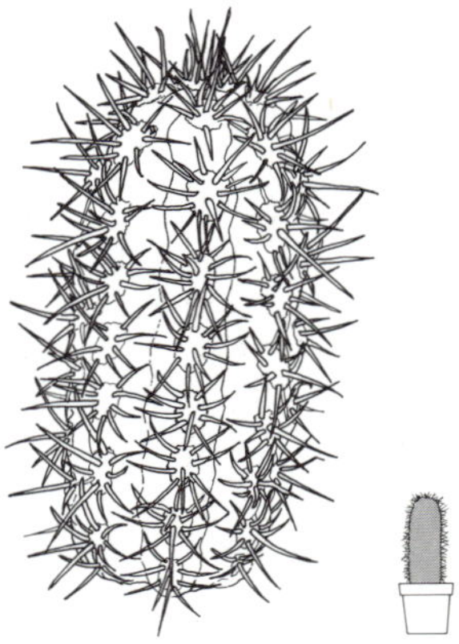

Trichocereus chilensis

- **Full sun**
- **Temp: 5-30°C (41-86°F)**
- **Keep dry in winter**

Trichocerei are pretty when small, but this cactus will not grow too large during the lifetime of its owner. This one is sometimes offered for sale and is well worth acquiring. With naturally large-growing cacti it is difficult to state a definite size but a good cultivated specimen would be about 20cm (8in) high and 5-8cm (2-3.2in) across after many years. But you are likely to buy this one at around 5cm (2in) high. The long golden-brown, stout spines arranged along the many-ribbed bright green stems make this a most attractive cactus, which is just as well, because it is of no use to expect flowers except on very large specimens. But the white flowers, when produced, are beautiful and pleasantly perfumed. Because the stem is unbranched, propagation from cuttings is not possible.

Any good standard peat- or loam-based potting mixture will do for this very tolerant cactus and you can water it freely in spring and summer.

Left: **Trichocereus chilensis**
All trichocerei are potentially large cacti. This is a beautiful one, with stout, sharp spines of an attractive colour. Flowers are unlikely so enjoy the plant for its appearance only.

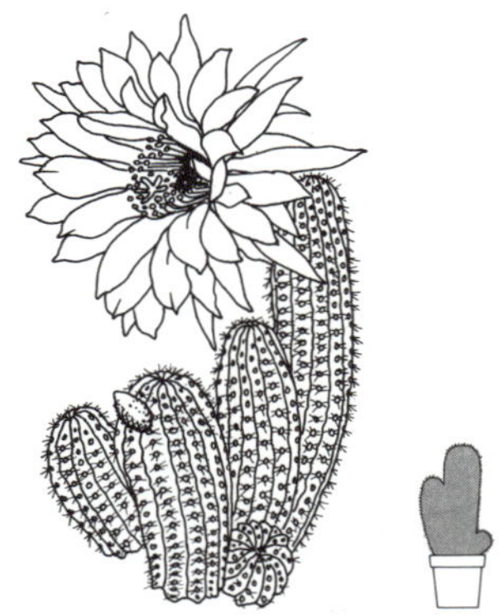

Trichocereus spachianus

- **Full sun**
- **Temp: 5-30°C (41-86°F)**
- **Keep dry in winter**

This trichocereus is another naturally large cactus that makes a good smaller specimen for a collection. It could easily reach a height of 30cm (12in), with bright green stems eventually branching from the base. The blunt ribs bear only quite short spines, and the plant is reasonably easy to handle. If allowed to become large enough it may well respond by producing large greenish-white flowers from the top, opening at night. But the main use for this plant is as a grafting stock for other cacti, and unless you want a large specimen, it is simplicity itself to produce many small ones. If any branch is cut off, not only will it root if given the usual few days' drying-off period, but the stump will send out a ring of offsets, which can be removed and potted up in their turn.

With a good standard porous potting mixture, peat- or loam-based, it is not necessary to add extra drainage material. Water freely in spring and summer.

Left: **Trichocereus spachianus**
This trichocereus will make a good pot specimen; and if it can be given enough space, it may well flower.

Trichopilia tortilis

- **Cool/intermediate: 10-13°C (50-55°F)**
- **Easy to grow and flower**
- **Summer flowering**
- **Evergreen/semi-rest**

About 30 species of *Trichopilia* are known, although only a few of these are available to growers today. Despite this, they remain very popular, partly because they are not difficult to cultivate and also because of their very showy flowers, which are large in comparison with the size of the plant. The plants are epiphytic and are found mainly in South America.

The plants, which never grow very tall, develop flattened pseudobulbs that may be rounded or elongated, and a solitary leathery leaf. Intermediate house conditions suit them well, with good shade during the summer months. The plants benefit from generous moisture at the root in full growth. After flowering, these orchids should be allowed a period of semi-rest.

This plant carries a single flower, up to 13cm (5in) across, on a pendent spike. The sepals and petals, which are narrow and twisted throughout their length, are brown, bordered by a narrow yellow-green band; the trumpet-shaped lip is white with some rose-red spotting.

Above: **Trichopilia tortilis**
A summer-flowering orchid of compact habit for the cool or intermediate greenhouse.

Tulipa

- **Good light**
- **Temp: 10-16°C (50-60°F)**
- **Keep moist**

Possibly the most colourful of all the spring bulbs, tulips can also be grown successfully indoors for that winter splash of colour. When selecting, choose only the finest quality bulbs if you wish to obtain the best results. Also, it is wise to choose the varieties that are normally recommended for rockeries, as these will be shorter and more appropriate for indoor decoration. Among the rockery varieties there are many fascinating colours, some with the added benefit of attractive foliage.

Plant the bulbs in shallow pans in a fibrous mixture in the autumn and keep them in a cool dark place. Just the tips of the bulbs should be visible above the moistened bulb fibre. When the developing leaves are about 7.5cm (3in) tall transfer the container to a cool light place. When flower buds are just evident, the plants can be transferred to a slightly warmer place, but high temperatures must be avoided. Discard the bulbs after flowering.

Above: **Tulipa (Triumph type)**
Tulips can be grown indoors in the same way as other spring bulbs. Be sure to keep them cool.

A practical hint
The compact habit and attractive waxy flowers of *Vanda cristata* make it a handsome orchid for indoors. Spray foliage in summer; water less in winter.

Vallota speciosa

- **Sunny location**
- **Temp: 13-18°C (55-65°F)**
- **Keep moist**

Given reasonable light, moderate temperature, and care to prevent the potting mixture becoming excessively wet, these attractive plants will go on for years with few problems. The bulbous plants have green strap-shaped leaves and attractive scarlet flowers borne on stems about 60cm (2ft) in height.

New plants can be raised from seed or, perhaps more easily, from offsets that form around the base of the parent bulb. The offsets, which are very small, should be removed in the autumn for planting in a group in a shallow pan of peaty mixture. They do not need frequent repotting.

Unlike many bulbs, a resting period is not required, so the mixture – a rich, loam-based one is best – should be kept moist throughout the year. However, at no time should it become excessively wet.

Left: **Vallota speciosa**
The spectacular scarlet flowers are produced in late summer and may last for several weeks in coolness.

A practical hint
In time, all perennial flowering plants need potting on. Most will benefit from a loam-based soil, but very large pots are not vital.

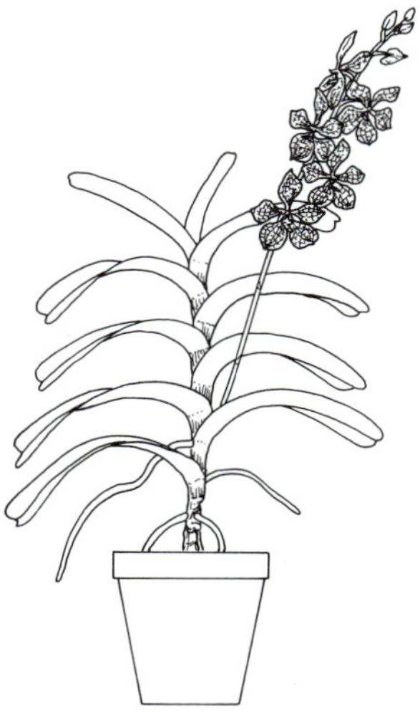

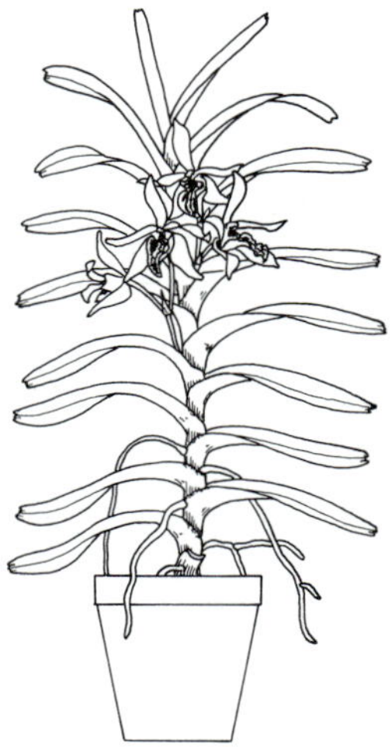

Vanda coerulea

- **Intermediate: 13°C (55°F)**
- **Moderately easy to grow**
- **Autumn/winter flowering**
- **Evergreen/semi-rest**

This is perhaps the showiest and most popular vanda for collectors. Blooming in autumn and winter with lovely pale blue flowers, *V. coerulea* is found wild in the Himalayas, Burma and Thailand, growing at about 1,220-1,830m (approx. 4,000-6,000ft). The leaves are leathery and rigid, about 25cm (10in) long and 2.5cm (1in) wide, and the flower stems are erect or arching to about 60cm (2ft) with from five to 20 flowers per spike.

The flowers can be variable in colour, shape and size, but are generally 10cm (4in) across with pale blue sepals and petals and a network of darker markings. The lip is purple-blue marked with white. Though most vandas revel in warmth, *V. coerulea* is a subject for the intermediate greenhouse.

Today this plant is seldom seen in collections owing to its rarity. Imported plants are no longer available and it is to the nurseryman that you should look for supplies of nursery-raised seedlings. These are not plentiful as the species is not easy to raise from seed.

Above right: **Vanda coerulea**
This blue-flowered species is for the intermediate house. Sprays of lovely flowers are produced in the autumn.

Vanda cristata

- **Cool/intermediate: 10-13°C (50-55°F)**
- **Easy to grow and flower**
- **Spring/summer flowering**
- **Evergreen/semi-rest**

This small orchid, which grows only to about 25cm (10in), is a good subject for indoor growing. It is native to high-altitude areas of Nepal and Bhutan. The leaves are 15cm (6in) long and the flowers waxy and fragrant, about 5cm (2in) across. The sepals and petals are mostly yellow-green, and the entire flower is marked with blood-red longitudinal stripes and spots. Blooming from early spring until mid-summer, this is a fine orchid for those with limited space.

This species is one of the few vandas suitable for beginners. It flowers very freely on a modestly sized plant and the flowers last for many weeks. Regular spraying of the whole plant, except when in bloom, will encourage the growth of fat, aerial roots, which grow at right angles from the stem. When the green tips of the roots become concealed by a white covering the plant is at rest and should be kept semi-dry.

This plant enjoys a position of good light in the cool or intermediate greenhouse.

Right: **Vanda cristata**
A small-growing species for cool or intermediate conditions. It blooms in the spring and summer months.

A practical hint
For indoors the miniature size of the orchid *Cymbidium devonianum* has much appeal, and produces green flowers that are speckled with red.

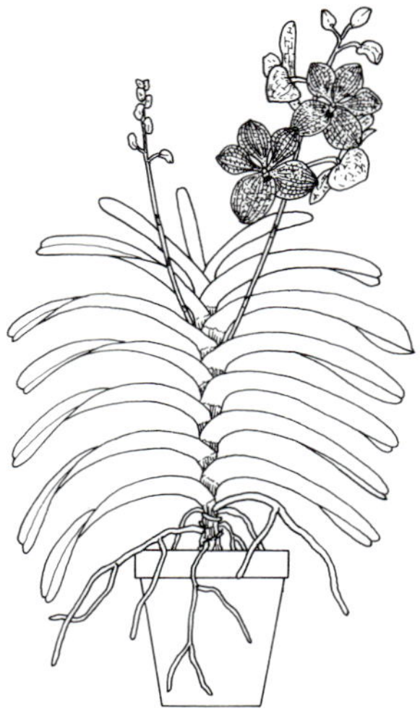

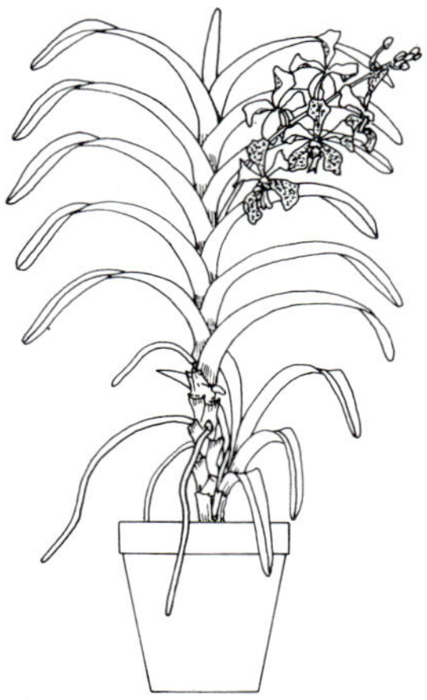

Vanda Rothschildiana

- **Warm: 18°C (65°F)**
- **Moderately easy to grow**
- **Winter flowering**
- **Evergreen/no rest**

Sometimes called a species but more often known as a hybrid, this cross between *V. coerulea* and *V. sanderana* is a display of nature at its finest. The plant has 25cm (10in) leaves, and grows to a height of about 75cm (30in). The flower spikes are arching and crowded with five to ten flowers of intense blue, almost crystalline in texture. The blooms, which are flat-faced and appear in mid-winter, are often 13-15cm (5-6in) across. This remarkable orchid can carry as many as three or four spikes of flowers.

Blue is an extremely rare colour in orchids and therefore any blue orchid carries a special appeal to growers. *Vanda* Rothschildiana is one of the finest deep blue orchids in the world. Being a robust grower, it is somewhat easier than many other hybrids and a good plant for a vanda fancier to start with. However, it requires warm and sunny conditions with a high humidity at all times. *V.* Rothschildiana was first raised in 1931, since when the cross has been remade many times.

Left: **Vanda Rothschildiana**
This warm-growing, winter-flowering hybrid is easier to grow than most Vanda *hybrids.*

Vanda suavis

- **Warm: 18°C (65°F)**
- **Moderately easy to grow**
- **Autumn/winter flowering**
- **Evergreen/semi-rest**

Coming from Java and Bali, this free-flowering strap-leaved epiphyte bears colourful flowers in autumn and early winter. The stems are densely leafy with curving leaves about 25cm (10in) long and 2.5cm (1in) wide. Flower spikes are horizontal, shorter than the leaves and carry five to ten flowers that vary in shape and colour. Typically they have whitish-yellow sepals and petals barred or spotted with red-brown, usually flushed with pale magenta near the base. The fragrant waxy flowers are about 7.5cm (3in) across. This vanda is moderately easy to coax into bloom in warm sunny conditions, although it should not be attempted by beginners. A well-grown plant can reach to a considerable height and in full leaf is a grand sight. It is also found under the name of *Vanda tricolor.*

Unobtainable from the wild, the few plants in cultivation are usually the result of propagating existing stock. New plants, complete with roots, are occasionally formed around the base of the parent.

Above left: **Vanda suavis**
A tall-growing species for the warm house. It flowers freely in the autumn and winter on long fragrant sprays.

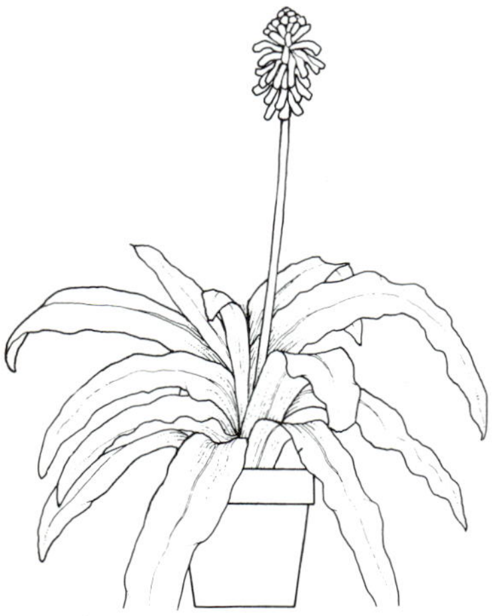

Veltheimia viridifolia

- **Good light**
- **Temp: 16-21°C (60-70°F)**
- **Keep moist and fed**

This bulbous plant from South Africa deserves to be more popular than it is at present. Leaves are large and soft green in colour. Its flowers – pink tinged with yellow – appear during the winter months.

Bulbs of *V. viridifolia* should be planted in early autumn to flower in winter. Place the bulbs in a loam-based mixture to which a liberal amount of peat has been added; just cover the bulbs with the mixture, ensuring that the potting is done with some firmness. Keep the soil on the dry side until new growth is under way, then water more liberally. Feed with a standard liquid fertilizer every month when in active growth.

They make good centrepiece plants provided they are given cool and light indoor conditions. During the summer place the plants in an unheated greenhouse until required again in the autumn.

Vriesea mosaica

- **Light shade**
- **Temp: 16-21°C (60-70°F)**
- **Water into urn of leaves**

Some of the vrieseas are quite small and produce their flowering bracts at an early age, whereas others, such as *V. mosaica,* are grown principally for their decorative foliage. The colouring of *V. mosaica* is a dull reddish-brown, and there are interesting variations of colour through and across the leaf, as the name suggests.

This plant is quite rare and seldom offered for sale, but others of similar type are seen occasionally. Most have intricate patterns and colours in their recurving leaves, and grow to considerable size. They also have the typical bromeliad rosette of recurving leaves that makes a watertight urn into which water can be poured for the plant to live on. The urn should be kept topped up and the water replenished occasionally, but there is seldom need to water the soil in the pot – spillage from the urn is usually enough to keep the soil moist enough. All bromeliads do better in a mix of peat and coarse leaf mould.

Right: **Veltheimia viridifolia**
The beautiful flower spike, up to 60cm (2ft) tall, appears after the glossy green leaves develop.

Above: **Vriesea mosaica**
A fine member of the bromeliad family with mainly reddish-brown colouring. Very decorative.

A practical hint
Plants preferring acid soil, such as azaleas and ericas, will also be the better for the use of rain water for watering and spraying.

Vriesea splendens

- **Good light; some sunshine**
- **Temp: 16-21°C (60-70°F)**
- **Keep moist; drier in winter**

This plant is a member of the splendid bromeliad family with a typical rosette of overlapping leaves that form a natural urn for holding water. The urn must be kept topped up at all times but needs to be cleaned out and freshly watered periodically.

The broad recurving leaves of *Vriesea splendens* are grey-green in colour with darker bands of brownish purple across the leaf. The flower spike usually develops in the summer and may last for many weeks. The bright red bracts enclosing the short-lived yellow flowers provide the main display of colour.

Grow this plant in a mixture of equal parts of loam-based growing medium and fir bark chips, or use a commercially prepared bromeliad mix. The main rosette flowers only once then dies, but as the plant deteriorates offsets form at the base of the trunk and, once rooted, these can be detached and potted separately to provide new plants.

Right: **Vriesea splendens**
This magnificent plant needs high humidity to flourish. Feed once a month when it is actively growing.

A practical hint
Adult orchid plants from which propagating material is taken should not be reduced to fewer than three or four pseudobulbs.

Vuylstekeara Cambria 'Plush'

- **Cool/warm: 10-16°C (50-60°F)**
- **Easy to grow and flower**
- **Varied flowering season**
- **Evergreen/no rest**

Every now and again a classic hybrid appears on the scene and *Vuylstekeara* Cambria 'Plush' is surely one of these. Although the cross was made in 1931, it was not until 1967 that the variety 'Plush' received a First Class Certificate from the Royal Horticultural Society, and 1973 when it obtained a First Class Certificate from the American Orchid Society – a unique double for a unique clone. Vuylstekearas are produced by introducing *Miltonia* (the pansy orchids) into *Odontioda* breeding, and they are characterized by large miltonia-type lips and glowing colours. This plant has 9cm (3.5in) dark red flowers, with large red and white lips.

Adaptability to various growing conditions has helped to make Cambria popular throughout the world; it is ideal for almost all collections, because it will grow well in cool, intermediate or warm environments. It also makes an ideal beginner's houseplant; the charming flowers never fail to please everyone.

Above left:
Vuylstekeara Cambria 'Plush'
Cool- or intermediate-growing, variable flowering. Very easy.

A practical hint
Besides foliage bugs there are also root mealy bugs, which are smaller in size; evidence of their presence is white powder around roots of plants.

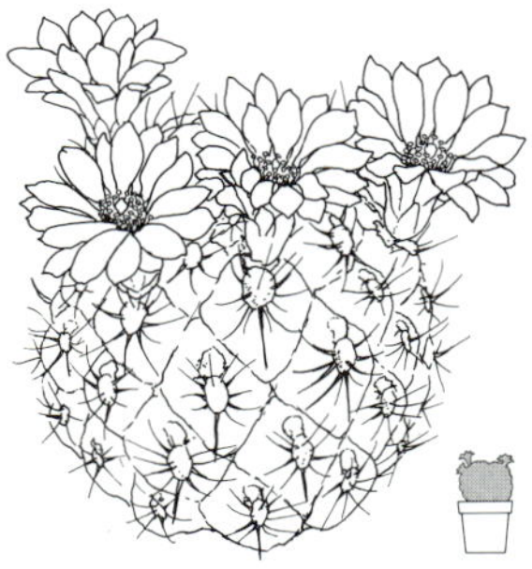

Weingartia cumingii

- **Full sun**
- **Temp: 5-30°C (41-86°F)**
- **Keep dry in winter**

This free-flowering small cactus is sometimes included with *Gymnocalycium*, because of also having hairless flower buds. But, apart from this, the resemblance is not very great. *W. cumingii* is a bright green, spherical plant with a maximum diameter of about 10cm (4in), and divided into a number of spiral, notched ribs. The golden spines are usually less than 1cm (0.4in) long and quite soft and bristly. Deep yellow flowers are freely produced around the top of the stem in spring and summer, about 3cm (1.2in) across.

If you keep this plant indoors, be sure to put it in the coldest room in winter (but with good light) in order to encourage flowering the following year. In a greenhouse there should be no problem. Grow this weingartia in a mixture of a good standard material and sharp sand or perlite in the proportion of three to one. Water freely in spring and summer, and give a feed every two weeks with a high-potassium fertilizer.

Right: **Weingartia cumingii**
A particularly free-flowering small cactus, producing masses of blooms in spring and summer.

A practical hint
Scented stephanotis needs less water in winter; it is also liable to mealy bug attack, so periodic inspection of the plant is vital.

Weingartia lanata

- **Full sun**
- **Temp: 5-30°C (41-86°F)**
- **Keep dry in winter**

The 'lanata' in the name of this delightful cactus is derived from the clumps of white wool scattered over the stem, which is roughly spherical and reaches a diameter of about 10cm (4in). The spiral ribs are deeply notched so that the appearance is of a mass of large tubercles rather than ribs. It is on the ends of these tubercles that the woolly hair appears, more towards the top of the plant, and also clumps of stiff but not very stout pale brown spines, about 2cm (0.8in) long. For sheer beauty the golden yellow flowers are unsurpassed. Although only about 3cm (1.2in) across, they are produced in profusion around the top of the stem, and in a good year spring or summer flowering is often followed by one in the autumn. The flowers last for several days, but unfortunately they are scentless.

This is not a demanding cactus, but to be on the safe side add about one third of extra sharp sand or perlite to a good standard mixture. Feed during the flowering period with a high-potassium fertilizer.

Above left: **Weingartia lanata**
The tufts of white wool give this cactus its name. Freely produced flowers appear over a long period.

A practical hint
Schlumbergera (Zygocactus) can spend the summer in the garden so that firmer and more attractive foliage will develop.

Wilsonara Widecombe Fair

- **Cool/intermediate: 10-13°C (50-55°F)**
- **Easy to grow and flower**
- **Varied flowering season**
- **Evergreen/no rest**

This hybrid between the small but many-flowered species *Oncidium incurvum* and *Odontioda* Florence Stirling produces long spikes and many 5cm (2in) white flowers, which are heavily marked with pink, and is well suited for the mixed collection. The plant can be grown in cool or intermediate conditions, and will tolerate fluctuations in temperature.

Although the individual flowers are smaller and more 'starry' than most intergeneric odontoglossums, they are uniquely pretty and when massed on the huge branching 'Christmas tree' flower spikes are quite breath-taking. This hybrid represents a different breeding line, characterized by the species *Oncidium incurvum*, which has dominated the size and shape of the individual flowers as well as the flowering habit. It is an unusual and charming addition to any collection. Its adaptability and ease of culture make it an ideal beginner's orchid.

It should be kept moist all year and lightly sprayed in summer.

Right: **Wilsonara Widecombe Fair**
An easy-to-grow, cool-house hybrid that produces hundreds of flowers on a long branching spike.

A practical hint
Foliage mealy bug is controlled by insecticide spray or methylated spirit, and root bug by drenching with liquid insecticide around the roots.

Yucca aloifolia

- **Good light**
- **Temp: 10-21°C (50-70°F)**
- **Keep on the dry side**

The woody lengths of stem are imported from the tropics in very large quantities; they come in an assortment of sizes and are rooted at their destination, then potted and sold with their attractive aloe-like tufts of growth at the top of the stem.

Further benefits of this plant are that they are pleasing to the eye when grouped together, and little trouble to grow.

They do best in well-lit, coolish rooms if given the minimum of attention. The soil should be allowed to dry out quite appreciably between waterings and feed should be given once every 10 days during the summer months.

Purchased plants are normally in pots relevant to their height, so the pot is often quite large; as a result of this, the plant is growing in a container in which it can remain for two years or more. Plants should be potted on only when they have well filled their existing pots with roots. Use loam-based soil for this job when it is done.

Above left: **Yucca aloifolia**
Stately plants ideal for difficult locations indoors, as they are very durable if not overwatered.

A practical hint
Fleshy-leaved succulents are generally freer growing and easier to propagate, from either rosettes or pieces of stem.

Zantedeschia rehmannii

- **Good light**
- **Temp: 10-16°C (50-60°F)**
- **Keep moist; dry in winter**

Frequently seen in flower borders out of doors, this compact arum with attractive leaves and pinkish flowers is also a fine plant for summer flowering indoors. It grows to a height of about 60cm (2ft). Ample water and frequent feeding are essential when plants are in leaf and flower.

In the autumn, when foliage begins to die down naturally, watering should be gradually discontinued until the soil is quite dry. Leave it in this condition until the following early spring. At this time the rhizomes should be repotted into fresh soil with reasonable body to it. A loam-based mixture would be suitable for potting, but a liberal amount of peat should be incorporated.

New plants can be started either from the small offshoots or by dividing the rhizomes when repotting.

Zebrina pendula

- **Good light**
- **Temp: 13-18°C (55-65°F)**
- **Keep moist and fed**

This very common member of the tradescantia family has extraordinary colouring in its leaves, all of which have a plain purple reverse. It is one of the easiest plants to care for indoors, but the ease of care sometimes results in the plant being neglected.

Plants are very easily started from cuttings taken at any time other than winter. These should go into small pots filled with peaty soil, six or seven cuttings in each pot. Once established, put three or four pots of cuttings into a small hanging basket filled with a good houseplant potting soil, and keep the basket at a low level until the plants have obviously got under way; then the basket can be suspended at about head level. (If baskets are suspended immediately after planting, their care is often neglected.) Put plants in a light position out of direct sunlight, and water and feed them well while they are active; keep them dryish in winter, with no feeding.

Above right:
Zantedeschia rehmannii
Elegant blooms of a delicate pink are produced during the summer months. Keep the plant fairly cool.

Right: **Zebrina pendula**
From the lowly tradescantia tribe, but a surprisingly colourful plant when seen as a well-grown specimen. An ideal plant for a hanging basket.

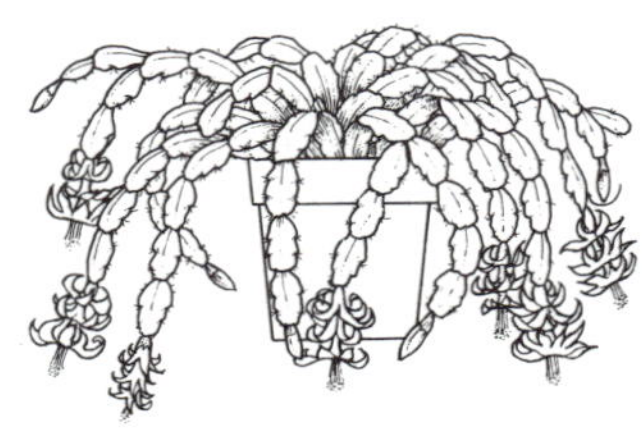

Zygocactus 'Margaret Koniger'

(Schlumbergera)
- **Partial shade**
- **Temp: 13-24°C (55-75°F)**
- **Keep slightly moist all year**

These plants are generally offered under both names, *Zygocactus* and *Schlumbergera.* In recent years we have seen many fine new coloured flowers being added to the original species *Zygocactus truncatus.* Colours now include pale salmon, pink (as here), red and a lovely variety 'White Christmas', which has white flowers with a cerise flush in the throat.

All produce pads of fleshy leaf growth that extend one from the other as the plant develops, with flowers appearing at the ends of the pads in winter. Plants flourish in coolish, light conditions, and will be better for spending the summer in a sunny, sheltered spot outdoors. Use a rich peaty mixture with one third coarse sand or perlite. Water freely and feed regularly while in bud and flower, reducing watering afterwards.

Pieces made up of two or three segments will root if inserted in peaty mixture. Take the cuttings in spring or summer.

Above:
Zygocactus 'Margaret Koniger'
Beautiful pink blooms are produced abundantly during winter. Do not disturb the plant while in bud.

Zygopetalum intermedium

- **Intermediate: 13°C (55°F)**
- **Moderately easy to grow**
- **Winter flowering**
- **Evergreen/dry rest**

This genus comprises 20 species, most of which come from Brazil. They are mainly terrestrial, producing rounded pseudobulbs with long but fairly narrow leaves.

These are plants for the intermediate house and require good light, with plenty of moisture at the root when in full growth. Air movement around the plant in conditions of high humidity is very important, otherwise the leaves soon become badly spotted; and, for this reason, they should never be sprayed.

Often known as *Z. mackayi,* this plant produces an upright flower spike, 45-60cm (18-24in) in height, from inside the first leaves of a new growth. The spike bears four to eight flowers, each 7.5cm (3in) across. The sepals and petals are of equal size, and bright green blotched with brown. The lip, in contrast, is broad, flat and basically white, heavily lined with purple. These heavily scented flowers last for four or five weeks during the winter months.

Left: **Zygopetalum intermedium**
A fragrant, winter-flowering species suitable for the intermediate house. It is important to provide high humidity with adequate ventilation.

Epiphyllum 'Ackermannii'

Common Name Index

Under each common name the botanical names of the plants featured in the book are listed in alphabetical order, together with the relevant page numbers. Alternative botanical names are shown in brackets. The index includes common names that are the same as the botanical names, such as Begonia and Chrysanthemum. In these cases the botanical names of all the plants featured in the book under that common name are listed.

Chlorophytum comosum variegatum

Credits

Line artwork
The drawings in this book have been prepared by the following people:
Foliage and flowering plants: Tyler/Camoccio
Design Consultants. Cacti and succulents: Maureen Holt.
Orchids: David Leigh. All drawings © Salamander Books Ltd.

Photographs
The publishers wish to thank the following photographers and agencies who have supplied photographs for this book. The photographs have been credited by page number and position on the page: (B) Bottom, (T) Top, (C) Centre, (BL) Bottom left etc.

A-Z Botanical Collection: 17 (TR), 26 (TL), 42 (BR), 62-3 (B), 167 (T), 176 (R), 178 (TL), 256-7 (C), 272 (TC), 296-7, 298 (TR), 301 (TC), 302 (TL)

Pat Brindley: 60 (L), 67 (R), 82 (TL, TC), 85 (B), 128-9 (B), 241 (TR, B), 288-9 (C)

Alec Bristow: 96 (B), 104 (TL)

Peter Chapman and Margaret Martin: 21 (TL), 22 (BR), 23 (BL), 27, 34 (T), 42 (TL), 64 (T), 65 (T), 66 (B), 78 (TC), 78-9 (C), 81 (TR), 96 (T), 109 (TR), 114 (TR), 114-5 (B), 115 (TL), 116 (TL), 118 (TL, TR), 118-9 (C), 120-1 (C), 121 (TR), 127 (TR), 133 (TR), 134 (TR, B), 139, 140 (TL), 149 (T), 154, 155, 156 (TL), 158 (TR), 178-9 (C), 188 (TR), 188-9 (B), 189 (T), 190-1 (C), 196, 197 (B), 208 (T), 212 (TR), 212-3 (B), 214 (T), 224, 225, 226-7 (T), 227 (TC), 238-9 (C), 261 (T), 268-9 (C), 269, 282 (TL), 294 (TL), 300-301 (B), 302-3 (C), 310 (T)

Eric Crichton: 14, 16, 17 (B), 18 (TC), 20 (TR), 24-5 (T), 24-5 (B), 29 (TR, BL), 30, 31, 32 (TR, BL), 36 (B), 44 (TL), 45 (T), 46 (B), 47 (L), 49 (TC), 51 (TR), 52, 53, 54, 55, 56-7 (T), 58-9 (T, B), 60 (TR), 62 (TL), 63 (TL), 68 (TL), 71, 72-3 (B), 74 (T), 74-5 (B), 76, 82-3 (B), 83 (TR), 88, 89, 90, 91, 92, 93, 94 (TL, TC), 97, 98 (TR, BR), 99, 100, 100-1 (C), 102, 103, 104 (TC), 104-5 (B), 108 (TR), 110-1 (C), 113 (TR), 122 (T), 123, 124, 128 (T), 130 (B), 135, 136, 137 (T), 146 (L), 150 (B), 151, 152 (T), 160-1 (T), 161 (BL), 165 (BL), 166 (TL), 168-9 (T, B), 171 (R), 175 (B), 177, 180, 181, 182, 183, 184, 191 (TR), 192, 193, 194 (TL), 198 (L), 200, 201 (B), 202 (TL), 204, 205, 208 (B), 210-1 (TC, BC), 214 (B), 215, 216, 217, 218, 219, 220, 221, 222-3 (C), 230, 231, 232, 233, 234, 235, 236, 237, 243 (T), 246-7 (C), 247, 248, 249, 260 (T), 260-1 (B), 264, 266 (TL), 271 (TR), 272 (TL), 273 (TR), 282 (R), 287 (R), 289 (TR), 290, 297 (TR), 304 (TR), 305 (R), 306, 307, 309 (T), 311 (B), 313 (B)

Eric Crichton (© Salamander Books Ltd.): 15, 18 (TL), 19 (TR), 24 (TL), 25 (TR), 26 (TR), 28, 32 (TL), 34 (B), 35, 36 (TL, TR), 38, 39, 40-1 (C), 42 (TR), 43 (L), 44 (TR), 44-5 (B), 46 (T), 47 (TR), 48, 49 (TL), 56, 56-7 (B), 57, 58 (TL), 65 (B), 67 (TL), 69 (TC), 72 (TL, TC), 72-3 (T), 77 (TR), 84, 85 (T), 86-7 (C), 94-5 (C), 95, 105 (TR), 106, 107, 108 (TL), 111 (TL, TR), 112, 113 (L), 130 (T), 131 (TR), 137 (B), 138 (TL), 141 (TR), 142, 143, 144, 145, 152 (B), 156 (TR), 158-159 (C), 159, 160 (BR), 162, 163, 164 (BR), 165 (TR), 170-1 (C), 172, 174 (T), 179 (TR), 186 (TL), 198-9 (C), 199, 203 (TL), 206 (T), 207, 209, 210 (TL), 228, 229, 242, 242-3 (B), 244, 252, 253, 254, 255, 257 (TC, TR), 258, 259, 262, 263, 267 (TC), 272-3 (C), 275, 276, 276-7 (C), 280, 280-1 (C), 286 (L), 292-3 (C), 293 (TC), 294 (TR), 298-9 (T, B), 298 (TC), 301 (TR), 302 (TC), 308 (TL), 311 (T), 312 (B), 313 (TR)

Jan van Dommelen: 66 (C), 119 (TR), 190 (TL), 284 (TL)

Alan Greatwood: 20-1 (C), 75 (T), 87 (TR), 122 (B), 129 (TL), 131 (T), 168 (TL), 201 (T), 203 (TR), 288 (TL)

Kees Hageman: 43 (TR), 148

B. J. van der Lans: 22 (TL), 51 (L), 153 (T), 175 (T), 285 (TR)

Louise Lippold: 117 (TR)

Josef Muench: 304 (L)

Frans Noltee: 17 (TL), 26 (CR), 33 (TL), 41 (TR), 65 (TR), 79 (TR), 115 (TR), 132 (TL), 140-1 (B), 153 (TR), 167 (B), 187 (TR), 188 (TL), 194 (TR), 194-5, 212 (TL), 213 (TR), 268 (TL), 281 (TR)

Orchid Society of Great Britain: 98 (TL)

Gerald Rodway: 63 (TR), 101 (TR)

Dr. Edward S. Ross: 61 (T)

Gordon Rowley: 18-9 (C), 22-3 (TC), 29 (T), 37 (B), 40 (TL), 66 (T), 80-1, 81 (TL), 132-3 (B), 140-1 (T), 186-7 (C), 197 (T), 222 (TL), 226-7 (B), 293 (TR), 298 (TL), 310 (B)

Harry Smith Photographic Collection: 20 (TL), 37 (T), 49 (TR), 68-9 (C), 108-0 (C), 132-3 (T), 161 (TR), 166 (R), 173 (TR), 174 (B), 187 (TL), 227 (TR), 240, 246 (TL), 256 (TL), 264-5, 270-1 (C), 291, 300-1 (T), 309 (B), 312-3 (T)

Daan Smit: 50 (TL), 61 (B), 70 (T), 129 (TR), 134 (TL), 138 (TR), 206 (B), 213 (TL), 213 (TC), 238 (TR), 278 (TL), 283, 305 (TL)

Michael Warren: 69 (TR), 116-7 (C), 126 (TL), 158 (TL), 185, 202-3 (C), 244-5 (C), 271 (TC), 278-9, 284-5 (C), 294-5 (B)

PRINTED IN BELGIUM BY proost INTERNATIONAL BOOK PRODUCTION